EFFECTIVE JUDICIAL PROTECTION IN CONSUMER LITIGATION

EFFECTIVE JUDICIAL PROTECTION IN CONSUMER LITIGATION

Article 47 of the EU Charter in Practice

Anna van Duin

INTERSENTIA
Cambridge – Antwerp – Chicago

Intersentia Ltd
8 Wellington Mews
Wellington Street | Cambridge
CB1 1HW | United Kingdom
Tel: +44 1223 736 170
Email: mail@intersentia.co.uk
www.intersentia.com | www.intersentia.co.uk

Distribution for the UK and
Rest of the World (incl. Eastern Europe)
NBN International
1 Deltic Avenue, Rooksley
Milton Keynes MK13 8LD
United Kingdom
Tel: +44 1752 202 301 | Fax: +44 1752 202 331
Email: orders@nbninternational.com

Distribution for Europe
Lefebvre Sarrut Belgium NV
Hoogstraat 139/6
1000 Brussels
Belgium
Tel: +32 (0)800 39 067
Email: mail@intersentia.be

Distribution for the USA and Canada
Independent Publishers Group
Order Department
814 North Franklin Street
Chicago, IL 60610
USA
Tel: +1 800 888 4741 (toll free) | Fax: +1 312 337 5985
Email: orders@ipgbook.com

Effective Judicial Protection in Consumer Litigation. Article 47 of the EU Charter in Practice

Artwork on cover: Piet Mondriaan, Flowering apple tree - Kunstmuseum Den Haag

ISBN 978-1-83970-194-8
D/2022/7849/10
NUR 822

British Library Cataloguing in Publication Data. A catalogue record for this book is available from the British Library.

FOREWORD

Justice for Both was the title of Anna van Duin's PhD thesis, which formed the basis for this monograph. Remindful of Eleanor Roosevelt's words, which are cited at the end of the concluding chapter, Anna's study of effective judicial protection in contractual relations between consumers and businesses aims to do justice to both sides. Anna's book provides a first comprehensive study of the manner in which the right to an effective remedy before a court, as laid down in Article 47 of the EU Charter of Fundamental Rights, affects the assessment of standard terms in consumer contracts. Based on a careful analysis of the case law of the Court of Justice of the European Union within the framework of the Unfair Contract Terms Directive, in combination with the comparison of Spanish and Dutch law on the subject, this book presents an insightful taxonomy of the functions that Article 47 of the Charter does and can fulfil in private law adjudication in Europe.

It is an honour for me to introduce Anna's work to a broader audience. As a supervisor of her research, together with Dr Joasia Luzak (University of Exeter), it was a pleasure to witness the development of Anna's thoughts on the role and functions of Article 47 of the Charter in the realm of private law. Her PhD research at the University of Amsterdam formed part of my project 'Judges in Utopia', funded by the Dutch Research Council (NWO Vidi 2014–2019). With a background of six years in legal practice and a keen interest in academic research, Anna was the ideal candidate for conducting a study encompassing both procedural and substantive aspects of effective protection of EU rights before national courts. Moreover, her fluency in Spanish allowed her to include an exploration of the national context of some of the most influential case law in the field, such as the well-known *Aziz* judgment. The comparison with Dutch law resulted in new insights into the national environments in which rights under EU law are sought to be effectuated. The outstanding nature of Anna's work was confirmed by the *cum laude* evaluation that she received at the occasion of her PhD defence on 23 October 2020 from a committee composed of experts in the field: Prof. Esther Arroyo Amayuelas (Professor of Civil Law at the University of Barcelona), Prof. Ruth de Bock (Advocate-General at the Dutch Supreme Court and Professor of Civil Adjudication at the University of Amsterdam), Prof. Fabrizio Cafaggi (judge in the Italian Council of State and former Professor of Private and Comparative Law at the University of Trento and the European University Institute), Prof. Aukje van Hoek (Professor of Private International Law and Civil Procedure at the University of Amsterdam) and Prof. Marco Loos (Professor of Private Law, in particular of European Consumer Law at the University of Amsterdam). After her PhD defence, Anna continued her academic path as an assistant professor at the Amsterdam Law School and she is currently working on questions of digitalisation and access to justice. The publication of her book with Intersentia, thus, concludes a time of in-depth study of the specific influence of Article 47 of the Charter in EU consumer law and opens up new avenues for research and exchange with legal scholars as well as practitioners.

A remarkable aspect of the book that you are about to start reading concerns its consideration of both theoretical and practical dimensions of judicial protection in consumer cases. Anna's research addresses a 'civil justice gap' in the protection of consumers against unfair contract terms imposed by professional parties, such as the Spanish mortgage cases. While the analysis is embedded in a thoughtful elaboration of Article 47's scope and normative content, it also makes visible the real-life problems that give rise to case law under the Unfair Contract Terms Directive. Anna convincingly demonstrates that Article 47 of the Charter, as an EU fundamental right, may contribute to establishing a more equal legal position for weaker parties, such as homeowners like Mr Aziz, in relation to stronger parties, such as banks. Insofar as Article 47, thus, adds procedural safeguards, it provides courts with a basis for granting and developing substantive remedies.

Anna concludes the book with the image of Article 47 of the Charter as a 'chameleon-like provision with many colours': depending on the context and interpretation by national courts, Article 47 can offer judges a basis for new remedies to redress the balance of parties' interests under the Unfair Contract Terms Directive. It does not impose solutions from above, but allows space for litigants and judges to define effective protection from below, within the dynamics of national private law, civil procedure and EU law. Similarly, Anna's reflections on the functions of Article 47 in European private law adjudication inspire the academic debate on the manner in which fundamental rights can contribute to procedural and substantive protection in private legal cases. At the same time, her work may provide judges with a framework that offers guidance for the application of EU law in national private legal contexts. Anna's ability to speak to both theorists and practitioners is just one of the many reasons that make this book an important read for anyone working within the field of European private law: it may help bridge the civil justice gap in EU consumer contract law by inviting us to think about judicial protection in different colours.

Amsterdam, 1 October 2021

Chantal Mak
Professor of Private Law, in particular
Fundamental Rights and Private Law
Amsterdam Centre for Transformative Private Law (ACT)
University of Amsterdam

ACKNOWLEDGEMENTS

This book is a revised version of my PhD thesis, which I defended on 23 October 2020 at the University of Amsterdam (*cum laude*). It could not have been written without the advice and support of my supervisors Chantal Mak and Joasia Luzak; thank you for your confidence in me. I am also grateful to my colleagues at the Amsterdam Centre for Transformative Private Law (ACT), who encouraged me to grow as an academic after having worked as an attorney, and to the students who have enriched my academic life. Special thanks to Candida Leone, Irina Domurath, Mirthe Jiwa and Sacha Tamboer, without whom the book would not be what it is today. To the members of my doctorate committee – Marco Loos, Aukje van Hoek, Ruth de Bock, Fabrizio Cafaggi and Esther Arroyo Amayuelas – thank you for taking the time to read my book, and for providing valuable comments. I would also like to thank the scholars who were willing to discuss my research with me, in particular Charlotte Pavillon, Bart Krans, Carla Sieburgh, Rob Widdershoven, Marieke Oderkerk, Padraic Kenna, Hanna Schebesta, Mateusz Grochowski, Janek Nowak, Fernando Gómez Pomar, Juan Antonio Mayoral, Alejandro Rubio González, Ruben de Graaff, Clark Warren, Irene Aronstein, Tim Staal, Betül Kas and Giulia Gentile.

At a crucial stage in my research I found myself surrounded by welcoming colleagues at the Universitat Pompeu Fabra. At the UB Facultat de Dret I had the opportunity of discussing my research with, amongst others, Esther Arroyo, Rosa Barceló Comte, Mariló Gramunt Fombuena, Vicente Pérez Daudí and Jordi Nieva Fenoll. I have also had the pleasure of meeting and talking to José Maria Fernández Seijo, Sandra Lange, Herman van Harten, Roland de Moor and other judges during two transnational judicial training projects I have participated in.[1] As one of the judges has observed, exploring the possibilities of Article 47 as a common EU-tool was no superfluous luxury.

1 ACTIONES, an EU-funded project under the coordination of the EUI Centre for Judicial Cooperation (see https://cjc.eui.eu/projects/actiones/), and Re-Jus, coordinated by the University of Trento (see https://www.rejus.eu/).

On a more personal note, I want to thank Jesús García González and Sara Dávila Castillo for being the best Spanish teachers I could wish for. Jesús, your energy and love have enabled me to start and finish this project. *Gracias por tu paciencia, la única sciencia.* Annechien Vink, literary scholar and my mother, has always stimulated my imagination. In the end, it was Leen van Duin, emeritus professor of architecture and my father, who convinced me to wrap up the thesis and let it go. Many thanks to Jessica van der Meer for the language edits, and to Fien de Ruiter for drafting the CJEU case law register. My peer support group consisted of other dear friends and (former) colleagues as well; I cannot thank you enough for being by my side along the way.

Lastly, I want to thank Ann-Christin Maak-Scherpe and Rebecca Moffat at Intersentia for helping me publish this book. For me, it is a stepping stone to further research in the field of access to justice, civil procedure and fundamental rights from a European and comparative perspective. I look forward also to continuing my work on digital justice and online dispute resolution, together with my colleagues from the 'Digital Transformation of Decision-Making' team. To the readers of this book: please do not hesitate to contact me if you would like to share your thoughts about these issues.

Anna van Duin
vanduin@uva.nl

CONTENTS

LIST OF CASES

COURT OF JUSTICE OF THE EUROPEAN UNION[1]

1 Cases concerning the UCTD are listed separately.

CASES CONCERNING THE UCTD[2]

[2] The cases marked with * refer to Article 47 of the Charter.

OPINIONS OF ADVOCATES GENERAL

CASES CONCERNING THE UCTD

EUROPEAN COURT OF HUMAN RIGHTS

SPAIN

TRIBUNAL CONSTITUCIONAL

TRIBUNAL SUPREMO

COURTS OF APPEAL

COURTS OF FIRST INSTANCE

NETHERLANDS

HOGE RAAD

OPINIONS OF ADVOCATES GENERAL

COURTS OF APPEAL

COURTS OF FIRST INSTANCE

CHAPTER 1
ARTICLE 47 IN UNFAIR TERMS CASES
Unchart(er)ed Territory

'Article 47 of the Charter seems to be a "sleeping beauty" which has not really been "kissed awake"'.[1]

1.1. ARTICLE 47 OF THE CHARTER: ON FIRST ACQUAINTANCE

1.1.1. VISIBILITY OF EFFECTIVE JUDICIAL PROTECTION AS AN EU FUNDAMENTAL RIGHT

Everyone whose rights and freedoms guaranteed by EU law are violated has the right to an effective remedy, and to a fair trial before a court of law. This is a fundamental right of all EU citizens, enshrined in Article 47 of the EU Charter of Fundamental Rights (Charter).[2] The high number of references to Article 47 by the Court of Justice of the European Union (CJEU), and

---

1 Norbert Reich, 'The Principle of Effectiveness and EU Private Law' in Ulf Bernitz, Xavier Groussot and Felix Schulyok (eds), *General Principles of EU Law and European Private Law* (Kluwer Law International 2013) 321.

2 The Charter is legally binding as of 1 December 2009, the date of entry into force of the Treaty of Lisbon amending the Treaty on European Union and the Treaty establishing the European Community (Lisbon Treaty), signed in Lisbon, 13 December 2007 (2007/C 306/01). Article 47 reads, 'Everyone whose rights and freedoms guaranteed by the law of the Union are violated has the right to an effective remedy before a tribunal in compliance with the conditions laid down in this Article.
Everyone is entitled to a fair and public hearing within a reasonable time by an independent and impartial tribunal previously established by law.
Everyone shall have the possibility of being advised, defended and represented. Legal aid shall be made available to those who lack sufficient resources in so far as such aid is necessary to ensure effective access to justice'.

by national courts in requests for preliminary rulings,[3] nevertheless suggests it cannot be taken for granted that effective judicial protection is always available and accessible. In EU consumer law, the rise of Article 47 coincided with a wave of crisis-induced litigation in the aftermath of the 2007/2008 'credit crunch'. Civil courts in Spain, Poland, Hungary and other EU Member States were confronted with large numbers of cases brought by financial institutions against indebted consumers. This triggered many questions to the CJEU on the meaning and scope of EU consumer protection legislation, as well as the need for effective judicial protection, in particular and most urgently for vulnerable consumer debtors. The referring courts questioned the adequacy of their own national legal frameworks, especially where the possibilities of judicial intervention were limited. Examples can be found in the CJEU's case law on mortgage enforcement and order for payment procedures.[4]

This book focuses on the role of Article 47 in cases concerning the Unfair Contract Terms Directive (UCTD or Directive),[5] where the number of references to Article 47 is relatively high. The Directive proved to be one avenue – an 'indirect remedy'[6] – to address structural imbalances in the civil justice system, both from a legal and a socio-economic point of view: 'a fountain of social justice in times of drought'.[7] As such, it was a portal to EU law and the applicability of the Charter. Since Reich referred to Article 47 as a 'sleeping beauty' in 2013, it has become no longer dormant. Unfair contract terms control is one of the areas of private law where effective judicial protection, as an EU fundamental right, has emerged in the past decade. In so far as Article 47 has become more visible in judicial decisions, this is in line with the Charter's aim of strengthening the protection of fundamental rights

3 Article 47 is the Charter provision most often referred to: European Commission, *2018 Report on the Application of the EU Charter of Fundamental Rights* 12. The report can be consulted at <https://ec.europa.eu/info/aid-development-cooperation-fundamental-rights/your-rights-eu/eu-charter-fundamental-rights/application-charter/annual-reports-application-charter_en> (last accessed 24 September 2021).

4 See further sections 3.2–3.3 and 4.2–4.3 of this book.

5 Council Directive 93/13/EEC of 5 April 1993 on unfair terms in consumer contracts (OJ L95, 21 April 1993, 29).

6 Immaculada Barral-Viñals, 'Aziz Case and Unfair Contract Terms in Mortgage Loan Agreements: Lessons to Be Learned in Spain' (2015) 4 Penn State Journal of Law & International Affairs 69, 71.

7 Daniela Caruso, 'Fairness at a Time of Perplexity' in Stefan Vogenauer and Stephen Weatherill (eds), *General Principles of Law: European and Comparative Perspectives* (Hart Publishing 2017) 346.

in the EU by increasing their visibility. Visibility is not just symbolic: when a problem is framed as a fundamental rights issue, the case gains a constitutional dimension.[8] For instance, where the rights of consumers to take legal action or to defend themselves are severely restricted or entirely excluded, Article 47 might be at stake.

According to the European Commission, '[p]romoting access to justice and the right to effective redress under Article 47 of the Charter is a precondition for the effective enjoyment of all rights under EU law'.[9] Article 47 confirms that where there is a right, there must be a remedy: *ubi ius, ibi remedium*,[10] the *condicio sine qua non* of 'a Union subject to the rule of law'.[11] The CJEU has recognised that Article 47 can be directly invoked by individuals: the effective judicial protection of their rights under EU law must be provided by national courts, regardless of the nature of the dispute (vertical or horizontal, public or private) between the parties.[12]

Article 47 holds the promise of an 'autonomous standard of effective judicial protection'[13] that superimposes on national (procedural) law in all cases falling within the scope of EU law, including unfair terms cases.[14]

---

8 The term 'constitutional' is used here in a narrow sense: it refers to the interpretation and application of EU law in accordance with EU fundamental rights, i.e. the Charter.

9 European Commission, *2017 Report on the Application of the EU Charter of Fundamental Rights*, 10.

10 See, e.g. Walter Van Gerven, 'Of Rights, Remedies and Procedures' (2000) 37 Common Market Law Review 501, 503.

11 Case C-682/15 *Berlioz Investment Fund v Directeur de l'administration des contributions directes*, Opinion of AG Wathelet, point 66. See also Explanations relating to the Charter of Fundamental Rights [2007] OJ C303/02, 29–30. See also Case C-14/08 *Roda Golf & Beach Resort*, Opinion of AG Ruiz-Jaracob Colomer, point 29: 'Access to justice is a fundamental pillar of western legal culture. "To no one will we sell, to no one will we deny right of justice" proclaimed the Magna Carta in 1215, expressing an axiom which has remained in force in Europe to the extent that it features in the European Convention of Human Rights, the Charter of Fundamental Rights of the European Union and the case law of the Court.' Article 47 of the Charter 'constitutes one of the fundamental guarantees for the respect of the rule of law and democracy and is inextricably linked to civil procedure as a whole': European Parliament resolution of 4 July 2017 with recommendations to the Commission on common minimum standards of civil procedure in the European Union (2015/2084(INL)).

12 Case C-414/16 *Egenberger v Evangelisches Werk Diakonie und Entwicklung*, paras. 78–79.

13 Marek Safjan and Dominik Düsterhaus, 'A Union of Effective Judicial Protection: Addressing a Multi-Level Challenge through the Lens of Article 47 CFREU' (2014) 33 Yearbook of European Law 3, 31, 36.

14 Article 47 of the Charter is binding on national (civil) courts when they adjudicate disputes under the UCTD: see, e.g. CJEU 21 February 2013, Case C-472/11 *Banif Plus Bank v Csaba Csipai* ECLI:EU:C:2013:88, para. 29. See further subsections 2.2.1, 2.3.3 and 3.5.2 of this book.

At the same time, Article 47 reinforces the link between substantive and procedural protection of EU rights. It emphasises the key role of courts in the enforcement and protection of those rights. Such a court-centred approach is not necessarily new; Article 47 could be seen as a confirmation, not a transformation, of a long-standing judicial practice.[15] Still, Article 47 grants constitutional status to the right to effective judicial protection in EU law. Its codification in the Charter, which has the same legal value as the Treaties,[16] could be seen as a 'substantial upgrade'.[17] Whether Article 47 provides a new frame of reference, or whether it reaffirms pre-existing rights, those rights have become more manifest, and possibly also more prominent.[18] A shortfall in judicial remedies or procedural safeguards may give rise to a fundamental rights violation, which implies an even more pressing need to address its consequences. Such a shortfall will be harder to overlook for all actors involved – at both EU and national level.

This book will explore what function(s) a reference to Article 47[19] can fulfil in the adjudication of disputes under the UCTD. It will be shown that the 'sleeping beauty' has not yet fully woken up. Moreover, another side (*altera parte*) of Article 47 is revealed that may seem counter-intuitive from the perspective of consumer protection: it is often invoked for the protection of the professional counterparties of consumers, even though such counterparties cannot derive rights from the Directive itself. Article 47 is not one-dimensional: it covers both the claimant's right of access to court and the defendant's rights of defence, and it contributes to ensuring procedural justice.[20] How the rights and interests on both sides,

---

15 Stephen Weatherill, Stefan Vogenauer and Petra Weingerl, 'Private Autonomy and Protection of the Weaker Party', *General Principles of Law: European and Comparative Perspectives* (Hart Publishing 2017) 263.

16 Article 6(1) of the Treaty of the European Union (TEU). See also Case C-279/09 *DEB v Bundesrepublik Deutschland* ECLI:EU:C:2010:811, para. 30; Sacha Prechal, 'The Court of Justice and Effective Judicial Protection: What Has the Charter Changed?' in Christophe Paulussen and others (eds), *Fundamental Rights in International and European law: Public and Private law Perspectives* (TMC Asser Press 2015) 145.

17 Dorota Leczykiewicz, '"Effective Judicial Protection" of Human Rights after Lisbon: Should National Courts Be Empowered to Review EU Secondary Law?' (2010) 35 European Law Review 326, 333.

18 Sara Iglesias Sánchez, 'The Court and the Charter: The Impact of the Entry into Force of the Lisbon Treaty on the ECJ's Approach to Fundamental Rights' (2012) 49 Common Market Law Review 1565, 1574–1575.

19 'Reference' means here that Article 47 is explicitly mentioned or alluded to by courts.

20 Procedural justice is generally understood as the fairness of the process resulting in a (judicial) decision, which legitimises the outcome: Nina Półtorak, *European Union Rights in National Courts* (Wolters Kluwer 2015) 11–12. See, for further references, Iris Benöhr, *EU Consumer Law and Human Rights* (1st ed., Oxford University Press 2013) 96.

and at different levels, must be balanced is a key question for civil courts in their roles as European courts.[21]

1.1.2. A UNIQUE PERSPECTIVE ON THE ROLE OF CIVIL COURTS IN CONSUMER LITIGATION

The role of national civil courts in providing effective judicial protection in the context of the UCTD is central to this book. For rights guaranteed by EU law, the premise is that effective legal protection must be ensured by the Member States and their national courts,[22] even – or especially – if remedies and procedures are not fully harmonised. For private parties, civil courts are the gateway to the enforcement of their subjective (EU) rights against each other. Courts operate as an 'intermediary' to prevent them from being deprived of their rights.[23] Judges in national civil courts are decentralised EU judges:[24] they are part of the EU's judicial system, and play an important part in the enforcement of EU law. While the choice and design of remedies and procedures are primarily the prerogatives of the (national) legislature, it is left to the judiciary to provide solutions in concrete cases, and to assess whether national law is up to standard.[25] Courts must not only interpret and apply national law in

---

21 Civil justice has a substantive and a procedural component: it means, in short, that a private party can obtain redress for a violation of their rights from the party responsible for that violation through civil litigation: Jason M Solomon, 'What is Civil Justice' [2010] William & Mary Law School Scholarship Repository – Faculty Publications, Paper 1149 317, 322–323, 329. The term 'EU civil justice' is mainly used to refer to (cross-border) civil proceedings. For the purposes of this book, the terms 'civil justice', 'civil procedure' and 'civil proceedings' refer to private law adjudication by civil (i.e. non-administrative and non-criminal) courts.

22 See, e.g. Article 19(1) TEU.

23 Fernanda Nicola and Evelyne Tichadou, '*Océano Grupo*: A Transatlantic Victory for the Consumer and a Missed Opportunity for European Law', *EU Law Stories: Contextual and Critical Histories of European Jurisprudence* (Cambridge University Press 2017) 378.

24 Urszula Jaremba, *National Judges as EU Law Judges: The Polish Civil Law System* (Martinus Nijhof Publishers 2014) 47.

25 See also Fabrizio Cafaggi and Paola Iamiceli, 'The Principles of Effectiveness, Proportionality and Dissuasiveness in the Enforcement of EU Consumer Law: The Impact of a Triad on the Choice of Civil Remedies and Administrative Sanctions' (2017) 25 European Review of Private Law 575, 580; Fabrizio Cafaggi, 'Towards Collaborative Governance of European Remedial and Procedural Law?' (2018) 19 Theoretical Inquiries in Law 235, 237.

conformity with EU law, they must also review its compatibility with EU law and, if necessary, set it aside, for example in the event that it conflicts with Article 47 of the Charter.[26]

Article 47 has been part of the Charter from the moment that it was first proclaimed.[27] However, its potential relevance for national civil courts is still largely uncharted territory.[28] Studies on Article 47 in the context of cross-border civil justice[29] typically do not account for the effect of (substantive) EU law in purely domestic cases. Studies on the 'horizontal' implications of the Charter[30] rarely focus on procedural safeguards, which distinguish Article 47 from other fundamental rights. Moreover, studies on 'private enforcement'[31] and *ex officio* application[32] of EU law rarely take a fundamental rights perspective.[33]

---

26 See further subsection 2.2.2 of this book.

27 Official Journal of the European Communities, 18 December 2000, 2000/C 364/01.

28 Chantal Mak, 'Unchart(er)ed Territory: EU Fundamental Rights and National Private Law' in Arthur Hartkamp and others (eds), *The Influence of EU Law on National Private Law* (Kluwer 2014).

29 See, e.g. Giangiuseppe Sanna, 'Article 47 of the EU Charter of Fundamental Rights and Its Impact on Judicial Cooperation in Civil and Commercial Matters' in Giacomo Di Federico (ed), *The EU Charter of Fundamental Rights* (Springer 2011); Monique Hazelhorst, *Free Movement of Civil Judgments in the European Union and the Right to a Fair Trial* (TMC Asser Press 2017).

30 The term 'horizontal' concerns the legal relationship between individuals, i.e. private parties. See, e.g. Sonja Walkila, *Horizontal Effect of Fundamental Rights in EU Law* (Europa Law Publishing 2016); Eleni Frantziou, 'The Horizontal Effect of Fundamental Rights in the European Union – A Constitutional Analysis' (Oxford University Press 2019).

31 See, e.g. Folkert Wilman, *Private Enforcement of EU Law Before National Courts* (Edward Elgar Publishing 2015); Arthur Hartkamp, *European Law and National Private Law: Effect of EU Law and European Human Rights Law on Legal Relationships between Individuals* (2nd ed., Intersentia 2016); Irene Aronstein, *Remedies for Infringements of EU Law in Legal Relationships between Private Parties* (Wolters Kluwer 2019).

32 See, e.g. Anthi Beka, *The Active Role of Courts in Consumer Litigation: Applying EU Law of the National Courts' Own Motion* (Intersentia 2018); Vicente Pérez Daudí, *La protección procesal del consumidor y el orden público comunitario* (Atelier 2018); Alain Ancery, *Ambtshalve toepassing van EU-recht* (Kluwer 2012).

33 A recent report by the Max Planck Institute Luxembourg for Procedural Law deals extensively with procedural protection and access to justice for consumers from a comparative perspective, but not specifically with the fundamental rights dimension, let alone Article 47 of the Charter: Burkhard Hess and Stephanie Law (eds), *Implementing EU Consumer Rights by National Procedural Law. Luxembourg Report of European Procedural Law: Volume II* (Beck 2019). This will hereinafter be referred to as '2019 Max Planck report'.

Most studies on effective judicial protection in EU law[34] do not elaborate in detail on the specific factual and legal context of a case[35] – its subject matter, the EU instrument(s) at hand, and the applicable national (substantive and procedural) rules, as well as the nature of the underlying (vertical or horizontal) relationship, all of which determine the court's tasks and powers. For civil courts, it matters how EU law has been implemented in their national legal systems. The level of judicial protection in civil proceedings, and the balance between the claimant's right of access to justice on the one hand, and the defendant's rights of defence on the other, are not harmonised across the EU[36] – at least not for all types of cases that fall within the scope of EU law, such as unfair contract terms cases. The adjudication of consumer disputes is, first and foremost, governed by rules of national private law and civil procedure, which constitute the primary frame of reference for civil courts. National procedural modalities – for example, questions of when the parties have access to particular procedures, what powers the courts have in the course of proceedings, and whether there is room for appeal – are essential to the level and scope of protection that courts can provide in practice. However, the distinct features of civil proceedings have been given surprisingly little attention, so far, in the literature on judicial protection in EU law, perhaps because they vary significantly across the Member States, or because they are less relevant from a top-down perspective.[37]

---

[34] See, e.g. Johanna Engström, *The Europeanisation of Remedies and Procedures through Judge-Made Law – Can a Trojan Horse Achieve Effectiveness?* (European University Institute 2009); Allison Östlund, *Effectiveness versus Procedural Protection: Tensions Triggered by the EU Law Mandate of Ex Officio Review* (Nomos 2019).

[35] See also Hans-W Micklitz, 'The ECJ between the Individual Citizen and the Member States: A Plea for a Judge-Made European Law on Remedies' in Hans-W Micklitz and Bruno De Witte (eds), *The European Court of Justice and the Autonomy of the Member States* (Intersentia 2012) 399.

[36] See, e.g. the 2019 Max Planck report (n 33). See also Magdalena Tulibacka, 'Europeanization of Civil Procedure: In Search of a Coherent Approach' (2009) 46 Common Market Law Review 1527, 1532–1533.

[37] The national qualification of measures (sanctions) as criminal, administrative or civil is not relevant for the purposes of EU law enforcement: see, e.g. Martin Ebers, *Rechte, Rechtsbehelfe Und Sanktionen Im Unionsprivatrecht* (Mohr Siebeck 2016) 291–292. Furthermore, the CJEU has held that the specific characteristics of court proceedings cannot constitute a factor liable to affect the legal protection of consumers under the UCTD: see e.g. Case C-169/14 *Sánchez Morcillo and Abril García v BBVA* ECLI:EU:C:2014:2099 ('*Sánchez Morcillo I*'), para. 47 and Case C-34/13 *Kušionová v SMART Capital* ECLI:EU:C:2014:2189, para. 53.

As a result, the (added) value of Article 47 of the Charter, in European private law adjudication,[38] remains unclear. This book aims to address this, by concentrating on a specific area of private law – unfair terms in consumer contracts – and the legal systems of two selected Member States: Spain and the Netherlands. An in-depth case study will be conducted to account for the dynamics between different levels (EU v. national, systemic v. case-specific) and different actors (judiciary v. other branches of government, courts v. litigating parties) at the crossroads of EU fundamental rights, consumer law and civil procedure. As such, this book provides a unique perspective on the role of civil courts in consumer litigation, in light of effective judicial protection as an EU fundamental right.

1.2. AN IN-DEPTH CASE STUDY: ARTICLE 47 IN UNFAIR TERMS CASES

1.2.1. A 'CIVIL JUSTICE GAP'

The reasons for conducting an in-depth case study are threefold.[39] First, Article 47 is a chameleon-like provision that may 'change colour' according to the context within which an action is brought.[40] It is open-ended and phrased broadly; it may give rise to different issues and be applied differently in different circumstances. To identify when a case is considered to have a constitutional dimension under Article 47, it is important to understand the factual and legal context, including the specific EU instrument

---

38 European private law adjudication is understood as litigation between private parties in a dispute on a matter of private law, e.g. contract law, that falls (partly or entirely) within the scope of EU law, before national civil courts of the EU Member States.

39 'Case study' means here an in-depth analysis of the relevant case law, legislation and literature on a specific area of law, as one of the many areas to which Article 47 of the Charter is applicable: see *infra* for my reasons for adopting this approach. Furthermore, the scope of this book is limited to two specific legal systems, chosen for the reasons provided below. On case studies in legal scholarship, see further Lisa L Miller, 'The Use of Case Studies in Law and Social Science Research' (2018) 14 Annual Review of Law and Social Science 381.

40 The term 'chameleon' is used to indicate that the meaning of a certain legal concept is context-related: see, e.g. Monica Claes, *The National Courts' Mandate in the European Constitution* (doctoral thesis, Maastricht University 2004) 339; Henk Snijders, 'Openbare orde, rechtspersonen en mensenrechten' [2014] Nederlands Juristenblad 1174; Stefan Grundmann, 'The Fault Principle as the Chameleon of Contract Law: A Market Function Approach' (2009) 107 Michigan Law Review 1583.

Article 47 is being read together with. This informs the implications of effective judicial protection, especially in comparison with the notion of effectiveness in EU law. Second, the application of Article 47 is connected to other EU rights. The requirement of an *effective* remedy highlights the link between substantive and procedural protections. Indeed, the effectiveness of remedies and procedures can only be understood in relation to the sector where they operate.[41] And, third, a comparison between the CJEU's approach and those of the Spanish and Dutch civil courts requires detailed knowledge of the applicable legal framework, as well as an awareness of other (legal) factors that might influence the application of EU law and Article 47 of the Charter in specific legal systems.[42]

The main reason for selecting the UCTD as a case study is that, after the Charter's entry into force, the CJEU – and national courts in its wake – started referring to Article 47 more and more frequently in the context of the UCTD.[43] The number of references to Article 47 is relatively high. Moreover, there is already an extensive body of case law, which allows for a comparison of cases with and without references to Article 47.

The regulation of unfair terms in consumer contracts is one of the fields where the legal discourse crystallises on the 'Europeanisation' of national private law and civil procedure, as well as the interactions between national (civil) courts and the CJEU.[44] The CJEU's case law has had a significant impact on national remedies and procedures, which would have been hard to foresee when the UCTD was adopted in 1993. Over time, the CJEU has developed several judge-made requirements for the effective (judicial) protection – on which the Directive itself is silent – of the rights that consumers derive from the Directive, in response to a wide range of issues raised by national (civil) courts. The CJEU's case law has unearthed ways in which national rules of civil procedure hinder the effectuation of consumer rights.[45] Examples of procedural issues that have

---

41 See further Michael Dougan, *National Remedies before the Court of Justice* (Hart Publishing 2004) 220–226.

42 See also Herman van Harten, *Autonomie van de nationale rechter in het Europees recht: een verkenning van de praktijk aan de hand van de Nederlandse Europeesrechtelijke rechtspraak over de vestigingsvrijheid en het vrijedienstenverkeer* (doctoral thesis, University of Amsterdam 2011) 18, 74.

43 See subsection 1.3.3 of this book for an overview.

44 Hans-W Micklitz and Norbert Reich, 'The Court and Sleeping Beauty: The Revival of the Unfair Contract Terms Directive (UCTD)' (2014) 51 Common Market Law Review 771, 808.

45 See also Joanna van Duin and Candida Leone, 'The Real (New) Deal: Levelling the Odds for Consumer-Litigants' [2019] European Review of Private Law 1227, 1236.

arisen under the UCTD are the unavailability of interim relief in mortgage enforcement proceedings,[46] the scope for judicial review of arbitral awards,[47] and third-party effects of collective actions.[48]

These issues may have, at first sight, nothing to do with unfair terms in consumer contracts, but they can still be brought within the scope of the Directive, based on the subject-matter of the case. The justification for this is that national remedies and procedures constitute the corollary to EU rights, including the rights that consumers derive from the UCTD.[49] Consumer rights are only as effective as their enforcement.[50] European consumer protection is not only about conferring substantive rights on consumers, but also about enforcing and protecting those rights through effective remedies and adequate procedures.

Despite the CJEU's progressive and consumer-friendly interpretation of EU consumer protection legislation, however, EU-wide reports suggest that there is still an 'enforcement deficit' or 'civil justice gap'.[51] Examples of this include a lack of incentives or opportunities for consumers to bring a claim; barriers, such as legal costs; uncertainty about the scope of the national court's *ex officio* powers; and inadequate mechanisms for the protection of collective interests. The CJEU's case law is voluminous but scattered, and appears to create more confusion than clarity, as evidenced by the continuing stream of preliminary references and a Guidance Notice on the interpretation and application of Directive 93/13/EEC, issued by the Commission in 2019.[52] This Notice is intended to present the CJEU's case law in a structured manner, to increase awareness, and to facilitate its application in practice. The Notice mentions the relevance of Article 47 of the Charter as regards procedural safeguards,[53] but does not discuss the constitutional dimension of the CJEU's case law, which this book aims to address.

---

46 See further subsection 3.3.2 of this book.

47 See further subsection 3.2.2.

48 See further subsection 4.5.3.

49 Verica Trstenjak and Erwin Beysen, 'European Consumer Protection Law: *Curia Semper Dabit Remedium*?' (2011) 48 Common Market Law Review 95, 110.

50 Geraint Howells and Stephen Weatherill, *Consumer Protection Law* (Routledge 2005) 660.

51 See 2019 Max Planck report (n 33) and *Study for the Fitness Check of EU consumer and marketing Law – Final report Part 1: Main report*, European Commission 29 May 2017 ('REFIT report'), available at <https://ec.europa.eu/newsroom/just/items/59332/en> (last accessed 24 September 2021). See also Benöhr (n 20) 177; Stefan Wrbka, *European Consumer Access to Justice Revisited* (Cambridge University Press 2015) 33.

52 Commission notice – Guidance on the interpretation and application of Council Directive 93/13/EEC on unfair terms in consumer contracts (2019/C 323/04).

53 Commission notice (n 52), 53.

1.2.2. JUSTICIABILITY OF EU (CONSUMER) RIGHTS

The potential significance of Article 47 in European private law adjudication has already been noted by other authors, but there has not yet been any comprehensive academic study on the question of what the actual (added) value, if any, is of Article 47 read in conjunction with the UCTD, despite the high number of references in this context. This is not just a theoretical question: access to justice has become a key issue in EU consumer law.[54] Access to justice is a broader concept than access to court, just as legal protection is broader than judicial protection. Whereas the role of courts in providing substantive protection to consumers is inherently limited,[55] and, in any case, part of a bigger enforcement palette, the importance of effective judicial protection – if only as a last resort – is widely acknowledged.

This book ties in with the strand of literature on the meaning of effective judicial protection vis-à-vis, in particular, the general principle of effectiveness in EU law and the *ex officio* application of EU consumer protection legislation, more specifically the UCTD. Effective judicial protection neither begins nor ends with *ex officio* control, as will be further elaborated in this study. Actual access to a court is a prerequisite for judicial protection. Any judicial intervention is based on the premise that a case can be, and is, brought before a competent court by one of the parties.[56] Therefore, judicial remedies and procedural safeguards are deemed to be essential for the enforcement and protection of EU consumer rights by national civil courts. A prominent example is the *Sánchez Morcillo* case from Spain, where the CJEU held that equality of arms – an integral element of the right to effective judicial protection as guaranteed by Article 47 – required the possibility of appeal for consumer debtors, as well as for creditors, in the course of mortgage enforcement proceedings.[57] When consumers cannot bring an appeal, the appellate

[54] See, e.g. Eva Storskrubb, *Civil Procedure and EU Law: A Policy Area Uncovered* (Oxford University Press 2008) 28; Benöhr (n 20) 105; Marco Loos, 'Access to Justice in Consumer Law' (2015) 36 Recht der Werkelijkheid 113; Remo Caponi and Janek Tomasz Nowak, 'Access to Justice' in 2019 Max Planck report.

[55] See, e.g. Irina Domurath, *Consumer Vulnerability and Welfare in Mortgage Contracts* (Hart Publishing 2017) 105–106.

[56] Case C-147/16 *Karel de Grote – Hogeschool Katholieke Hogeschool Antwerpen v Kuijpers*, Opinion of AG Sharpston, point 32.

[57] Case C-169/14 *Sánchez Morcillo I* (n 37), para. 48; further discussed in sections 3.4 and 4.4 of this book.

court cannot perform unfair terms control either and, thus, it cannot remedy an infringement of their rights in the first instance, if necessary.

The application of Article 47 in unfair terms cases is linked to problems with the enforceability and justiciability of consumer rights. Both of these terms refer to the possibilities for private parties to effectuate their legally recognised rights, but the term 'justiciability' specifically relates to the capacity (i.e. standing) to invoke a right *in court*. Understood broadly, justiciability also means that courts must be able to take EU consumer rights into account when they adjudicate consumer disputes.[58] Article 47 places the emphasis on the responsibility of courts to enforce and protect EU consumer rights, which presupposes a genuine opportunity for consumers to exercise their rights in court. If access to court only exists on paper, if consumers are denied a proper chance to take legal action, or if there is no remedy available at all, the fundamental right to effective judicial protection might be at stake. Even if a reference to Article 47 does not immediately change the outcome of a concrete case, it puts the spotlight on a potential fundamental rights violation. As such, a reference to Article 47 may indicate or signal systemic issues that transcend the UCTD, and might possibly lead to structural changes in the long run.

1.3. AIM AND METHODOLOGY

1.3.1. FUNCTION(S) OF A REFERENCE TO ARTICLE 47 IN JUDICIAL DECISIONS

1.3.1.1. Bridging the Gap Between Theory and Practice

The main question this book seeks to answer is what function(s) a reference to Article 47 of the Charter can fulfil in European private law adjudication, more particularly in cases concerning the UCTD.[59] This question ties in with other studies on fundamental rights in private law and other studies on

58 See also Van Duin and Leone (n 45) 1229. This understanding of 'justiciability' is broader than the direct effect of (subjective) EU rights or the mere existence of a (procedural) means of recourse. It includes rights originating from directives that have been implemented in national legal systems. Practical and legal obstacles, such as a lack of knowledge or financial means, as well as restrictive procedural conditions, may equally stand in the way of the justiciability of those rights.

59 A 'function' expresses how a particular concept works or operates in a certain way and reveals its purpose or (intended) role. This use of the term 'function' must be distinguished from the functionality of the EU single market, which is associated

general principles of EU law, which refer to 'functions' as well.[60] Against the background of these studies, this book aims to identify, analyse and classify the functions of a reference to Article 47 by the CJEU and by national civil courts when they decide cases under the UCTD. It rests on the premise that these functions cannot be analysed in isolation, separately from the EU rights the case pertains to, and the case's national setting. Therefore, these functions will be addressed as part of an in-depth case study on the UCTD and two specific legal systems: Spain and the Netherlands.

This book aims to bridge the gap between theory and practice in respect of the application of Article 47 at EU and national levels. As such, it makes a vital contribution to the conceptualisation and explanation of Article 47 as a legal phenomenon.[61] It adopts a bottom-up, case-driven approach by looking at the practice of courts, as exposed by their judicial decisions. It takes an internal, comparative perspective[62] and examines the EU's multi-level legal order from within, i.e. on its own terms. The normative background provided by the objectives of the UCTD and the Charter is taken as a given. The functions of Article 47 of the Charter are described as they emerge from the literature review, and the analysed case law in its factual, legal and national contexts. All references to Article 47 – the common denominator[63] – in the case law of the CJEU, and of the Spanish and Dutch civil courts on the UCTD, are mapped out and compared. The comparison is, first of all, vertical, in the sense that it examines similarities and disparities between the way the CJEU refers to Article 47, and the way Article 47 is referred to by national courts. The differences and dynamics between these become particularly clear in the case law pertaining to Spain. Second, a horizontal comparison is made between two Member States, Spain and the Netherlands. This is done through a doctrinal analysis of the domestic legal framework in each country. The selection of legal systems and relevant case law will be further explained below.

---

with instrumentality: see, e.g. Christoph Schmid, 'The Instrumentalist Conception of the Acquis Communautaire in Consumer Law and its Implications on a European Contract Law Code' [2005] European Review of Contract Law 211.

60 See further sections 2.4 and 2.5 of this book.

61 On the importance of doctrinal legal expertise: Rob Van Gestel and Hans-W Micklitz, 'Revitalizing Doctrinal Legal Research in Europe: What About Methodology?' EUI Law Working Papers 2011/05 25.

62 Martijn Hesselink, 'A European Legal Method? On European Private Law and Scientific Method' (2009) 15 European Law Journal 20, 33.

63 Marieke Oderkerk, 'The Need for a Methodological Framework for Comparative Legal Research – Sense and Nonsense of "Methodological Pluralism" in Comparative Law' (2015) 79 Rabels Zeitschrift für ausländisches und internationales Privatrecht 589, 610.

In so far as courts explicitly refer to Article 47 and/or effective judicial protection as a fundamental right, this tells us, firstly, what type of issues they are confronted with, and what triggers a reference to Article 47. Secondly, this reflects, at least to some extent, the perceived (added) value of a reference to Article 47 when it is read in conjunction with the UCTD. For each case, answers are sought to the questions of how and why a reference to Article 47 has been made, what the meaning of such a reference is vis-à-vis the notion of effectiveness (which has been the main parameter in the CJEU's case law so far), and whether it makes a difference in outcome and/or judicial reasoning. From these answers, various functions can be inferred, which will be placed in the broader debate outlined above. The exact labelling of certain functions is mostly semantic. What matters, for the purposes of this book, is what a reference to Article 47 can do, what is behind it, and what the commonalities or disparities are in the way that it is used.

1.3.1.2. Focus on Civil Procedure

The scope of this book extends to the functions of a reference to Article 47 of the Charter in the contexts of the UCTD and the two selected Member States. Whereas the findings cannot be automatically extrapolated to other areas of (private) law or other Member States, they may still provide guidance to national civil courts on how to apply Article 47. The CJEU's interpretation of EU law is binding, even if it is given in preliminary rulings pertaining to other legal systems. Moreover, judicial decisions from other Member States may provide an example or inspiration for the application of Article 47 as an EU fundamental right.

While this is a book on the impact of Article 47 on national procedural law, its focus is specifically on civil procedure. Administrative enforcement falls outside its scope. It should be noted that the term 'enforcement' may refer to a public (administrative or judicial) authority securing that a rule or policy is followed properly, but may also refer to private parties realising their subjective rights against each other. Broadly speaking, enforcement, in the former meaning, is geared towards *law* enforcement, compliance and deterrence in the public interest, whereas in the latter meaning it predominantly revolves around *rights* enforcement in the (private) self-interest of the right-holder.[64] Whereas the legal protection

[64] Colin Scott, 'Enforcing Consumer Protection Laws' in Geraint Howells, Ian Ramsay and Thomas Wilhelmsson (eds), *Handbook of Research on International Consumer Law* (Edward Elgar Publishing 2010) 539; Johanna Engström, 'The Europeanization

and vindication of subjective rights could be seen as the primary function of civil procedure, civil procedure also has a regulatory dimension.[65] Law enforcement and rights enforcement are not opposites: rather, they coexist and interact.[66] Individual litigants may, thus, contribute to the public interest of upholding EU law, especially where mandatory rules or fundamental rights are at stake.[67] Wilman has called this a 'duality' of purpose: offering redress to private parties for infringements of EU law is expected to contribute to enhancing compliance with EU law.[68] In the context of the UCTD, both meanings of enforcement are relevant: the enforcement of the UCTD and the achievement of its objectives both largely depend on the justiciability of consumer rights and private parties enforcing them in court.[69]

There may be parallels between the Charter and other instruments, such as the European Convention on Human Rights (ECHR), or between the Charter and national constitutional rights, but those are not the focus of this book, and will only be discussed in so far as they are relevant for an understanding of the analysed case law. No separate analysis has been carried out of the case law of the European Court of Human Rights (ECtHR) in Strasbourg or the Spanish Constitutional Court in Madrid.

---

of Remedies and Procedures – The Principle of Effective Judicial Protection in the Swedish Judicial Habitat' (2011) 23 European Review of Public Law 577, 593–594; Candida Leone, *The missing stone in the Cathedral: of unfair terms in employment contracts and coexisting rationalities in European contract law* (doctoral thesis, University of Amsterdam 2020) 13.

65 See, e.g. Storskrubb (n 54) 296. See also Laura Ervo, 'Party Autonomy and Access to Justice' in Laura Ervo, Minna Gräns and Antti Jokela (eds), *Europeanization of Procedural Law and the New Challenges to Fair Trial* (Europa Law Publishing 2009) 24–25; Gerhard Wagner, 'Harmonisation of Civil Procedure: Policy Perspectives' in XE Kramer and CH Van Rhee (eds), *Civil Litigation in a Globalising World* (Springer/TMC Asser Press 2012) 109; Simon Whittaker, 'Who Determines what Civil Courts Decide? Private Rights, Public Policy and EU Law' in Dorota Leczykiewicz and Stephen Weatherill (eds), *The Involvement of EU Law in Private Law Relationships* (Hart Publishing 2013) 89–90.

66 Zampia Vernadaki, *EU Civil Procedure and Access to Justice after the Lisbon Treaty: Perspectives for a Coherent Approach* (doctoral thesis, University College London 2013) 21 <http://discovery.ucl.ac.uk/1399838/> (last accessed 24 September 2021); Wilman (n 31) 457; Engström (n 64) 591; Beka (n 32) 80.

67 Östlund (n 34); Norbert Reich, *General Principles of EU Civil Law* (Intersentia 2014) 122; Olha Cherednychenko, *Fundamental Rights, Contract Law and the Protection of the Weaker Party* (European Law Publishers 2007) 63.

68 Folkert Wilman, 'The End of the Absence? The Growing Body of EU Legislation on Private Enforcement and the Main Remedies It Provides For' (2016) 53 Common Market Law Review 887, 931.

69 Ebers (n 37) 319.

The ECtHR is sometimes asked to rule on issues adjoining EU law, such as State liability for a national court's failure to make a preliminary reference,[70] or national legislation that implements (the CJEU's case law on) the UCTD.[71] Indirectly, State liability may influence the application of the UCTD, for instance when a court fails to comply with its duty to perform *ex officio* control.[72] However, State liability, as such, falls outside the scope of this book. Almost all relevant CJEU cases concern horizontal disputes between private parties. The CJEU hardly refers to the ECHR in the context of the UCTD at all.

A follow-up question for future research would be whether the findings presented in this book are consistent with the views and experiences of the judges involved. In addition to a contextual analysis of the cases in which judges *do* refer to Article 47, it could then be examined why they *do not* in other cases – within and beyond the scope of the UCTD. This book forms a stepping stone for such future research. Another follow-up question that could be addressed concerns the influence of judicial culture and civil courts' familiarity with fundamental rights reasoning, also in areas other than the UCTD. In particular, the interplay between Article 47 of the Charter, on the one hand, and the ECHR (Articles 6 and 13) and national constitutions, on the other, could be investigated further. Furthermore, this book does not question the legitimacy of judicial lawmaking as such. Neither does it necessarily strive for consistency, coherence or integration.[73] Rather, it attempts to explain the function(s) of a reference to Article 47 by uncovering the variables at play when it comes to its application in practice.

1.3.2. SELECTION OF NATIONAL LEGAL SYSTEMS: SPAIN AND THE NETHERLANDS

This book aims to explain how and why the impact of the CJEU's case law on Article 47 may diverge between Member States; it does not seek to identify a common core. From a top-down perspective, all national

---

70 ECtHR 8 April 2014, Appl. No. 17120/09 *Dhahbi v Italy.*

71 ECtHR 20 December 2018, Appl. No. 22853/15 *Merkantil Car Zrt. v Hungary*: further discussed in subsection 3.3.3 of this book.

72 Case C-168/15 *Tomášová v Slovenská republika – Ministerstvo spravodlivosti SR and Pohotovosť.*

73 See also Jan Vranken, 'Methodology of Legal Doctrinal Research' in Mark van Hoecke (ed), *Methodologies of Legal Research: Which Kind of Method for What Kind of Discipline?* (Hart Publishing 2010).

courts are equally bound by Article 47. However, different issues arise in different settings. The explanations for these issues are not purely legal: other dimensions, for example political, cultural and socio-economic, are relevant as well.

This book focuses on the legal and factual contexts of the analysed case law, in particular the implementation of the UCTD, the reception that the CJEU's case law has met with in national private law and civil procedure, and specific issues with judicial protection that have arisen in this context. Different remedies have been recognised, with a great variety of modalities, in the Member States' legal systems. The role of courts and the litigating parties also varies significantly. Moreover, whether, and to what extent, fundamental rights are used in judicial reasoning is related to the institutional positions, tasks and powers of civil courts in their respective jurisdictions. Their willingness to frame an issue in terms of EU fundamental rights also depends on systemic factors such as monist or dualist views on the interplay between EU law, fundamental rights and private law.[74] Colombi Ciacchi has distinguished a legal family of States that became totalitarian at some point in the twentieth century, such as Germany, Spain and Poland. In her view, this explains 'judicial activism' by civil courts there, which often apply national constitutional norms.[75] By contrast, in the Netherlands, there is no centralised system of constitutional review by the judiciary, and the ECHR plays a much bigger role than the national constitution.[76] This may shape the perception of the (added) value of Article 47, which is why the role of civil courts in the protection of fundamental rights is a relevant factor at the national level as well.

Spain was selected because it has the highest number of references to Article 47 in the CJEU's case law. Spanish civil courts have contributed significantly to the constitutionalisation of consumer protection under the UCTD, i.e. the integration of fundamental rights reasoning – and more specifically the Charter – in the adjudication of unfair terms cases. It could even be said they have been catalysts of the development of the

---

[74] On the structural relation between fundamental rights and private law, see Hugh Collins, 'On the (In)Compatibility of Human Rights Discourse and Private Law' in Hans-W Micklitz (ed), *Constitutionalization of European Private Law* (Oxford University Press 2014).

[75] Aurelia Colombi Ciacchi, 'European Fundamental Rights and Private Law: The Dutch System in the Context of Different Legal Families' in Bettina Heiderhoff, Sebastian Lohsse and Reinier Schulze (eds), *EU-Grundrechte und Privatrecht: EU Fundamental Rights and Private Law* (Nomos 2016) 209.

[76] Colombi Ciacchi (n 75) 218.

CJEU's case law in this respect.[77] The Spanish experience informs the CJEU's interpretation of the UCTD read in conjunction with Article 47. An analysis of the functions of a reference to Article 47 requires an understanding of the national background and the impact of the case law, not only in the relation between the CJEU and Spanish civil courts, but also in the inferences that can be drawn as to its meaning for civil courts in other Member States. This book aims to place the Spanish cases in their national setting, and to connect the Spanish and the European debates on effective judicial protection in unfair terms cases.

The Netherlands represents a legal system where Article 47 is less visible, at least in the case law on the UCTD. A comparison between Spain and the Netherlands may reveal how different court systems can impact on the role of Article 47. In the Netherlands, unlike in Spain, no clear (added) value of Article 47 has been recognised in unfair terms cases. Dutch civil courts seem to have found other ways to achieve effective judicial protection of consumers, which could be informative for courts in other Member States as well. Perhaps Dutch courts do not see a need to refer to Article 47, or perhaps they are simply unaware of its potential functions, despite their perceived 'loyalty' to the CJEU.[78] This book, therefore, aims to contribute to creating more awareness about these functions.

1.3.3. SELECTION OF CASE LAW

There is CJEU case law on the UCTD with explicit reference to Article 47 of the Charter,[79] whether made by the referring court, the CJEU or the

---

77 Juan Antonio Mayoral Díaz-Asensio, Dimitri Berberoff Ayuda and David Ordóñez Solís, 'El juez español como juez de la Unión Europea' [2013] Revista española de derecho europeo 127, 129.

78 Jasper Krommendijk, 'De civiele kamer en de prejudiciële procedure: kritisch doch loyaal aan het Hof van Justitie' [2019] Tijdschrift voor Civiele Rechtspleging 1, 13–14.

79 These are the various judgments with 'Directive 93/13/EEC' or 'Directive 93/13' in the title, which apparently do not include, e.g. cases in which the CJEU found it had no jurisdiction (such as *Margarit Panicello* and *Garzón Ramos* – see below). Therefore, the total number may be even higher. All cases before the CJEU cited in this book can be found in the *Répertoire de jurisprudence* (Digest of case law) on curia.europa.eu. The cut-off date for the case law analysis is 31 July 2019, except for three CJEU decisions, a Spanish Supreme Court judgment and a Dutch Supreme Court judgment, which came out afterwards. The dates and ECLI numbers of the CJEU decisions and AG Opinions can be found in the list of cases at the beginning of this book.

Advocate General (AG), originating from Spain,[80] Poland,[81] Slovakia,[82] Hungary,[83] Italy[84] and Romania.[85] In eight cases, the CJEU found either the UCTD to be inapplicable, or that the Court lacked jurisdiction, and/or the reference for a preliminary ruling was inadmissible.[86] In five cases, the compatibility of national legislation with Article 47, in light of the UCTD, was discussed only by the AG, not by the CJEU.[87] In one case, neither the CJEU nor the AG addressed a question regarding Article 47, presumably because they deemed it unnecessary to give an answer.[88] In 12 cases, the CJEU gave substantive consideration to Article 47, which will be elaborated in Chapter 3.[89] In six of those, it was the CJEU that brought up Article 47, not the referring court, and thus, the CJEU itself that acknowledged a fundamental rights dimension.[90]

---

80 Case C-40/08 *Asturcom Telecomunicaciones v Rodríguez Nogueira*; Case C-169/14 *Sánchez Morcillo I* (n 37) and Case C-539/14 *Sánchez Morcillo v BBVA* ('*Sánchez Morcillo II*', pertaining to the same case); Case C-49/14 *Finanmadrid v Albán Zambrano*; Case C-380/15 *Garzón Ramos v Banco de Caja España de Inversiones*; Case C-7/16 *Banco Popular Español v Giráldez Villar*; Joined Cases C-154/15, C-307/15 and C-308/15 *Gutiérrez Naranjo v Cajasur Banco, Palacios Martínez v BBVA, Banco Popular Español v Irles López and Torres Andreu*; Case C-503/15 *Margarit Panicello v Hernández Martínez*; Case C-426/17 *Barba Giménez v Carrión Lozano.*

81 Case C-119/15 *Biuro podróży 'Partner' v Prezes Urzędu Ochrony Konkurencji i Konsumentów*; Case C-176/17 *Profi Credit Polska v Wawrzosek*; Case C-632/17 *PKO Bank Polski v Michalski*; Case C-266/18 *Aqua Med v Skóra; Case C-495/19 Kancelaria Medius v RN.*

82 Case C-433/11 *SKP v Polhošová*; Case C-34/13 *Kušionová* (n 37); Case C-470/12 *Pohotovosť v Vašuta*; Case C-153/13 *Pohotovosť v Soroka*; Case C-485/19 *LH v Profi Credit Slovakia.*

83 Case C-472/11 *Banif Plus Bank v Csaba Csipai*; Case C-483/16 *Sziber v ERSTE Bank Hungary*; Case C-51/17 *OTP Bank v Ilyés*; Case C-118/17 *Dunai v ERSTE Bank Hungary*; Case C-34/18 *Lovasné Tóth v ERSTE Bank Hungary.*

84 Case C-344/17 *IJDF Italy Srl v Fernando Dionisio.*

85 Case C-92/14 *Tudoran v SC Suport Colect.*

86 Case C-433/11 *SKP*, Case C-153/13 *Pohotovosť v Soroka;* Case C-7/16 *Banco Popular Español;* Case C-92/14 *Tudoran;* Case C-380/15 *Garzón Ramos;* Case C-503/15 *Margarit Panicello;* Case C-344/17 *IJDF Italy;* Case C-426/17 *Barba Giménez.*

87 Case C-40/08 *Asturcom;* Case C-49/14 *Finanmadrid;* Case C-503/15 *Margarit Panicello;* Case C-51/17 *OTP Bank;* Case C-34/18 *Lovasné Toth.*

88 Case C-308/15 *Irles López.*

89 Case C-472/11 *Banif Plus Bank*, Case C-470/12 *Pohotovosť*; Case C-34/13 *Kušionová;* Case C-169/14 *Sánchez Morcillo I* and Case C-539/14 *Sánchez Morcillo II* (pertaining to the same case); Case C-119/15 *Biuro;* Case C-483/16 *Sziber;* Case C-632/17 *Profi Credit Polska;* Case C-632/17 *PKO Bank Polski;* Case C-118/17 *Dunai;* Case C-266/18 *Aqua Med;* Case C-495/19 *Kancelaria Medius.*

90 Case C-472/11 *Banif Plus Bank;* Case C-470/12 *Pohotovosť*; Case C-34/13 *Kušionová;* Case C-632/17 *Profi Credit Polska;* Case C-632/17 *PKO Bank Polski;* and Case C-266/18 *Aqua Med.* In *Kušionová*, the referring court had mentioned only Article 38 of the Charter, but the CJEU found the request related in essence to Article 47 of the Charter.

Chapters 2 and 3 also contain references to case law on the UCTD that does not mention Article 47, and, conversely, case law on Article 47 in other cases that do not pertain to the UCTD. Those references fall outside the scope of this book. They only serve to place the analysed case law in a broader setting, to get a better understanding of the distinguishing features of Article 47 in the context of the UCTD.

In Chapter 4, several hundred (published) decisions of Spanish civil courts that refer to Article 47 in unfair terms cases have been analysed.[91] All decisions encountered date from March 2013 onwards, i.e. after *Banif Plus Bank* (21 February 2013). Most decisions date from July 2014 or later, i.e. after *Sánchez Morcillo I* (17 July 2014) and *Kušionová* (10 September 2014). *Sánchez Morcillo* is the CJEU judgment that is referred to the most in the analysed case law from Spain.

In Chapter 5, the few (published) decisions of Dutch civil courts that refer to Article 47 of the Charter in unfair terms cases are discussed.[92] Possible explanations are sought for the low number of explicit references to Article 47 in the Netherlands compared to Spain. Whereas the CJEU's case law has led directly to legislative changes in Spain, its impact on Dutch (procedural law) can only be discovered through an analysis of judicial decisions and guidelines that are largely focused on the *ex officio* doctrine. Drawing parallels between Dutch and Spanish case law is expected to lay bare the different ways civil courts provide effective

91 The database used for the Spanish case law analysis is Aranzadi, with the following search terms: '*art. 47*' or '*artículo 47*' + '*Carta*' or '*Carta de los Derechos Fundamentales*' + '*consumidor*' or '*consumidores*'. Aranzadi is a database operated by Thomson Reuters; it is said to be the most widely used database by legal professionals in Spain for searching and citing case law. A similar search was conducted in CENDOJ, the public database of the Spanish Judiciary (*Poder Judicial*), but the earliest decision that appeared in this search was dated 18 December 2014, whereas the earliest decision in Aranzadi dated from 25 March 2013. Aranzadi has more filter options than CENDOJ. It also provides short summaries in the overview of search results, and references to related decisions. In both databases, almost all published decisions are from *Audiencias Provinciales* (Courts of Appeal). Due to the high number of cases and the names of natural persons being mostly anonymised, only the names of high-profile cases are mentioned. The other cases can be identified by the Aranzadi reference (JUR\) or the ECLI number, if available.

92 The database used for the Dutch case law analysis is rechtspraak.nl, the public database of the Dutch Judiciary (*De Rechtspraak*), with the following search terms: '*artikel* 47' of 'art. 47' + '*Handvest*' of '*Grondrechtenhandvest*' + '*consument*'. Some judgments are also published in legal journals, sometimes with annotations. References to these journals are provided on rechtspraak.nl as well. In this book, annotations are only mentioned when they have been consulted as a separate source. Due to the names of natural persons being mostly anonymised, only the names of high-profile cases are mentioned. The other cases can be identified by the ECLI number.

judicial protection in light of the Directive. This may also show the different civil courts how they could learn from one another.

Both chapters also give brief descriptions of the impact of the UCTD on national civil procedure, and the role of civil courts in the system of constitutional review and the protection of fundamental procedural rights and safeguards. This provides relevant background information, and places the analysed case law in its applicable national context.

1.4. STRUCTURE

The analytical framework will be set out in Chapter 2. Firstly, the chapter examines the normative content of Article 47 – its core components, on which the structure of the three subsequent chapters is modelled – as well as its scope of application and direct effect. This translates into the functions ascribed to Article 47 in the literature, which will be discussed in the second part of the chapter. After briefly discussing the emergence of Article 47 in the context of the CJEU's case law concerning the UCTD, which will be further elaborated in Chapter 3, the chapter catalogues the functions attributed to Article 47 by other authors. It thus provides a basis for the case law analysis that forms the core of this book.

Chapter 3 examines all decisions of the CJEU and Opinions of the AG that explicitly refer to Article 47 in the context of the UCTD. It concentrates on the cases where the CJEU, the AG or both have given extensive consideration to Article 47. Chapter 4 maps out the references to Article 47 by Spanish civil courts and discusses these in light of several procedural issues that have arisen under the UCTD. A particular focus will be on the cases that led to a preliminary ruling of the CJEU. Chapter 5 focuses on the references to Article 47 by Dutch civil courts or, rather, the lack thereof.

Chapter 6 contains a synthesis of the key findings, in answer to the research questions. It critically evaluates the analysed case law by contrasting the conclusions from Chapters 4 and 5 with the functions of Article 47, as mapped out in Chapter 2, and further identified in the CJEU's case law, discussed in Chapter 3. It also takes a comparative perspective that sheds light on discrepancies between the CJEU's case law on Article 47 and the way Spanish civil courts refer to the provision in unfair terms cases, which leads to valuable insights for Dutch civil courts as well. Chapter 6 closes with a few observations as to the unfulfilled potential of Article 47, and considerations for its (future) application by national civil courts.

CHAPTER 2

ANALYTICAL FRAMEWORK

Normative Content, Scope and Functions Ascribed to Article 47

This chapter places the emergence of Article 47 of the Charter in the context of the UCTD. It introduces the main legal characteristics and constraints of Article 47, which inform its functions in unfair terms cases. It also outlines the views and expectations voiced in the literature as to these functions. The questions and issues raised in this chapter will be revisited and further explored in the following chapters.

The first part of this chapter sets out the normative content of Article 47, i.e. its core components (section 2.1). It also dives into its scope of application and direct effect (section 2.2). The second part considers the functions ascribed in legal doctrine to Article 47, which must be understood against the background of the CJEU's case law concerning national remedies and procedures under the UCTD (section 2.3). These functions range from a function largely parallel to the notion of effectiveness, to a positive standard of effective judicial protection with a separate identity (sections 2.4 and 2.5). The different views are distilled into five main categories (section 2.6), which will be referenced throughout this book.

2.1. NORMATIVE CONTENT OF ARTICLE 47: A MULTI-FACETED PROVISION

2.1.1. RIGHTS, REMEDIES AND PROCEDURES

Article 47 of the Charter guarantees, first and foremost, the fundamental right to an effective (judicial) remedy. The term 'remedy' has many meanings: a medicine that alleviates, eliminates or prevents disease; a cure; a right 'born of a wrong' or 'injustice'; a cause of action; or an enforceable court order or judgment.[93] The CJEU does not use the term 'remedy' univocally. In general, it could be said that *rights* create substantive legal positions for individuals and *remedies* are intended to enforce rights, or to redress infringements of rights.[94] As Zuckerman has put it:

> 'In a society governed by the rule of law, we all have an interest in rights being respected and wrongs being remedied. For in the absence of redress for wrong there is no value to rights and no reason to behave according to the law'.[95]

In this respect, a distinction can be made between primary remedies, intended to enforce a right, and secondary remedies, which constitute new claims (secondary rights) in response to the infringement of a (primary) right.[96] The term 'remedy' may refer to a substantive remedy – a claim-right or cause of action – for example the provision that unfair terms are voidable. It may also refer to a procedural remedy – a means of recourse giving access to court – for example the possibility of requesting interim relief or bringing an appeal.[97]

Whereas substantive remedies (for example one party paying damages to another) are generally considered as part of private law, procedural remedies could be regarded as part of public law. Civil courts are public institutions that perform the public function of the administration of civil justice.[98] Civil procedure pertains to a State's judicial organisation, jurisdiction and the conduct of court proceedings.[99] The distinction between substantive and procedural remedies is, nevertheless, not clear-cut,

---

93 Peter Birks, 'Rights, Wrongs and Remedies' (2000) 20 Oxford Journal of Legal Studies 1, 9.

94 Engström (n 64) 577, 582–583; Van Gerven (n 10) 502–503. This reflects the view that enforcement is a consequence of subjective rights, but not a precondition for their existence: Ebers (n 37) 96.

95 Adrian Zuckerman, Professor of Civil Procedure at the University of Oxford, 'Comment on: The principle of effective judicial protection in EU law', 18 June 2010 (PDF on file with the author).

96 Thomas Eilmansberger, 'The Relationship between Rights and Remedies in EC Law: In Search of the Missing Link' (2004) 41 Common Market Law Review 1199, 1199.

97 Reich (n 67) 123; Ebers (n 37) 52–53.

98 Peter Rott, 'The Court of Justice's Principle of Effectiveness and its Unforeseeable Impact on Private Law Relationships' in Dorota Leczykiewicz and Stephen Weatherill (eds), *The Involvement of EU Law in Private Law Relationships* (Hart Publishing 2013) 89–90. See also Storskrubb (n 54) 296; Zampia Vernadaki, 'Civil Procedure Harmonization in the EU: Unravelling the Policy Considerations' (2013) 9 Journal of Contemporary European Research 298, 298.

99 Tulibacka (n 36) 1532.

and not uniformly established across all EU Member States.[100] It can be said that, taken together, remedial and procedural rules determine when, for what, by whom and how – i.e. under what conditions – a legal action can be brought.[101] The CJEU mainly refers to Article 47 of the Charter as encompassing procedural rights and safeguards, as this chapter and the next will show. Therefore, the term 'remedy' will hereinafter be used to refer to *procedural* or *judicial* remedies, unless indicated otherwise.[102]

2.1.2. CORE COMPONENTS OF ARTICLE 47

Article 47 of the Charter is multifaceted: it comprises both the right to an effective remedy before a tribunal (first paragraph) and fair trial or due process requirements (second and third paragraphs). Pursuant to Article 52(1) of the Charter, the essence of Charter rights, including Article 47, must always be respected: Dougan has referred to 'an irreducible core of protection'.[103] Restrictions on those rights must be justified, and should not undermine their essential content.[104] Which components constitute the core of Article 47, and to what extent they can be restricted, are subject to judicial interpretation.[105] Most requirements following from Article 47 have been interpreted and construed judicially.[106] To the extent that there is consensus, the following list gives an indication of Article 47's core components:[107]

(i) The right of access to an independent and impartial tribunal.
(ii) The right to an effective remedy.

---

[100] See further Van Gerven (n 10) 502, 525; Reich (n 1) 323; Ebers (n 37) 52; Olivier Dubos, 'The Origins of the Proceduralisation of EU Law: A Grey Area of European Federalism' (2015) 8 Review of European Administrative Law 7, 8.

[101] Van Gerven (n 10) 524; Hanna Schebesta, 'Procedural Theory in EU Law' in Kai Purnhagen and Peter Rott (eds), *Varieties of European Economic Law and Regulation: Liber Amicorum for Hans Micklitz* (Springer 2014) 853; Półtorak (n 20) 9–10.

[102] On substantive remedies in private law from an EU law perspective, see further Aronstein (n 31).

[103] Michael Dougan, 'The Vicissitudes of Life at the Coalface: Remedies and Procedures for Enforcing Union Law before the National Courts' in Paul Craig and Gráinne De Búrca (eds), *The Evolution of EU Law* (Oxford University Press 2011) 431.

[104] Joined Cases C-569/16 and C-570/16 *Stadt Wuppertal v Bauer*, para. 59. See further subsection 2.4.1 of this book.

[105] Takis Tridimas and Giulia Gentile, 'The Essence of Rights: An Unreliable Boundary?' (2019) 20 German Law Journal 794, 812.

[106] Vernadaki (n 66) 61; Malu Beijer, *The Limits of Fundamental Rights Protection by the EU. The Scope for the Development of Positive Obligations* (Intersentia 2017) 309.

[107] See, e.g. Case C-199/11 *Otis*, para. 48. For an extensive overview, see, e.g. Laurent Pech and Debbie Sayers, 'Article 47 –Right to an Effective Remedy. D. Analysis. VII–VIII.

(iii) The principle of equality of arms.
(iv) The rights of defence, in particular the right to be heard.
(v) The right to legal aid.
(vi) The right to adjudication within a reasonable time.

A short introduction as to what these core components entail, in so far as they are relevant to this book, is provided below. These components will be further elaborated in the subsequent chapters. Not all of them play equally important roles in the analysed case law. The right to legal aid and the right to adjudication within a reasonable time are not explicitly addressed as such. Therefore, they will be discussed only briefly here, and not separately in Chapter 3.

2.1.2.1. Access to an Independent and Impartial Tribunal

The first core component of Article 47 of the Charter is the right of access to court.[108] Article 47 refers to 'an independent and impartial tribunal established by law'. The CJEU's case law on Article 267 of the Treaty on the Functioning of the European Union (TFEU) clarifies when a body is considered a court or tribunal within the meaning of EU law. This depends on certain conditions, inter alia whether it is established by law, is permanent, has compulsory jurisdiction, has *inter partes* (i.e. contentious) procedure, applies rules of law, is independent and gives judgment in proceedings leading to decisions of a judicial nature.[109] A court or tribunal must exercise its functions autonomously and

Article 47(2)' in Steve Peers and others (eds), *The EU Charter of Fundamental Rights: A Commentary* (Hart Publishing 2014); Vernadaki (n 66). See also European Union Agency for Fundamental Rights and Council of Europe, *Handbook on European law relating to access to justice* (2016), which can be consulted on <https://fra.europa.eu/en/publication/2016/handbook-european-law-relating-access-justice> (last accessed 24 September 2021); Fabrizio Cafaggai and Federica Casarosa (eds), *ACTIONES Handbook on the Techniques of Judicial Interactions in the Application of the EU Charter. Module 3 – Right to an Effective Remedy* (EUI 2017), available via <https://cjc.eui.eu/projects/actiones/actiones-platform/> (last accessed 24 September 2021).

108 See, e.g. Joined Cases C-317/08, C-318/08, C-319/08 and C-320/08 *Alassini*, para. 62; C-199/11 *Otis*, paras. 48-49; Case C-470/12 *Pohotovosť*, para. 53; Case C-112/13 *A v B*, para. 51; Case C-437/13 *Unitrading v Staatssecretaris van Financiën*, para. 20; Case C-34/13 *Kušionová*, para. 59.

109 See, e.g. Case C-64/16 *Associação Sindical dos Juízes Portugueses v Tribunal de Contas*, para. 38; Case C-503/15 *Margarit Panicello*, paras. 27–28. See also Recommendations of the CJEU to national courts and tribunals in relation to the initiation of preliminary ruling proceedings, 25 November 2016, OJ 2016, C 439/01 No. 9.

impartially, with no interest in the outcome of the proceedings apart from the strict application of the rule of law.[110] To be able to determine a dispute concerning rights and obligations arising under EU law, a court or tribunal must have the power to consider all the questions of fact and law that are relevant to the case before it.[111]

The right of access to court is not absolute. An example of a restriction on the right of access to court that could be justified is the introduction of additional procedural steps before an action can be brought. The case of *Alassini*, for instance, concerned an out-of-court settlement procedure under Italian law, which formed a mandatory step for individuals to bring a claim against, in this case, a telecom provider. The CJEU balanced this restriction on the right of access to court against objectives of general interest, i.e. the facilitation of quicker and less expensive settlement of disputes, and alleviation of the burden on the court system.[112] The legislation at issue pursued a legitimate aim and was not disproportionate. The CJEU also referred to the principle of effectiveness: it was not practically impossible or excessively difficult for individuals to exercise their rights derived from, in this case, the Universal Service Directive.[113] This may be different if the national court were to find that the settlement procedure could be accessed only by electronic means, or that no interim measures were available in urgent situations.[114] The CJEU adopted a similar reasoning in *Menini*, which concerned a mandatory mediation procedure under Italian law. The Consumer ADR Directive (ADR Directive)[115] does not preclude mediation as a mandatory preliminary step, as long as it does not prevent the parties from exercising their rights of access to the judicial system. The CJEU based its conclusion on the principle of effective judicial protection, with reference to *Alassini*,[116] and the ADR Directive itself, which explicitly refers to Article 47 of the Charter.[117]

---

110 See, e.g. Case C-503/15 *Margarit Panicello*, paras, 37–38.

111 Case C-199/11 *Otis*, para. 49; Case C-403/16 *El Hassani v Minister Spraw Zagranicznych*, para. 39.

112 Joined Cases C-317/08, C-318/08, C-319/08 and C-320/08 *Alassini*, paras. 63–64.

113 Directive 2002/22/EC on Universal Service and users' rights relating to electronic communications networks and services (OJ L108, 24 April 2002, p. 51).

114 Joined Cases C-317/08, C-318/08, C-319/08 and C-320/08 *Alassini*, paras. 53–60.

115 Directive 2013/11/EU on alternative dispute resolution for consumer disputes (OJ L165, 18 June 2013, p. 63).

116 Case C-75/16 *Menini and Rampanelli v Banco Popolare Società Cooperative*, paras. 55 and 61.

117 Recital 45: 'The right to an effective remedy and the right to a fair trial are fundamental rights laid down in Article 47 of the Charter of Fundamental Rights of the European Union. Therefore, ADR procedures should not be designed to replace court procedures

Other examples of restrictions on the right of access to court are time limits and the costs of judicial proceedings.[118] Costs must not represent an insurmountable obstacle to access to the courts:[119] 'prohibitively expensive justice means no justice'.[120] The question of to what extent restrictions to the right of access to court and other core components of Article 47 can be justified will be considered further below.[121]

2.1.2.2. *An Effective (Judicial) Remedy*

As observed above, the right to an effective (judicial) remedy is generally associated with the opportunity of obtaining actual redress for an infringement of one's rights, which presupposes access to justice.[122] What constitutes an *effective* remedy depends on the circumstances of the case, as long as the remedy is effective in practice, as well as in law.[123] In the words of AG Kokott:

> '[Article 47 of the Charter] is invoked mainly on account of its procedural requirements, but they are merely a means to an end, namely to guarantee an *effective* remedy. However, a remedy is effective only if the finding of infringements of the law has appropriate consequences'.[124]

Article 47 requires the availability of a *means of recourse* to realise the appropriate consequences of a rights violation. What those consequences

---

and should not deprive consumers or traders of their rights to seek redress before the courts. This Directive should not prevent parties from exercising their right of access to the judicial system. In cases where a dispute could not be resolved through a given ADR procedure whose outcome is not binding, the parties should subsequently not be prevented from initiating judicial proceedings in relation to that dispute.' On ADR and procedural safeguards, see further Anne Kamphorst, 'The Right to a Fair Trial in Online Consumer Dispute Resolution' [2019] Journal of European Consumer and Market Law 175.

118 See, e.g. Case C-73/16 *Puškár v Finančné riaditeľstvo Slovenskej republiky and Kriminálny úrad finančnej správy*, para. 76. The fact that the claimant has not been deterred, in practice, from asserting the claim is not, in itself, sufficient to establish that the proceedings are not prohibitively expensive: Case C-260/11 *The Queen, on the application of David Edwards v Environment Agency*, para. 43.

119 Case C-279/09 *DEB*, para. 61.

120 Case C-470/16 *North East Pylon Pressure Campaign Limited and Maura Sheehy v An Bord Pleanála Minister for Communications, Climate Action and Environment*, Opinion of AG Bobek, point 34.

121 See subsection 2.4.1 of this book.

122 Handbook on European law relating to access to justice (n 107), 92.

123 Handbook on European law relating to access to justice (n 107), 95.

124 Case C-411/17 *Inter-Environnement Wallonie ASBL v Conseil des ministres*, Opinion of AG Kokott, point 199.

are does not follow from Article 47 itself. An effective (judicial) remedy might be understood as the possibility of appeal before a court against an administrative decision or the annulment of a legislative act. This type of judicial review does not normally occur in private law adjudication.[125] Nevertheless, access to a competent court to seek redress for an infringement of one's EU rights is also an important prerequisite here.

Another prerequisite is the finality of judicial decisions. The effectiveness of a (judicial) remedy would be illusory if a judicial decision that is final and binding remains inoperative. There must be a means of securing observance of the judgment.[126] In the words of AG Bobek:

> '[Article 47] cannot be reduced to the "input" stage leading to a court's decision, namely the mere possibility to "access the court building", institute proceedings, and be allowed to plead one's case. It naturally also includes certain requirements as to the "output" of the entire endeavour, that is, the stage of execution of the final decision'.[127]

The execution of a judgment is, therefore, an integral part of the right to a fair trial.[128]

2.1.2.3. Equality of Arms

Article 47 includes the principle of equality of arms, which is 'a corollary of the very concept of a fair hearing'.[129] It constitutes a specific expression of the general principle of equality before the law, or non-discrimination, laid down in Article 20 of the Charter.[130] Each party must be afforded a reasonable opportunity to present their case under conditions that do not place them at a substantial disadvantage vis-à-vis their opponent.[131] The aim is to ensure a procedural balance between the parties, inter alia by guaranteeing that any document submitted to the court may be examined and challenged by any party to the proceedings.[132]

---

125 Storskrubb (n 54) 296–298.

126 Case C-752/18 *Deutsche Umwelthilfe v Freistaat Bayern*, para. 35. See also Wagner (n 65) 34.

127 Case C-556/17 *Torubarov v Bevándorlási és Menekültügyi Hivatal*, Opinion of AG Bobek, point 59.

128 Case C-205/15 *Direcţia Generală Regională a Finanţelor Publice Braşov (DGRFP) v Toma and Biroul Executorului Judecătoresc Horaţiu-Vasile Cruduleci ('Toma')*, para. 43.

129 Case C-205/15 *Toma*, para. 47.

130 Case C-205/15 *Toma*, para. 36.

131 See also Case C-169/14 *Sánchez Morcillo I*, para. 49; Case C-682/15 *Berlioz*, para. 96.

132 Case C-199/11 *Otis*, paras. 71–72.

The right of access to court, the right to legal aid and the principle of equality of arms are closely related. The case of *Toma*, for instance, was about an exemption from court fees for legal persons governed by public law that did not apply to legal persons governed by private law. This could be framed as an issue of access, but also of equality before the law.[133] The CJEU considered the case under Article 47, but ultimately found no violation: the applicants were not placed in a clearly less advantageous position compared with their opponents, and the fairness of the procedure was not, therefore, called into question.[134]

2.1.2.4. Rights of Defence

The rights of defence occupy a prominent position in the organisation and conduct of a fair hearing.[135] The right to be heard – also referred to as the principle of *audi alteram partem*[136] – and the so-called adversarial principle both form part of the rights of defence, which are inherent to Article 47.[137] In *Banif Plus Bank*, the CJEU reiterated that:

> '[I]n order to satisfy the requirements associated with the right to a fair hearing, it is important for the parties to be apprised of, and to be able to debate and be heard on, the matters of fact and of law which will determine the outcome of the proceedings'.[138]

The right to be heard applies in all judicial proceedings,[139] and entails that everyone should have the possibility of setting out their views before a decision is taken that could adversely affect their interests.[140] The time period within which the right to be heard must be exercised should be sufficient to allow the parties to make known their views effectively.[141]

---

133 Case C-205/15 *Toma*, paras. 45–46 and paras. 35–36, respectively.

134 Case C-205/15 *Toma*, para. 54.

135 See, e.g. Case C-325/11 *Alder and Alder v Orlowska and Orlowski*, para. 35.

136 Literal translation: 'hear the other side'.

137 Case C-300/11 *ZZ v Secretary of State for the Home Department*, paras. 55 and 57.

138 Case C-472-11 *Banif Plus Bank*, para. 30, with reference to Case C-89/08 *European Commission v Ireland*, paras. 55–56.

139 Case C-277/11 *MM v Ministry for Justice, Equality and Law Reform*, para. 82.

140 Case C-418/11 *Texdata Software*, para. 83; C-119/15 *Biuro*, Opinion of AG Saugmandsgaard Øe, point 61, referring to settled case law of the CJEU.

141 See, e.g. Case C-69/10 *Samba Diouf v Ministre du Travail, de l'Emploi et de l'Immigration*, paras. 66–67: the period prescribed must be sufficient, in practical terms, to enable the applicant to prepare and bring an effective action.

2.1.2.5. *Other Components*

The requirement of adjudication within a reasonable time aims to protect the parties against excessive procedural delays, but there are no set time frames to determine what is reasonable:[142] this depends on the circumstances of each case, such as its complexity and the conduct of the parties.[143]

Furthermore, Article 47 specifically provides that everyone shall have the possibility of being advised, defended and represented, and that legal aid shall be made available to those who lack sufficient resources, in so far as such aid is necessary to ensure effective access to justice. In the case of *DEB*, the CJEU held that the national court assessing the conditions for granting legal aid – in the form of assistance by a lawyer or an exemption from costs – must take several factors into account, including the importance of what is at stake for the applicant, the applicant's capacity to represent themselves effectively, and the costs of the proceedings.[144] The bottom line is that it is important for litigants not to be denied the opportunity to present their cases effectively before the court.[145]

2.1.3. ARTICLE 47 OF THE CHARTER AND THE ECHR

Within the EU, the rights to an effective remedy and a fair hearing are also protected by national constitutions and, in particular, Articles 6 and 13 ECHR. However, the right to effective judicial protection, recognised as part of EU law by virtue of Article 47 of the Charter, has acquired a separate identity and content that is partly shaped, but not defined, by Articles 6 and 13 ECHR.[146] The CJEU has held that Article 47 must be 'interpreted in its context, in light of other provisions of EU law, the law of the Member States and the case law of the European Court of Human Rights'.[147] To clarify the normative content of Article 47 and, in particular, its embedding in EU law, it is helpful to contrast it with the ECHR.

---

142 Handbook on European law relating to access to justice (n 107), 135–136.

143 Case C-58/12 *Groupe Gascogne v European Commission*, para. 85; Case C-385/07 *Der Grüne Punkt – Duales System Deutschland v Commission of the European Communities*, para. 186.

144 Case C-279/09 *DEB*, para. 61.

145 Case C-279/09 *DEB*, para. 45.

146 Case C-69/10 *Samba Diouf*, Opinion of AG Cruz Villalón, point 39. See also Safjan and Düsterhaus (n 13) 38.

147 C-279/09 *DEB*, para. 37. Pursuant to Article 6(3) TEU, the fundamental rights as guaranteed by the ECHR constitute general principles of EU law.

All current EU Member States are parties to the ECHR, but its effect in national law – in particular, its role in judicial reasoning by national civil courts as reflected in their decisions – may vary. In Spain, Article 24 of the Spanish Constitution serves as the primary basis to assess alleged infringements in consumer cases where the right to effective judicial protection is at stake.[148] This provision recognises the individual right to effective judicial protection, which is then interpreted in light of the ECHR. The dual regime of fundamental rights protection – at the national level and at EU level – led to a preliminary reference in *Melloni*. The CJEU held that the Member States could apply a higher fundamental rights standard than the Charter, provided that the primacy, unity and effectiveness of EU law were not compromised.[149] The protection of fundamental rights within the EU must be ensured within the framework of the structure and objectives of the EU.[150] National authorities and courts are allowed more room for manoeuvre where an EU legal act, for example a minimum harmonisation directive like the UCTD, calls for national implementing measures, as long as these can be realised with respect for both the effectiveness of EU law and the fundamental rights protected by the Charter, as interpreted by the CJEU.[151] In Chapter 4, examples will be given of cases where the CJEU provided a higher level of protection, in the context of the UCTD, than the Spanish Constitutional Court.[152]

In the Netherlands, Article 6 ECHR appears to be the primary reference. Dutch civil courts generally assume that Article 47 of the Charter and Article 6 ECHR are interchangeable.[153] Even though there is overlap between the two provisions, the Dutch courts' assumption is not entirely correct, for various reasons.

Firstly, Article 47 of the Charter has direct effect, irrespective of the status accorded to it in national law.[154]

Secondly, unlike Article 6 ECHR, the right to a fair hearing of Article 47 of the Charter is not confined to disputes concerning civil rights and

148 See further subsections 4.1.2 and 4.1.3 of this book.

149 Case C-399/11 *Melloni v Ministerio Fiscal*, para. 60, with reference to Article 53 of the Charter. See also Case C-206/13 *Siracusa v Regione Sicilia – Soprintendenza Beni Culturali e Ambientali di Palermo*, paras. 31–32; Case C-112/13 *A v B*, para. 44.

150 Case C-399/11 *Melloni v Ministerio Fiscal*, Opinion of AG Bot, point 107.

151 Case C-399/11 *Melloni v Ministerio Fiscal*, Opinion of AG Bot, points 124 and 127; Case C-476/17 *v Hütter and Schneider-Esleben*, paras. 79–80. See also Hilde K Ellingsen, 'Effective Judicial Protection of Individual Data Protection Rights: *Puškár*' (2018) 55 Common Market Law Review 1879, 1089, 1091.

152 See subsections 4.3.2 and 4.4.2 of this book.

153 See subsection 5.1.2.

154 See further subsection 2.2.2 below.

obligations or criminal charges, but extends to all areas of EU law, including administrative law.[155] At the same time, Article 6 ECHR is cross-sectoral: it applies to everyone within the jurisdiction of the State parties (Article 1 ECHR), and to all civil proceedings regardless of the subject matter. The Charter only binds the Member States when they are implementing EU law (Article 51(1) of the Charter). Thus, the application of Article 47 is confined to the scope of EU law.[156] This could be seen as a limitation. However, it could also be seen as an extension: EU law may provide a higher level of protection (Article 52(3) of the Charter). Article 47 of the Charter may impose more demanding requirements than Articles 6 and 13 ECHR. Examples will be given in subsequent chapters where Article 47 seems to go beyond a minimum level of protection when read in conjunction with the UCTD.[157]

Thirdly, Article 47 also protects the right to an effective remedy before a tribunal. Unlike Article 13 ECHR, Article 47 of the Charter may be relied upon in respect of any EU rights, not only the rights set forth in which it is contained.[158] While the ECHR does not explicitly provide for any specific consumer rights,[159] EU law does. This emphasises the special importance of Article 47 of the Charter in the context of EU consumer law. Article 47 is not connected to weaker party protection as such, but in unfair terms cases it is read in conjunction with the Directive.

And, lastly, the ECtHR and the CJEU have different institutional positions, although there is no formal hierarchy between their decisions.[160] The ECtHR may find a violation of the ECHR in a concrete case and provide a 'safety net', in the form of compensation, to an individual applicant when domestic remedies have been exhausted.[161]

155 Explanations relating to the Charter of Fundamental Rights [2007] OJ C303/02, 29–30.

156 See further subsection 2.2.1 below.

157 See, more specifically, e.g. subsections 4.4.2 and 5.2.1 below.

158 Sacha Prechal, 'The Court of Justice and Effective Judicial Protection: What Has the Charter Changed?' in Christophe Paulussen and others (eds), *Fundamental Rights in International and European Law: Public and Private Law Perspectives* (TMC Asser Press 2015) 148.

159 Benöhr (n 20) 49; Collins (n 74) 33. On weaker party protection and the ECtHR, see Jan Zglinski, 'Doing Too Little or Too Much? Private Law Before the European Court of Human Rights' (2018) 37 Yearbook of European Law 1, 25–27.

160 See, e.g. Aida Torres Pérez, *Conflicts of Rights in the European Union: A Theory of Supranational Adjudication* (Oxford University Press 2009) 31–32.

161 Martin Kuijer, 'Fundamental Rights Protection in the Legal Order of the European Union', in Adam Lazowski and Steven Blockmans (eds), *Research Handbook on EU Institutional Law* (Elgar Publishing 2016) 244.

But its case law is case-specific, and not the only source of interpretation for the CJEU. The CJEU may assess the validity of EU law and interpret it, in response to a request of a national civil court for a preliminary ruling about a question of EU law (Article 267 TFEU). Exhaustion of local remedies is not required. Many cases do not, or only partially, concern fundamental rights issues.

In short, it could be argued that the Charter should now be the primary point of reference as regards fundamental rights in EU law. In cases involving the right to effective judicial protection, the CJEU has repeatedly stated that it is necessary to refer only to Article 47 of the Charter.[162] This does not mean that other instruments have become irrelevant. On the contrary, the ECHR still offers a minimum level of protection, which cannot be restricted or adversely affected (Article 53 of the Charter). Moreover, the interpretation of the ECHR remains instructive for the CJEU.

2.2. SCOPE AND DIRECT EFFECT OF ARTICLE 47 IN THE CONTEXT OF THE UCTD

2.2.1. SCOPE OF APPLICATION

2.2.1.1. Scope Ratione Materiae: *Applicability of Article 47 in Unfair Terms Cases*

The applicability of Article 47 of the Charter to the adjudication of disputes under the UCTD was not immediately evident. National rules of civil procedure have often not been specifically designed for consumer litigation. The EU does not have a general competence in the field of civil procedure. Moreover, the Member States have retained the competence to lay down detailed procedural rules for the enforcement and protection of the subjective rights that the UCTD confers on consumers.[163] Therefore, the question was whether national procedural law could be seen as an implementation of EU consumer law for the purposes of engaging Article 47.

[162] Case C-682/15 *Berlioz*, para. 54; Case C-199/11 *Otis*, para. 47; Case C-386/10 *Chalkor AE Epexergasias Metallon v European Commission*, para. 51.

[163] See further section 2.3 below.

The Charter does not fully harmonise fundamental rights protection in the EU; it is not an all-embracing fundamental rights regime.[164] Charter provisions cannot, in and of themselves, trigger their own application, or form the basis of any new powers of the EU or the CJEU.[165] The CJEU's fundamental rights jurisdiction is limited to interpreting provisions of (primary and secondary) EU law in light of the Charter.[166] Article 47 expressly refers to the protection of rights (and freedoms) guaranteed by EU law. This indicates that it has an accessory character: its application requires a connecting link with another instrument of EU law.[167]

At the same time, the CJEU interprets Article 51(1) of the Charter broadly: situations covered by EU law cannot exist without the fundamental rights guaranteed by the Charter being applicable.[168] In other words, the applicability of EU law triggers the applicability of Article 47, regardless of the existence or absence of harmonised remedies and procedures.[169] Article 47 encompasses several procedural rights and safeguards that must be observed in all cases covered by EU law, including cases concerning unfair terms in consumer contracts.[170]

---

164 Weatherill, Vogenauer and Weingerl (n 15) 267; Olha Cherednychenko, 'The EU Charter of Fundamental Rights and Consumer Credit: Towards Responsible Lending?' in Hugh Collins (ed), *European Contract Law and the Charter of Fundamental Rights* (Intersentia 2017) 143. On the limits of the EU fundamental rights regime, see Beijer (n 106).

165 Prechal (n 158) 146.

166 See, e.g. Case C-403/16 *El Hassani*, para. 33. See further Malu Beijer, 'Active Guidance of Fundamental Rights Protection by the Court of Justice of the European Union: Exploring the Possibilities of a Positive Obligations Doctrine' (2015) 8 Review of European Administrative Law 127, 132, 136.

167 Pech and Sayers (n 107) 1215.

168 Case C-617/10 *Åklagaren v Åkerberg Fransson*, paras. 18–21; Case C-206/13 *Siracusa v Regione Sicilia – Soprintendenza Beni Culturali e Ambientali di Palermo*, paras. 24–25; Case C-205/15 *Toma*, para. 23. See also Beijer (n 166) 137.

169 See, e.g. Case C-243/15 *Lesoochranárske zoskupenie tegen Obvodný úrad Trenčín (Brown Bears II)*, para. 65. Safjan and Düsterhaus (n 13) 25; Janek Tomasz Nowak, 'Considerations on the Impact of EU Law on National Civil Procedure: Recent Examples from Belgium' in Vesna Lazić and Steven Stuij (eds), *International Dispute Resolution: Selected Issues in International Litigation and Arbitration (Short Studies in Private International Law)* (TMC Asser Press 2018) 8; Koen Lenaerts, 'The Court of Justice of the European Union and the Protection of Fundamental Rights' [2011] Polish Yearbook of International Law 79, 87.

170 The *Sánchez Morcillo* case, for instance, related to mortgage enforcement proceedings where unfair terms were not initially even at issue. AG Wahl had concluded that the case did not concern the implementation of EU law. This may be true to the extent that the applicable procedural rules pertained to enforcement against *all* mortgage debtors, not only consumers. However, the CJEU held that enforcement proceedings may fall within the scope of the UCTD, where they are based on mortgage loan

It can, nevertheless, be debated whether Article 47 may impose more far-reaching requirements than the instrument of EU law that triggers its application.[171] The UCTD is a minimum harmonisation directive. The Charter is arguably not applicable where the Member States may provide a higher level of (substantive) protection,[172] or where EU law leaves contractual autonomy untouched, for instance in respect of B2B contracts,[173] or in other cases – such as property and non-contractual liability – not covered by the Directive.[174]

However, directives must be implemented and interpreted in conformity with Article 47.[175] National procedural rules can have an impact on the 'protection guarantees' resulting from the UCTD read in light of Article 47.[176] It could, therefore, be submitted that the Member States and their national civil courts are bound by Article 47 even where they have procedural autonomy, and are free to choose 'adequate and effective means' to combat unfair terms.[177] As Bobek put it in his much-cited article 'Why There is no Principle of "Procedural Autonomy" of the Member States', once a right originates in EU law, its effective enforcement potentially covers all aspects of national procedural law.[178] It could be said that the same applies to Article 47; if so, this would have potentially wide ramifications. This will be further explored in Chapter 3.

---

agreements concluded with consumers. In that event, those proceedings are subject to the requirements arising out of the CJEU's case law on the effective protection of consumers under the UCTD. This implies a requirement of judicial protection, guaranteed by Article 47 of the Charter, that is binding on national courts: Case C-169/14 *Sánchez Morcillo I*, paras. 25 and 35.

171 See, e.g. Case C-193/17 *Cresco Investigation v Achatzi*, where the CJEU went beyond the requirements of the applicable directive to impose an obligation on national courts to guarantee individuals the legal protection afforded to employees under Article 21 of the Charter (paras. 78 and 80).

172 Marija Bartl and Candida Leone, 'Minimum Harmonisation after *Alemo-Herron*: The Janus Face of EU Fundamental Rights Review' (2015) 11 European Constitutional Law Review 140. See, differently, Leczykiewicz (n 17) 484.

173 Reich (n 67) 122.

174 Case C-349/18 *Nationale Maatschappij der Belgische Spoorwegen v Kanyeba*, paras. 72–73; Case C-598/15 *Banco Santander v Sánchez López*, discussed further in subsection 3.3.2 of this book.

175 Case C-73/16 *Puškár*, para. 59; Case C-214/16 *King v The Sash Window Workshop Ltd and Richard Dollar*, para. 41.

176 Case C-118/17 *Dunai*, paras. 38 and 60.

177 Iglesias Sánchez (n 18) 1594.

178 Michal Bobek, 'Why There is no Principle of "Procedural Autonomy" of the Member States' in Hans-Wolfgang Micklitz and Bruno De Witte (eds), *The European Court of Justice and the Autonomy of the Member States* (Intersentia 2012) 320.

In *Associaçião Sindical dos Juízes Portugueses*, the CJEU seemed to go even further. It reiterated that effective judicial protection is essential for the rule of law.[179] Therefore, Member States must ensure that all national courts and tribunals within their judicial system that deal with cases in the fields covered by EU law meet the requirements of effective judicial protection, including judicial independence.[180] The CJEU not only referred to the application or interpretation of EU law, but also to the task of adjudication and the autonomous exercise of judicial functions, to which the guarantee of independence is inherent.[181] This would imply that all national courts in all Member States must meet the requirements of Article 47 of the Charter at an institutional level: not only in cases falling within the scope of EU law, but always.

AG Bobek has distinguished this 'transversal' case from remedy- or procedure-specific issues, which do not structurally concern the entire judicial function.[182] One could further distinguish the applicability of Article 47 at a systemic level, which requires the Member States to maintain a system of effective remedies and adequate procedures, and in a concrete case, which requires the observation of procedural safeguards in cases covered by EU law. The CJEU's case law on the UCTD mainly pertains to remedy- or procedure-specific issues on a systemic level: it concerns the question as to the compatibility of national procedural law with Article 47, in the context of the Directive.

2.2.1.2. *Scope* Ratione Personae: *Protection of Both Consumers and Traders*

Consumers are entitled to effective judicial protection in respect of the rights the UCTD confers on them. The UCTD is not aimed at the protection of traders, but that does not mean they enjoy no judicial protection in unfair terms cases at all. It should be considered whether traders can also rely on Article 47, or whether it can only be invoked by individuals who derive specific subjective rights from EU consumer law.

AG Bobek has pointed out that Article 47 alone does not create standing (i.e. active legitimacy to bring a claim): it is not 'universally applicable'.[183]

---

[179] Case C-64/16 *Associação Sindical dos Juízes Portugueses*, paras. 30 and 36. See also Case C-362/14 *Schrems v Data Protection Commissioner*, para. 95 and Case C-279/09 *DEB*, para. 58.

[180] Case C-64/16 *Associação Sindical dos Juízes Portugueses*, paras. 37 and 41.

[181] Case C-64/16 *Associação Sindical dos Juízes Portugueses*, paras. 40 and 42–44.

[182] Case C-556/17 *Torubarov*, Opinion of AG Bobek, points 54–55.

[183] Case C-403/16 *El Hassani*, Opinion of AG Bobek, points 74–82.

However, the applicability of the Charter already implies a connection with EU law, whether EU law is invoked by or enforced *against* individuals. In the words of AG Wathelet:

> 'To require that that rule of EU law, which entails the applicability of the Charter, should also confer a specific subjective right capable of having been breached in the case of the person concerned seems to me to contradict the liberal intention that underpins Article 47 of the Charter'.[184]

In the same vein, the CJEU reiterated that the Charter is applicable in all situations governed by EU law.[185] Article 47 pertains not only to protective norms.[186] Its protection extends to parties adversely affected by measures that are based on national provisions implementing a directive, even if they cannot derive any rights from it.[187] Here, Article 47 operates as a shield, not a sword. Similarly, the protection of Article 47 in unfair terms cases is not limited to consumers; traders can also rely on it. Even if there is no other basis in EU law that provides for a scheme of effective judicial protection for traders, they still have a right to be heard.[188] The key question is whether a case falls within the scope of the UCTD.

It has been argued that Article 47 should be applicable as soon as one of the parties relies on substantive EU law, i.e. before the scope of the case has been established by a court. The very fact that there is a dispute over alleged EU rights should suffice for the purposes of Article 47.[189] The above-cited case of *Banif Plus Bank* seems to confirm this; the right to be heard must be observed before the court takes a final decision regarding a potentially unfair term.[190]

184 Case C-682/15 *Berlioz*, Opinion of AG Wathelet, point 63.

185 Case C-682/15 *Berlioz*, paras. 48–49. See also Case C-664/15 *Protect Natur-, Arten- und Landschaftsschutz Umweltorganisation v Bezirkshauptmannschaft Gmünd*, Opinion of AG Sharpston, point 88.

186 See also Półtorak (n 20) 241–242.

187 Case C-682/15 *Berlioz*, para. 59.

188 Case C-119/15 *Biuro*, para. 26.

189 See, e.g. Herwig Hofmann, 'Article 47 – Right to an Effective Remedy. D. Analysis. III. Specific Provisions (Meaning)' in Steve Peers and others (eds), *The EU Charter of Fundamental Rights: A Commentary* (Hart Publishing 2014) 1213; Prechal (n 158) 148. Hofmann refers to the requirement of an arguable complaint, in respect of Article 13 ECHR: a court must be able to assess whether an infringement has occurred and, if so, provide redress, but Article 47 of the Charter does not guarantee a favourable outcome.

190 See subsection 2.1.3 of this book.

A follow-up question would be whether Article 47 also guarantees the right to an effective judicial remedy against a violation of procedural safeguards in and of themselves, not just a violation of other EU rights. The CJEU has held that a procedural irregularity that infringes a fundamental right guaranteed by Article 47 gives the party concerned an entitlement to a remedy – again, as long as the case falls within the scope of EU law.[191] In *Kadi*, for instance, the CJEU found an independent violation of the applicants' rights of defence, especially their right to be heard.[192] It emphasised 'the need to accord the individual a sufficient measure of procedural justice', in the course of a judicial review of restrictive measures taken against persons and entities associated with al-Qaeda and the Taliban.[193]

In *Tomášová*, the CJEU acknowledged the possibility of State liability for damages in the event of a national court's failure to exercise *ex officio* control under the UCTD.[194] It can be submitted that a manifest infringement of Article 47, despite the existence of well-established CJEU case law, also constitutes a sufficiently serious breach of EU law.[195] However, it is questionable whether State liability constitutes a truly effective remedy, not only because it is seen as a last resort, but also because it is not the same as the correct application of the law in a concrete case;[196] it does not provide redress in the (contractual) relationship between the consumer and the trader.

2.2.2. DIRECT EFFECT

2.2.2.1. Vertical and Horizontal Dimensions of Article 47

The EU legal order relies strongly on the cooperation of the Member States and their national courts. These 'contribute to the attainment of the objective ...

---

191 Case C-58/12 *Groupe Gascogne*, para. 72, with reference to ECtHR 26 October 2000, Appl. No. 30210/96 *Kudla v Poland*. For instance, an action for damages can be brought (before the General Court itself) for a failure of the General Court of the European Union to adjudicate within a reasonable time: *Groupe Gascogne*, paras. 81–83; Case C-385/07 *Der Grüne Punkt*, para. 195. The reopening of the case or the setting aside of the judgment are not required on this ground alone, because these does not necessarily change the outcome of the initial dispute: *Groupe Gascogne*, paras. 74 and 78.

192 Joined Cases C-402/05 P and C-415/05 P *Kadi*, paras. 352–353.

193 *Kadi*, para. 344.

194 Case C-168/15 *Tomášová*, para. 36.

195 Where a supreme court is responsible for such a breach, this could constitute a ground for State liability: Case C-224/01 *Gerhard Köbler v Republik Österreich*.

196 Jerfi Uzman, *Constitutionele remedies bij schending van grondrechten: over effectieve rechtsbescherming, rechterlijk abstineren en de dialoog tussen rechter en wetgever* (Kluwer 2013) 333, 361.

of ensuring effective judicial protection of an individual's rights' under EU law.[197] The effects of EU law in the legal systems of the Member States have been the subject of an extensive debate on 'the complex cooperative relationship'[198] between the CJEU and national courts. The focus is on the solutions the CJEU has developed for conflicts (norm collisions) between EU law and national law. The supremacy (or primacy) and direct effect of EU law play important roles in this respect. The CJEU has confirmed in *Egenberger* that Article 47 of the Charter has direct effect, in the sense that it can be invoked directly by individuals, provided that their cases fall within the scope of EU law.[199] The fundamental right to effective judicial protection, as laid down in Article 47, is sufficient in and of itself and does not need to be made more specific by provisions of EU law or national law to confer on individuals a right on which they may rely. National courts must ensure, within their jurisdictions, the judicial protection for individuals that flows from Article 47, and guarantee its full effectiveness by disapplying contrary provisions of national law if necessary.[200] Thus, Article 47 may provide a ground for courts to set aside national law if an interpretation that is compatible with EU law is not possible.[201]

The above-mentioned direct effect of EU law could be seen as a different concept from direct horizontal effect in private law, which is understood as meaning that subjective rights (and obligations) are created, modified or extinguished between private parties.[202] Article 47 can be invoked against the Member States and their national (civil) courts, but it does not have direct horizontal (or interpersonal) effect in the sense of imposing

197 See, e.g. Case C-106/89 *Marleasing v La Comercial Internacional de Alimentación*; Case C-432/05 *Unibet*, para. 44; Case C-50/00 *Unión de Pequeños Agricultores v Council of the European Union*, para. 42.

198 Case C-137/08 *Pénzügyi Lízing*, Opinion AG Trstenjak, point 59.

199 Case C-414/16 *Egenberger*, para. 78. See also Case C-176/12 *Association de médiation sociale v Union locale des syndicats*, para. 47. This is not the same concept as a subjective right: Uzman (n 196) 306.

200 Case C-414/16 *Egenberger*, para. 79.

201 Joined Cases C-569/16 and C-570/16 *Bauer*, para. 65.

202 Arthur Hartkamp, 'The Effect of the EC Treaty in Private Law: On Direct and Indirect Horizontal Effects of Primary Community Law' [2010] European Review of Private Law 527, 529, 536; David Ramos Muñoz, 'Fundamental Rights and Private Law – A Blueprint for Analysis with Spanish Eyes' in Bettina Heiderhoff, Sebastian Lohsse and Reinier Schulze (eds), *EU-Grundrechte und Privatrecht / EU Fundamental Rights and Private Law* (Nomos 2016) 229. 'Direct horizontal effect' may also be understood as meaning that courts can give effect to EU (fundamental) rights in private disputes and, if need be, set aside national law. On the 'horizontality' of EU fundamental rights in the latter sense, and Article 47 of the Charter, in particular, see Frantziou (n 30) 106–107.

obligations on private parties vis-à-vis other private parties. In private law adjudication, it takes effect indirectly via the interpretation and application of national private law and civil procedure by the courts.[203] It is the *courts* that must provide effective judicial protection, not the private parties themselves.

It is hard to imagine how private parties could be required to comply directly with Article 47. For instance, Article 47 does not entail that parties cannot use a jurisdiction clause in their standard terms and conditions. In the context of the UCTD, they must, however, refrain from using unfair terms. Accordingly, Article 47 could potentially be a parameter for the assessment of substantive unfairness in light of the Directive: a jurisdiction clause may make it difficult for consumers to take legal action or exercise their rights of defence.[204] Thus, Article 47 could, indirectly, have a *horizontal* dimension. Judicial control of unfair terms must, nevertheless, be distinguished from judicial or legislative review on the basis of Article 47, which inserts a *vertical* dimension in the adjudication of horizontal disputes.[205]

The provisions of the UCTD do not have direct (horizontal) effect in either sense. Even if they confer subjective rights on individuals, they require implementation in national private law and cannot be directly relied on against other individuals.[206] Member States must take all appropriate measures to ensure fulfilment of their obligations arising out of EU law (Article 4 of the Treaty on European Union (TEU)), in addition to such measures as are necessary to implement legally binding EU acts (Article 291(1) TFEU). But they have considerable leeway as to the implementation and application of directives, especially in case of minimum harmonisation. Directives are binding as to the result to be achieved, but the choice of form and method is left to the Member States (Article 288(3) TFEU). National courts, in turn, have a duty to interpret national law in

[203] Leczykiewicz (n 17) 491; Dorota Leczykiewicz, 'Horizontal Application of the Charter of Fundamental Rights' (2013) 38 European Law Review 479, 491; Chantal Mak, 'Rights and Remedies: Article 47 EUCFR and Effective Judicial Protection in European Private Law Matters' in Hans-Wolfgang Micklitz (ed), *The Constitutionalization of European Private Law (Collected Courses of EUI Summer School)* (Oxford University Press 2014) 242; Cherednychenko (n 164) 145.

[204] See, e.g. Joined Cases C-240/98 to C-244/98 *Océano*, para. 24. See further subsection 3.2.4 below on Case C-266/18 *Aqua Med*.

[205] Mak (n 203) 242; Cherednychenko (n 164) 145.

[206] Joined Cases C-569/16 and C-570/16 *Bauer*, para. 76. See also Ebers (n 37) 89; Aronstein (n 31) 21ff.

conformity with a directive, to ensure that the directive is fully effective, and to achieve an outcome consistent with the objectives it pursues.[207] However, they are not obliged to apply national law *contra legem*,[208] or to set national provisions aside solely on the basis of a directive.[209]

2.2.2.2. *Obligation to Apply Article 47* Ex Officio?

The direct effect of Article 47 empowers national courts to provide effective judicial protection, and to set national law aside if necessary. This gives rise to the question of whether they are obliged to apply Article 47 *ex officio*, i.e. if it has not been explicitly invoked by the parties. Article 47 requires the existence of a judicial remedy and several other procedural safeguards. The right to be heard, for instance, must be respected by courts, particularly when they decide a dispute on a ground identified of their own motion.[210] In this sense, it could be said that the court must apply – or rather, observe – Article 47 *ex officio*. A failure to do so in a concrete case may constitute a procedural breach and an infringement of Article 47.

A violation of Article 47 may also be found on a systemic level, for instance where the applicable procedural rules do not sufficiently guarantee an opportunity to exercise the rights of defence. The question, thus, arises as to whether the court is obliged to check *ex officio* whether national procedural law is compatible with the requirements of Article 47 and, if not, set it aside. *Egenberger* implies that such an obligation only exists 'where the national court is called on [by one of the parties] to ensure that Article 47 of the Charter is observed'.[211] That a court is not obliged to raise a potential violation of Article 47 *ex officio* – notwithstanding the obligation of courts at last instance to make a preliminary reference to the CJEU under Article 267 TFEU – does not mean that it cannot do so. The above-mentioned *Sánchez Morcillo* case provides an example of a national civil court reframing a preliminary reference in terms of the fundamental

---

207 See, e.g. Case C-377/14 *Radlinger*, para. 79; Case C-407/18 *Kuhar v Addiko Bank*, paras. 65-66.

208 Case C-282/10 *Dominguez v Centre informatique du Centre Ouest Atlantique and Préfet de la région Centre*, para. 42; Case C-26/13 *Kásler and Káslerné Rábai v OTP Jelzálogbank*, para. 65. See also Case C-414/16 *Egenberger*, para. 71.

209 Ebers (n 37) 267.

210 Case C-89/08 *European Commission v Ireland*, para. 54; see also Case C-472/11 *Banif Plus Bank*, para. 29 (cited above in subsection 2.1.3).

211 Case C-414/16 *Egenberger*, para. 81.

right to effective judicial protection.[212] It was the referring court that brought up Article 47 of the Charter,[213] not the parties themselves. And the CJEU has 'recast' a request for a preliminary ruling, on a few occasions, by reference to Article 47.[214]

The *ex officio* application of Article 47 must be distinguished from the *ex officio* application of EU consumer protection legislation. Article 47 does not entail a general requirement for courts to conduct *ex officio* reviews in order to safeguard the rights that parties derive from EU law. The duty of the court to apply EU consumer law of its own motion seems to depend on the EU instrument at issue.[215] The CJEU refers neither to the principle of effective judicial protection nor to Article 47, in this respect. It simply emphasises that *ex officio* control is the only way to attain effective consumer protection under the UCTD. To get a better understanding of the difference between effective judicial protection and *ex officio* control, the next section will take a closer look at the CJEU's case law concerning national remedies and procedures under the UCTD pre- and post-Lisbon (2009).

2.3. REMEDIES AND PROCEDURES UNDER THE UCTD

2.3.1. IN PRINCIPLE: PROCEDURAL AUTONOMY OF THE EU MEMBER STATES

The UCTD is a minimum harmonisation directive that has been received and transposed in national legal systems in different ways.[216] It contains only minimum requirements, and does not regulate the detailed remedial and procedural rules governing its decentralised enforcement. The Directive

212 Case C-169/14 *Sánchez Morcillo I*, further discussed in subsections 3.4.2 and 4.4.2 of this book.

213 Mr. Alejandro Rubio González, (former) State Attorney, representing the Government of Spain at the CJEU, speech delivered in Brussels on 17 December 2014, available at <http://www.academia.edu/9846524/The_application_of_the_Charter_of_Fundamental_Rights_of_the_European_Union_by_legal_practitioners> (last accessed 14 September 2021). See also subsections 3.4.2 and 4.4.2 of this book.

214 See, e.g. Case C-279/09 *DEB*, para. 33.

215 Van Duin and Leone (n 45) 1244.

216 See, e.g. the 2019 Max Planck report (n 33) and the REFIT report (n 51).

was adopted in 1993, on the basis of Article 100A of the EEC Treaty.[217] This is the predecessor of Article 114 TFEU, which calls for the adoption of harmonisation measures in order to achieve a high level of consumer protection for the establishment and functioning of the internal market. The Directive aims to protect consumers against unfair standard terms and conditions that have not been individually negotiated when they enter into a contracts. As the CJEU has repeatedly held, the system of protection introduced by the Directive is based on the idea that consumers are in a weak position vis-à-vis their professional counterparties – i.e. traders[218] – as regards both bargaining power and level of knowledge. The Directive aims to replace 'the formal balance which the contract establishes between the rights and obligations of the parties with *an effective balance that re-establishes equality between them*' (italics added).[219]

Article 6(1) of the UCTD provides that unfair terms are not binding on consumers.[220] While Article 6(1) shows the correlation between rights of consumers and obligations of traders, it does not constitute a private law remedy as such; consumers must still rely on national private law and civil procedure to effectuate their rights vis-à-vis traders. Article 7(1) obliges the Member States to provide for adequate and effective means to prevent the continued use of unfair terms in consumer contracts, but the Directive itself does not define what measures may constitute such means (apart from injunctions: see Article 7(2) UCTD).

---

217 Treaty Establishing the European Economic Community, signed in Rome, 25 March 1957.

218 The term 'trader' will hereinafter be used to refer to the professional counterparties of consumers in business-to-consumer contracts, i.e. sellers or suppliers (Article 2(c) UCTD) who use standard terms and conditions.

219 See, e.g. Case C-137/08 *VB Pénzügyi Lízing v Ferenc Schneider*, para. 47; C-169/14 *Sánchez Morcillo I*, paras. 22–23; Joined Cases C-154/15, C-307/15 and C-308/15 *Gutiérrez Naranjo*, paras. 53 and 55; Case C-453/10 *Pereničová and Perenič v SOS financ*, para. 28.

220 The CJEU has held that Article 6(1) must be regarded as a provision of equal standing to national rules of public policy: see, e.g. Case C-243/08 *Pannon v Sustikné Győrfi*, para. 32; C-40/08 *Asturcom*, paras. 51–52; Case C-421/14 *Banco Primus v Gutiérrez García*, para. 42. Moreover, the CJEU has interpreted Article 6(1) in such a way that there is little room left for the Member States and their national courts to determine the substantive legal consequences of a finding of unfairness: see, e.g. Case C-618/10 *Banco Español de Crédito v Calderón Camino (Banesto)*; Joined Cases C-482/13, C-484/13, C-485/13 and C-487/13 *Unicaja Banco v Rueda and Caixabank v Rueda Ledesma*; Joined Cases C-96/16 and C-94/17 *Banco Santander v Mahamadou Demba and Mercedes Godoy Bonet and Rafael Ramón Escobedo Cortés v Banco de Sabadell*. See also Ebers (n 37) 888–894; Thomas Wilhelmsson, 'Unfair Contract Terms' in Geraint Howells, Christian Twigg-Flesner and Thomas Wilhelmsson, *Rethinking EU Consumer Law* (Routledge 2018) 154.

In the absence of full harmonisation, the Member States, in principle, have procedural autonomy in respect of the choice and design of remedies for (alleged) infringements of EU law.[221] The assumption behind this seems to be that all Member States are subject to the rule of law and, thus, national remedies and procedures should suffice for the purposes of EU law.[222] Article 47 of the Charter mirrors the Member States' obligations to provide remedies (Article 19 TEU) by granting individuals the fundamental right to effective judicial protection.[223] According to Micklitz and Reich, it is implicitly recognised in the 'tandem' of Article 19 TEU and Article 47 that consumers need effective legal protection and, more particularly, *courts* to defend their rights under the UCTD.[224] However, courts may not always be able to do so, as demonstrated by the CJEU's case law on procedural issues that have arisen in the context of the Directive.

2.3.2. IN PRACTICE: JUDGE-MADE PROCEDURALISATION

2.3.2.1. Contours of a Common Procedural Law for Consumers

Whereas the UCTD may initially have been a 'toothless tiger',[225] this is no longer the case. It has become the subject of widespread litigation between consumers and consumer organisations, on the one hand, and traders, on the other. It has also become the focal point of many requests

---

221 As Prechal and Widdershoven have observed, procedural autonomy encompasses remedial autonomy: Sacha Prechal and Rob Widdershoven, 'Redefining the Relationship between "*Rewe*-Effectiveness" and Effective Judicial Protection' (2011) 4 Review of European Administrative Law 31, 31. See further on the concept of 'procedural autonomy' in the context of the UCTD, e.g. Trstenjak and Beysen (n 49) 99; Beka (n 32) 19ff.

222 Wilman (n 31) 27. On the issue of 'mutual trust' in this respect, see Dominik Düsterhaus, 'Judicial Coherence in the Area of Freedom, Security and Justice – Squaring Mutual Trust with Effective Judicial Protection' (2015) 8 Review of European Administrative Law 151. On the 'rule of law' concept in the case law of the CJEU, see Koen Lenaerts, 'The Rule of Law and the Coherence of the Judicial System of the European Union' (2007) 44 Common Market Law Review 1625; Thomas Von Danwitz, 'The Rule of Law in the Recent Jurisprudence of the ECJ' (2014) 35 Fordham International Law Journal 1311.

223 See also Case C-682/15 *Berlioz Investment Fund v Directeur de l'administration des contributions directes*, para. 44; Case C-619/18 *European Commission v Republic of Poland*, para. 54. See also Pech and Sayers (n 107) 1213.

224 Micklitz and Reich (n 44) 803–804.

225 Micklitz and Reich (n 44) 775.

for preliminary rulings, which has led to a 'judicial dialogue'[226] between national civil courts and the CJEU on the Directive's interpretation and application at the national level. The CJEU has promoted the Directive's effective enforcement by dealing with matters of national procedural law that are, strictly speaking, not covered by the Directive. It has done so in response to preliminary references from national civil courts who were confronted with (perceived) shortfalls in their own legal frameworks. For instance, the CJEU has assessed national regimes for mortgage enforcement, even though the UCTD does not regulate mechanisms for the enforcement of claims, let alone security rights.[227] As a result, the Member States' procedural autonomy has been qualified, or even 'severely curtailed'.[228]

The CJEU has developed various requirements for the enforcement and protection, by national (civil) courts, of the rights that consumers derive from the UCTD. It has done so mainly on the basis of the general principles of equivalence and effectiveness, which entail – in short – that rights should not be treated less favourably under EU law than under national law, and that national law must not render the exercise of EU rights practically impossible or excessively difficult.[229] These principles define the outer limits of the Member States' procedural autonomy.[230] In addition, the CJEU has held that national courts must ensure the practical or useful effect – also referred to as *effet utile* or full effectiveness – of the

---

[226] See, e.g. Engström (n 64) 625; Mak (n 203) 255; Cafaggi and Iamiceli (n 25) 579.

[227] Case C-415/1 *Aziz v Catalunyacaixa*, para. 50; Case C-34/13 *Kušionová*, paras. 36 and 49; Case C-280/13 *Barclays Bank v Sánchez García and Chacón Barrera*, para. 37.

[228] Micklitz and Reich (n 44) 784.

[229] See, inter alia, Case C-33/76 *Rewe-Zentralfinanz en Rewe-Zentral v Landwirtschaftskammer für das Saarland*, para. 5; Case C-45/76 *Comet v Produktschap v Siergewassen*, paras. 13–16; Joined Cases C-430/93 and C-431/93 *Van Schijndel and Van Veen v Stichting Pensioenfonds voor Fysiotherapeuten*, para. 17; Case C-312/93 *Peterbroeck, Van Campenhout & Cie v Belgian State*, para. 12; Case C-432/05 *Unibet (London) Ltd and Unibet (International) Ltd v Justitiekanslern*, para. 43. The CJEU's assessment of equivalence is, in principle, unrelated to its assessment of effectiveness, and the case law on the principle of effectiveness has a bigger impact on national (procedural) law: see Janek Tomasz Nowak, 'De bevoegdheid van EU-lidstaten voor de aanname van regels van nationaal procesrecht: grenzen in de rechtspraak van het Hof van Justitie' in Nicolas Cariat and Janek Tomasz Nowak (eds), *Le droit de l'Union européenne et le juge belge – Het recht van de Europese Unie en de Belgische rechter* (Bruylant 2015) 37.

[230] Bobek has observed that the term 'autonomy' is misguiding, because it minimalises the impact of EU law on national procedural law: Bobek (n 178) 321–322. Van Gerven has proposed the use of the term 'procedural competence' instead, to make clear that procedural matters remain the prime responsibility of the Member States.

UCTD, which demands positive action from them.[231] They must apply their internal procedural rules in such a way as to achieve the outcome that unfair terms are not binding on consumers.[232]

The role of the CJEU consists of an ad hoc examination of procedural rules that, according to the referring court, might impair the effective protection of consumers under the UCTD. There has been a shift from a substance-focused to a more procedure-oriented approach ('proceduralisation').[233] It has been a gradual and fragmented process, on the basis of a substantive competence (Article 114 TFEU and Articles 6 and 7 UCTD). As a consequence, there is now a considerable body of case law – a 'judicial *acquis*'[234] – in connection with procedural issues, which has changed the roles and responsibilities of national civil courts in consumer cases.[235] This judicial *acquis* constitutes an 'invisible pillar'[236] of judge-made requirements, which has been said to affect consumer litigation more significantly than harmonised procedural mechanisms like the European Small Claims Regulation.[237] In the words of AG Szpunar:

> 'Consumer protection has become *one of the essential fields of EU law* which ... affects the everyday lives of EU consumers ... [A]s a result of Directive 93/13, the degree of protection afforded to EU consumers is quite high ... conferring on them rights which must be protected by the national courts'.[238]

---

231 See, e.g. Case C-147/16 *Karel de Grote – Hogeschool Katholieke Hogeschool Antwerpen v Kuijpers*, para 41; Case C-377/14 *Radlinger and Radlingerová v Finway*, para. 79.

232 Case C-397/11 *Jőrös v Aegon Magyarország Hitel*, para. 52.

233 Federico Della Negra, 'The Uncertain Development of the Case Law on Consumer Protection in Mortgage Enforcement Proceedings: *Sánchez Morcillo* and *Kušionová*' (2015) 52 Common Market Law Review 1009, 1010; Magdalena Tulibacka, 'Proceduralisation of EU Consumer Law and its Impact on European Consumers' (2015) 8 Review of European Administrative Law 51, 53. Tulibacka specifically refers to 'judicial proceduralisation'. The term 'proceduralisation' has also been used to refer to the adoption of EU procedural rules in legislative instruments. The CJEU's progressive interpretation of the UCTD has led to a more indirect, judge-made 'Europeanisation' of national remedies and procedures: Beka (n 32) 10, 17. It could be said that the CJEU has initiated the 'proceduralisation' process: Dubos (n 100) 53–54.

234 Oliver Gerstenberg, 'Constitutional Reasoning in Private Law: The Role of the CJEU in Adjudicating Unfair Terms in Consumer Contracts' [2015] European Law Journal 599, 603.

235 Gerstenberg (n 234) 604; Cafaggi (n 25) 242–243.

236 Bart Krans, 'EU Law and National Civil Procedure Law: An Invisible Pillar' (2015) 23 European Review of Private Law 567.

237 Regulation (EC) No. 861/2007 establishing a European Small Claims Procedure, OJ L199, 31 July 2007, p. 1–22; Dubos (n 100) 51–52; Nowak (n 169) 2.

238 Case C-70/17 *Abanca v Salamanca Santos*, Opinion of AG Szpunar of 13 September 2018, point 53.

The CJEU's case law adds a layer of procedural rules of European origin to the adjudication of domestic cases, arguably to the extent that the contours of a common 'European consumer procedural law' can be discerned.[239] Remedies and procedures are (re)interpreted and developed in light of the EU consumer rights they serve to protect; they are upgraded and turned into 'hybrids', in the sense that they take up both national and European elements.[240] Examples of such hybrids will be given in Chapters 4 and 5.

2.3.2.2. *A More Active Role for Courts*

Under the UCTD, consumers have the subjective right to bring legal actions requesting courts to examine whether standard terms of contracts to which they are parties are unfair.[241] They must be able to take such action in relation to contracts themselves, or against their enforcement.[242] However, consumers are not always the *claimants* who initiate an action. On the contrary, they are often likely to find themselves on the 'receiving end' – as *defendants* in proceedings – and this will affect their legal positions whether they participate in the proceedings or not.[243] In such cases, they must at least be able to contest the merits of claims arising from contracts that contain terms likely to be unfair.[244]

Often, the challenge for consumers is not so much to win their cases on the substance, as to get their cases before a competent court despite procedural gaps or obstacles.[245] What many of the preliminary references to the CJEU have in common is that they concern the scope for judicial intervention, especially if consumers do not stand up for their rights of their own accord.[246] Various factors other than mere 'inertia' may cause

---

239 Hans-W Micklitz, '*Mohamed Aziz* – sympathetic and activist, but did the court get it wrong?' in Anna Sodersten and Joseph HH Weiler, *When the ECJ Gets it Wrong* (European Constitutional Law Network 2013) 1.

240 Reich (n 1) 308–309.

241 Joined Cases C-381/14 and C-385/14 *Sales Sinués and Drame Ba v Caixabank and Catalunya Caixa (Catalunya Banc)*, paras. 21 and 42.

242 See, e.g. Case C-32/14 *ERSTE Bank Hungary v Sugár*, para. 59; C-176/17 *Profi Credit Polska*, para. 63; C-266/18 *Aqua Med*, para. 53.

243 Case C-147/16 *Karel de Grote*, Opinion of AG Sharpston, point 32.

244 Case C-377/14 *Radlinger*, para. 56.

245 Mónika Józon, 'Unfair Contract Terms Law in Europe in Times of Crisis: Substantive Justice Lost in the Paradise of Proceduralisation of Contract Fairness' [2017] Journal of European Consumer and Market Law 157, 162.

246 See also Micklitz and Reich (n 44) 781; Ebers (n 37) 920.

consumers 'to forego any legal remedy or defence',[247] for example a lack of information about their legal options or the costs involved with litigation.[248] In *Océano*, the very first preliminary ruling on the UCTD, the CJEU highlighted the 'real risk' that consumers do not challenge unfair terms because they are unaware of their rights or encounter difficulties in enforcing them.[249] This was the rationale behind the introduction of a duty of *ex officio* control: national civil courts have to compensate for procedural omissions on the part of consumers by performing unfair terms control of their own motion.[250] In this respect, Micklitz and Reich have referred to a 'compensatory function' of civil procedure,[251] and Beka to an 'active court doctrine'.[252] Thus, the new balance the UCTD introduced in business-to-consumer (B2C) relationships extends into the procedural realm. The substantive and procedural aspects of consumer protection are intertwined, to the extent that the latter is a necessary precondition for the former.

The CJEU's case law has created tension between the role that civil courts fulfil within their own legal systems and what the CJEU expects from them. A more active role may be at odds with, in particular, the principle of party autonomy, i.e. that parties define which issues are to be decided by the court, and on what factual basis.[253] In the words of

---

247 Joined Cases C-240/98 to C-244/98 *Océano Grupo Editorial v Murciano Quintero*, para. 22; Case C-137/08 *Pénzügyi Lízing*, para. 54. As Anthi Beka has observed, the term 'inertia' implies an indifference that does not correspond with the notion of overindebted and vulnerable consumers; 'inertia' should not be equated with a renouncement of rights: Beka (n 32) 298–299.

248 See, e.g. Loos (n 54).

249 Joined Cases C-240/98 to C-244/98 *Océano*, para. 26; Case C-473/00 *Cofidis v Fredout*, para. 33; Case C-168/05 *Mostaza Claro v Centro Móvil Milenium*, para. 28.

250 See also Case C-40/08 *Asturcom*, para. 47 and, more recently, Case C-147/16 *Karel de Grote*, para. 31; Case C-51/17 *OTP Bank and OTP Faktoring Követeléskezelő v Ilyés and Kiss*, para. 88. In Case C-377/14 *Radlinger*, the duty of *ex officio* control is phrased broadly: courts must examine, of their own motion, 'infringements of EU consumer protection legislation' (para. 62). Their role is not limited to a mere power to rule on compliance with the requirements flowing from that legislation; it also consists of the obligation to examine the issue, and to establish the consequences (paras. 70 and 73).

251 Micklitz and Reich (n 44) 803–804. See also Josep Maria Bech Serrat, 'Cláusulas suelo y autonomía procesal en la Unión Europea: ¿por qué no hacer una excepción a la cosa juzgada?' [2018] InDret 55 <https://www.raco.cat/index.php/InDret/article/view/332601> (last accessed 24 September 2021).

252 Beka (n 32) 129.

253 See, e.g. Rott (n 98) 89–90; Hanna Schebesta, 'Does the National Court Know European Law? A Note on *Ex Officio* Application after *Asturcom*' [2010] European Review of Private Law 847, 849.

AG Trstenjak, 'the principle that the subject-matter of the case is delimited by the parties' – the so-called 'dispositive principle' – has been departed from 'in order to ensure the effectiveness of consumer protection desired by the EU legislature'.[254] The specific characteristics of court proceedings have become subordinate to the protection intended by the UCTD. This reflects a top-down, instrumental approach: national civil courts and civil procedure are merely a means to an end.[255] It will be investigated, in this book, to what extent Article 47 of the Charter entails a paradigm shift, since it contains autonomous procedural safeguards.

2.3.3. PROCEDURALISED CONSTITUTIONALISATION

The start of the judge-made proceduralisation process under the UCTD predates the Charter.[256] A constructive reading of the Directive has allowed the CJEU to 'infuse a common standard of effective judicial protection into the national procedural orders'.[257] Whereas it could be said that the Charter has arrived 'late at the party'[258] in the debate on weaker party protection and access to justice, Article 47 of the Charter is far from obsolete, as shown by multiple references in the CJEU's more recent case law.[259] In 2013, the CJEU explicitly recognised for the first time, in the case of *Banif Plus Bank*, that Article 47 is binding on national civil courts when they adjudicate disputes under the UCTD. The CJEU held that:

> 'in implementing European Union law, the national court must also respect the requirements of effective judicial protection of the rights that individuals derive from European Union law, as guaranteed by Article 47 of the Charter of Fundamental Rights of the European Union. Among those requirements is the

---

254 Case C-618/10 *Banesto*, Opinion of AG Trstenjak, point 33. See also Beka (n 32) 79. Beka observes that this principle is the reflection of a legal culture that respects party autonomy, participation and individuality, as well as judicial impartiality.

255 See also Storskrubb (n 54) 39; Tulibacka (n 36) 1533–1534; Półtorak (n 20) 11; Wilman (n 31) 470.

256 The Charter was proclaimed on 18 December 2000 (six months after the landmark judgment in Joined Cases C-240/98 to C-244/98 *Océano*), and entered into force on 1 December 2009 (seven months after Case C-243/08 *Pannon*).

257 Safjan and Düsterhaus (n 13) 13–14.

258 Weatherill, Vogenauer and Weingerl (n 15) 257.

259 A reference to Article 47 of the Charter was made in almost 30 per cent of cases on the UCTD that came before the CJEU. See subsection 1.3.3 of this book for an overview.

> principle of *audi alteram partem*, as part of the rights of defence and which is binding on that court, in particular when it decides a dispute on a ground that it has identified of its own motion'.[260]

It appears that effectiveness is no longer the sole parameter for the assessment of national procedural law in light of EU consumer law. The rights of defence are elevated to the level of EU fundamental rights. The fact that the CJEU now refers to Article 47 more regularly suggests an increased attention to procedural safeguards. In so far as a lack of effective judicial protection is framed as a fundamental rights issue, a move towards 'proceduralised constitutionalisation' can be detected:[261] proceduralisation with a constitutional dimension.

As regards the UCTD, key issues identified in the case law and academic debate are the duty of *ex officio* control, substantive issues, such as the legal consequences of a finding of unfairness, and the interaction between judicial and other ways of enforcement. Article 47 places the emphasis on the former, i.e. an effective remedy and a fair hearing before a *court*. While *ex officio* control could be seen as a manifestation of effective judicial protection,[262] the assessment of a norm infringement – the substantive unfairness test – must be distinguished from the procedural preconditions that make such an assessment possible, and subsequent (substantive) remedies. As will become apparent in this book, Article 47 predominantly plays a role in respect of *judicial remedies*, in the sense of a (procedural) means of recourse, and *procedural safeguards*. It is not so much about determining what private parties are substantively entitled to as it is about facilitating them to exercise their EU rights in court.

The interrelation between Article 47 and the notion of effectiveness is a key issue in the case law and literature. One explanation for this can be found in the historical origins of Article 47, which spring from two different sources.[263] There is the line of case law developed by the CJEU to test the compliance of national remedies and procedures with EU law, in particular the principles of equivalence and effectiveness. In addition, Article 47 reaffirms the principle that Member States must guarantee

260 Case C-472/11 *Banif Plus Bank*, para. 29.

261 Domurath (n 55) 172.

262 See, e.g. Pech and Sayers (n 107) 1222.

263 Angela Ward, 'Article 47 – Right to an Effective Remedy. E. Evaluation' in Steve Peers and others (eds), *The EU Charter of Fundamental Rights: A Commentary* (Hart Publishing 2014) 1273.

'real and effective judicial protection'.[264] The principle of effective judicial protection in EU law stems from 'the constitutional traditions common to the Member States' and the right to a fair trial and an effective remedy enshrined in Articles 6 and 13 ECHR.[265] This principle has been codified as an EU fundamental right: Article 47 is its written, statutory expression.[266]

This twofold origin results in an inherent dichotomy, which becomes particularly visible in civil proceedings, and will be explored further in this book. Whereas the full effectiveness of the UCTD demands that the court performs unfair terms control *ex officio*, it follows from *Banif Plus Bank* that the requirements of a fair hearing must be observed before a decision is given. The core components of Article 47 could be interpreted in ways that go beyond the goals of specific instruments of EU law such as the UCTD, or the laws of the Member States. Against this background, the question arises of whether Article 47 may operate as a separate (negative) yardstick or a (positive) standard for the adjudication of EU consumer rights.

2.4. ARTICLE 47 AS A NEGATIVE YARDSTICK OR POSITIVE STANDARD?

2.4.1. RESTRICTIONS TO ARTICLE 47: AN ELIMINATORY FUNCTION

The fundamental right to effective judicial protection is not absolute, but it cannot be denied altogether either.[267] In so far as Article 47 of the Charter precludes unjustified restrictions of its core components, it may

264 Case C-14/83 *Von Colson and Kamann v Land Nordrhein-Westfalen*, para. 23. For an extensive study on the pre-Lisbon principle of effective judicial protection in EU law, see Engström (n 34).

265 See, e.g. Case C-222/84 *Marguerite Johnston v Chief Constable of the Royal Ulster Constabulary*, para. 18; Case C-432/05 *Unibet*, para. 37; Joined Cases C-402/05 P and C-415/05 P *Kadi*, para. 335; Joined Cases C-317/08, C-318/08, C-319/08 and C-320/08 *Alassini*, para. 61; Case C-199/11 *Otis*, paras. 46-47; Case C-93/12 T *Agrokonsulting-04-Velko Stoyanov v Izpalnitelen direktor na Darzhaven fond 'Zemedelie' – Razplashtatelna agents*, para. 59.

266 Johanna Engström, 'The Principle of Effective Judicial Protection after the Lisbon Treaty. Reflection in the Light of Case C-279/09 *DEB Deutsche Energiehandels- Und Beratungsgesellschaft MbH*' (2011) 4 Review of European Administrative Law 53, 53; Prechal (n 158) 145.

267 Prechal and Widdershoven (n 221) 36; Ellingsen (n 151) 1983.

operate as a (negative) yardstick for national procedural law. Where it is used to eliminate procedural rules – or, in its horizontal dimension, contract terms – that impinge on the fundamental right to effective judicial protection, it could fulfil an *eliminatory function*.[268] Such an eliminatory function could be seen as largely parallel to the principle of effectiveness, but also separate to the extent that Article 47 entails a different test.[269]

Pursuant to Article 52(1) of the Charter, restrictions must be provided for by law, and must respect the essence of the rights recognised by the Charter. In addition, they must be necessary and proportionate, and genuinely meet objectives of general interest recognised by the EU, or the need to protect the rights (and freedoms) of others. Article 52(1) resembles a classic fundamental rights assessment in the vertical relationship between citizens and the State, i.e. fundamental rights as defences for individuals against unjustified interferences by the government. However, Article 47 of the Charter has acquired a separate identity, because of its connection to EU law. As Safjan and Düsterhaus have observed, ensuring the effectiveness of EU law and effective judicial protection at the same time requires 'a novel and original balancing approach'.[270]

In respect of secondary EU legislation, the CJEU has held that national courts must take into account the balance the EU legislature has struck between the various interests involved, when determining the implications of Article 47 in the circumstances of each case.[271]

A further complicating factor is that, in civil proceedings, a balance must be struck between the competing (fundamental) rights of both private parties involved.[272] As Prechal has observed, this differs from balancing the protection of an individual right and an objective of general interest.[273] The protection of one party's rights may entail a restriction of the other party's rights. For horizontal relationships, Collins has, therefore,

---

268 The label 'eliminatory function' was introduced by Reich: see subsection 2.5.2 below. Other possible labels that express the same function are 'derogating' or 'corrective' function: Carla Sieburgh, 'Principles in Private Law: From Luxury to Necessity – Multi-Layered Legal Systems and the Generative Force of Principles' (2012) 22 European Review of Private Law 295, 301.

269 See further subsection 2.5.1 below.

270 Safjan and Düsterhaus (n 13) 37.

271 Case C-414/16 *Egenbeger*, para. 81.

272 Case C-275/06 *Productores de Música de España (Promusicae) v Telefónica de España*, para. 68.

273 Prechal (n 158) 153. See also Karl Riesenhuber, 'Interpretation of EU Secondary Law' in Karl Riesenhuber (ed), *European Legal Methodology* (Intersentia 2017) 252–253.

proposed a double proportionality test: not only must an interference with a protected right be justified in the general interest, but the interference with competing rights must also be minimised.[274] This seems to be in line with what the CJEU has held: where several fundamental rights are at issue, the proportionality assessment must be carried out in accordance with the need to reconcile the requirements of the protection of those various rights, striking a fair balance between them.[275]

Under Article 47 of the Charter, the claimant's right to an effective judicial remedy and the defendant's rights of defence both deserve protection.[276] The question arises as to how these rights should be balanced against each other. In *Hypoteční banka*, a case concerning the Brussels I Regulation,[277] the CJEU considered the following:

> '49. [T]he requirement that the rights of the defence be observed, as laid down also in Article 47 of the Charter of Fundamental Rights of the European Union, must be implemented in conjunction with respect for the right of the applicant to bring proceedings before a court in order to determine the merits of its claim ...
>
> 51. In that regard, it must be borne in mind that the Court has already held that the objective of avoiding situations of denial of justice, which the applicant would face should it not be possible to determine the defendant's domicile, constitutes such an objective of public interest ... it being a matter for the referring court to determine whether that objective is in fact pursued by the national provision at issue'.

A balance was struck between the procedural rights of the parties: a restriction of the defendant's rights of defence was justified in light of the applicant's right to bring proceedings, which would have been meaningless in the absence of a competent court.[278] Substantive consumer protection

---

274 Hugh Collins, 'The Constitutionalization of European Private Law as a Path to Social Justice?' in Hans-W Micklitz (ed), *The Many Concepts of Social Justice in European Private Law* (Edward Elgar Publishing 2011) 155; Collins (n 74) 49.

275 Case C-752/18 *Deutsche Umwelthilfe* C-752/18, para. 50.

276 Case C-199/11 *Otis*, para. 48; Case C-327/10 *Hypoteční banka v Lindner*, para. 46.

277 Regulation 44/2001 on jurisdiction and the recognition and enforcement of judgments in civil and commercial matters (Brussels I Regulation). As of 10 January 2015, Regulation 44/2001 has been replaced by Regulation 1215/2012 on jurisdiction and the recognition and enforcement of judgments in civil and commercial matters (recast) (also referred to as the 'Brussels I *bis* Regulation').

278 Case C-327/10 *Hypoteční banka*, para. 53. The CJEU did not answer the question regarding a jurisdiction clause that was arguably unfair within the meaning of the UCTD.

under the UCTD did not play a role: the requirements of the rights of defence were interpreted within the scheme and for the purposes of the Brussels I Regulation.[279] The CJEU's interpretation of Article 47 in the context of this Regulation cannot, therefore, simply be transposed to other areas of law.[280]

The balance may play out differently in the context of the UCTD, where the protection of consumers as weaker parties is prioritised, in order to restore the transactional balance. The aim of restoring this balance extends into the procedural sphere. Judicial protection under the UCTD is inevitably more one-sided, because it is focused on consumer rights. There does not seem to be much space for a true balancing process of all substantive and procedural rights and interests involved.[281] AG Wahl has, nevertheless, submitted that 'certain legitimate interests have a better claim to outweigh the protection of consumers than others', such as the principle of *res judicata*.[282] In addition, traders have invoked fair trial rights to argue that 'preferential treatment' of consumers is at odds with their right to be heard, equality of arms, and judicial impartiality.[283] This other side of Article 47, where it is used as an argument *against* increased judicial protection of consumers, will be further explored below, and in subsequent chapters.

2.4.2. TOWARDS A GENERATIVE FUNCTION?

One of the main topics of debate is whether Article 47 sets a positive standard for the adjudication of EU rights, i.e. whether it can fulfil a *generative function*.[284] On the one hand, it is clear that the Member States

279 Case C-327/10 *Hypoteční banka*, para. 48. See also Case C-112/13 *A v B*, paras. 51, 56, 58.

280 On Article 47 of the Charter in the context of the recognition and enforcement of foreign judgments, see further Hazelhorst (n 29) 292.

281 Collins, 'The Constitutionalization of European Private Law as a Path to Social Justice?' (n 274) 160–161; Nowak (n 229) 36.

282 Case C-482/12 *Macinský and Macinská v Getfin and Financreal*, Opinion of AG Wahl, point 76.

283 See, e.g. ECtHR 20 December 2018, Appl. No. 22853/15 *Merkantil*, discussed in subsection 3.3.3 of this book, and cases on the right to be heard, discussed in sections 3.5, 4.5 and 5.5. See also Beka (n 32) 141.

284 Label introduced by Gerstenberg (n 234), 617. In this function, Article 47 is used not only to interpret or explain existing rules, but also as a source for generating new ones: see also Sieburgh (n 268) 301.

have positive obligations to guarantee effective judicial protection.[285] They must establish a system that provides remedies capable of addressing (alleged) infringements of EU rights, alongside procedures allowing actual access to a court, and granting fair prospects for a case to be adjudicated.[286] Procedural rights and safeguards must be guaranteed and observed by all authorities of the Member States, including judicial bodies. In this respect, Cafaggi has distinguished a systemic, institutional function of Article 47, which requires coordination between modes of enforcement and the content of remedies.[287] Further, Mak has recalled the '*Schutzgebotsfunktion*' or protective function of fundamental rights, in so far as these entail an 'obligation to protect' that requires positive action from public authorities, including courts.[288]

On the other hand, it is contested to what extent the Member States and their national courts are required to take any further (positive) action on the basis of Article 47 alone.[289] The right of access to court, for instance, does not necessarily imply that access to court must be actively facilitated.[290] Moreover, Article 47 does not prescribe any specific measures, and leaves choices to be made with regard to the measures that can be taken.[291]

There is a fear that if Article 47 derives legal authority from being a written source of law, the CJEU might become more interventionist.[292]

285 Jasper Krommendijk, 'Is There Light on the Horizon? The Distinction between *Rewe* Effectiveness and the Principle of Effective Judicial Protection in Article 47 of the Charter after *Orizzonte*' (2016) 53 Common Market Law Review 1395, 1413; Beijer (n 106) 270. Article 47 of the Charter is not the only source of procedural positive obligations in EU law, as Beijer (n 106) 306 notes. See, e.g. Case C-213/89 *The Queen v Secretary of State for Transport, ex parte: Factortame*, para. 20 (pre-Lisbon Treaty): national courts must have the power do 'everything necessary' to ensure that national law does not prevent EU law from having 'full force and effect'.

286 Pech and Sayers (n 107) 1216; Beijer (n 166) 138.

287 Cafaggi (n 25) 257.

288 Mak (n 203) 242–243. Mak refers to the work of Canaris on fundamental rights in (German) private law. See also the 'protective' function of Charter provisions discerned by Olha Cherednychenko and Norbert Reich, 'The Constitutionalization of European Private Law: Gateways, Constraints, and Challenges' [2015] European Review of Private Law 797, 818.

289 Beijer (n 106) 204–205.

290 Case C-403/16 *El Hassani*, Opinion AG Bobek, point 110.

291 Beijer (n 166) 145; Wilman (n 68) 892.

292 Dorota Leczykiewicz, '"Where Angels Fear to Tread": The EU Law of Remedies and Codification of European Private Law' [2012] European Review of Contract Law 47, 58–59. See also Collins, 'The Constitutionalization of European Private Law as a Path to Social Justice?' (n 274) 157; Micklitz (n 35) 363; Reich (n 1) 323.

The Charter was adopted to enhance the visibility of fundamental rights protection in the EU, not to expand the EU's powers, or to extend the scope of application of EU law. It expressly stipulates that it does not extend or modify the competences of the EU (Article 51(2) of the Charter), and rights recognised by the Charter must be exercised under the conditions and within the limits defined by the Treaties (Article 52(2) of the Charter). The Treaties – and, by extension, the Charter – are not intended to create new remedies, unless the structure of the national legal system is such that there is no remedy making it possible, even indirectly, to ensure respect for the rights that individuals derive from EU law.[293] The CJEU has used this as a justification to 'invent' new remedies, such as interim relief. Furthermore, in *DEB*, it relied on Article 47 to introduce an EU-wide standard for the assessment of national conditions for granting legal aid. This may add fuel to the fear that Article 47 will be used as a 'Trojan Horse', with the language of rights as a legitimising pretext for enhancing the general effectiveness of EU law.[294]

It nevertheless seems unlikely that Article 47 is capable, on its own, of overriding all limitations to (EU or CJEU interference in the enforcement of EU rights at the national level.[295] Rather, as Van Cleynenbreugel has suggested, Article 47 offers a constitutional basis for 'guided deference': the CJEU may develop a blueprint for national procedural law that allows for diversified rules, as long as they conform to judge-made standards that shape and refine the right to an effective remedy and a fair hearing. Such a standard still leaves a margin of appreciation to national procedural systems in order to render it operational.[296] In this respect, national rules of civil procedure could be seen as an expression of the fundamental right to effective judicial protection. Article 47 is relevant for the interpretation

293 See also, e.g. Case C-583/11 *Inuit Tapiriit Kanatami v European Parliament and Council of the European Union*, paras. 103–104; Case C-432/05 *Unibet*, para. 40. See also Prechal and Widdershoven (n 221) 41–42; Pech and Sayers (n 107) 1215–1216.

294 Engström (n 34) 3.

295 Leczykiewicz (n 292) 58.

296 Pieter Van Cleynenbreugel, 'Judge-Made Standards of National Procedure in the Post-Lisbon Constitutional Framework' (2012) 37 European Law Review 90, 97, 99. See also Reich (n 1) 324. On guidance and deference, see further Takis Tridimas, 'Bifurcated Justice: The Dual Character of Judicial Protection in EU Law' in Allan Rosas, Egil Levits and Yves Bot (eds), *The Court of Justice and the Construction of Europe: Analyses and Perspectives on Sixty Years of Case-law* (Springer 2013) 369.

and (dis)application of those rules, but does not provide remedies as such. Even when the CJEU imposes a certain interpretation, or insists upon the availability of a remedy, it is ultimately for the referring court to resolve the matter. The same is true when a provision is set aside on the basis of Article 47 of the Charter. The conclusions to be drawn in the case at hand are still governed by national law.[297] It very much depends on the national legal systems how far courts are able and willing to go; this will be further examined in Chapters 4 and 5.

2.5. ARTICLE 47 VIS-À-VIS EFFECTIVENESS

2.5.1. A DIFFERENT RATIONALE

2.5.1.1. A Rights-Based, Court-Centred Approach

The relationship between Article 47 of the Charter and the notion of effectiveness in EU law is a recurring issue in both the CJEU's case law and legal scholarship. Many attempts have been made to clarify the differences between three manifestations of effectiveness in the CJEU's case law: the principle of effectiveness, *effet utile* and effective judicial protection.[298] In practice, however, the difference is not as clear-cut. There is consensus that the CJEU is inconsistent: it does not offer any clear guidance on the question of which test should be applied in what cases.[299] There seems to be no obvious hierarchy between the concepts either.[300] It cannot be said that one should precede the other, and not even that one entails a higher threshold than the other.[301] The CJEU has held that the principle of effectiveness implies effective judicial protection,[302] which suggests both concepts embody the same legal principle.[303] Both account for the effective protection of EU rights. On other occasions, however, the CJEU

297 See also Engström (n 64) 595–596.

298 See, e.g. Koen Lenaerts and others, *EU Procedural Law* (Oxford University Press 2014) 110; Ebers (n 37) 249–250.

299 See, e.g. Wilman (n 31) 32; Nowak (n 229) 30–31; Krommendijk (n 285) 1408.

300 Wilman (n 31) 472.

301 Östlund (n 34) 211.

302 Case C-169/14 *Sánchez Morcillo I*, para. 61; Case C-61/14 *Orizzonte Salute – Studio Infermieristico Associato v Azienda Pubblica di Servizi alla persona San Valentino – Città di Levico Terme*, para. 48.

303 See also C-73/16 *Puškár*, Opinion of AG Kokott, point 51.

has differentiated between the two,[304] or even rephrased a preliminary reference pertaining to the principle of effectiveness in terms of effective judicial protection.[305]

Certain differences become apparent at the outset. According to Prechal, the scope and content of Article 47 are more sharply defined than (unwritten) principles.[306] Compliance with the fundamental right itself is what matters first and foremost.[307] Article 47 contains autonomous procedural safeguards, as *Banif Plus Bank* exemplifies.[308] It reflects a rights-based conception of the rule of law: EU citizens have individually enforceable rights that must be upheld by courts.[309] This intensifies the duty of national civil courts to interpret rules of national procedural law in accordance with EU law and, if necessary, set those rules aside.[310]

The justifications cited for restrictions also differ.[311] The test under Article 52(1) of the Charter has been discussed above.[312] Unlike Article 47, the principle of effectiveness does not guarantee any procedural rights in and of itself. It removes obstacles *to* protection, but it does not create remedies *for* protection.[313] The test is rule-based, i.e. whether a certain rule is justified in the legal system as a whole: the so-called procedural rule of reason.[314] The rule at issue must be analysed by reference to its role in the procedure, its progress and its special features before the various national instances. The basic principles of the domestic judicial system, such as the protection of the rights of defence, the principle of legal certainty, and

304 See, e.g. Joined Cases C-317/08, C-318/08, C-319/08 and C-320/08 *Alassini*; Case C-93/12 *Agrokonsulting*, paras. 59–60. See also Krommendijk (n 285) 1409–1410.

305 See also subsection 2.3.2 above.

306 Prechal (n 158) 156.

307 Prechal and Widdershoven (n 221) 43; Tridimas and Gentile (n 105) 806.

308 Case C-472/11 *Banif Plus Bank*: see subsection 2.1.3 above.

309 Micklitz (n 35) 358, 363; Vernadaki (n 66) 20. See also Case C-556/17 *Torubarov*, Opinion of AG Bobek, point 56: '[I]t might be useful to recall that all those institutional and constitutional guarantees are not an end in themselves. Nor are they put in place for the benefit of judges. They are the means to another end: to ensure effective judicial protection of EU-law rights for individuals at national level, and thus, again, the essence of the rule of law.'

310 Collins (n 274) 156–157.

311 Sacha Prechal, 'The European Acquis of Civil Procedure: Constitutional Aspects' (2014) 19 Uniform Law Review 179, 194–195.

312 See subsection 2.4.1 of this book.

313 Reich (n 1) 303. See also Östlund (n 34), 105.

314 Schebesta (n 253) 859; Krommendijk (n 285) 1407.

the proper conduct of procedure, must be taken into consideration where appropriate.[315]

The principle of effectiveness marks the borders between EU law and national legal systems, without reflecting substantive ideas of justice.[316] As AG Jääskinen has put it, the principle of effectiveness 'came into being as a function of the limitations placed by EU law on the procedural autonomy of the Member States'.[317] It is inextricably linked to the decentralised enforcement of EU law, and only applies in the absence of specific EU rules on remedies and procedures.[318] There is no normative yardstick beyond or below the existence (or otherwise) of remedies and procedures.[319] To the extent that the concept of *effet utile* has been used by the CJEU to require positive action, effectiveness as such is still an empty, amorphous concept.[320] It has no internal limits, which makes it volatile and potentially intrusive.[321] It can be used to legitimise any result, as long as it serves the purposes of the EU legal order.[322]

2.5.1.2. *Contrasting Dynamics*

The needs to ensure the full effectiveness of EU law and effective judicial protection are not necessarily driven by the same rationale.[323] The former is specifically geared towards, for example, the protection of consumers

---

315 See, e.g. Case C-40/08 *Asturcom*, para. 39; Case C-470/12 *Pohotovosť*, para. 51; Case C-169/14 *Sánchez Morcillo I*, para. 34; Case C-32/14 *ERSTE Bank Hungary*, para. 51; Case C-49/14 *Finanmadrid*, para. 44.

316 Eric Tjong Tjin Tai, 'Effectiviteitsbeginsel en nationaal privaatrecht' [2011] Weekblad voor privaatrecht, notariaat en registratie 790.

317 Case C-61/14 *Orizzonte Salute*, Opinion of AG Jääskinen, point 33.

318 Nowak (n 169) 8. See also Safjan and Düsterhaus (n 13) 32; Ebers (n 37) 258–259, 325; Östlund (n 34) 106.

319 Micklitz (n 35) 397–398.

320 Engström (n 64) 588; Bobek (n 178) 316.

321 Della Negra (n 233) 1020; Dougan (n 103) 424.

322 Bobek (n 178) 316; Półtorak (n 20) 48.

323 I have already tentatively explored the difference in 'Metamorphosis? The Role of Article 47 of the EU Charter of Fundamental Rights in Cases Concerning National Remedies and Procedures under Directive 93/13/EEC' [2017] Journal of European Consumer and Market Law 190. See also Prechal and Widdershoven (n 221) 50; Engström (n 64) 592–593; Prechal (n 311) 196; Della Negra (n 233) 1026; Krommendijk (n 285) 1405; Katri Havu, 'EU Law in Member State Courts: Adequate Judicial Protection and Effective Application: Ambiguities and Nonsequiturs in Guidance by the Court of Justice?' (2016) 8 Contemporary Readings in Law and Social Justice 158; Ellingsen (n 151) 1890.

against unfair terms,[324] whereas effective judicial protection could be seen as both a process and a goal.[325] Procedural rights are 'enabling' rights: they enable 'individuals to protect themselves against infringements of their rights' and 'to remedy civil wrongs'.[326] In this sense, procedural rights could be seen as derivative subjective rights.[327] Procedural rights could also be seen as independent, self-contained rights, implementing the idea of procedural justice and maintaining the rule of law.[328] This leads to contrasting dynamics.[329] Article 47 may even be invoked *against* the EU: judicial remedies must be guaranteed in order to contest enforcement measures based on EU law,[330] which inevitably distinguishes Article 47 from the notion of effectiveness in EU law. In consumer litigation, a challenge to an EU act is usually not the basis for legal action: Article 47 can be applied within the framework of the UCTD. Still, Article 47 and effectiveness are not always completely aligned in this context either, as will be further elaborated in Chapter 3.

As observed earlier, the CJEU has mainly taken an instrumental approach, so far, towards the proceduralisation of consumer protection under the UCTD.[331] This approach is functional and sectoral,[332] aimed at the enforcement of substantive EU consumer protection legislation, rather than the development of overarching EU procedural standards.[333] This instrumentality has been criticized for its narrow focus.[334] Civil justice is traditionally regarded as a bastion of state sovereignty.[335] Civil procedure, in particular, has its own internal logic and policy goals, which

324 Ebers (n 37) 100, 106; Riesenhuber (n 273) 250; Trstenjak and Beysen (n 49) 124; Della Negra (n 233) 1021.

325 Dougan (n 103) 431; Krommendijk (n 285) 1406.

326 Handbook on European law relating to access to justice (n 107), 16.

327 Półtorak (n 20) 12–13.

328 Vernadaki (n 98) 310; Östlund (n 34) 250, 290.

329 Safjan and Düsterhaus (n 13) 37–38.

330 Safjan and Düsterhaus (n 13) 15. See, for instance, Joined Cases C-402/05 P and C-415/05 P *Kadi*: see subsection 2.2.1 of this book.

331 See subsection 2.3.2.

332 Nowak (n 169) 30; Adelina Adinolfi, 'The "Procedural Autonomy" of Member States and the Constraints Stemming from the ECJ's Case-Law: Is Judicial Activism Still Necessary?' in Hans-Wolfgang Micklitz and Bruno De Witte (eds), *The European Court of Justice and the Autonomy of the Member States* (Intersentia 2012) 303.

333 Engström (n 64) 594. See also Case C-618/10 *Banesto*, Opinion of AG Trstenjak, point 58.

334 See, e.g. Hugh Collins, 'The Revolutionary Trajectory of EU Contract Law towards Post-National Law' in Sarah Worthington, Andrew Robertson and Graham Virgo (eds), *Revolution and Evolution in Private Law* (Hart Publishing 2018) 320–322; Dubos (n 100) 25.

335 Vernadaki (n 98) 299.

have not been clearly and uniformly established across Europe.[336] It is often trans-substantive:[337] there may be different procedures for the same substantive issues (for example a contractual claim can be brought in an expedited order for payment procedure, or in ordinary proceedings on the merits). Similarly, the same procedure (for example summary proceedings to obtain interim relief) may be followed for different substantive issues. The CJEU's approach is the opposite of trans-substantive. The duty of *ex officio* control following from the UCTD applies in all types of proceedings, as long as the case concerns potentially unfair terms falling within the scope of the Directive.[338] It can be regarded as a procedural tool to realise the Directive's objectives.[339] Such a 'one-size-fits-all' template does not fit seamlessly into a trans-substantive procedural framework that has not been specifically designed for consumer litigation.

The question arises as to what extent EU rights should shape national remedies and procedures,[340] especially in the area of civil justice. Moreover, it could be contended that reaching a fair and just decision requires a more tailored approach from the national civil court, with due regard to the circumstances of the case.[341] In private law adjudication, unfair terms are often only one aspect of a case; there are usually other rights and interests involved as well, such as security rights and/or efforts to render the administration of justice more efficient.[342] It has also, rightly, been observed that private parties are deprived of their personalities as legal subjects when they are merely defined as functional

---

336 Nowak (n 169) 33–34.

337 Schebesta (n 101) 852–853; Nowak (n 169).

338 Case C-137/08 *Pénzügyi Lízing*, para. 56 (*inter partes* proceedings); Case C-147/16 *Karel de Grote* (default proceedings, equivalence); Case C-618/10 *Banesto*, para. 57 (order for payment, effectiveness); Case C-415/11 *Aziz* (mortgage enforcement proceedings); Case C-377/14 *Radlinger*, para. 59 (insolvency proceedings); Case C-488/11 *Asbeek Brusse and de Man Garabito v Jahani* (appeal); Case C-168/05 *Mostaza Claro* (annulment of arbitral award).

339 See, e.g. Wrbka (n 51) 267; Nowak (n 169) 31. Micklitz has called *ex officio* control a 'procedural remedy': Hans-W Micklitz, 'Unfair Contract Terms – Public Interest Litigation before European Courts' in Evelyne Terryn, Gert Straetmans and Veerle Colaert (eds), *Landmark Cases of EU Consumer Law: In Honour of Jules Stuyck* (Intersentia 2013) 640.

340 Micklitz (n 35) 385.

341 Tulibacka (n 36) 1539. See further subsection 5.4.2 of this book.

342 See, e.g. Case C-618/10 *Banesto*, Opinion of AG Trstenjak. See also Jarich Werbrouck, 'Another Brick in the Wall: The Court's Judgment in *KdG/Susan Kuijpers*, 17 May 2018 [C-147/16]' [2019] European Review of Private Law 135, 154.

entities,[343] for example as consumers. Their rights, too, are turned into instruments when they are merged with policy objectives.[344]

Article 47 of the Charter can be conceived of as not merely ancillary to the goals of specific instruments of EU law. It appears to be less instrumental, and to leave more space to take other procedural factors into account than just the objectives of, for example, the UCTD.[345] It is about the fundamental right to effective judicial protection of EU citizens at large, not just in their capacity as consumers or market actors.[346] In the words of Reich, Article 47 'shares the concept of protecting individual rights as subjective rights in a liberal spirit'.[347] As such, it might better fit into, and possibly enrich, the private law discourse.[348]

2.5.2. OTHER FUNCTIONS ASCRIBED TO ARTICLE 47

2.5.2.1. A Merely Legitimising Function, or a Strengthening/Empowering Function?

How close or far from effectiveness one positions Article 47 influences the perception of its (potential) functions. A reference to Article 47 could be seen as merely reinforcing effectiveness, with no function other than legitimising (further) CJEU interference.[349] Reich has discerned three functions of the notion of effectiveness in European private law. The first is an eliminatory function.[350] The second is an interpretative or hermeneutical function, which serves to give an expansive, remedy-oriented

---

343 Collins (n 334) 318; Hans-W Micklitz, 'The Consumer: Marketised, Fragmentised, Constitutionalised' in Dorota Leczykiewicz and Stephen Weatherill (eds), *The Images of the Consumer in EU Law: Legislation, Free Movement and Competition Law* (Hart Publishing 2016) 25–26; Marija Bartl, 'Internal Market Rationality, Private Law and the Direction of the Union: Resuscitating the Market as the Object of the Political' (2015) 21 European Law Journal 572, 581.

344 Hans-W Micklitz, 'The Constitutional Transformation of Private Law Pillars through the CJEU' in Hugh Collins (ed), *European Contract Law and the Charter of Fundamental Rights* (Intersentia 2017) 69–70. See also Östlund (n 34), 215; Wilman (n 31) 470.

345 Östlund (n 34), 239, 255.

346 Micklitz (n 343) 41.

347 Reich (n 1) 322.

348 Cherednychenko (n 164) 157.

349 See also subsection 2.4.1 of this book.

350 Reich (n 1) 302. See also subsection 2.4.1.

interpretation of national law.[351] The third is a remedial function, which leads to an 'upgrade' of remedies under national law.[352] The first and third functions are reminiscent of the eliminatory and generative functions ascribed to Article 47. Reich himself has connected Article 47 to the positive side of effectiveness by reference to the link between substantive and procedural protection of EU rights.[353] A functional interpretation of Article 47 could, thus, contribute to a constructive approach towards remedies and procedures.[354]

This gives rise to the question of what the added value, if any, of Article 47 could be, beyond a *legitimising function*. Other authors have observed that Article 47 pertains not only to the effective enforcement of EU consumer rights, but also to the concept of EU citizenship, and to expectations of a fair and efficient justice system.[355] It reflects the importance attached by the EU legal order to court-based justice for EU citizens.[356] Instead of comparing the (added) value of Article 47 vis-à-vis effectiveness, the argument could also be turned around by positing that Article 47 should be the 'umbrella provision' or 'anchor point' for the adjudication of cases falling within the scope of EU law.[357] This would leave only a residual role for effectiveness, for instance in respect of the duty of *ex officio* control of unfair terms that does not follow (directly) from Article 47.[358]

While that point has not yet been reached, it could be said that Article 47 operates as a strengthened benchmark of effective access to justice within the EU.[359] From the perspective of EU citizens (consumers), Article 47 could, thus, fulfil a *strengthening function* that may go beyond effectiveness, in so far as the fundamental rights dimension of (a restriction of) its core components is expressly recognised. From the perspective of the courts, Article 47 could also fulfil an *empowering function*,[360] whereby it accentuates the primary role of courts as protectors of individual rights,

351 Reich (n 1) 305–307.
352 Reich (n 1) 308. See also subsection 2.3.2.
353 Reich (n 1) 322–323.
354 Cherednychenko and Reich (n 288) 819.
355 Tulibacka (n 36) 1535; Storskrubb (n 54) 83. See also subsection 2.4.2 above.
356 Tulibacka (n 36) 1530; Micklitz (n 343) 41.
357 Case C-562/12 *Liivimaa Lihaveis v Eesti-Läti programmi*, Opinion of AG Jaäskinen, point 57, reiterated in his Opinion in Case C-61/14 *Orizzonte Salute*, para. 24; Case C-93/12 *Agrokonsulting*, Opinion of AG Bot, points 29–30. See also, e.g. Ward (n 263) 1273; Prechal (n 158) 156; Krommendijk (n 285) 1416–1417.
358 See, e.g. Nowak (n 229) 36.
359 Sanna (n 29) 173.
360 Label derived from Gerstenberg (n 234), 621.

rather than policy enforcers.[361] The direct effect of Article 47 authorises the courts to step in and correct the legislature's errors or omissions, if necessary, by reference to its eliminatory or generative function. Both the strengthening and empowering functions of Article 47 reflect the rights-based, court-centred approach discussed above. These functions could be seen as an elaboration of an interpretative or hermeneutical function: they specify what effective judicial protection entails.

2.5.2.2. A Signalling or Transformative Function: Open Constitutionalisation

A conceptualisation of Article 47 as a provision with intrinsic value moves away from the principle of effectiveness, and in the direction of a self-standing yardstick or standard. In this respect, Tridimas and Gentile have argued that a fundamental right has its own identity ('essence'), as opposed to the notion of effectiveness, which seeks to augment a right's functionality.[362] They observe a strong *signalling* effect of constitutional language that pays tribute to the rule of law. A reference to Article 47 is more than symbolic: it indicates the seriousness of the issue. A similar 'leverage' or 'signal' function is also ascribed to fundamental rights in private law, which may indicate that an essential societal issue is at stake, and incite a desired legal development.[363] According to Mak, fundamental rights may mediate between the legal and political spheres, where they raise policy questions or make the deliberation of policy choices more explicit. As such, the interplay between fundamental rights and private law may help to 'open up' fixed or established rules that do not provide satisfactory solutions.[364] Wielsch has also pointed out such a function of fundamental rights in European private law, in the sense that they are used by courts as a check on lawmaking powers and processes.[365]

---

361 Ebers (n 37) 123–124. See also Engström (n 64) 592; Micklitz (n 35) 389. A rights-based approach does not necessarily involve a complete exclusion or rejection of policy-based reasoning: Donal Nolan and Andrew Robertson, 'Rights and Private Law' in Donal Nolan and Andrew Robertson (eds), *Rights and Private Law* (Hart Publishing 2012) 7.

362 Tridimas and Gentile (n 105) 804–805, 815.

363 Jan Smits, 'Constitutionalisering van het vermogensrecht', *Preadviezen uitgebracht voor de Nederlandse Vereniging voor Rechtsvergelijking* (Kluwer 2003) 51, 65.

364 Chantal Mak, *Fundamental Rights in European Contract Law* (Kluwer Law International 2008) 282. Mak refers to the work of Duncan Kennedy, *A Critique of Adjudication* (Harvard University Press 1997) 319–320.

365 See, e.g. Dan Wielsch, 'The Function of Fundamental Rights in EU Private Law' (2014) 10 European Review of Contract Law 365, 368, 382.

Similarly, Article 47 may operate as a correction mechanism when national procedural law is deemed to offer insufficient protection.[366] Moreover, as Sieburgh has observed, judicial reasoning in a discursive manner is important where national law meets EU law, especially in the event of (perceived) tension. Conflicts and discrepancies should be discussed openly, to motivate why, and on what basis, a certain path is chosen.[367] Article 47 has discursive value in this respect.

The signalling function of effective judicial protection as an EU fundamental right resonates with the meaning of rights and 'rights talk' as a discursive framework.[368] There is a difference between fundamental rights protection by means of structural (legislative and policy) reforms, and adjudication on a case-by-case basis. Civil courts may be hesitant to interfere directly in the lawmaking process, but a reference to fundamental rights in judicial decisions can, indirectly, play a role in public discussions about rights implementation. The signal could be a trigger for change, and instigate a 'trialogue', as Cafaggi has aptly called it,[369] about an upgrade of the procedural framework between the referring court, the CJEU and the national legislature. In this respect, a reference to Article 47 could fulfil a *transformative function*, as Gerstenberg has suggested.[370]

In a sense, the signalling function of Article 47 also has a systemic, institutional dimension. It is closely connected to the generative function of Article 47, except that it is used to indicate a problem and encourage a debate on potential solutions; finding a (systemic) solution is only the next step, not necessarily prescribed by Article 47 alone, and often left to the national legislature. Thus, Article 47 is not, directly, the source of positive requirements. Like Reich, Gerstenberg connects Article 47 to the positive side of effectiveness, but he also refers to 'an imperative commitment to an EU-wide, shared understanding of a fundamental right'.[371]

---

366 See also Półtorak (n 20) 50.

367 Carla Sieburgh, 'Legitimiteit van de confrontatie van Europees recht en burgerlijk recht van nationale origine', *Controverses rondom legaliteit en legitimatie* (Kluwer 2011) 240.

368 Barbara Oomen, 'The Contested Homecoming of Human Rights in the Netherlands' (2013) 31 Netherlands Quarterly of Human Rights 41, 72.

369 Fabrizio Cafaggi, 'On the Transformations of European Consumer Enforcement Law: Judicial and Administrative Trialogues, Instruments and Effects', in Fabrizio Cafaggi and Stephanie Law (eds), *Judicial Cooperation in European Private Law* (Edward Elgar Publishing 2017) 228, 237.

370 Gerstenberg (n 234) 603, 613. See also the 'transformative' function attributed to EU consumer law by Spanish courts, discussed in subsection 4.1.3 of this book.

371 Gerstenberg (n 234) 617.

This resonates with the 'guided deference' envisaged by Van Cleynenbreugel,[372] as well as Micklitz's view that Article 47 could be one of the building blocks for an 'autonomous constitutionally "safe" European private legal order'.[373]

Whether Article 47 will live up to its potential to be such a building block remains to be seen. Frantziou observes a 'mismatch' between the horizontal application of EU fundamental rights across a common constitutional order and a functional approach to ensure the effectiveness, uniformity and primacy of EU law.[374] To the extent that the term 'constitutional' refers to the EU and CJEU's own outlooks on fundamental rights protection, openly constitutional reasoning has been largely absent from the CJEU's case law.[375] Therefore, calls have been made for a more transparent or well-developed approach towards the application of EU fundamental rights, including Article 47 of the Charter.[376] Open constitutionalisation,[377] i.e. the explicit recognition of fundamental rights issues, could clarify both the purpose of judicial protection and the balancing of rights and interests at stake, even if no violation is found. It is the different rationale of Article 47 that could make it truly stand out in judicial reasoning: a rights-based, court-centred approach, a rule of law connotation, and due process as an end in itself.

2.6. INTERIM CONCLUSION: OVERVIEW OF FUNCTIONS OF ARTICLE 47 IN LEGAL DOCTRINE

This chapter has recounted the core components of Article 47 – access to court, an effective judicial remedy, equality of arms and the right to be heard – that inform the structure of the subsequent chapters. All authors who have written about proceduralisation under the UCTD, or Article 47 of the Charter as a new instrument in EU law, have proposed different views on Article 47's (potential) functions and, in particular, its (added)

[372] See subsection 2.4.2 of this book.

[373] Micklitz (n 239) 14–15.

[374] Eleni Frantziou, 'The Horizontal Effect of the Charter of Fundamental Rights of the EU: Rediscovering the Reasons for Horizontality' (2015) 21 European Law Journal 657, 665–666.

[375] Frantziou (n 374) 672.

[376] See, e.g. Cherednychenko (n 164) 162; Reich (n 67) 94.

[377] Micklitz and Reich (n 44) 801; Della Negra (n 233) 1024; Micklitz (n 344) 74.

value vis-à-vis effectiveness. Exactly how these functions are labelled is less relevant for the purposes of this book than what they express about the use of (references to) Article 47 in response to different issues.

To operationalise the various functions ascribed to Article 47 in legal doctrine, the overview below distils them into five main categories that reflect the debate outlined in this chapter. The indicators that can be expected, in view of these functions, are listed as well. The overview starts with the function that is closest to the notion of effectiveness; the other functions slowly move beyond it, and may even go against it.

Table 1. Overview of functions of Article 47 in literature

	Function (label)	Indicators
1.	LEGITIMISING FUNCTION (subsection 2.5.1)	– Reference to Article 47 merely serves as legitimation for CJEU interference – Parallel or supplementary to effectiveness; other functions cannot be (clearly) discerned
2.	STRENGTHENING FUNCTION (subsection 2.5.1)	Reinforcing effectiveness, but may go further: – Express recognition of (and restriction of) core components of Article 47 as fundamental rights issue – Rights-based: focus on procedural rights – Emphasis on consumer's perspective: availability of recourse
	EMPOWERING FUNCTION (subsection 2.5.1)	Overlap with strengthening function, but: – Court-centred: focus on responsibility of courts – Emphasis on court's perspective: power or duty to intervene
3.	SIGNALLING FUNCTION (subsection 2.5.2)	– Court could have opted to refer to effectiveness but referred (instead or additionally) to Article 47 to signal an issue in the design of procedure – More than ornamental: potential fundamental rights violation indicates seriousness – Aim is to make deliberation explicit and/or to trigger debate (trialogue) about the need for change
	TRANSFORMATIVE FUNCTION (subsection 2.5.2)	Overlap with signalling function, but: – Reference to Article 47 (is a factor that) triggers debate about an upgrade of national procedural law

(continued)

Table 1 *continued*

	Function (label)	Indicators
4.	ELIMINATORY FUNCTION (subsection 2.4.1)	– Separate test from effectiveness, although outcome may be the same – Not necessarily a higher threshold, but different rationale – Vertical: basis to set restrictive procedural rules aside (judicial review) – Horizontal: parameter for substantive assessment of unfair terms (judicial control)
5.	GENERATIVE FUNCTION (subsection 2.4.1)	– Article 47 as separate source of positive requirements – Compliance with autonomous procedural safeguards may go *against* effectiveness (see also subsection 2.5.2)

Source: Compiled by the author.

These functions are not mutually exclusive; they may be mutually reinforcing. The same reference to Article 47 (in the same case) may have two or more different functions. These functions may have different purposes or effects for different entities, and on different levels. For instance, a reference to Article 47 in its legitimising function pertains mainly to the division of competences between the EU and CJEU, on the one hand, and the Member States (and their national courts), on the other. Here, the overarching question is to what extent the CJEU can interfere in the choice and design of national remedies and procedures and/or impose any additional requirements. The eliminatory function pertains to the role of civil courts in proceedings that involve two or more private parties on opposite sides, i.e. the claimant and the defendant. It allows courts to offer immediate protection to the parties at the level of a concrete case. But this function also has an institutional dimension, whereby Article 47 operates as a correction mechanism on a systemic level: it is, thus, closely related to its signalling function. This institutional dimension pertains to the position of the judiciary vis-à-vis the legislature. Here, the question is whether and, if so, in what way(s) a shortfall in existing remedies and procedures can be addressed by *courts*.

The labels and indicators set out above provide a basis for the case law analysis in the subsequent chapters. Examples of all five categories, with some important nuances, will be discussed. Chapter 6 contains an overview that includes two additional functions identified in Chapters 4 and 5: a reconciliatory function and a rhetorical function.

CHAPTER 3

CASE LAW OF THE COURT OF JUSTICE ON ARTICLE 47 AND THE UCTD

This chapter examines the functions of Article 47 of the Charter in the case law of the CJEU on the UCTD, using the labels and indicators set out in the preceding chapter (section 2.6). The same reference in the same case may have different functions. Therefore, the cases will not be grouped according to function, but according to the core component(s) of Article 47 to which they pertain. The focus will be on four core components in particular: the right of access to court (section 3.2), the right to an effective remedy (section 3.3), the principle of equality of arms (section 3.4) and the right to be heard (section 3.5). Special attention will be paid to the (added) value of Article 47 vis-à-vis the notion of effectiveness. Finally, a summary will be given of the various functions of Article 47 that can be detected in the analysed case law (section 3.6).

3.1. FOCUS ON FOUR CORE COMPONENTS OF ARTICLE 47

In this chapter, the CJEU's case law referring to Article 47 of the Charter in the contxt of the UCTD will be analysed. The cases where substantive consideration was given to Article 47 by the Advocate General and/or the CJEU[378]

---

378 See the cases listed in subsection 1.3.3, footnotes 89 and 91. The Opinion of AG Tanchev in Case C-51/17 *OTP Bank* will be mentioned in relation to Case C-118/17 *Dunai*. The Opinion of AG Hogan in Case C-34/18 *Lovasné Tóth* will be mentioned in relation to Case C-34/13 *Kušionová*.

will be discussed by virtue of the core components that they pertain to, as per the table below:

Table 2. Overview of cases discussed in Chapter 3

Core component	Cases	Subsection
Access to court	*Asturcom*	3.2.2
	Finanmadrid; *Margarit Panicello*	3.2.3
	Profi Credit Polska and *PKO Bank Polski*; *Aqua Med*	3.2.4
Effective remedy	*Aziz*; *Kušionová*	3.3.2
	Sziber; *Dunai*	3.3.3
Effective judicial protection	*ERSTE Bank Hungary*; *Banco Santander*[379]	3.3.2
Equality of arms	*Sánchez Morcillo I & II*	3.4.2
	Pohotovosť	3.4.3
Right to be heard	*Banif Plus Bank*; *Biuro podróży 'Partner'*	3.5.2

Source: Compiled by the author.

The right to adjudication within a reasonable time and the right to legal aid do not (yet) play separate roles of significance in unfair terms cases.[380] Cases that do not contain a reference to Article 47 will only be discussed where the CJEU itself draws a parallel (for example between *Kušionová* and *Aziz*), or where this is necessary to get a better understanding of the analysed case law (for example, *Finanmadrid* pertains to the same Spanish order for payment procedure as *Banesto*, and *Aqua Med* and *Baczó* both concern procedural rules on jurisdiction with a potential deterrent effect on consumers).

---

379 Case C-34/18 *Lovasné Tóth* (para. 59) also refers to 'effective judicial protection', but only as part of a reference to Case C-32/14 *ERSTE Bank Hungary*. Case C-495/19 *Kancelaria Medius* merely reconfirms the CJEU's case law on *ex officio* control in default proceedings, and repeats the reference to Article 47 of the Charter in Case C-176/17 *Profi Credit Polska* and Case C-266/18 *Aqua Med* (paras. 17 and 32).

380 One of the questions in Case C-426/17 *Barba Giménez* pertained to legal aid, but the case did not concern unfair terms (or unfair commercial practices) and, thus, did not fall within the scope of EU consumer law. In Case C-567/13 *Baczó and Vizsnyiczai v Raffeissen Bank* (3.2.4) and Case C-407/18 *Addiko Bank* (3.3.2), legal aid was a relevant factor in light of the costs of proceedings, but these cases do not contain an explicit reference to Article 47 of the Charter.

The four core components listed above are closely related. In so far as the scope for judicial intervention is excluded or severely limited, the right of access to court, the right to an effective judicial remedy and the rights of defence might all be at stake. The first group of cases (section 3.2) concern consumer arbitration and order for payment procedures that are either extrajudicial or expedited. A distinction can be made between a delegation of judicial functions to non-judicial bodies (for example an arbitral tribunal or a court registrar) and restrictive procedural conditions (for example time limits). Both can be considered as restrictions on the right of access to court and an effective judicial remedy, especially when a remedy is understood as a (procedural) means of recourse. While these cases almost exclusively concern consumer defendants and, thus, could also be framed as pertaining to the rights of defence, they will be discussed under the heading of access to court. What they have in common is that they concern the risk that consumers are, in one way or another, prevented or deterred from exercising their rights in court. This is particularly problematic when the consumer is the defendant, and the possibility of judicial intervention – and unfair terms control – depends on them lodging an objection against the enforcement of a contract.

The second group of cases (section 3.3) concern the impossibility of the court granting a remedy against unfair terms once the case comes before it. Here, the main problem is a limitation of the ambit of the dispute and/or the court's power to provide interim relief in pending proceedings. Given that such a limitation may prevent the court from offering an effective remedy under the UCTD, these cases will be discussed under the heading of an effective remedy. While Article 47 of the Charter is not explicitly mentioned in *ERSTE Bank Hungary* and *Banco Santander*, the CJEU refers, in both decisions, to 'effective judicial protection' in the context of the UCTD. These cases are included in the analysis to distinguish *judicial* protection from other types of protection.

The cases in the third group (section 3.4) are related to the ones in the second group that concern a lack of judicial remedies in the context of mortgage enforcement. They will be discussed separately, because Article 47 is explicitly linked to the need to ensure procedural equality between consumers and traders.

Finally, the fourth group of cases (section 3.5) concern the right to be heard, which can be invoked by consumers as well as traders.

3.2. ACCESS TO COURT

3.2.1. INTRODUCTION: ACCESS AS A PREREQUISITE FOR JUDICIAL PROTECTION

As observed in Chapter 1, access to justice is a broader concept than access to court. Legal protection can, for instance, also be provided by non-judicial bodies like notaries or administrative authorities, or via mechanisms for alternative dispute resolution (ADR). Judicial remedies are not the only 'adequate and effective means' to ensure the effective protection of consumers against unfair terms (Articles 6 and 7 UCTD). At the same time, the right of access to court is one of the core components of Article 47 of the Charter, and a prerequisite for judicial protection. This section examines the meaning of access to court, in the context of the UCTD.

The case law in this section concerns consumer arbitration (*Asturcom*) and order for payment procedures that are either extrajudicial (*Finanmadrid, Margarit Panicello*) or impose restrictive procedural conditions (*Profi Credit Polska, PKO Bank Polski, Aqua Med*). The fact that consumers must meet certain procedural requirements to assert their rights does not automatically mean they do not enjoy effective judicial protection.[381] However, in so far as access to court is severely restricted or even excluded entirely, it may become a fundamental rights issue.

All of the above-mentioned cases concern procedures where the role of the court is limited, compared to the ordinary model of adversarial proceedings with corresponding procedural safeguards. These procedures all entail a reversal of the dispute or shift of procedural initiative.[382] The burden is placed on the defendant to initiate court proceedings and/or trigger a contentious debate between the parties: by asking for annulment of an arbitral award, by filing an objection against the claim, or by opposing enforcement of an arbitral award or order for payment. If the defendant does not take any action, no (full) judicial review or examination of the merits takes place, let alone unfair terms control. In this respect, the right of access to court and the rights of defence could be regarded as two sides of the same coin.

---

[381] See, e.g. Case C-483/16 *Sziber*, para. 50 (discussed in subsection 3.3.3 below); Case C-176/17 *Profi Credit Polska*, Opinion of AG Kokott, points 71–73 (subsection 3.2.4).

[382] Case C-49/14 *Finanmadrid*, Opinion of AG Szpunar, point 72; Case C-503/15 *Margarit Panicello*, Opinion of AG Kokott, point 41.

In the Spanish cases, adjudicative competences, i.e. decision-making powers, were delegated to an arbitral tribunal (*Asturcom*) or a court registrar (*Finanmadrid* and *Margarit Panicello*). In the Polish cases, the court's role was limited to a formality check; it was up to the debtor to challenge the claim and/or the terms of the underlying contract. The delegation aspect that features in the Spanish cases differs from normal proceedings upon default, i.e. when a consumer defendant fails to appear in court. In that situation, the case is usually still adjudicated by a *court*. But even then, it must be investigated – as the Polish cases show – whether the consumer's default of appearance is the result of a deterrent (or preclusive) effect of procedural rules as regards, for example, time limits and costs.

Unlike the Advocate Generals, the CJEU did not explicitly address the constitutional dimension of the Spanish cases, i.e. the consumer debtors' fundamental rights under Article 47 of the Charter. This dimension will be further elaborated on in Chapter 4. The Polish cases are a step towards open constitutionalisation, because the CJEU acknowledged that restrictive procedural conditions can also be problematic from a fundamental rights perspective.

3.2.2. CONSUMER ARBITRATION: A RESIDUAL ROLE OF COURTS?

3.2.2.1. Horizontal and Vertical Dimensions of Article 47 in Respect of Arbitration Clauses

Consumer arbitration, as such, is not the topic of this book. ADR can help to strengthen the effectiveness of consumer protection, where it offers a simple, fast and low-cost out-of-court solution to disputes between consumers and traders.[383] The cases of *Alassini* and *Menini* show that restrictions on the right of access to court may be justified in favour of ADR.[384] When consumers are claimants and can choose freely between bringing their claim in court or submitting it to an ADR body, there is prima facie no problem in respect of the right of access to court.[385]

---

383 See, e.g. Andrea Fejős and Chris Willett, 'Consumer Access to Justice: The Role of the ADR Directive and the Member States' (2016) 24 European Review of Private Law 33.

384 Discussed in subsection 2.1.2.1 above.

385 The ADR Directive contains quality requirements for ADR bodies, including expertise, independence, impartiality, fairness, liberty and legality. An agreement to submit complaints to an ADR entity is not binding on the consumer if it was concluded

There is, nevertheless, tension between ADR and the effective judicial protection of consumers against unfair terms,[386] especially when the consumer is the defendant. This tension becomes even more visible in the case of arbitration, which has a more adjudicative nature than mediation; arbitration normally entails the exclusion of the jurisdiction of (State) courts and results in a binding decision.[387] Private arbitral tribunals are not bound by the law in the same way as courts. It is unclear whether they can, or can be obliged to, exercise unfair terms control; they certainly cannot make a preliminary reference to the CJEU.[388]

Arbitration clauses in consumer contracts generally exclude the right of access to court. The UCTD does not prohibit arbitration clauses in consumer contracts as such, and the CJEU has not exercised the same scrutiny in respect of arbitration clauses as it has towards, for example, jurisdiction clauses.[389] This does not mean that arbitration clauses cannot be considered unfair. Terms excluding or hindering the consumer's right to take legal action, or to exercise any other legal remedy, are on the indicative and non-exhaustive list of unfair terms (Article 1(q) of the Annex to the UCTD). There could also be an issue of consent: are consumers aware of the arbitration clause when they enter into the contract, and, if so, are they able to make a well-considered choice to waive their rights of access to court?[390] In *Sebestyén*, a consumer

before the dispute had arisen, and if it deprives the consumer of the right to go to court (Article 10). Moreover, the solution imposed must not deprive the consumer of the protection afforded by provisions of national law that cannot be derogated from (Article 11).

386 See, e.g. Norbert Reich, 'More Clarity after "*Claro*"? Arbitration Clauses in Consumer Contracts as an ADR (Alternative Dispute Resolution) Mechanism for Effective and Speedy Conflict Resolution, or as "Deni de Justice"?' [2007] European Review of Contract Law 41; Marco Loos, 'Enforcing Consumer Rights through ADR at the Detriment of Consumer Law' [2016] European Review of Private Law 61, 74.

387 See, e.g. Lorna McGregor, 'Alternative Dispute Resolution and Human Rights: Developing a Rights-Based Approach through the ECHR' (2015) 26 European Journal of International Law 607.

388 See, e.g. Case C-125/04 *Denuit v Transorient-Mosaïque Voyages et Culture*; Case C-185/19 *KE v LF*.

389 Discussed in subsection 2.3.2 above: see further subsection 3.2.4 below on Case C-266/18 *Aqua Med*. See also Micklitz (n 339) 640.

390 Case C-342/13 *Sebestyén v OTP Bank*, para. 36. See also Horst Eidenmüller and Martin Fries, 'Against False Settlement: Designing Efficient Consumer Rights Enforcement Systems in Europe' in Hans-W Micklitz and Andrea Wechsler (eds), *The Transformation of Enforcement: European Economic Law in a Global Perspective* (Hart Publishing 2016) 100–101. A follow-up question is whether the right of access to court and to a fair trial (Article 6 ECHR) can be waived altogether: see Marte Knigge and Pauline Ribbers, 'Waiver of the Right to Set-Aside Proceedings in Light of Article 6 ECHR: Party-Autonomy on Top?' (2017) 34 Journal of International Arbitration 775.

had asked the referring court to declare an arbitration clause in a mortgage agreement void, because it unjustifiably limited her constitutional right to initiate legal proceedings; the arbitral tribunal had exclusive jurisdiction and there was no judicial remedy against its decisions. The CJEU held that the court must take Article 1(q) of the Annex into account, as well as the fact that the communication to the consumer of general information on the difference between arbitration and ordinary legal proceedings alone cannot rule out the unfairness of that clause.[391]

Arbitration clauses in consumer contracts touch on both the horizontal and vertical dimensions of Article 47. Horizontally, Article 47 could be a parameter for the (substantive) unfairness assessment of potentially unfair terms under the UCTD: a few examples will be given in Chapter 5.[392] Vertically, it could provide a basis for the judicial review of national (procedural) law that allows for such terms and/or prevents the court from performing unfair terms control (*ex officio*). Courts fulfil a residual role in this respect. They may be required to assess the unfairness or invalidity of an arbitration clause in three situations: (i) the defendant invokes an arbitration clause to argue that the court lacks jurisdiction to hear the claim; (ii) an action for annulment of an arbitral award is brought before the court; or (iii) the court is requested to grant leave for the enforcement of an arbitral award. The scope for judicial review of arbitral awards is usually limited.[393] However, extra scrutiny may be warranted in consumer cases, as became clear in *Asturcom*.

3.2.2.2. Asturcom: *An Empowering Function of Article 47?*

Asturcom concerned the enforcement of an arbitral award that was based on a presumably unfair arbitration clause in a contract between a consumer

[391] Case C-342/13 *Sebestyén*, para. 36. Thus, information is crucial. See Case C-191/15 *Verein für Konsumenteninformation v Amazon EU*, para. 69: a choice of law term that leads consumers into error by giving them the wrong impression about the law applicable to the contract is unfair; see also Aukje van Hoek, 'Eén voor allen en allen voor één: individuele versus collectieve handhaving van het consumentenrecht in het IPR' [2016] Ars Aequi 957; Marco Loos and Joasia Luzak, 'Wanted: A Bigger Stick. On Unfair Terms in Consumer Contracts with Online Service Providers' (2016) 39 Journal of Consumer Policy 63, 85. This does not mean that the trader must inform the consumer of the general procedural provisions of domestic law, if the terms concerned do not alter or prejudice the consumer's legal position: Case C-34/18 *Lovasné Tóth*, paras. 53, 56 and 66.

[392] More specifically, in subsection 5.2.1.

[393] See, e.g. Case C-126/97 *Eco Swiss China Time v Benetton International*, para. 34; Case C-168/05 *Mostaza Claro*, para. 34. See also Schebesta (n 253) 870.

and a mobile telephone company. The award had obtained the force of *res judicata*, because the consumer had not brought an action for annulment within the prescribed period of two months. The referring Spanish court asked the CJEU whether it should still refuse to enforce the arbitral award of its own motion, in the absence of the consumer.[394]

The principle of *res judicata* – literally, a matter (already) judged – means that a matter that has already been decided by a competent court or tribunal, resulting in a final and binding decision, may not be subject to litigation again between the same parties. This principle serves to ensure the stability of the law and legal relations as well as the sound administration of justice.[395] It has two aspects: procedural *res judicata* means that a decision has become final and cannot be appealed and/or reviewed; substantive *res judicata* means that the decision is binding upon the parties, which precludes them from relitigating the matter in new proceedings. Procedural *res judicata* usually entails substantive *res judicata*.[396] In principle, EU law does not require a national court to disregard national procedural rules conferring a *res judicata* effect on a decision, even if doing so would enable it to remedy an infringement of EU law.[397] The question of to what extent, and under what circumstances, this runs counter to the principle of effectiveness was at issue in *Asturcom*, as well as in some other (non-UCTD) cases that will not be discussed here.[398]

In *Asturcom*, the CJEU found that the principle of effectiveness does not automatically entail that an arbitral award with *res judicata* effect must be set aside. When a national court is asked to enforce such an award, it must only assess *ex officio* whether the arbitration clause is unfair within the meaning of the UCTD if national rules of procedure require *ex officio* control under domestic rules of public policy (pursuant to the principle of equivalence), and where the legal and factual elements necessary for that task are available to the court.[399] Under Spanish procedural law, public

---

394 Case C-40/08 *Asturcom*; see further subsection 4.2.2 of this book, on the national background and follow-up.

395 See, e.g. Case C-503/15 *Margarit Panicello*, Opinion of AG Kokott, points 30–31; Case C-224/01 *Köbler*, para. 38.

396 See, for an exception, e.g. the type of decision at issue in Case C-503/15 *Margarit Panicello* (subsection 3.2.3 below).

397 Case C-126/97 *Eco Swiss*, paras. 46–47; Case C-421/14 *Banco Primus*, para. 47.

398 On this topic, see further e.g. Hartkamp (n 31) 106–109. In the context of the UCTD, see Case C-831/19 *Banco di Desio e della Brianza and Others v YX, ZW* (pending).

399 Case C-40/08 *Asturcom*, paras. 51–53 and 59. See also Case C-168/15 *Tomášová*, para. 32 and Case C-470/12 *Pohotovosť*, point 42. Article 6 UCTD must be regarded as a provision of equal standing to domestic rules of public policy: see subsection 2.3.1 above.

policy was not listed as a ground for the court to refuse enforcement of the arbitral award, let alone *ex officio*. Thus, the principle of equivalence did not require *ex officio* control of unfair terms either. According to the CJEU, the need to comply with the principle of effectiveness cannot be stretched so far as to mean that the national court should make up fully for 'total inertia' on the part of the consumer. In principle, it is for the parties to take the initiative for legal proceedings.[400] Furthermore, it is compatible with EU law to establish reasonable time limits in the interest of legal certainty.[401] The CJEU held that a time limit of two months to bring an action for annulment of an arbitral award did not make it virtually impossible or excessively difficult for consumers to exercise their rights and, thus, did not run counter to the principle of effectiveness.[402]

By contrast, it could also be argued that maintaining legal certainty must not lead to upholding unfair arbitration clauses,[403] regardless of whether the consumer brings an action for annulment or not. Unlike the CJEU, AG Trstenjak concluded that the national court must always have the power of *ex officio* control, given the aim of the UCTD to protect consumers, and the obligation of the Member States to effectively guarantee the rights granted to individuals by EU law. She suggested that the principle of *res judicata* must be disregarded in favour of consumer protection.[404] According to her, the consumer could not be expected to take part in invalid arbitration proceedings based on an unfair arbitration clause, in order to have the clause annulled. In this respect, the referring court had highlighted distance – the arbitral tribunal was located 300 kilometres from the consumer's domicile[405] – and costs as potential deterrent factors. Trstenjak referred to Article 47, even though the Charter had not yet entered into force. The right to be heard must be safeguarded in all proceedings, initiated against a person, which are

---

[400] See, e.g. C-300/17 *Hochtief v Budapest Főváros Önkormányzata*, para. 52.

[401] Case C-40/08 *Asturcom*, para. 41. See also Case C-8/14 *BBVA v Peñalva López*, para. 28; Joined Cases C-154/15, C-307/15 and C-308/15 *Gutiérrez Naranjo*, para. 69.

[402] Case C-40/08 *Asturcom*, paras. 46–47. In the case at hand, the consumer had been notified of both the arbitration proceedings and the arbitral award that was sought to be enforced. She had an opportunity to take legal action and, thus, there was no need for *ex officio* control.

[403] Christopher Hodges, 'Consumer Protection and Procedural Justice' in Evelyne Terryn, Gert Straetmans and Veerle Colaert (eds), *Landmark Cases of EU Consumer Law – In Honour of Jules Stuyck* (Intersentia 2013) 624.

[404] Case C-40/08 *Asturcom*, Opinion of AG Trstenjak, points 58–59 and 74–75.

[405] See also the Commission's written observations of 4 July 2008 (JURM(2008)88 RVP), para. 40.

liable to culminate in a measure adversely affecting that person, including arbitration proceedings.[406] This meant that it could not be held against the consumer that she did not participate in the arbitration proceedings.[407] Trstenjak also expressed doubts as to the independence and neutrality of the arbitrators, where the arbitration clause in question was drafted by the arbitral tribunal itself. She found that the assessment of the clause must be the responsibility of a court, 'which fully guarantees the judicial impartiality required in a State governed by the rule of law'.[408] Although the referring court and the Commission[409] shared these doubts, they were passed over by the CJEU.

It has been observed that the CJEU's hesitation to interfere in consumer arbitration, perhaps due to its politically sensitive nature, overshadows its pursuit of a high level of consumer protection.[410] This could be partially explained by the CJEU's institutional position and its role in the preliminary reference procedure: it is primarily asked to interpret the Directive, and must be sensitive to the division of competences between the EU and the Member States. In *Achmea*, a non-consumer case concerning international arbitration under a bilateral investment treaty, the CJEU, nevertheless, stressed the importance of judicial review of arbitral awards from the perspective of the interpretation and application of EU law,[411] which cannot be ensured if the courts and tribunals of the Member States are sidelined. The CJEU recalled that the requirements of efficient arbitration proceedings may justify judicial review being limited in scope, provided that the fundamental provisions of EU law can be examined.[412] It could be argued that Article 47 of the Charter is a fundamental provision that warrants judicial review of arbitral awards in other cases as well,[413] including unfair terms cases.

---

406 Opinion of AG Trstenjak, point 61. See also subsection 2.1.2.4 on the rights of defence.

407 Opinion of AG Trstenjak, point 64.

408 Opinion of AG Trstenjak, point 66. See also Norbert Reich, 'Party Autonomy and Consumer Arbitration in Conflict: A "Trojan Horse" in the Access to Justice in the E.U. ADR-Directive 2013/11?' (2015) Penn State Journal of Law & International Affairs 290, 320.

409 Commission's written observations, para. 37.

410 Chantal Mak, 'Judgment of the Court (First Chamber) of 6 October 2009, *Asturcom Telecomunicaciones SL v Cristina Rodríguez Nogueira*, Case C-40/08' [2010] European Review of Contract Law 437, 438, 443; Schebesta (n 253) 871.

411 Case C-284/16 *Slovak Republic v Achmea*, paras. 42 and 50.

412 Case C-284/16 *Achmea*, para. 54.

413 See also Bettina Heiderhoff, 'Die Selbstbeschränkung des Anwendungsbereichs der EU-Charte in Art. 51 und die Ausbildung eines anerkennungsrechtlichen europäischen ordre public' in Bettina Heiderhoff, Sebastian Lohsse and Reinier

The Opinion of AG Trstenjak shows how *Asturcom* might have had a different outcome if it had been framed as an issue of effective judicial protection. The CJEU did not consider the fundamental rights dimension of the case. Rather, it focused on the existence of an opportunity to bring an action for annulment, and the role of the national court under domestic law. Trstenjak went a step further and questioned whether consumers can be expected to challenge an unfair arbitration clause at all, let alone an arbitral award based on that clause.[414] She referred to Article 47 as a standard for national procedural law, beyond the threshold of the principles of equivalence and effectiveness. Article 47 could create space for judicial intervention, in so far as national procedural law does not allow for it. As such, it could fulfil an empowering function where it authorises national civil courts to step in. For the referring court in *Asturcom* this might have made a difference, as will be shown in Chapter 4.

3.2.3. EXPEDITED ORDER FOR PAYMENT PROCEDURES: A LIMITED ROLE FOR COURTS[415]

3.2.3.1. Delegation of Judicial Functions to Non-Judicial Bodies

The CJEU has repeatedly emphasised the special responsibility of national courts to ensure the judicial protection of the rights that EU law confers on individuals, with reference to Article 47 of the Charter. Access to court comes with procedural guarantees, such as judicial independence, and ensures the application of national and EU law.[416] This gives rise to the question of whether, and to what extent, judicial tasks and/or competences may be delegated to other, non-judicial bodies. Such a delegation of competences may take place for various reasons, for example to ease the burden on the courts. In *Alassini*, this was deemed a legitimate aim: as long as the parties could still exercise their right of access to the judicial system, they could be required to resort to ADR first.[417] However, in

Schulze (eds), *EU-Grundrechte und Privatrecht / EU Fundamental Rights and Private Law* (Nomos 2016) 91.

414 See also Schebesta (n 253) 862.

415 The analysis in this and the following subsection has also been included in Van Duin and Leone (n 45) 1238–1242.

416 See also Case C-284/16 *Achmea*, paras. 35–36.

417 Joined Cases C-317/08, C-318/08, C-319/08 and C-320/08 *Alassini*, discussed in subsection 2.1.2.1 above.

Finanmadrid, a Spanish order for payment procedure that was handled by the *Secretario Judicial* (court registrar or clerk[418]) instead of a judge was found to be liable to undermine the effectiveness of the UCTD.[419] The CJEU did not make an assessment under Article 47 of the Charter, despite an express reference to the right to effective judicial protection by the referring court. Still, the Opinion of AG Szpunar and the Commission's written observations shed more light on the potential (added) value of Article 47 in the context of the UCTD.

Finanmadrid is a sequel to *Banco Español de Crédito* (*Banesto*), a landmark case on the UCTD. In both cases, the debtors were consumers who had entered into credit agreements for the purchase of motor vehicles. Both cases concerned the same Spanish order for payment procedure, aimed at granting creditors easy and rapid access to justice for uncontested pecuniary claims.[420] The creditor had to provide prima facie evidence of the claim, i.e. the existence of a debt, by the submission of a contract or invoices. If the debtor did not lodge an objection, the procedure was non-contentious, and it merely had to be ascertained whether the formal requirements were met. *Banesto* was about the lack of unfair terms control by the court before it issued an order for payment, *Finanmadrid* about the lack of unfair terms control by the court when it was asked to enforce an order for payment issued by the court registrar.

In *Banesto*, the CJEU famously held that national courts are, in principle, not allowed to modify the contract by revising the content of unfair terms. But the case was also about a shift of procedural initiative under restrictive procedural conditions. The CJEU found there was a significant risk that consumer debtors would not lodge an objection, for the following reasons:

- Due to the particularly short period provided for that purpose (20 days).
- Consumers might be dissuaded from defending themselves, in view of the costs that legal proceedings would entail, in comparison to the amount of the disputed debt.

418 Since 2015 called *Letrado de la Administración de Justicia*: see further subsection 4.3.2 of this book, on the national background, and follow-up events to C-49/14 *Finanmadrid*. See also Fernando Gascón Inchausti, 'Between Reform and Dejudicialization: Current Trends in Spanish Civil Litigation' in Alan Uzelac and Remco van Rhee (eds), *Transformation of Civil Justice* (Springer International Publishing 2018) 135.

419 Case C-49/14 *Finanmadrid*, paras. 46–47.

420 Case C-618/10 *Banesto*, para. 51.

- Consumers might be unaware of, or fail to appreciate, the extent of their rights.
- Due to the incomplete nature of the information available to consumers, owing to the limited content of the request for the order for payment submitted by the creditor.[421]

According to the CJEU, to deprive consumer debtors of the benefit of the protection intended by the UCTD, it was sufficient for creditors (traders) to initiate an order for payment.[422] They could simply count on the consumer's passivity, and circumvent judicial control through what Gerstenberg has called 'opportunistic exercises of party autonomy'.[423] Therefore, the court performs *ex officio* control where it has the necessary legal and factual elements available to it.[424]

This time, AG Trstenjak doubted whether it was really necessary to change the order for payment procedure. In her view, the introduction of *ex officio* control – a 'preventive judicial protection mechanism' – would eliminate an important efficiency benefit.[425] Trstenjak emphasised that procedures must be established that take the interests of both parties equally into account, including the creditor's right of access to justice. She considered that the case law of the CJEU up until then (2012) allowed for judicial protection to be dependent on consumers revealing their intentions to make legal challenges. It was sufficient that they could lodge an objection, which gave them the opportunity to decide whether they wished to avail themselves of the protection offered to them.[426]

The factors listed by the CJEU in *Banesto* nevertheless make it clear that, even if such an opportunity exists, there are many reasons – de facto (for example unawareness) and *de jure* (for example time limits) – why

421 Case C-618/10 *Banesto*, para. 54.

422 Case C-618/10 *Banesto*, para. 55. See also Case C-473/00 *Cofidis*, para. 29: to prevent the court from performing unfair terms control, the trader merely had to wait for expiry of a time limit before bringing an action for payment against the consumer.

423 Gerstenberg (n 234) 610. The trader would get away with a breach of EU consumer law by profiting from the consumer's lack of legal knowledge: Rott (n 98) 193. A focus on party autonomy, without taking the weaker position of consumers into account, may facilitate aggressive debt collection and repossession practices: Daniela Caruso, 'Fairness at a Time of Perplexity' in Stefan Vogenauer and Stephen Weatherill (eds), *General Principles of Law: European and Comparative Perspectives* (Hart Publishing 2017) 349.

424 Case C-618/10 *Banesto*, para. 60.

425 Case C-618/10 *Banesto*, Opinion of AG Trstenjak, point 56.

426 Case C-618/10 *Banesto*, Opinion of AG Trstenjak, points 68–69, 73 and 75.

consumers might fail to make use of it.[427] In that event, the opportunity may be a mere formality, not a genuine opportunity for consumers to exercise their rights in court.[428] *Ex officio* control is one way to fix this; a broad understanding of access to court and justiciability of EU consumer rights is another, as will be further elaborated on below.

3.2.3.2. Finanmadrid: *A Blind Spot Where Article 47 is Concerned*

Finanmadrid concerned the follow-up issue that *court* involvement had been made dependent on the consumer debtor lodging an objection, otherwise the order would be issued by a court registrar instead of a judge.[429] The referring court, which was subsequently requested to enforce the order, wanted to know whether the procedure was compatible with the fundamental right to effective judicial protection. The court could have opted to raise only the principle of effectiveness, but it additionally, and explicitly, referred to Article 47.

In essence, there were four problems. Firstly, the court registrar could only check whether the formal admissibility requirements had been met; there was no unfair terms control (*Banesto* had not yet been implemented).[430] The matter would only be referred to a judge where the documents indicated that the claimed amount was incorrect, or where the debtor contested the claim. Secondly, the referring court assumed that the order had acquired the force of *res judicata* and was endowed with effects analogous to those of a judicial decision.[431] This meant that the debtor could not oppose enforcement of the order on the ground of unfair terms in the underlying contract, and that the court could not make an assessment of this issue on its own motion either.[432] The order was effectively immune from judicial review. Thirdly, the court registrar was not an independent judicial authority and did not enjoy the same constitutional status as a court.

A fourth, additional problem – drawn attention to by the Commission in its written observations[433] – was that there appeared to be procedural

---

427 See also subsection 3.2.1 above.

428 Dougan (n 103) 412, 424; Beka (n 32) 172, 355.

429 Case C-49/14 *Finanmadrid*, paras. 37–39.

430 Case C-49/14 *Finanmadrid*, para. 50.

431 Case C-49/14 *Finanmadrid*, paras. 24 and 47.

432 Case C-49/14 *Finanmadrid*, para. 24. See also the Commission's written observations of 19 May 2014 (sj.c(2014)1686122), para. 33.

433 Case C-49/14 *Finanmadrid*, paras. 71–73, with reference to Case C-472/11 *Banif Plus Bank*, paras. 29–31.

defects in the order for payment procedure at issue, i.e. no valid service or notification on two of the defendants, which cast doubt on the possibility of them exercising their rights of defence, as guaranteed by Article 47 of the Charter. The case concerned one main debtor and three guarantors; in respect of two of those guarantors, it was unclear whether they had actually been informed of the pending order for payment procedure against them.

While the CJEU dealt with the first and second problems, it did not address the third and fourth. It focused on unfair terms control at the enforcement stage, and not on the delegation of judicial competences, or potential violation of the rights of defence, in the preceding stage. The CJEU held that, when the authority hearing the request for an order for payment (i.e. the court registrar) did not have the power to assess unfair terms, the court ruling on enforcement of the order must have that power.[434] Thus, the CJEU seemed to agree with AG Szpunar's view that the onus is on the enforcement court as a last resort to ensure that unfair terms control takes place.[435] This was reiterated in *EOS KSI Slovensko*: the conferral of jurisdiction regarding payment procedures to officials who do not have the status of a magistrate, and cannot perform unfair terms control, is permissible, so long as judicial control is ensured at the enforcement stage (*ex officio*), or when an objection is lodged.[436]

The mere fact that an order has *res judicata* effect because the consumer has not challenged the claim (in time) cannot justify the complete absence of judicial review.[437] In the words of AG Szpunar, a balance must be struck 'between the notion that a court should compensate for a procedural omission on the part of a consumer who is unaware of his rights and the notion that it should not make up fully for the consumer's total inertia'.[438] In so far as the principle of *res judicata* makes it impossible or excessively difficult to ensure the protection conferred on consumers by the UCTD, it runs counter to the principle of effectiveness.[439] Time limits must be sufficient, in practical terms, to enable the applicant to prepare and bring

---

434 Case C-49/14 *Finanmadrid*, paras. 46 and 55.
435 Case C-49/14 *Finanmadrid*, Opinion of AG Szpunar, points 62 and 72.
436 Case C-448/17 *EOS KSI Slovensko v Danko and Danková*, para. 50.
437 Case C-49/14 *Finanmadrid* para. 48.
438 Case C-49/14 *Finanmadrid*, Opinion of AG Szpunar, point 43, with reference to Case C-40/08 *Asturcom Telecomunicaciones*, para. 47.
439 Case C-49/14 *Finanmadrid*, para. 54. See also Case C-122/14 *Aktiv Kapital Portfolio v Egea Torregrosa*, paras. 31 and 36.

an action.[440] If the time limit is too short, there is a significant risk that the consumer will not lodge an objection.[441] The referring court had also mentioned the additional obstacle of mandatory legal representation, but the CJEU did not take this into consideration.

The question regarding Article 47 remained unanswered in *Finanmadrid*, although the referring court considered this to be a pertinent issue.[442] This is peculiar, in view of the CJEU's own statement in *Åkerberg Fransson* that, when requested to give a preliminary ruling, it must provide all the interpretative guidance the national court needs in order to determine whether legislation falling within the scope of EU law is compatible with EU fundamental rights.[443] Unlike the CJEU, the Commission did discuss the third and fourth problems mentioned above. According to the Commission, the court registrar could not be considered as an 'independent and impartial tribunal, established by law'. Therefore, orders issued by the court registrar required to be subject to judicial review.[444] This was a different rationale for judicial intervention: it was not only about ensuring that unfair terms control took place, but also about ensuring that the case came before a court. It was questionable whether the delegation of judicial competences was justified in light of the aim it pursued, i.e. streamlining the procedure. Moreover, the Commission noted that the procedure at issue could be contrary to Article 47 in respect of the two defendants who had not been duly notified.[445]

In so far as the referring court and the Commission used Article 47 in its strengthening or signalling function, the CJEU did not pick up on this. Consequently, the decision in *Finanmadrid* has a blind spot where Article 47 is concerned. From the perspective of the Directive's effectiveness, the possibility of judicial control at the enforcement stage might be sufficient. However, this neither diminishes the fact that disputes are resolved in a procedure of a (quasi-)judicial nature *outside* the judicial

---

440 Case C-8/14 *BBVA*, para. 29, with reference to Case C-69/10 *Samba Diouf*, para. 66. In this respect, the service of a specific procedural notice is significant: Case C-8/14 *BBVA*, Opinion of AG Szpunar, point 56.

441 Case C-448/17 *EOS KSI Slovensko*, paras. 52–53.

442 Case C-49/14 *Finanmadrid*, paras. 46 and 56–57, respectively.

443 Case C-617/10 *Åkerberg Fransson*, para. 19.

444 Case C-49/14 *Finanmadrid*, Commission's written observations, para. 67. The CJEU adopted similar reasoning in a (non-consumer) case under the Brussels I Regulation regarding a writ of execution issued by a notary: Joined Cases C-267/19 and C-323/19 *Parking v Sawal and Interplastics v Letifico*, paras. 52–53.

445 Case C-49/14 *Finanmadrid*, Commission's written observations, para. 75.

system, nor addresses a potential violation of the rights of defence at the preceding stage. As AG Szpunar observed, even if Article 47 provides only a *minimum* level of protection, there might be a violation in cases where the consumer defendant did not have access to an effective remedy due to, for example, a restrictive calculation of the time period for lodging an objection, the prohibitive costs of the procedure, or the absence of recourse against an order adopted without the defendant's knowledge. In this respect, Szpunar drew a parallel with the Brussels I Regulation.[446] This Regulation also recognises explicitly that consumers deserve special protection: for that reason, it contains additional procedural guarantees in cross-border disputes.[447] According to Szpunar, however, the order for reference did not contain enough information to answer the question of whether the defendant had had access to an effective remedy.[448]

3.2.3.3. Margarit Panicello: *Another Instance of a Signalling Function of Article 47*

The solution offered by the CJEU in *Finanmadrid* – *ex officio* control at the enforcement stage – does not address a lack of judicial involvement, or a potential violation of procedural rights, in the proceedings leading up to the order for payment. In *Margarit Panicello*, another Spanish case concerning a similar type of procedure (*jura de cuentas*: 'unpaid fee recovery procedure'[449]), AG Kokott explained why judicial review at the enforcement stage might be too late. The pressure that the very existence of an enforceable instrument exerts on consumers to discharge their (alleged) payment obligations must not be underestimated. If the consumer 'voluntarily' complies with a decision, albeit based on unfair terms, it does not even need to be enforced. This was one of the reasons why AG Kokott

446 Case C-49/14 *Finanmadrid*, Opinion of AG Szpunar, point 95, where a parallel is drawn with Regulation 44/2001. See also, e.g. Case C-519/13 *Alpha Bank Cyprus*, paras. 30–31: the objectives of improving the efficiency and speed of judicial procedures and ensuring the proper administration of justice cannot be attained by undermining the rights of defence.

447 Case C-347/18 *Salvoni v Fiermonte*, para. 21. On the special protective rules for consumers under the Brussels I Regulation, see, e.g. Aukje van Hoek, 'CJEU – *Pammer and Alpenhof* – Grand Chamber, 7 December 2010, Joined Cases 585/08 and 144/09' [2012] European Review of Contract Law 93.

448 Case C-49/14 *Finanmadrid*, Opinion of AG Szpunar, point 96.

449 Case C-503/15 *Margarit Panicello*, Opinion AG Kokott, point 1. See further subsection 4.3.3 of this book, on the national background and follow-up.

concluded that the procedural rules at issue were contrary to the UCTD, as well as to Article 47 of the Charter.[450]

The *jura de cuentas* is a special administrative procedure before the court registrar. The procedure is designed for lawyers to recover unpaid fees from their clients; while it is voluntary for the lawyer, it is mandatory for the client. It should be noted that the UCTD applies to contracts for legal services between lawyers and natural persons acting for purposes outside their trade, business or profession.[451] The request for a preliminary ruling was made by a Spanish court registrar, who questioned his own exclusive competence in the procedure. Paradoxically, this is also why the CJEU found the case to be inadmissible: the court registrar was not an independent 'court or tribunal' in the sense of Article 267 TFEU. In AG Kokott's view, by contrast, it did not matter that a decision adopted by a court registrar in another procedure was not classified as 'a judicial act *within the meaning of Spanish constitutional procedural law*':[452] the court registrar acts with sufficient independence. Moreover, an order of the court registrar is of a judicial nature: it establishes an enforceable claim to payment.[453] In any case, it is questionable whether consumers are able to tell the difference between a registrar's order and a 'real' judicial decision.

According to AG Kokott, several elements of the procedure were problematic from the perspective of the UCTD read in conjunction with Article 47. The court registrar could not perform unfair terms control, but, more importantly, Kokott also found that the notion of deferring such control to the enforcement stage must be rejected on grounds of both procedural economy and the effective implementation of the UCTD. Even if unfair terms control could take place at the enforcement stage, the initial claim would still have been awarded, and there would be the threat of enforcement of the decision. The pressure that the very existence of an enforceable decision exerts on consumers to discharge their (alleged) payment obligations must not be underestimated.[454] Consumers may not

---

450 Case C-503/15 *Margarit Panicello*, Opinion of AG Kokott, points 136–137.

451 Case C-537/13 *Šiba v Devėnas*. See also Marien Aguilera Morales, '¿*Quo vadis* "jura de cuentas"? ¿*quo vadis* Europa? El estatus y función de los Secretarios Judiciales a examen por el TJUE' (2017) 41 Revista General de Derecho Procesal 6–7.

452 Case C-503/15 *Margarit Panicello*, Opinion of AG Kokott, point 63. Kokott refers to a national debate about the question of whether it was compatible with the rule of law to transfer quasi-judicial powers to bodies responsible for the administration of justice: see point 86.

453 Opinion of AG Kokott, points 81, 91 and 95.

454 Opinion of AG Kokott, points 136–137.

be able to tell the difference between a real judicial decision and an order for payment issued by a court registrar, and this promotes the settlement of claims founded on unfair terms.[455] Therefore, it could be argued that judicial intervention should already be possible at an earlier stage.

As AG Kokott indicated, the design of the procedure may give rise to concerns under Article 47, in light of the risk that consumers will not challenge the claim, the decision, or its enforcement. This might encourage traders to take their chances with claims that are based on unfair terms, or otherwise unfounded.[456] From the perspective of the UCTD, *ex officio* control at the enforcement stage might be acceptable as a last resort, but Kokott relied on Article 47 to go one step further: effective judicial protection would entail that judicial control should take place *before* a decision is issued.[457] She seemed to consider *judicial* protection in the preceding procedure as an additional, positive requirement.[458] Article 47 fulfils a signalling function here, too: it was meant to incite a more fundamental reconsideration of the procedure at issue.

The CJEU, nevertheless, concluded that the procedure lacked a clear judicial nature, and that the case was, therefore, inadmissible. A similar question in a different case was also declared inadmissible, because the case was pending before the court registrar and not before the referring court.[459] The issue was left unresolved until it was picked up by the Spanish Constitutional Court in 2019, as will be discussed in Chapter 4.[460]

3.2.4. OTHER RESTRICTIVE PROCEDURAL CONDITIONS

3.2.4.1. Profi Credit Polska: *A Strengthening Function of Article 47*

Whereas *Finanmadrid* was a missed opportunity for the CJEU to clarify the meaning of effective judicial protection in the context of the UCTD, the CJEU did explicitly refer to Article 47 of the Charter in two more

455 Opinion of AG Kokott, points 133–136.

456 In this respect, Beka has rightly noted that there is a fundamental distinction between a debt that is owed, but which the consumer is unable to pay, and a debt that has resulted from an unfair term, and/or consumer protection legislation not having been observed: Beka (n 32) 252.

457 See also Case C-426/17 *Barba Giménez*, para. 28.

458 Case C-503/15 *Margarit Panicello*, Opinion of AG Kokott, point 117.

459 Case C-426/17 *Barba Giménez*, para 45–46.

460 See subsection 4.2.3 of this book.

recent cases – *Profi Credit Polska* and *PKO Bank Polski* – that concerned an order for payment procedure in Polish law. In both cases, a financial institution had brought a claim against a consumer debtor on the basis of a promissory note or a bank ledger that provided security for a credit agreement. Unlike in *Banesto* and *Finanmadrid*, the agreement itself was not in the case file; the procedure was *ex parte* and rested on the presumption that the promissory note fully proved the factual basis for the claim. The court only had to establish that it was formally valid. It was up to the debtor to contest not only the obligation arising from the promissory note, but also the underlying contractual relationship.

According to AG Kokott, it was not problematic per se that consumers were required to lodge an objection; they could reasonably be expected to have to take this step to assert their rights.[461] The assumption that the creditor must have access to an expedited procedure was not called into question either: to do so would be an excessive intrusion on the Member States' procedural autonomy.[462] Moreover, the creditor has an interest in seeking enforcement quickly. What was problematic, however, was a constellation of restrictive procedural conditions: a time limit of only two weeks for consumers to substantiate their complaints, a limitation of the scope of the court's assessment of those complaints, and relatively high court fees. These were all capable of making it excessively difficult for consumers to exercise their rights.[463]

The CJEU held that Article 7(1) UCTD – the need to provide 'adequate and effective means' – entailed an obligation to lay down detailed procedural rules that ensured observance of the rights individuals derived from the Directive, which also implied a requirement that there was an effective remedy: a requirement 'also enshrined' in Article 47 of the Charter.[464] The right to an effective remedy would be infringed if national procedural law gave rise to a significant risk that consumers would not lodge the required objection.[465] The decision confirmed and consolidated *Banesto* and *Finanmadrid*. The CJEU reiterated that

---

461 Case C-176/17 *Profi Credit Polska*, Opinion of AG Kokott, points 71–73. See also Case C-32/14 *ERSTE Bank Hungary*, para. 63.

462 Opinion of AG Kokott, point 76.

463 Opinion of AG Kokott, points 77–81. See also the Commission's written observations of 27 July 2017 (sj.j(2017)4286930), para. 75.

464 Case C-176/17 *Profi Credit Polska*, para. 59; Case C-632/17 *PKO Bank Polski*, para. 45. See also Case C-483/16 *Sziber*, para. 49.

465 Case C-176/17 *Profi Credit Polska*, paras. 61 and 69, with reference to Case C-49/14 *Finanmadrid*, para. 52 and Case C-122/14 *Aktiv Kapital Portfolio*, para. 37.

the exercise of consumers' substantive rights must not be subject to unreasonable procedural conditions: in particular, time limits or costs.[466] A time limit of two weeks, by which time consumers not only had to raise their complaints, but also to adduce facts and evidence, when combined with strict admissibility requirements and a court fee that was three times higher for the consumer than for the other party, was found to be unreasonable.[467] The procedural rules at issue allowed for an order for payment to be granted in the absence of a genuine opportunity for the consumer debtor to file an opposition, or a possibility for the court to perform *ex officio* control.[468]

The CJEU seemed to consider Article 47 as largely synonymous with the principle of effectiveness.[469] It also cited the procedural rule of reason as the relevant test, not Article 52(1) of the Charter. Still, this reference to Article 47 was more than symbolic, even if it did not necessarily lead to a different outcome in the case at hand and could, thus, be seen as merely supporting the UCTD's effectiveness. It was the CJEU, not the referring court, that brought up Article 47, which appears to fulfil not only a legitimising function but also a strengthening function in respect of procedural rights as enabling rights. *Ex officio* control is meant to compensate for procedural omissions that cannot be imputed to consumers; due, for example, to restrictive procedural conditions.[470] It is only part of the solution:[471] it does not remove procedural obstacles, such

466 Case C-176/17 *Profi Credit Polska*, paras. 63–64. The UCTD itself does not cover the allocation of the costs of legal proceedings, as provided for by national legislation: Case C-433/11 *SKP*, para. 34.

467 Case C-176/17 *Profi Credit Polska*, paras. 65–68.

468 The court may require the trader to produce underlying documents – in particular, the credit agreement – in order to verify that the rights consumers derive from the UCTD and the Consumer Credit Directive are observed: Joined Cases C-419/18 and C-483/18 *Profi Credit Polska v Włostowska*, para. 77; Case C-632/17 *PKO Bank Polski*, paras. 51–52; Case C-495/19 *Kancelaria Medius*, para. 45. See also Joined Cases C-453/18 and C-494/18 *Bondora v VC and XY*, para. 54 (on the European order for payment procedure).

469 Case C-176/17 *Profi Credit Polska*, para. 57; Case C-632/17 *PKO Bank Polski*, para. 43. See, more recently, Case C-485/19 *Profi Credit Slovakia*, paras. 36 and 54–55. In that case, AG Szpunar observed that the approach based on Article 47 is difficult to distinguish from that based on the principle of effectiveness. He nevertheless preferred the latter, because the rules at issue must then be assessed as a whole, to determine whether a time limit is reasonable: Opinion of AG Szpunar, points 38–39 and 66–67. On limitation periods, see further section 5.3.2 of this book.

470 See, e.g. Case C-147/16 *Karel de Grote*, para. 31.

471 Case C-8/14 *BBVA*, Opinion of AG Szpunar, point 70. *Ex officio* control is an imperfect response to a combination of restrictive procedural rules and a reliance on party initiative: Van Duin and Leone (n 45) 1240.

as excessive court fees. Article 47 calls for a different balance between the creditor's right of access to justice and the consumer debtor's right to effective judicial protection. Restrictive procedural conditions may be harder to justify when EU consumer rights are at stake. Expedited procedures should not turn into an avenue for depriving consumers of their (substantive and procedural) rights. The Polish cases show clearly that the judicial protection of consumers against unfair terms presupposes that the right of access to court can be exercised effectively, which is explicitly recognised as a fundamental rights issue.

3.2.4.2. Aqua Med: *An Eliminatory Function of Article 47?*

Aqua Med, another Polish case, seems to confirm that the core components of Article 47 of the Charter deserve protection in and of themselves, also in the context of the UCTD. The CJEU reiterated that national procedures under the UCTD must be in conformity with the principle of equivalence and the right to an effective remedy, as required by Article 47. The CJEU distinguished a restriction of the right of consumers to an effective remedy from the exercise of the rights conferred on them by the UCTD.[472] Procedural difficulties may deter or prevent consumers from exercising their *substantive* rights, but excessive restrictions of their *procedural* rights are also (in and of themselves) prohibited.

The case was about a jurisdiction clause that referred to national provisions governing the arrangements for determining jurisdiction in domestic disputes. The clause allowed the claimant to choose between either the court that had jurisdiction in the place where the defendant (consumer) was domiciled, or the court that had jurisdiction in the place where the contract was to be performed. Contractual terms that reflect mandatory statutory or regulatory provisions are excluded from the scope of the UCTD (Article 1(2)). The rationale behind this is that the national legislature is already supposed to have struck a balance between all the rights and obligations of the parties to the contract.[473] However, the CJEU found that the clause at issue could not be understood as merely reflecting a specific provision; rather, it referred to a set of procedural rules.[474] Questions relating to the impact of national legislation on the

---

472 Case C-266/18 *Aqua Med*, paras. 50–51.

473 Case C-266/18 *Aqua Med*, para. 33. See also Joined Cases C-96/16 and C-94/17 *Banco de Sabadell*, para. 43.

474 Case C-266/18 *Aqua Med*, paras. 35–37.

'protection guarantees' resulting from the UCTD do fall within the scope of the UCTD.[475] In the end, the CJEU assessed the national procedural rules at issue, not the clause itself. Like jurisdiction clauses, procedural rules on jurisdiction may make it more difficult for consumers to take legal action. The CJEU found that rules on jurisdiction – and by extension a jurisdiction clause referring to those rules – could give rise to an 'excessive restriction'[476] of the consumer's right to an effective remedy under Article 47 of the Charter.

Again, it was the CJEU itself, not the referring court, that brought up Article 47. It held that the rules at issue did not exclude the possibilities for consumers to participate in proceedings brought against them, and to assert the rights that they derive from the UCTD. However, overly high travel costs could deter them from entering an appearance and properly defending their rights, if the court is very far away from their place of residence.[477] In this respect, the Commission has drawn a comparison with Article 18 of the Brussels I Regulation, which stipulates that proceedings against a consumer may only be brought in the courts of the Member State where the consumer is domiciled.[478] Even though *Aqua Med* concerned a domestic dispute, the distance between the court and the consumer's place of residence was approximately 200 kilometres, almost the same distance as between Amsterdam and Brussels.

In so far as Article 47 precludes excessive restrictions, it may fulfil an eliminatory function. It is, nevertheless, unclear whether the excessive restriction test is an implicit reference to the proportionality test of Article 52(1) of the Charter. A comparison between *Aqua Med* and another case on jurisdiction, *Baczó*, shows that it matters whether procedural rules are solely assessed in light of the need to ensure protection of *substantive* consumer rights, or whether those rules are also considered as potential restrictions of the *procedural* rights that form the core components of Article 47.

In *Baczó*, which is referred to in *Aqua Med*, the designation of specialised courts for actions seeking to have unfair contract terms set aside was considered to be a legitimate aim, even though this might

---

475 Case C-118/17 *Dunai*, para. 38. See further subsection 3.3.3.

476 Case C-266/18 *Aqua Med*, para. 52.

477 Case C-266/18 *Aqua Med*, paras. 53–54. See also Joined Cases C-240/98 to C-244/98 *Océano*, paras. 22–23; Case C-243/08 *Pannon*, para. 41; Case C-137/08 *Pénzügyi Lízing*, para. 54.

478 Case C-266/18 *Aqua Med*, Commission's written observations of 27 July 2018 (sj.a(2018)4465858 SK), paras. 19 and 48.

burden consumers with higher costs.[479] The CJEU held that the aim of ensuring 'uniform practice and a more effective protection of consumer rights' by specialised courts could prevail over procedural difficulties such as costs, distance and the mandatory assistance of a lawyer, which did not necessarily make the exercise of *substantive* rights excessively difficult. According to the CJEU, measures aiming to compensate for the consumer's financial difficulties, such as legal aid, may help to offset the (extra) costs of the proceedings. Moreover, consumers, in their capacity as applicants, did not need to be present at all stages.[480]

In *Aqua Med*, the CJEU came to a slightly different conclusion, with reference to Article 47, than it did in *Baczó*. The CJEU held that the consumer's right to an effective remedy should not be excessively restricted by procedural conditions such as costs or time limits.[481] This suggests that procedural difficulties are harder to justify under Article 47 than under the UCTD's effectiveness. Nevertheless, it remains to be seen whether the excessive restriction test actually differs from the tests applied in other cases.

3.3. EFFECTIVE (JUDICIAL) REMEDY

3.3.1. INTRODUCTION: A BROAD UNDERSTANDING OF JUSTICIABILITY

The cases discussed in the previous section have already illustrated the importance that the availability and accessibility of judicial remedies have for the exercise of consumer rights under the UCTD. In *Profi Credit Polska*, the right to an effective remedy under Article 47 of the Charter was phrased as a parallel requirement to Article 7 UCTD; in *Aqua Med*, it was formulated as an additional requirement. As will become apparent in the present section, not all restrictive procedural conditions are infringements of Article 47. A differentiation can be made between, on the one hand, rules that obstruct access to an effective judicial remedy and, thus, impinge on the core elements of Article 47, and, on the other hand, rules that merely

479 Case C-567/13 *Baczó*, paras. 46–47.

480 Case C-567/13 *Baczó*, para. 55 with reference to Case C-413/12 *Asociación de Consumidores Independientes de Castilla y León v Anuntis Segundamano España*, para. 42 and paras. 57–59.

481 See, specifically, Case C-266/18 *Aqua Med*, paras. 51 and 53.

complicate subsequent legal proceedings.[482] AG Wahl made a similar distinction in his Opinion on a Slovakian case concerning extrajudicial enforcement, comparable to *Kušionová*. According to Wahl, consumers do not need to be subject to a particularly favourable treatment. Some rules may make it difficult for consumers to protect their rights effectively, which, Wahl seems to imply, might not necessarily be a problem, but in other cases it may become outright *impossible* for them to do so.[483] As an example of why this is problematic, Wahl referred to the well-known *Aziz* case.[484] In that case, the CJEU held that Spanish procedural law was incompatible with the UCTD, because the referring court could not adopt interim measures to suspend the enforcement and guarantee the full effectiveness of its final decision. In other cases, however, the distinction between difficult and impossible might not always be as clear, as the difference between the Commission's view and the CJEU's judgment in *Kušionová* shows.[485]

In *Kušionová*, which, like *Aziz*, pertained to mortgage enforcement against the consumer's family home, the CJEU openly referred to the Charter. The CJEU insisted that the possibility of interim relief must be available, in order to ensure the right to an effective judicial remedy under the UCTD, by reference to Articles 7 and 47 of the Charter.[486] This begs the question of whether Article 47 may give any further constructive guidance as to what an effective remedy requires, in the context of the UCTD. As we saw in Chapter 2, a positive or generative function of Article 47 of the Charter is controversial. There is a delicate balance between the Scylla of reducing the Member States' procedural autonomy and the Charybdis of denying consumers a high level of (judicial) protection.[487] It will be shown in this section that the requirement of an effective *judicial* remedy under the UCTD has been given further substance in the CJEU's case law. The analysed case law reaffirms that access to court is not a mere formality: there must be a genuine opportunity for consumers to take legal action. Moreover, once a case comes before a court, that court must also be able to grant an actual remedy for an infringement of the rights that it is meant to

---

482 Nowak (n 229) 34–35; Krommendijk (n 285) 1413.

483 Case C-482/12 *Macinský*, Opinion of AG Wahl, points 73 and 77, referring to the principle of effectiveness. The case was withdrawn before the CJEU could give a decision.

484 Case C-415/11 *Aziz*, further discussed in subsections 3.4.2 and 4.4.2 of this book.

485 See subsection 3.3.2 below.

486 Case C-34/13 *Kušionová*, paras. 47 and 66.

487 Gerstenberg (n 234) 601.

protect. This is in line with a broad understanding of justiciability, and also echoes the call made by Van Gerven for a standard of sufficient or adequate judicial protection.[488]

What constitutes an effective *substantive* remedy ultimately depends on the factual and legal context. In *Kušionová*, it was the possibility of preventing the definitive and irreversible loss of the consumer's family home.[489] In *Sziber*, it was the availability of an 'effective procedural path' to obtain restitution of amounts unduly paid.[490] This follows from Article 47 of the Charter, read in conjunction with Articles 6 and 7 UCTD. Unlike Article 7 UCTD, which requires 'adequate and effective means', Article 47 requires a *judicial* remedy, as *ERSTE Bank Hungary* confirms.[491]

3.3.2. THE ROLE OF THE COURT IN MORTGAGE ENFORCEMENT PROCEEDINGS

3.3.2.1. Aziz: *Hidden Constitutionalisation*

The case of *Aziz* revealed a missing link between substantive and procedural consumer protection in Spanish law. It revolved around a mortgage loan agreement, which constituted an extrajudicial title that gave the creditor direct access to mortgage enforcement proceedings. The possibility for consumers to allege that the agreement contained unfair terms was deferred to separate declaratory proceedings before a different court. Here, the problem was not so much a lack of court involvement (*ex officio* control) per se, as a shortfall in judicial remedies. The referring court could declare the terms of the mortgage loan agreement unfair, but it could not suspend – let alone reverse – mortgage enforcement proceedings based on those terms. Thus, it asked the CJEU for a reconsideration of the applicable procedural framework against the background of a common understanding of the fundamental right to an effective remedy.[492]

The dispute at issue in *Aziz* was directly concerned with the powers of the referring court to determine whether contractual terms were

---

488 Van Gerven (n 10) 530. See also Micklitz (n 35) 395; Reich (n 1) 308–309.

489 Case C-34/13 *Kušionová*: see subsection 3.3.2 below.

490 Case C-483/16 *Sziber*: see subsection 3.3.3 below.

491 See subsection 3.3.2 below.

492 Gerstenberg (n 234) 616–617, 620–621. See further subsection 4.3.2 on the national background and follow-up of *Aziz*.

unfair.[493] The CJEU emphasised that a judicial remedy must not only be available to consumers: its effectiveness must also be guaranteed.[494] In Spanish mortgage enforcement proceedings, the ambit of the dispute was restricted. Consumer debtors could only file an opposition on a limited number of (procedural) grounds, which did not include unfair terms. The CJEU observed that the creditor could deprive consumers of the protection intended by the UCTD, simply by initiating the enforcement proceedings.[495] The possibilities for consumers to obtain subsequent compensation were insufficient, especially where the mortgaged property was their family home.[496] Compensation was not an effective remedy: it could not prevent the loss of the home. In this respect, the CJEU referred to *Unibet*, where the need for interim relief was recognised as necessary to give full effect to EU rights.[497]

The CJEU highlighted the link between substantive and procedural protection in an additional way. Certain terms may make it more difficult for consumers, given the procedural means at their disposal, to take legal action, and to exercise their rights of defence.[498] The court's unfairness assessment should, therefore, include a consideration of the procedural means available to consumers to ensure that unfair terms are not binding on them.[499] For instance, a so-called early maturity or acceleration clause in the mortgage loan agreement allowed the creditor to call in the totality of the loan on expiry of a stipulated time limit. The referring court found this time limit to be disproportionately short in light of the long-term (lifelong) contract.[500]

Unlike the Commission,[501] the CJEU did not explicitly mention the Charter, but *Aziz* could be seen as an instance of 'hidden

---

493 Case C-280/13 *Barclays Bank*, para. 38.

494 Case C-415/11 *Aziz* paras. 59–60.

495 Case C-415/11 *Aziz*, para. 62, with reference to Case C-618/10 *Banesto*, para. 55. See also Joined Cases C-537/12 and C-116/13 *Banco Popular Español v Rivas Quichimbo and Banco de Valencia v Valldeperas Tortosa*, para. 60; Case C-169/14 *Sánchez Morcillo I*, para. 28; Case C-32/14 *ERSTE Bank Hungary*, para. 45.

496 Case C-415/11 *Aziz*, paras. 60–61.

497 Case C-423/05 *Unibet*, paras. 37 and 77. See also subsection 2.4.1 of this book.

498 Case C-415/11 *Aziz*, para. 75. See also Joined Cases C-537/12 and C-116/13 *Banco Popular Español*, paras. 70–71.

499 Case C-415/11 *Aziz*, para. 68.

500 Case C-415/11 *Aziz*, paras. 21 and 31.

501 Case C-415/11 *Aziz*, Commission's written observations of 5 December 2011 (sj.j (2011)1426399), para. 44.

constitutionalisation':[502] it indirectly set a higher standard of fundamental rights protection than the national constitutional standard.[503] It provoked the creation of a new judicial remedy at the national level; a 'hybridisation' in the procedural sphere. In a way, the right to an effective remedy could be said to fulfil a transformative function, by leading to the introduction of unfair terms as an opposition ground in mortgage enforcement proceedings.[504] In Chapter 4 it will be explained why it cannot be maintained that it was the CJEU that 'invented' a new remedy,[505] i.e. interim relief, if only because the Spanish legislature opted for a different solution: unfair terms control – if necessary *ex officio* – in mortgage enforcement proceedings.

3.3.2.2. Kušionová: *Open Constitutionalisation*

In *Kušionová*, a Slovakian case, the CJEU confirmed that the right to an effective judicial remedy, as safeguarded by Article 47 of the Charter, is a mandatory requirement applicable to the implementation of the UCTD.[506] The CJEU reformulated the question submitted by the referring court, which mentioned only Article 38 of the Charter but pertained to the judicial remedies available to consumers. An important difference from *Aziz* was that, in *Kušionová*, there was no court involvement at all, unless the consumer debtor challenged the enforcement.[507] A reference to Article 47 was used to stress the need for an effective judicial remedy against the *extrajudicial* enforcement of a loan secured by a charge.[508] Article 47, thus, fulfils a strengthening function in support of the Directive's full effectiveness, and possibly even a generative function, where it underlines the need for *judicial* remedies.

The CJEU held that where the choice of remedies remains within the discretion of the Member States, they must ensure that those remedies are effective, proportionate and dissuasive.[509] The national court must be able to adopt protective interim measures to prevent the enforcement

[502] Micklitz (n 339) 649; Micklitz and Reich (n 44) 800; Iglesias Sánchez (n 18) 970; Della Negra (n 233) 1024.

[503] See further subsection, 4.3.2 of this book. See also Iglesias Sánchez (n 18) 963, 970.

[504] See further subsection 4.3.3.

[505] As submitted by Micklitz (n 339) 641.

[506] Case C-34/13 *Kušionová*, para. 47.

[507] Della Negra (n 233) 1023.

[508] Case C-34/13 *Kušionová*, para. 45.

[509] Case C-34/13 *Kušionová*, para. 59.

from going ahead.[510] This applies all the more strongly where the property at issue is the family home of the consumer whose rights have been infringed. The loss of a home after unlawful enforcement, resulting in eviction, would seriously undermine consumer rights (including the right to respect for the home protected by Article 7 of the Charter), and place the consumer's family in a particularly vulnerable position.[511] In this respect, it has been observed that fundamental rights have the potential to expose underlying socio-economic concerns.[512] These concerns transcend the issue of unfair terms control: the vulnerability of consumers vis-à-vis financial institutions is magnified where: (i) the case concerns the family home, which distinguishes mortgage enforcement from regular order for payment procedures;[513] *and* (ii) there is a lack of effective remedies and/or procedural safeguards, which puts consumer debtors in an even more subordinated position vis-à-vis creditors.[514]

The CJEU did not answer the sensitive question, asked by the referring court,[515] of whether extrajudicial enforcement, without any court involvement, is a way for the trader to effectively circumvent unfair terms control. It merely concluded that a contractual term, for example one that enables the creditor to use extrajudicial means of enforcement, falls outside the scope of the UCTD if it reflects the content of a mandatory statutory or regulatory provision (Article 1(2) UCTD).[516] Here, the term referred to the existence of an extrajudicial enforcement procedure under national law; in its absence, the creditor would still have been entitled to employ the procedure. According to AG Hogan in his Opinion on *Lovasné Tóth*, such terms do not exclude the right to an effective remedy under Article 47 of the Charter.[517] A term that does not affect the consumer's legal position, even if it gives the false impression that the consumer's legal remedies are limited, is not a possibly unfair term in the sense of the Annex, Article 1(q).[518]

---

510 Case C-34/13 *Kušionová*, paras. 58 and 60.

511 Case C-34/13 *Kušionová*, paras. 63 and 66. See also Case C-415/11 *Aziz*, para. 61.

512 See, e.g. Aurelia Colombi Ciacchi, 'European Fundamental Rights, Private Law, and Judicial Governance' in Hans-W Micklitz (ed), *Constitutionalization of European Private Law* (Oxford University Press 2014) 126.

513 Case C-176/17 *Profi Credit Polska*, Opinion of AG Kokott, point 62.

514 Maribel González Pascual, 'Social Rights Protection and Financial Crisis in Europe. The Right to Housing in Spain: a Cautionary Tale' (2016) 9 Inter-American and European Human Rights Journal 260, 269–272.

515 Case C-34/13 *Kušionová*, para. 30.

516 Case C-34/13 *Kušionová*, para. 80.

517 Case C-34/18 *Lovasné Tóth*, Opinion of AG Hogan, points 73 and 78.

518 Case C-34/18 *Lovasné Tóth*, paras. 53–54.

The CJEU ultimately found that, in Slovakia, *ex ante* and *ex post* remedies were available to the consumer to challenge the enforcement, albeit under time limits (within 30 days and three months, respectively).[519] It was possible for the national court to adopt interim measures, and to declare the enforcement void, which would retrospectively place consumers in a situation almost identical to their original situation.[520] The CJEU might have come to a different conclusion if either the prospect of having to make a deposit by way of guarantee or the costs of legal representation without the possibility of seeking legal aid would have deterred consumers from seeking a suspension of the enforcement. Protection *a posteriori* would most likely also have been insufficient if the home would definitely have been lost.[521]

The Commission argued that the only way to achieve actual consumer protection was judicial control *ex ante*, i.e. before the enforcement took place.[522] It also argued that 30 days was too short, and that the three-month time period after the enforcement should not count.[523] Furthermore, it could be observed that, given what was at stake in *Kušionová* – the loss of a family home – the 30-day time-limit was not significantly longer than the 20-day time limit in *Banesto*.[524]

Despite its reference to the Charter, and to the case law of the ECtHR,[525] the CJEU did not engage in a proportionality assessment under Article 52(1) of the Charter. Accordingly, it should have assessed whether a restriction of the consumer's right to an effective remedy (Article 47 of the Charter) or interference with Article 7 of the Charter could be justified in light of, for example, the need to ensure the efficiency of enforcement proceedings, or the creditor's interest in swift enforcement of the debt.[526]

---

519 Case C-34/13 *Kušionová*, para. 55.

520 Case C-34/13 *Kušionová*, para. 67.

521 See Case C-407/18 *Addiko Bank*, paras. 60 and 62.

522 Case C-34/13 *Kušionová*, Commission's written observations of 14 May 2013 (sj.h(2013)1140700), para. 16. The Commission had doubted whether unfair terms did, indeed, constitute a ground to declare the sale void: see its written observations, paras. 17 and 20.

523 Case C-34/13 *Kušionová*, Commission observations, para. 48. According to AG Wahl, the total of four months was not comparable to the 20-day time limit in *Banesto*: Case C-482/12 *Macinský*, Opinion of AG Wahl, point 91.

524 Della Negra (n 233) 1024. The significance of what is at stake for the parties is a relevant factor for time limits: Case C-8/14 *BBVA*, Opinion of AG Szpunar, point 41.

525 Case C-34/13 *Kušionová*, para. 64.

526 Della Negra (n 233) 1024, 1030. The ECHR considers procedural guarantees (Article 6 ECHR) as crucial for the proportionality assessment of a breach of the right to respect for the home (Article 8 ECHR). See further González Pascual (n 514) 263; Padraic

Instead, the CJEU considered whether a suspension or termination of the enforcement proceedings was proportionate to the aim of consumer protection against unfair terms.[527] Thus, *Kušionová* might be an instance of open constitutionalisation, but the CJEU did not strike a real balance between all competing rights and interests involved.[528]

3.3.2.3. *Judicial Protection as a Mandatory (Minimum) Requirement*

Two CJEU decisions will be considered that refer to 'effective judicial protection', but do not expressly mention Article 47 of the Charter. They pertain to extrajudicial enforcement, like *Kušionová*, and show that the actual availability of a judicial remedy constitutes a mandatory (minimum) requirement.

In *ERSTE Bank Hungary*, the CJEU confirmed that extrajudicial enforcement is allowed, as long as effective judicial protection is guaranteed.[529] In so far as a role is assigned to public notaries, this falls within the Member States' procedural autonomy: the CJEU's case law on the exercise of the judicial function – *ex officio* control of unfair terms – cannot be transposed to notaries.[530] According to AG Cruz Villalón, notaries have a particular responsibility to inform and advise consumers about potentially unfair terms and subsequent procedural options.[531] Without the intervention of the notary, consumers may not have all the relevant information enabling them to take legal action and/or defend themselves. As an impartial advisor, the notary can assist the parties in the exercise of their rights and the fulfilment of their obligations, in order to prevent litigation. As such, notaries may play a preventive role with respect to unfair terms, and must also ensure equal treatment when giving their advice. Thus, they may contribute to compliance with Articles 6 and 7 UCTD, and the effectiveness of the Directive.[532]

Kenna and Héctor Simón Moreno, 'Towards a Common Standard of Protection of the Right to Housing in Europe through the Charter of Fundamental Rights' (2019) 25 European Law Journal 608.

527 Luca Ettore Perriello, 'Right to Housing and Unfair Contract Terms' [2018] Journal of European Consumer and Market Law 96, 99.

528 See also Cherednychenko (n 164) 162; Perriello (n 527) 102.

529 Case C-32/14 *ERSTE Bank Hungary*, paras. 36 and 65. See also Case C-34/18 *Lovasné Toth*, para. 59.

530 Case C-32/14 *ERSTE Bank Hungary*, paras. 47–49. The Commission had argued that the notary should take the responsibility of unfair terms control, because the notarial deed constitutes an enforceable title with effects analogous to a judicial decision: written observations, paras. 43 and 46.

531 Case C-32/14 *ERSTE Bank Hungary*, Opinion of AG Cruz Villalón, points 80 and 81.

532 Case C-32/14 *ERSTE Bank Hungary*, paras. 54–58.

Nevertheless, the CJEU held that effective *judicial* protection must be guaranteed by making it possible for consumers to bring legal proceedings in relation to the disputed contract, including in the enforcement phase, and under reasonable procedural conditions.[533] The CJEU explicitly referred to, inter alia, *Kušionová* and *Aziz*. Notarial and judicial protection supplement each other, but the latter is not optional. In *Addiko Bank*, the CJEU repeated that a preventive check by the notary in respect of unfair terms is not sufficient: consumers must be enabled to bring legal proceedings, including in the enforcement phase.[534]

In *Banco Santander*, the referring Spanish court was considering whether, in practice, the notary may not be the 'sole effective remedy' for protecting consumer rights in respect of extrajudicial enforcement procedures, especially in the situation at issue in that case.[535] In Spain, the sale of the mortgaged property may take place in front of a notary instead of a judge, if the parties have agreed to an extrajudicial auction.[536] In the case of *Banco Santander*, the mortgage loan agreement also contained a clause by which the consumer authorised the bank to execute the sale of the mortgaged property on her behalf. Thus, the bank could represent the consumer before the notary without her attendance or participation. After the bank acquired the property for less than 60 per cent of its value, it brought a claim seeking an order for eviction. By then, it was too late for *ex officio* control of the unfairness of the terms of the underlying mortgage agreement: the transfer of ownership had already taken place. Thus, the mortgage agreement no longer existed. The court could not review the unfairness of its terms: it was merely required to enforce and protect the bank's property right.

The CJEU found that the case was inadmissible:[537] the scope of application of the UCTD and the CJEU's competence were limited to proceedings concerning *contractual* relationships, not property rights. Against a third party, the consumer debtor cannot invoke a defence based on a contract between her and the bank. AG Wahl referred in his Opinion to the principle of legal certainty and the security of acquired property

---

533 Case C-32/14 *ERSTE Bank Hungary*, para. 59. See also Case C-598/15 *Banco Santander*, para. 38; Case C-377/14 *Radlinger*, para. 46.

534 Case C-407/18 *Addiko Bank*, paras. 56–57.

535 Case C-598/15 *Banco Santander*, para. 27.

536 Koldo Casla, 'The Rights We Live in: Protecting the Right to Housing in Spain through Fair Trial, Private and Family Life and Non-Retrogressive Measures' (2016) 20 The International Journal of Human Rights 285, 287.

537 Case C-598/15 *Banco Santander*, para. 31.

rights.[538] However, the CJEU's reasoning has been criticised for being too formal, and distracting from the conflicting norms and interests at stake.[539] It has also been observed that it is often the bank itself (or a proxy), and not a third party acting in good faith, that acquires the property.[540] The real problem in *Banco Santander* was that the clause at issue limited the consumer's practical ability to take legal action and, thus, her right to effective judicial protection. While she had had a legal opportunity to challenge the enforcement,[541] she might have refrained from using it because she had not been aware of her rights, or what would follow if she did not exercise them in time. In so far as notaries can play a preventive role, that was not the case here, because the consumer's presence before the notary was not required.

Banco Santander exemplifies how the Directive's limited scope can be a constraint for the application of Article 47 as well. The requirement of effective judicial protection only applies in cases where there is a nexus with EU law, as illustrated by other cases where the UCTD – and, therefore, also Article 47 of the Charter – was found to be inapplicable.[542]

3.3.3. ADDITIONAL PROCEDURAL REQUIREMENTS

3.3.3.1. Sziber: *No Further Guidance on What Constitutes an Effective Procedural Path*

The cases discussed so far show that consumers must have access to an effective *judicial* remedy. Article 47 itself does not prescribe the remedy's (substantive) content, but it reinforces the link between rights and

538 Case C-598/15 *Banco Santander*, Opinion of AG Wahl, point 77.

539 Wolfgang Faber and Claes Martinson, 'Can Ownership Limit the Effectiveness of EU Consumer Contract Law Directives? A Suggestion to Employ a "Functional Approach"' [2019] Austrian Law Journal 85, 88.

540 Ángel Francisco Carrasco Perera and Karolina Lyczkowska, 'STJUE de 17 de Julio de 2014, *Asunto* C-169/14, Banco Bilbao Vizcaya Argentaria: un nuevo (y esta vez defectuoso) pronunciamiento del TJEU sobre el procedimiento hipotecario español' [2014] Revista CESCO de Derecho de Consumo 1, 11; Helena Díez García, 'Igualdad de Armas y Tutela Judicial Efectiva En El Art. 695.4 LEC Tras El Real Decreto-Ley 11/2014, de 5 de Septiembre: Crónica de Una Reforma Legislativa Anunciada (de Los AATC 70/2014, 71/2014, 111/2014, 112/2014 y 113/2014 a La STJUE de 17 de Julio de 2014)' [2014] Derecho Privado y Constitución 247.

541 Case C-598/15 *Banco Santander*, para. 49.

542 See, e.g. Case C-380/15 *Garzón Ramos*, para. 27; Case C-7/16 *Banco Popular Español*, para. 27.

remedies – between substantive and procedural protection. In the context of the UCTD, it must be ensured that unfair terms are not binding on consumers. In *Sziber*, the CJEU clarified that the goal is to 'restore the legal and factual situation that the consumer would have been in had those unfair terms not existed', which includes 'restitution of advantages wrongly obtained' by the trader.[543]

The case was about a loan agreement denominated in a foreign currency with no clear stipulation of the exchange rate. In response to CJEU case law,[544] ad hoc legislation was adopted in Hungary to deal with the large number of cases regarding foreign currency loans. This legislation remedied specific unfair terms, with retroactive effect, inter alia by converting the outstanding amount into a loan denominated in the national currency.[545] If consumers wished to request the invalidity of the entire loan agreement, they were obliged to specify the legal consequences, and to submit a settlement of accounts showing the amounts unduly charged. The referring court wanted to know whether it was contrary to Article 47 to impose such additional procedural requirements on consumers.[546] The Commission also doubted whether consumers could be expected to provide the court with specification of the legal consequences of invalidity of the agreement, and complex mathematical calculations.[547]

The CJEU held that these requirements did not appear to be so complex or onerous that they disproportionately affected the consumers' rights to effective judicial protection. The additional effort required from consumers was intended to 'unblock the judicial system', as 'a response to an exceptional situation' in Hungary, which pursued 'a general interest in the proper administration of justice'. Such an objective may prevail over private interests, provided that it does not go beyond what is necessary.[548] Interestingly, the ECtHR came to a similar conclusion in a case brought by five companies, i.e. traders, that were part of the OTP Banking Group, arguing that the new legislation violated their right to a fair trial (Article 6 ECHR). The ECtHR found that the accelerated, simplified processing of cases pursued the legitimate aims of consumer protection and the

543 Case C-483/16 *Sziber*, para. 53.
544 In particular, Case C-26/13 *Kásler*.
545 Case C-118/17 *Dunai*, para. 36.
546 Case C-483/16 *Sziber*, para. 27.
547 Case C-483/16 *Sziber*, Commission's written observations of 9 February 2017 (sj.h(2017)742229), paras. 35–37.
548 Case C-483/16 *Sziber*, paras 51–52.

efficient administration of justice. According to the ECtHR, the applicant companies had not been prevented from challenging the presumption of unfairness of the terms at issue. The fact that their arguments had been rejected did not violate the guarantees of a fair trial, such as equality of arms. They must also have been aware for a long time of the potentially unfair nature of the terms in question: the UCTD became applicable in Hungary in 2004.[549]

In *Sziber*, the CJEU found that where there is an 'effective procedural path' open to the consumer to request reimbursement and seek reparation, the effectiveness of the protection intended by the UCTD does not preclude the procedural rules at issue.[550] A relevant factor may have been that, in this case, the consumer was the applicant, who could reasonably be requested to provide the court with further details and quantification of the claim. It was, ultimately, for the national court to ascertain whether the procedural rules at issue were contrary to the right to effective judicial protection.[551]

Congruous with *Profi Credit Polska*, the CJEU appeared to consider effective judicial protection, as provided for in Article 47, as largely synonymous with the principle of effectiveness.[552] Its reference to Article 47 mainly fulfilled a strengthening function, not an eliminatory or generative one. While the *Sziber* case could be seen as an example of guided deference, the CJEU did not give any further guidance on what constitutes an 'effective procedural path'. However, the test applied in *Sziber* does resemble that contained in Article 52(1) of the Charter. Additional procedural requirements may be justified, as long as these are proportionate, and consumers are still offered an effective procedural path to obtain a substantive remedy. This provides more support for a broad understanding of justiciability, in the context of the UCTD.

3.3.3.2. Dunai: *An Empowering Function of Article 47*

In *Dunai*, which revolved around the same Hungarian ad hoc legislation as *Sziber*, the CJEU held that, while terms reflecting mandatory statutory provisions did not fall within the scope of the UCTD (Article 1(2)), questions relating to the impact of national legislation on the 'protection

549 ECtHR 20 December 2018, Appl. No. 22853/15 *Merkantil*, paras. 72 and 78–80.
550 Case C-483/16 *Sziber*, para. 54.
551 Case C-483/16 *Sziber*, paras. 53–55. See also Case C-118/17 *Dunai*, paras. 44–45.
552 Case C-483/16 *Sziber*, para. 35.

guarantees' resulting from Article 6(1) UCTD did.[553] In short, those guarantees entailed that Article 6(1) precluded (substantive and procedural) provisions that prevented consumers from not being bound by the unfair term concerned.[554] National legislation could be used to put an end to the use of unfair terms, as was done in Hungary, but it must respect the requirements of the UCTD. If it fell outside the Directive's scope, the legislative response of a Member State to CJEU case law would be immune from judicial review, as AG Tanchev also observed in *OTP Bank*.[555] This would erode the rights that the UCTD confers on consumers, and cause tension with the right to effective judicial protection. Tanchev's reference to Article 47 of the Charter could be seen as an example of its legitimising function. It provides an extra argument for CJEU interference with national legislation but does not play any separate role.

Furthermore, *Dunai* concerned the question of whether lower courts can be formally bound, in the exercise of their judicial functions, by general and abstract decisions adopted by a supreme court, to ensure consistency in the interpretation of the law.[556] The referring court wanted to know whether the UCTD precluded this, in light of Article 47. It had doubts about the appointment of judges as members of the Hungarian Supreme Court's standardisation panel, which was not transparent (i.e. not public). The CJEU had earlier held that the supreme courts of the Member States may elaborate certain criteria for the examination of unfair terms, in compliance with the Directive.[557] In *Dunai*, it added that lower courts must not be prevented from ensuring the Directive's full effect by making a preliminary reference, or by setting aside conflicting legislative provisions or judicial practices.[558] The CJEU referred to previous case law, where it had held that national courts must refuse to apply any conflicting provision of national legislation when they are called upon to apply provisions of EU law.[559] This is not (directly) the case when they apply *national* provisions implementing a directive. Unlike the UCTD, however, Article 47 has direct effect: it is a 'concrete provision of EU law', as opposed

553 Case C-118/17 *Dunai*, para. 38. See also Case C-51/17 *OTP Bank*, para. 54 and Case C-266/18 *Aqua Med*, para. 34: Article 1(2) UCTD is to be strictly construed.
554 Case C-118/17 *Dunai*, para. 53.
555 Case C-51/17 *OTP Bank*, Opinion of AG Tanchev, points 63–64.
556 Case C-118/17 *Dunai*, paras. 57 and 63.
557 Joined Cases C-96/16 and C-94/17 *Banco de Sabadell*, para. 68.
558 Case C-118/17 *Dunai*, para. 61.
559 Case C-689/13 *Puligienica Facility Esco (PFE) v Airgest*, para. 40.

to a set of general principles.[560] Thus, it has an empowering function for national civil courts, not only vis-à-vis the legislature, but also vis-à-vis higher courts in their own jurisdiction. *Dunai* empowers these lower courts to apply Article 47 in its eliminatory function, in so far as they may disregard or set aside (a certain interpretation of) national law.

The wording of the CJEU implies that ensuring the Directive's full effect and offering consumers an effective remedy are distinct, but overlapping, aims.[561] National legislative provisions or judicial practices should not undermine the full effect of the UCTD, in particular Article 6(1) and the consumer's right to restitution. In this respect, it is for the CJEU alone to decide upon any limitations on the effects of an interpretation of a rule of EU law.[562] Where national courts are prevented from offering an effective remedy, Article 47 of the Charter may be at stake, and this requires courts to set aside conflicting national provisions or practices, if necessary. Article 47 provides them with a procedural tool to achieve substantive consumer protection.

In *Dunai*, the CJEU found there was nothing in the case file to suggest that the referring court would not be able to offer an effective remedy for the purpose of protecting the rights that consumers could derive from the Directive.[563] Still, the decision makes it clear that national (civil) courts are, ultimately, responsible for providing an effective remedy in a concrete case. Moreover, legislative or judicial guidance does not discharge them from their tasks as decentralised EU judges. In this respect, Józon has referred to a 'new allocation of roles between the courts and the legislature': civil courts find themselves exercising a more regulatory function, especially where legislative action appears to be inadequate.[564] Article 47 reinforces the mandate of national courts to uphold the subjective rights that EU law confers on citizens: in this case, in their role as consumers.[565]

---

560 Case C-118/17 *Dunai*, para. 58. See subsection 2.3.2 of this book.

561 Case C-118/17 *Dunai*, para. 64: 'do not prevent the competent court from ensuring the full effect … *and* from offering consumers an effective remedy' [italics added]. See also the duality of purpose discussed in subsection 1.3.1 of this book.

562 Joined Cases C-154/15, C-307/15 and C-308/15 *Gutierrez Naranjo*, para. 70; see further subsection 4.5.2.

563 Case C-118/17 *Dunai*, para. 62.

564 Józon (n 245) 160.

565 Collins (n 334) 327. See also Micklitz (n 35) 363; Beka (n 32) 276.

3.4. EQUALITY OF ARMS

3.4.1. INTRODUCTION: WEAKER POSITION EXACERBATED BY PROCEDURAL INEQUALITIES

Restrictive procedural conditions, such as time limits or limitations on grounds of opposition, may prevent consumers from obtaining, or courts from providing, an effective judicial remedy under the UCTD, as read in conjunction with Article 47 of the Charter. While such conditions may be justifiable in themselves, they may be problematic where the consumer is the weaker party, not only from a substantive, but also from a procedural point of view. Procedural inequalities exacerbate the consumer's disadvantageous position vis-à-vis the trader. A de facto inequality might exist in terms of knowledge or financial means; a *de jure* inequality might consist of differences in the legal remedies that are available to the parties.[566] The case of *Sánchez Morcillo*, for instance, concerned an asymmetric restriction of the right to appeal in mortgage enforcement proceedings.[567] It was the first case in which the CJEU found a (prima facie) violation of Article 47 in the context of the UCTD. It did not matter whether the consumers involved were represented or assisted by a lawyer. Legal representation could, arguably, countervail a lack of legal knowledge,[568] but could not fix a lack of legal remedies, in this case the right to appeal.

Article 47 in itself does not guarantee the right to appeal, i.e. access to a higher instance (second jurisdictional level). However, if such a right exists, its exercise cannot compromise the primacy, unity and effectiveness of EU law.[569] Moreover, Article 47 encompasses the principle of equality of arms, which requires that litigating parties should not be placed in clearly less advantageous procedural positions compared to their opponents.[570] This does not mean that expedited procedures, such as mortgage enforcement

---

566 See also subsection 3.2.3 above.

567 Case C-169/14 *Sánchez Morcillo I* and Case C-539/14 *Sánchez Morcillo II* (pertaining to the same proceedings).

568 It should, nevertheless, be noted that legal representation or legal assistance constitutes a specific factual circumstance that is irrelevant for the interpretation of EU (consumer) law: Case C-429/05 *Rampion and Godard Rampion v Franfinance*, para. 65; Case C-497/13 *Faber v Autobedrijf Hazet Ochten*, para. 47.

569 Case C-169/14 *Sánchez Morcillo I*, paras. 35–36; C-169/14 *Sánchez Morcillo I*, View of AG Wahl, paras. 42–43. See also Case C-421/14 *Banco Primus*, para. 48.

570 Case C-205/15 *Toma*, para. 54, discussed in subsection 2.1.2.3. See also Case C-199/11 *Otis*, paras. 71–72.

proceedings, can never be justified. There may be good reasons to give mortgage creditors direct access to enforcement on the basis of a non-judicial, enforceable instrument, to restrict the opposition grounds and/or to limit the possibility of appeal. However, questions may be asked, as happened in Spain, about the balance struck between the interests at stake, in particular in light of the vulnerable position of consumer debtors.[571] In this respect, *Sánchez Morcillo* can be seen as a sequel of *Aziz*. Article 47 was used as the basis for an argument to correct a procedural inequality between the parties; the Article amplifies the duty on the part of the legislature and the judiciary to compensate for the consumer's weaker position.[572]

Unlike individual consumers, consumer protection organisations are not automatically considered to be in a disadvantageous position vis-à-vis traders.[573] They do not enjoy the same level of protection as individual consumers. Moreover, individual and collective actions have different purposes and different legal effects.[574] While the CJEU has not ruled out that consumer protection organisations might be able to rely on Article 47, it has held that Article 47 does not create standing for them to intervene in individual proceedings.[575] This confirms that Article 47 does not provide a stand-alone basis to bring a claim.

3.4.2. RESTORING THE PROCEDURAL BALANCE

3.4.2.1. Sánchez Morcillo I: *A Transformative Function of Article 47*

In *Sánchez Morcillo*, the CJEU reiterated that the principle of equality of arms is an integral element of effective judicial protection, and a corollary of the concept of a fair hearing, as guaranteed by Article 47 of the

---

571 Irene Sabaté, 'The Spanish Mortgage Crisis and the Re-Emergence of Moral Economies in Uncertain Times' (2016) 27 History and Anthropology 107, 118–119. See further subsection 4.1.1 of this book.

572 Manuel Medina Guerrero, 'Derecho a la vivienda y desahucios: la protección del deudor hipotecario en la jurisprudencia del TJUE' [2015] Teoría y Realidad Constitucional 261, 273.

573 Case C-413/12 *Asociación de Consumidores Independientes de Castilla y León*, paras. 49–50; Joined Cases C-381/14 and C-385/14 *Sales Sinués*, paras. 26–27; Case C-169/14 *Sánchez Morcillo I*, para. 46.

574 Joined Cases C-381/14 and C-385/14 *Sales Sinués*, para. 30; Case C-472/10 *Nemzeti Fogyasztóvédelmi Hatóság v Invitel Távközlési*, para. 37.

575 Case C-470/12 *Pohotovosť*, para. 54.

Charter. Consumers must have a reasonable opportunity to present their cases in conditions that do not place them in a clearly less advantageous position.[576]

After *Aziz*, a new ground for opposition against mortgage enforcement was introduced, on the basis of unfair terms.[577] *Sanchez Morcillo* concerned a follow-up issue: while the creditor could bring an appeal against a ruling that, upholding an objection raised by the debtor, terminated the enforcement, debtors were *not* allowed to bring an appeal in the reverse situation that their objection was dismissed. Even if they were consumers, they could not appeal the ruling on the basis of (alleged) unfair terms in the mortgage contract, or on any other ground. Thus, there was a difference in treatment between consumers and traders in their positions as parties to the proceedings.[578]

It was the referring court in *Sánchez Morcillo* that linked the case to Article 47, read together with the UCTD. By doing so, it reframed a constitutional question as a consumer protection issue. A similar question had already been asked by another Spanish court, but without explicit reference to Article 47. That court had only mentioned the need for 'adequate and effective means' and 'the [consumer's] right to take action'.[579] One possible reason for the reformulation of the question as an issue of *equality of arms* is that it could be argued that the right of access to court and an effective judicial remedy was already sufficiently guaranteed, after the legislative reform following *Aziz*.[580] Indeed, AG Wahl argued that the provision at issue already complied with the principle of effectiveness.[581]

The Commission submitted that the case was not about a lack of legal remedies or *ex officio* control of unfair terms as such, but, rather, about a procedural disadvantage for consumers that was contrary to the principle of equality of arms. This was particularly problematic in light of the UCTD, which is aimed at restoring the balance between consumers and traders.[582]

---

576 Case C-169/14 *Sánchez Morcillo I*, paras. 48–49.

577 See further section 4.4 on the national background and follow-up.

578 Case C-169/14 *Sánchez Morcillo I*, para. 30.

579 Case C-645/13 *Cajas Rurales Unidas v Méndez Sena*. Case C-169/14 *Sánchez Morcillo* was, ultimately, decided earlier than Case C-645/13, because the CJEU had ordered that it be adjudicated under the expedited procedure: ECLI:EU:C:2014:1388.

580 Case C-169/14 *Sánchez Morcillo I*, View of AG Wahl, points 65–67.

581 View of AG Wahl, point 77.

582 See Case C-169/14, Commission's written observations of 6 June 2014 (sj.c(2014)2009262), paras. 66–67.

According to the Commission, there should be 'adequate and effective means' for consumers to take legal action and exercise their rights under the UCTD, as well as *ex officio* control of unfair terms. Moreover, once a case comes before a court, procedural equality between the parties must be ensured. Article 47 constituted an additional requirement that could be violated independently from the principle of effectiveness.[583]

The CJEU held that the effectiveness of the rights that the parties, i.e. consumers, derived from the UCTD implied a requirement of judicial protection. It found that the asymmetric appeal provision was, indeed, contrary to the principle of equality of arms or procedural equality.[584] In this respect, it was relevant that the object of enforcement was the consumer's family home, that the enforcement was based on an enforceable notarial instrument not subject to judicial scrutiny, and that the enforcement proceedings were expedited, i.e. subject to time constraints.[585] The imbalance between procedural rights accentuated the contractual imbalance between the parties.[586] Thus, the applicable procedural rules were incomplete and inadequate. The UCTD, read in conjunction with Article 47 of the Charter, precluded a system that reinforced the inequality of arms between traders (as creditors) and consumer debtors in mortgage enforcement proceedings.[587] This could be seen as an instance of the eliminatory function of Article 47.

Article 47 also fulfilled a transformative function in *Sánchez Morcillo*, by triggering a trialogue about an upgrade of the procedural framework between the referring Spanish civil court, the CJEU and the Spanish legislature. While this transformative function manifested itself at the national level, it was instigated by the CJEU. The UCTD's effectiveness only required a remedy, in the sense of a procedural means of recourse and/or *ex officio* control, in one instance. But the CJEU went a step further. Arguably it went too far, because Article 47 does not guarantee a right to appeal, and initially the case did not even concern unfair terms.[588] The consumers involved lodged their objection before unfair terms could be raised in the mortgage enforcement proceedings. The court of first

[583] See Case C-169/14, Commission's written observations of 6 June 2014 (sj.c(2014)2009262), paras. 20, 30, 41 and 63.

[584] Case C-169/14 *Sánchez Morcillo I*, paras. 50–51. In its written observations, the Commission also referred to the right of non-discrimination in respect of the principle of procedural equality (para. 56).

[585] Case C-169/14 *Sánchez Morcillo I*, paras. 38 and 41.

[586] Case C-169/14 *Sánchez Morcillo I*, para. 46.

[587] Case C-169/14 *Sánchez Morcillo I*, para. 50.

[588] Della Negra (n 233) 1031. See also subsection 2.3.1 of this book.

instance had failed to perform *ex officio* control, and its ruling was given three days after the transitional period of one month for lodging a new objection had passed.[589] Thus, unfair terms did not play a role in the first instance. It was the referring appellate court that linked the case to the UCTD, thereby also providing a link to Article 47.[590]

It has been observed that the real issue in this case was not so much a procedural inequality as irreversibility, as in *Aziz*. The problem had simply been shifted to the phase of appeal. If there had been no possibility of appeal at all, i.e. for none of the parties, there might have been no violation of Article 47.[591] Perhaps an asymmetry in the parties' recourse to legal remedies – giving one party a second chance while denying it to the other – could even be justified in light of the creditor's privileged position as a mortgage holder.[592] But consumer debtors would be in the same situation as they had been pre-*Aziz* once the creditor had brought an appeal, or, as in the case of *Sánchez Morcillo*, the court had failed to perform unfair terms control. In this respect, the CJEU's decision is in line with *Aziz*, and confirms that Article 47 is concerned with problems of justiciability.

3.4.2.2. Sánchez Morcillo II: *Accessory Character of Article 47 as its Strength and Weakness*

After a subsequent legislative amendment that introduced a right to appeal for consumers on the basis of unfair terms,[593] the referring court in the case of *Sánchez Morcillo* found that it still could not declare the appeal admissible. Under the amended provision, an appeal was only

---

[589] Case C-169/14 *Sánchez Morcillo I*, View of AG Wahl, points 50–51. The Commission noted this in its written observations, but found that the court's failure to exercise *ex officio* control did not render the procedural rules at issue contrary to the principle of effectiveness: see, respectively, paras. 18–19 and 51, paras. 33 and 39–40. The purpose of the principle of effectiveness is not to prevent the incorrect application of substantive legal norms by the national court. However, it was the lack of procedural equality that made it impossible for the appellate court to examine unfair terms *ex officio* and, thus, unable to provide effective judicial protection (para. 70). On the transitional period, see Case C-8/14 *BBVA*.

[590] See further subsection 4.4.2.

[591] Díez García (n 540) 229–230, 241, 249. See also Case C-169/14 *Sánchez Morcillo I*, paras. 44–45; Commission's written observations, para. 69.

[592] See also C-169/14 *Sánchez Morcillo*, View of AG Wahl, points 61–63. Wahl referred to 'the preferential nature of the enforceable instrument which the creditor has relied upon'.

[593] See further subsection 4.4.3 of this book.

allowed against a ruling terminating the enforcement, disapplying an unfair term, or rejecting an objection based on an unfair term. In the case at hand, none of these grounds applied. Therefore, the referring court made a new preliminary reference to the CJEU.[594] Apparently, the referring court was not prepared to give an expansive or *contra legem* interpretation, on its own, of the amended provision at issue: it wanted the CJEU to conclude that the amended provision was still incomplete and inadequate. This is a sign that national courts do not perceive the empowering function of Article 47 to be as strong as *Dunai* suggests.

It is questionable whether it should be held against consumers that a court, at first instance, has failed to perform unfair terms control (*ex officio*), and whether it is justifiable that this cannot be remedied on appeal, especially if the consumers have actively sought judicial protection. It could even be argued that an appellate court should always be able to assess unfair terms (of its own motion), as long as the case falls within the scope of the UCTD. However, in *Jőrös* and *Asbeek Brusse*, the CJEU had already made clear that this depended on national procedural rules (under the principle of equivalence).[595] If the appellate court has the power to examine, of its own motion, any grounds for invalidity of contract terms – either because they are contrary to public policy or a mandatory statutory provision – that are clearly apparent from the elements submitted at first instance, it must also perform *ex officio* control under the Directive. In Dutch civil procedure this is the case,[596] but in Spanish mortgage enforcement proceedings it is not. In this respect, *Sánchez Morcillo I* is an exception to the CJEU's deference to the Member States' national procedural laws in respect of appeal.

In a follow-up order, referred to here as *Sánchez Morcillo II*, – the CJEU found that the second question was identical to the one already answered. From the perspective of the UCTD, consumers were provided with a reasonable opportunity to take legal action in conditions that did not place them in a clearly less advantageous position. Now that the court responsible for the enforcement could assess the unfairness of contract terms and declare the proceedings invalid, consumer debtors were no longer exposed to the risk of final and irreversible loss of their homes, and their legal protection was sufficiently guaranteed.[597] An objection based on grounds other than unfair terms did not fall within the scope

594 Case C-539/14 *Sánchez Morcillo II*, para. 50.

595 Case C-397/11 *Jőrös*, paras. 35–36 and 38; Case C-488/11 *Asbeek Brusse*, paras. 45 and 51.

596 See further section 5.4 of this book.

597 Case C-539/14 *Sánchez Morcillo II*, paras. 40–41 and 47–48.

of the UCTD.[598] The principle of equality of arms does not require that the parties are put on an equal footing in all circumstances.[599] Thus, the grounds for an appeal brought by consumer debtors could legitimately be restricted to unfair contract terms, and the amended provision was found to be in compliance with the Directive.

Sánchez Morcillo I and *II* reveal that the accessory character of Article 47 can be both its strength and its weakness. The CJEU cannot provide a comprehensive solution for legal and socio-economic issues that transcend the UCTD:[600] its competence is tied to EU (consumer) law. The applicability of Article 47 cannot be stretched beyond the scope of EU law, to the UCTD.[601] *Sánchez Morcillo* also shows how the CJEU's case law can 'invade' national procedural law, without entirely solving the underlying issue. The CJEU did not follow the same 'generous approach'[602] as in *Aziz*, even though *Sánchez Morcillo* also concerned a shortfall in procedural safeguards against the final and irreversible loss of the consumer's family home. One explanation is that the CJEU intentionally restrained itself from further interference with Spanish civil procedure, or that it simply – but wrongly[603] – assumed that the consumers involved had had a genuine opportunity to exercise their rights. In the end, consumers in the position of Mr. Sánchez Morcillo and Mrs. Abril García were left only with the possibility of bringing declaratory proceedings that would not suspend enforcement, which is precisely the situation that, according to the CJEU, must be prevented.[604] The case of *Sánchez Morcillo*, therefore, gave rise to multiple follow-up questions, which will be further discussed in Chapter 4.

3.4.3. FOCUS OF ARTICLE 47 ON INDIVIDUAL RIGHTS: *POHOTOVOST'*

The imbalance that exists between consumer protection organisations and traders is not the same as that which exists between traders and

598 Case C-539/14 *Sánchez Morcillo II*, paras. 43–44.

599 See also Case C-543/14 *Ordre des barreaux francophones et germanophone v Conseil des ministres*, paras. 40 and 42.

600 Sara Iglesias Sánchez, 'Unfair Terms in Mortgage Loans and Protection of Housing in Times of Economic Crisis: *Aziz v. Catalunyacaixa*' (2014) 51 Common Market Law Review 955, 973; González Pascual (n 514) 275–276.

601 See also C-598/15 *Banco Santander*, discussed in subsection 3.3.2 above.

602 Case C-482/12 *Macinský*, Opinion of AG Wahl, point 41.

603 Carrasco Perera and Lyczkowska (n 540) 10–12. See further subsection 4.4.3 of this book.

604 Case C-539/14 *Sánchez Morcillo II*, para. 31.

consumers themselves.[605] In *Pohotovosť*, the CJEU held that a refusal to grant such organisations leave to intervene in individual proceedings in support of a consumer neither infringes the individual consumer's right to an effective judicial remedy, nor affects the organisation's rights to collective action, as recognised by Article 7(2) UCTD.[606]

Pohotovosť concerned the enforcement of an arbitral award against a consumer in Slovakia. A local consumer protection organisation (HOOS) sought leave to intervene in the enforcement proceedings on the ground that the appointed bailiff, who was the enforcing authority, had, in the past, been employed by the creditor, Pohotovosť, and so was not impartial. HOOS also claimed that the court had failed to provide the consumer with protection against unfair terms under the UCTD. They were denied leave to intervene, not only because the organisation was a third party, but also because the enforcement proceedings were considered not to be (fully) contentious.[607]

Consumer protection organisations can contribute to ensuring effective access to justice for consumers.[608] However, the CJEU found there was not yet any EU legislation governing the role of such organisations in individual proceedings.[609] In the absence of such legislation, the CJEU found that neither Article 38 nor Article 47 of the Charter imposed an interpretation of the UCTD that would encompass a right to intervene. The intervention of a consumer protection association is, according to the CJEU, not comparable to legal aid, which under Article 47 must be made available to those who lack sufficient resources. Moreover, in so far as consumer protection organisations can rely on Article 47, their rights to collective action are not affected, and they can still represent individual consumers directly if mandated to do so.[610]

Pohotovosť illustrates, firstly, that the focus of Article 47 lies on individual litigants and individual rights, although many cases brought

605 See, e.g. Case C-413/12 *Asociación de Consumidores Independientes de Castilla y León*, paras. 49–50; Joined Cases C-381/14 and C-385/14 *Sales Sinués*, paras. 26–27.

606 Case C-470/12 *Pohotovosť*, paras. 53–54. See also Case C-448/17 *EOS KSI Slovensko*, para. 41.

607 See Case C-470/12 *Pohotovosť*, para. 17.

608 See, e.g. Directive 2020/1828 on representative actions for the protection of the collective interests of consumers, adopted on 25 November 2020.

609 Case C-470/12 *Pohotovosť*, para. 46.

610 Case C-470/12 *Pohotovosť*, paras. 52–55. On the relation between individual and collective actions, see further subsection 4.5.3 of this book.

before the CJEU have an impact that goes beyond the individual case.[611] Secondly, *Pohotovosť* shows that Article 47's application has boundaries: the CJEU cannot single-handedly introduce a procedural link between individual and collective litigation on the basis of that Article. In so far as Article 47 has a signalling function in this respect, it is primarily directed at (European or national) legislatures as an argument to regulate collective actions.[612]

3.5. RIGHT TO BE HEARD

3.5.1. INTRODUCTION: A GENERATIVE FUNCTION OF ARTICLE 47

The case law that will be discussed in this section 3.5 confirms that the concepts of the fundamental right to effective judicial protection and effectiveness are not synonymous. The core components of Article 47 of the Charter cannot be bypassed simply by reference to the UCTD's objectives. Certain measures may be justified to enhance the effectiveness of consumer protection under the Directive, but not at the expense of essential procedural safeguards, such as the trader's right to be heard.

The right to be heard has an external dimension: the effects of a judicial decision cannot be extended to the detriment of third parties that have not participated in the proceedings,[613] at least not without giving them an opportunity to be heard, too (*Biuro podróży 'Partner'*).[614] The right to be heard also has an internal dimension, i.e. within the process itself: the parties must be given an opportunity to set out and contradict

611 See also Micklitz and Reich (n 44) 807.

612 See further Reich (n 67) 128. Directive 2020/1828 on representative actions for the protection of the collective interests of consumers refers in its preamble to Article 47 of the Charter, but only to the extent that protecting the collective interests of consumers should be without prejudice to the right to an effective remedy of (individual) consumers and traders. On the different purpose and character of collective actions, see further subsection 4.5.3 of this book.

613 See also Case C-472/10 *Invitel*, Opinion of AG Trstenjak, point 60: '[A]n *erga omnes* effect adversely affecting persons not party to the proceedings would be difficult to reconcile with the principles of a fair trial, particularly as such persons would be denied an opportunity to express their views on the accusation of using unfair terms in contracts before a judgment affecting them was delivered'.

614 Case C-119/15 *Biuro*; see further subsection 3.5.3.

each other's views (*Banif Plus Bank*).[615] In this respect, a requirement for adversarial proceedings or contentious debate could be discerned.[616] In civil proceedings, both parties – consumers and traders – must have the chance to present their views to the court, otherwise this may result in a denial of justice.[617]

The wording of the CJEU judgments in *Banif Plus Bank* and *Biuro* implies that Article 47 provides autonomous procedural safeguards for the adjudication of EU rights that are not completely aligned with the principle of effectiveness. This is Article 47 in its generative function: in both cases, the CJEU specified the substantive aspects that the parties should be heard on. This is another manifestation of the connection between substantive and procedural protection that characterises Article 47, as well as its different rationale: it pertains to the adjudication of EU rights, even when it does not contribute to the effectiveness of EU law per se. Article 47 also appears to guarantee the right to an effective remedy in the event of an alleged infringement of its core components, especially the right to be heard.[618] Litigants can invoke such infringements when attempting to overturn decisions that are unfavourable to them, as *Biuro* shows.

3.5.2. *BANIF PLUS BANK*: QUALIFYING THE DUTY OF *EX OFFICIO* CONTROL

Banif Plus Bank was the first judgment in which the CJEU confirmed that Article 47 was binding on national courts when they adjudicate cases under the UCTD. Such courts must observe the rights of defence, in particular where they apply EU (consumer) law of their own motion.[619] In earlier case law, the CJEU had already recognised the principle of *audi alteram partem* – the right to be heard – as a basic principle of the Member States' legal systems, under the procedural rule of reason test,[620] which may justify a certain procedural rule in light of the principle of effectiveness. Under

---

615 Case C-472/11 *Banif Plus Bank*; see further subsection, 3.5.2.

616 See, e.g. Beka (n 32) 199; Gerstenberg (n 234) 610.

617 On the concept of denial of justice and the notion of *indefensión* in the Spanish legal system, see further in particular, section 4.5 below.

618 See subsection 2.3.1 of this book.

619 Case C-472/11 *Banif Plus Bank*, para. 29. See also subsection 2.3.1.

620 See subsection 2.5.2.

the principle of equivalence, the right to be heard can also be regarded as a matter of public policy, if national law classifies it as such. In *Banif Plus Bank*, it was formulated as an EU fundamental right, irrespective of, or in addition to, national procedural rules. This may not seem revolutionary, but the impact of *Banif Plus Bank* at the national level should not be underestimated, as will be shown in Chapters 4 and 5.

The CJEU emphasised that it is important for the parties to a court action to be apprised of, and to be able to debate and be heard on, the matters of fact and law which will determine the outcome of their proceedings, especially when the court decides a dispute on grounds that it has identified of its own motion.[621] Thus, the court must invite each party to the dispute to present their views, with the opportunity of challenging the views of the other party, in accordance with national procedural rules,[622] but presumably also if those rules do not (explicitly) provide for this. In the context of the UCTD, this means that the parties must be able to respond to the court's finding that there are grounds for invalidity of contractual terms.[623] This presumably encompasses both the unfair nature of the terms, as well as the legal consequences of such a finding.

In so far as *ex officio* control of unfair terms is an expression of the full effectiveness of the UCTD,[624] this can be limited – or, rather, qualified – by Article 47 of the Charter.[625] The CJEU has held that consumers can give their (free and informed) consent to the terms in question, even if the court finds that they are unfair.[626] This could be seen as a counterbalance to the CJEU's determination to enhance the Directive's effectiveness.[627] It would, nevertheless, go too far to derive from *Banif Plus Bank* that observation of the right to be heard would compromise the protection provided by the UCTD for the benefit of consumers. There is no one-on-one relationship between an improvement of the procedural position of one party and a deterioration of the substantive position of the other.[628] Indeed, the CJEU

621 Case C-472/11 *Banif Plus Bank*, paras. 29–30, with reference to C-89/08 *Commission v Ireland*, paras. 50 and 54 – but that case pertained to proceedings before the EU Court of First Instance, not a national court.

622 Case C-472/11 *Banif Plus Bank*, para. 36. See also Case C-488/11 *Asbeek Brusse*, para. 52.

623 Case C-472/11 *Banif Plus Bank*, para. 32.

624 Case C-472/11 *Banif Plus Bank*, para. 28.

625 Della Negra (n 233) 1026; Nowak (n 169) 8; Safjan and Düsterhaus (n 13) 17.

626 Case C-472/11 *Banif Plus Bank*, para. 35. See also Case C-243/08 *Pannon*, para. 35; Case C-260/18 *Dziubak*, para. 53–54.

627 Leone (n 64) 75.

628 Wilman (n 31) 483.

found that the right to be heard is 'not incompatible' with the principle of effectiveness.[629] The level of consumer protection is not necessarily diminished when both parties to the dispute – consumers as well as traders – are heard: in the same proceedings, the court can still declare the terms at issue to be unfair and, therefore, not binding if the trader cannot successfully defend their use. Rather than limiting the Directive's (*ex officio*) application, hearing the parties gives the court the opportunity to align its decision with their submissions. Article 47's function(s) in this respect will be further explored in section 4.5 of the next chapter.

3.5.3. *BIURO PODRÓŻY 'PARTNER'*: GIVING SUBSTANCE TO THE RIGHT TO BE HEARD

The divergence between the effectiveness of the UCTD, on the one hand, and Article 47 of the Charter, on the other, became even more visible in *Biuro podróży 'Partner'*, a Polish case about a national register of standard contract terms that have been declared unfair in individual or collective proceedings. This register is aimed at enhancing the effectiveness of the prohibition on the use of unfair terms.[630] This should not, however, come at the cost of depriving the parties of effective judicial protection. While it may be effective to impose fines on traders who use terms that are deemed to be equivalent to those in the register, this may be at odds with their right to be heard. When the case concerns a national scheme transposing the UCTD and, therefore, its implementation, the fundamental rights of the EU legal order must be observed.[631] The CJEU confirmed that *any* person whose rights guaranteed by EU law might be infringed is entitled to an effective remedy. In the absence of a scheme of effective judicial protection for traders, the UCTD must be interpreted in light of Article 47.[632]

In *Biuro*, the CJEU found that, where traders were not a party to the proceedings that culminated in the entry of certain terms in the register, they must have the opportunity to challenge both the

[629] Case C-472/11 *Banif Plus Bank*, paras. 33–34.

[630] Case C-119/15 *Biuro*, para. 34. For a more detailed and elaborate description of the case, see Joasia Luzak, 'You Too Will Be Judged: Erga Omnes Effect of Registered Unfair Contract Terms in Poland' (2017) 6 Journal of European Consumer and Market Law 120.

[631] Case C-119/15 *Biuro*, para. 25.

[632] Case C-119/15 *Biuro*, paras. 26–27. See also subsection 2.3.1 of this book.

equivalence of their own terms to the previously registered terms, as well as the amount of the applicable fine.[633] AG Saugmandsgaard Øe stated that traders should also be able to contest whether the terms they use are unfair, which is broader than a mere equivalence assessment, and would possibly require courts to assess the same set of terms multiple times.[634] In his view, the trader's right under Article 3(2) of the UCTD to furnish arguments and evidence in order to discharge the burden of proof forms part of the more general and extensive right to a hearing, arising from Article 47 of the Charter.[635] The objective to put a 'swift and effective stop' to the use of unfair terms, and to avoid a 'multiplicity of judicial procedures', could not justify a restriction of the trader's right to a hearing.[636]

A relevant distinction from *Banif Plus Bank* is that *Biuro* concerned administrative proceedings. In civil proceedings, it is about invalidity of the terms at issue, rather than a fine. Still, the right to be heard applies equally in civil proceedings; it could be submitted that, parallel to *Biuro*, it pertains to the (alleged) unfair nature of contract terms, and to the legal consequences of a finding of unfairness. The added value of the CJEU's reference to Article 47 mainly appears to be that its link with EU law gives *substance* to the right to be heard.

3.6. INTERIM CONCLUSION: FUNCTIONS OF ARTICLE 47 IN CJEU CASE LAW

The case law analysed in this chapter exemplifies how the functions of Article 47 of the Charter may play out in the CJEU's case law. It also shows how Article 47 has had an impact upon what the CJEU requires from the Member States and, in particular, from national courts, in the context of the UCTD.

In *Profi Credit Polska*, *Kušionová* and *Sziber*, Article 47 fulfilled a strengthening function vis-à-vis the (full) effectiveness of consumer protection under the UCTD. Not every procedural issue is a fundamental rights issue, but it might become one in cases where the right to take legal

[633] Case C-119/15 *Biuro*, paras. 42–43.

[634] Case C-119/15 *Biuro*, Opinion of AG Saugmandsgaard Øe, point 64. See also Luzak (n 630) 121–122.

[635] Opinion of AG Saugmandsgaard Øe, point 60.

[636] Opinion of AG Saugmandsgaard Øe, point 67.

action is severely limited or entirely excluded. Article 47 highlights the importance of access to judicial remedies, which should not be a mere formality. If consumers cannot exercise their substantive rights under reasonable procedural conditions, this might give rise to a violation of Article 47. Both *Profi Credit Polska* and *Kušionová* can be seen as steps towards open constitutionalisation: the CJEU acknowledges, or at least shows awareness of, the fundamental rights dimension. Even if no violation is found, a reference to Article 47 indicates that the justiciability of EU (consumer) rights might be at stake.

Article 47 may be used as a negative yardstick to preclude a constellation of restrictive procedural conditions, such as time limits and costs. In *Aqua Med*, Article 47 fulfilled an eliminatory function where the emphasis was placed on an 'excessive restriction' of *procedural* rights. The core components of Article 47 deserve protection, in themselves. At the same time, Article 47 stresses the link between substantive and procedural protection. In *Sziber*, the CJEU found that an 'effective procedural path' to the obtainment of a substantive remedy must be offered to consumers. This could be regarded as a positive requirement, just like the existence of an effective judicial remedy against unfair terms in mortgage enforcement proceedings (*Kušionová*, *ERSTE Bank*). In this respect, Article 47 could be said to have a generative function, too.

In *Dunai*, Article 47 fulfilled an empowering function in respect of the role of courts. They must provide effective judicial protection under EU (consumer) law, if necessary by setting aside restrictive procedural conditions or disregarding judicial practices that are contrary to Article 47 (in its eliminatory function). The empowering function of Article 47 is also reflected in AG Trstenjak's Opinion in *Asturcom*, where she referred to Article 47 as an argument to widen the scope for the judicial review of arbitral awards in respect of unfair terms. In its judgment, the CJEU, nevertheless, showed deference to the laws of the Member States.

In *Finanmadrid*, the CJEU was not inclined to attach any independent meaning to Article 47 either, as long as unfair terms control was ensured at some stage of the proceedings. AG Szpunar's Opinion and the Commission's observations in *Finanmadrid*, nevertheless, demonstrate how Article 47 may provide a different rationale for judicial intervention: courts not only ensure the application of EU (consumer) law, but also the observance of procedural safeguards, such as the rights of defence (see also *Banif* and *Biuro*). The CJEU's case law reveals a generative function of Article 47, whereby it gives content to procedural safeguards in the context of UCTD, in particular the right to be heard. If the parties – consumers as well as traders – do not have genuine opportunities to present their cases to the court, this may result in the denial of justice.

Effective judicial protection and effectiveness are not opposites: they may converge, complement or even amplify each other. But the two types of protection also diverge. *Ex officio* control does not (fully) remedy a shortfall in procedural rights and safeguards. In this respect, Article 47 may also fulfil a signalling function, as it did in AG Kokott's Opinion in *Margarit Panicello*. Kokott referred to Article 47 to highlight a flaw in the design of the procedures at issue, which, in addition to allowing traders to circumvent unfair terms control, might also be at odds with the consumer's rights of defence. To some extent, Article 47 even has transformative potential: this will be further explored in Chapter 4. Where *Profi Credit* triggered a debate on order for payment procedures in Poland, *Aziz* and *Sánchez Morcillo* did the same for mortgage enforcement proceedings in Spain. *Sánchez Morcillo I* shows how Article 47 can play a role in restoring the balance between consumers and traders by removing unjustified procedural inequalities that deter or prevent consumers from exercising their rights.

The question remains of when restrictions of the right to an effective judicial remedy are excessive: or, phrased more positively, what exactly constitutes an effective procedural path. Article 47, in and of itself, does not provide any further guidance. Therefore, the two subsequent chapters will examine how the CJEU's case law is received and implemented at the national level, as well as whether, and to what extent, the above-mentioned functions of Article 47 trickle down to the case law of national civil courts.

CHAPTER 4

ARTICLE 47 IN UNFAIR TERMS CASES IN SPAIN

This chapter examines the role that Article 47 of the Charter has played in unfair terms cases before the Spanish civil courts. Almost all references to Article 47 have been part of broader citations of the CJEU's case law, to justify certain interpretations and/or explain why procedural rules were changed. The impact of the CJEU's case law on Spanish civil procedure will be discussed first, as well as possible explanations for the high number of preliminary references from Spain (section 4.1). Special attention will be paid to the position of civil courts vis-à-vis the Constitutional Court, with a view to understanding what is behind, in particular, *Sánchez Morcillo* and *Finanmadrid*.

The rest of this chapter follows the same structure as Chapter 3. The national background and implementation of key CJEU judgments – *Asturcom*, *Finanmadrid* and *Margarit Panicello* – will be examined in respect of the right of access to court (section 4.2). *Aziz* and *Sánchez Morcillo*, which specifically concern the Spanish mortgage enforcement regime, will be analysed separately, in respect of the right to an effective judicial remedy and the principle of equality of arms (sections 4.3 and 4.4). Lastly, a landmark judgment of the Spanish Supreme Court and the preliminary reference in *Irles López* on so-called *cláusulas suelo* ('floor clauses') will be further explored in respect of the right to be heard (section 4.5). Here, Article 47 operates as a hinge between EU (consumer) law and national (procedural) law. It may fulfil a reconciliatory function in cases where there is a (perceived) conflict, where it can be used to open up rigid or restrictive rules with due regard for the principles underpinning civil procedure.

4.1. BACKGROUND: MANY PRELIMINARY REFERENCES FROM SPANISH CIVIL COURTS

4.1.1. IMPACT OF THE UCTD ON SPANISH CIVIL PROCEDURE

4.1.1.1. A Missing Link Between Substantive and Procedural Protection

In 2008, 15 years after the adoption of the UCTD, the Spanish government believed that Spain was among the EU Member States that offered the strongest legislative protection to consumers against unfair terms.[637] Over the next 12 years (2008 to 2020), the CJEU held, on various occasions, that Spanish procedural law, in particular, did not offer sufficient protection. Spanish civil courts have been very active in asking questions to the CJEU about the interpretation and implementation of the UCTD, in particular as regards the role of national courts. There have been many cases before the CJEU concerning the compatibility or otherwise of procedural rules with the UCTD, some of which have explicitly referred to Article 47 of the Charter.[638] This does not necessarily mean that Spanish civil courts tend to rely on the CJEU to resolve interpretative issues, or that they are particularly committed to a judicial dialogue; compared with the total number of unfair terms cases adjudicated in Spanish courts, the number of cases before the CJEU is still low.[639] Still, of all decisions of the CJEU regarding the UCTD, Spain has had more than any other Member State.[640] Many of these have related to procedural issues that have surfaced after the 2008 financial crisis, in particular:

---

637 Written observations of the Kingdom of Spain, submitted to the CJEU in Case C-40/08 *Asturcom* on 11 August 2008 (*Observaciones del Reino de España en el asunto C-40/08 Asturcom* (not published)).

638 Case C-40/08 *Asturcom*; Case C-169/14 *Sánchez Morcillo I* and Case C-539/14 *Sánchez Morcillo II* (pertaining to the same dispute); Case C-49/14 *Finanmadrid*; Case C-7/16 *Banco Popular Español*; Case C-380/15 *Garzón Ramos*; Case C-308/15 *Irles López* (part of the CJEU's judgment in Joined Cases C-154/15, C-307/15 and C-308/15 *Gutiérrez Naranjo*, but hereinafter separately referred to as *Irles López*); Case C-503/15 *Margarit Panicello*; C-426/17 *Barba Giménez*; Case C-869/19 *L v Unicaja Banco*, request for a preliminary ruling from the Tribunal Supremo (pending).

639 Klaus Jochen Albiez Dohrmann and Sixto Sánchez Lorenzo, 'National Perspectives: Spain' in Karl Riesenhuber (ed), *European Legal Methodology* (Intersentia 2017) 702–703.

640 In EUR-Lex, 24 judgments (out of 85) and 12 orders (out of 33), on 4 October 2021.

- the (im)possibility of *ex officio* control with regard to the unfairness of jurisdiction and arbitration clauses;[641]
- the (im)possibility of unfair terms control – whether *ex officio* or at the consumer's request – and the lack of court involvement in special expedited procedures;[642]
- the (im)possibility of unfair terms control in mortgage enforcement proceedings;[643]
- the binding (*res judicata*) force of a judicial decision on the same subject matter between the same parties;[644]
- the procedural position of consumer protection associations;[645]
- the relation between collective actions and individual actions;[646] and
- legal costs.[647]

Consumer protection is recognised as a basic principle in Article 51 of the Spanish Constitution (Constitución Española 1978).[648] This principle does not grant subjective rights to individuals, and leaves the legislature a wide margin for enacting consumer protection laws.[649] Article 51 of the Constitution has led to the introduction of the General Act for the Defence of Consumers and Users (Ley General 26/1984 para la Defensa de los Consumidores y Usuarios or LGDCU), which enacted domestic regulation of unfair terms in consumer contracts. For the transposition

---

641 Joined Cases C-240/98 to C-244/98 *Océano*; Case C-168/05 *Mostaza Claro*; C-40/08 *Asturcom*.

642 Case C-618/10 *Banesto*; Case C-49/14 *Finanmadrid*; Case C-122/14 *Aktiv Kapital Portfolio*; Case C-503/5 *Margarit Panicello*.

643 Case C-415/11 *Aziz*; Joined Cases C-537/12 and C-116/13 *Banco Popular Español*; Case C-169/14 *Sánchez Morcillo I* and Case C-539/14 *Sánchez Morcillo II* (pertaining to the same dispute); Case C-8/14 *BBVA*; Case C-421/14 *Banco Primus*; Case C-598/15 *Banco Santander*.

644 Case C-421/14 *Banco Primus*.

645 Case C-413/12 *Asociación de Consumidores Independientes de Castilla y León*.

646 Joined Cases C-381/14 and C-385/14 *Sales Sinués*; Case C-568/14 *Fernández Oliva and Others v Caixabank*; Case C-308/15 *Irles López* C-308/15.

647 See, e.g. Case C-385/20 *EL and TP v Caixabank*, request for a preliminary ruling from Juzgado de Primera Instancia de Barcelona (pending).

648 Article 51.1 of the Spanish Constitution reads, 'The public authorities shall guarantee the protection of consumers and users and shall, by means of effective measures, safeguard their safety, health and legitimate economic interests' [English translation: <https://www.boe.es/legislacion/documentos/ConstitucionINGLES.pdf> (last accessed 3 October 2021)].

649 Jordi Ribot and Judith Conrad, 'National Report: Spain' in Gert Brüggemeijer, Aurelia Colombi Ciacchi and Giovanni Comandé (eds), *Fundamental Rights and Private Law in the European Union, Volume I: A Comparative Overview* (Cambridge University Press 2010) 651–652.

of the UCTD, the Spanish legislator opted for a dual approach, through both an amendment of the LGDCU and the adoption of a law on general contractual conditions (Ley 7/1998 sobre condiciones generales de la contratación or LCGC).[650] The LCGC governs all kinds of contracts; the LGDCU only applies to consumer contracts. The former mainly contains rules on the incorporation of general terms and conditions; the latter specifically regulates unfair terms that are not individually negotiated.

In 2004, the CJEU held that Spain had failed to correctly transpose Articles 5 and 6(2) of the UCTD into national law.[651] The LGDCU was subsequently modified,[652] and a consolidated version (*texto refundido* or TR-LGDCU) was adopted in 2007.[653] Pursuant to Article 83 TR-LGDCU (and Article 8.2 LCGC), unfair contract terms are automatically void.[654] However, it is one thing to make statutory provision for this, but quite another to ensure that unfair terms are neither used nor invoked in practice, as *Océano* famously shows.[655]

For the purposes of this book, it is relevant to consider why Spanish civil courts resorted to the CJEU in unfair terms cases, especially after the 2008 financial crisis. Several explanations have been given, by Spanish scholars and by the courts themselves in their judicial decisions, that help to give an understanding of the case law discussed in this chapter. A first explanation is that it was a judicial response to a social emergency: a 'judicial mobilisation'[656] triggered by the socio-legal context in Spain.

---

650 See Albiez Dohrmann and Sánchez Lorenzo (n 639) 709.

651 Case C-70/03 *Commission of the European Communities v Kingdom of Spain*.

652 Ley 44/2006, de mejora de la protección de los consumidores y usuarios, Boletín Oficial del Estado (BOE) no. 312 of 30 December 2006, p. 46601.

653 Real Decreto Legislativo 1/2007, por el que se aprueba el texto refundido de la Ley General para la Defensa de los Consumidores y Usuaris y otras leyes complentarias, BOE no. 287 of 30 November 2007, p. 48181.

654 The first sentence of Article 83, TR-LGDCU reads (as from 29 March 2014) as follows: 'Unfair contractual terms shall automatically be void and deemed not to have formed part of the contract. For those purposes, having heard the parties, the court shall rule that the unfair terms included in the contract are invalid, though the contract shall continue to bind the parties upon those terms if it is capable of continuing in existence without the unfair terms' [English translation is taken from Joined Cases C-154/15, C-307/15 and C-308/15 *Gutiérrez Naranjo*, para. 14].

655 Joined Cases C-240/98 to C-244/98 *Océano* (on jurisdiction clauses). See further Esther Arroyo Amayuelas, 'No vinculan al consumidor las cláusulas abusivas: del Derecho civil al procesal y entre la prevención y el castigo' in Esther Arroyo Amayuelas and Ángel Serrano de Nicolás (eds), *La Europeización del Derecho privado: cuestiones actuales* (Marcial Pons 2016) 73–74. The relevant legislative provisions on territorial competence and jurisdiction clauses are Articles 52.3 and 54.2 LEC, as well as Article 90.2 TR-LGDCU.

656 Juan A Mayoral and Aida Torres Pérez, 'On Judicial Mobilization: Entrepreneuring for Policy Change at Times of Crisis' (2018) 40 Journal of European Integration 719.

Secondly, and more importantly from the perspective of Article 47 of the Charter, Spanish civil procedure is said to be too rigid for the judges in these courts to be able to fulfil their roles as decentralised EU judges. Crisis-induced litigation highlighted a missing link between the substantive and procedural protection of consumers. Until the crisis, consumers were considered as ordinary debtors, and severe restrictions of their procedural rights were not seen as problematic. This prevented courts from offering effective judicial protection against infringements of substantive rights. Thirdly, the CJEU has assumed a role that the Spanish Constitutional Court (Tribunal Constitucional) has declined to take, in respect of the protection of fundamental rights of mortgage debtors, in particular.[657] These explanations are interrelated, and not exhaustive. The position of civil courts vis-à-vis the Tribunal Constitucional will be discussed separately,[658] because this also specifically concerns the fundamental right to effective judicial protection in the Spanish Constitution (Article 24), which, according to the Spanish Supreme Court (Tribunal Supremo) is the 'functional equivalent' of Article 47 of the Charter.[659]

4.1.1.2. Judicial Response to a Social Emergency

During the financial crisis, Spanish civil courts were confronted with a social emergency. The Spanish economy was heavily dependent on construction, and Spain had high levels of home ownership and mortgage debt.[660] Spanish law is said not to be very protective or supportive of

657 Fernando Esteban de la Rosa, 'The Treatment of Unfair Terms in the Process of Foreclosure in Spain: Mortgage Enforcement Proceedings in the Aftermath of the ECJ's "Ruling of the Evicted"' [2015] Zeitschrift für Europäisches Privatrecht 366; Teresa Jiménez París, 'El incidente de oposición en la ejecución hipotecaria por existencia de cláusulas abusivas y las SSTJUE de 17 de julio de 2014 y 21 de enero de 2015' [2015] Revista Crítica de Derecho Inmobiliario 982/1004, 985.

658 See subsection 4.2.2 below.

659 Case C-869/19 *L v Unicaja Banco*, request for a preliminary ruling from the Tribunal Supremo (pending), discussed in subsection 4.5.3 below.

660 Pablo Gutiérrez de Cabiedes Hidalgo and Marta Cantero Gamito, 'Spain' in Irina Domurath, Guido Comparato and Hans-W Micklitz (eds), *The over-indebtedness of European consumers: a view from six countries* (EUI LAW 2014/10) 108 <http://cadmus.eui.eu//handle/1814/32451> (last accessed 3 October 2021); Fernando Gómez Pomar and Karolina Lyczkowska, 'Spanish Courts, the Court of Justice of the European Union and Consumer Law: A Theoretical Model of Their Interaction' (2014) 4 InDret 6 <www.indret.com/pdf/1093.pdf> (last accessed 3 October 2021); Casla (n 536) 285; Esther Arroyo Amayuelas, 'Mortgage Credit in Spain' [2017] Journal of European Consumer and Market Law 132, 132.

over-indebted consumers in (mortgage-secured) loan contracts.[661] Large numbers of foreclosures affecting thousands of citizens, as well as the government's reluctant response, and a lack of guidance from the highest courts, all increased the number of cases in lower courts.[662] Some legislative measures were taken to mitigate the harsh consequences for vulnerable mortgage debtors who could no longer meet their contractual obligations, but those measures were generally considered to be inadequate, and have even been called 'palliative'.[663] Macroeconomic challenges affecting the Spanish financial system and the mortgage market were major concerns for the Spanish legislator, the Tribunal Constitucional, and the Tribunal Supremo, and these challenges were deemed to outweigh the needs of debtors.[664] Meanwhile, demonstrations organised by the Platform for Mortgage Victims (Plataforma de Afectados por la Hipoteca) were held all over the country.[665] The creditor–debtor relationship came to be viewed as asymmetrical, unbalanced, exploitative and predatory.[666] Lower courts found it unfair that the burden of decreases in values of houses was being borne entirely by the debtors.[667] The Spanish mortgage enforcement regime gave creditors a double benefit: they could acquire the mortgaged property for a fraction of its original value and sell it on to a third party, while still claiming the residual debt from the original mortgage debtor.

Spanish civil courts started having questions about the precarious position of mortgage debtors and the balance struck between the interests at stake.[668] Inequalities between parties – natural persons (consumers)

---

661 Fernando Gómez Pomar and Karolina Lyczkowska, 'Spanish Courts, the European Court and Consumer Law: Some Thoughts on Their Interaction' in Fabrizio Cafaggi and Stephanie Law (eds), *Judicial Cooperation in European Private Law* (Edward Elgar Publishing 2017) 115–117.

662 Gómez Pomar and Lyczkowska (n 661) 95–97; González Pascual (n 514) 273; Barral-Viñals (n 6) 70; Iglesias Sánchez (n 600) 955–956.

663 Díez García (n 540) 203–205. See also Juana Marco Molina, 'Spanish Law in 2010–2012: The Influence of European Union Law and the Impact of the Economic Crisis' (2013) 6 Journal of Civil Law Studies 401, 430–433; Iglesias Sánchez (n 600) 955–956; Esteban de la Rosa (n 657); Sabaté (n 571) 112; Miriam Anderson and Héctor Simón Moreno, 'The Spanish Crisis and the Mortgage Credit Directive: Few Changes in Sight' in Esther Arroyo Amayuelas and Miriam Anderson (eds), *The Impact of the Mortgage Credit Directive in Europe: Contrasting Views From Member States* (Europa Law Publishing 2017) 95–98.

664 See, e.g. Joined Cases C-154/15, C-307/15 and C-308/15 *Gutiérrez Naranjo*, Opinion of AG Mengozzi, point 72. See also Díez García (n 540) 234.

665 Gutiérrez de Cabiedes Hidalgo and Cantero Gamito (n 660) 115.

666 Sabaté (n 571) 118–119; González Pascual (n 514) 262, 281.

667 Marco Molina (n 663) 427.

668 Gómez Pomar and Lyczkowska (n 661) 116; Beka (n 32) 257.

and financial institutions (traders) – were aggravated by a lack of effective judicial remedies and procedural safeguards for mortgage debtors.[669] However, the Tribunal Supremo ruled that as long as the foreclosure took place in accordance with the legal procedure, it was not an abuse of rights when creditors exercised the rights conferred on them by law.[670] The Tribunal Constitucional confirmed this: it was up to the Spanish legislature to make changes in the law, not the judiciary.[671] Against this background, lower courts began to doubt whether the applicable legislation was compatible with EU consumer law, by referring the 'cracks' that they had identified in their national legal system upwards for consideration at EU level.[672] They resorted to the CJEU to mitigate some of the harsh effects of mortgage enforcement proceedings.[673] In a way, such judges be seen as 'judicial entrepreneurs' who resorted to EU law to induce policy change and legislative reform when the Spanish legal order failed to give satisfactory solutions.[674] Courts were seen as a last resort – the 'last trench'[675] – to provide protection against the enforcement of (mortgage) loan agreements that could be challenged in light of, for example, the UCTD.

The CJEU has, indeed, adopted a more consumer-friendly approach. The judgment in *Aziz*, in particular, has been described of being of 'enormous social significance'.[676] This has not been received with unanimous support. The protection of consumer debtors by Spanish courts has been called 'Robinhoodian'; it has helped to rebalance the consumer-creditor relationship, but has also, allegedly, distorted the civil law system and caused legal uncertainty.[677] Perhaps due partly to the ad hoc nature of

---

669 González Pascual (n 514) 269–272.

670 Tribunal Supremo (Sala de lo Civil), judgment no. 681/2006 of 16 February 2006, ECLI:ES:TS:2006:681. See also Marco Molina (n 663) 429–430.

671 See, e.g. Tribunal Constitucional, order no. 113/2011 of 19 July 2011, ECLI:ES:TC:2011:113A, discussed further below, in subsection 4.3.2.

672 Marien Aguilera Morales, 'TJUE, proceso civil y tutela del consumidor: repaso de un año que termina y previsiones en torno a otro que comienza' (2018) 44 Revista General de Derecho Procesal 29; Gómez Pomar and Lyczkowska (n 660) 11.

673 Iglesias Sánchez (n 18) 970; Pérez Daudí (n 32) 81.

674 Mayoral and Torres Pérez (n 656) 720; Joaquim Bosch Grau and Ignacio Escolar, *El secuestro de la justicia: Virtudes y problemas del sistema judicial* (Roca Editorial de Libros 2018) 106–116.

675 Javier Álvarez and Luis Fernando Rodríguez, *La última trinchera* (Planeta 2016) 107.

676 Case C-415/11 *Aziz*, introduced in subsection 3.3.2 of the preceding chapter. See, e.g. AP Lleida (Sección 2ª), order no. 55/2013 of 25 March 2013, JUR\2014\294266.

677 Sergio Nasarre-Aznar, '"Robinhoodian" Courts' Decisions on Mortgage Law in Spain' (2015) 7 International Journal of Law in the Built Environment 127, 128, 138.

the CJEU's case law,[678] the Spanish legislature's efforts to implement this case law have not cleared all the doubts either, as will become apparent in this chapter. While, in theory, codification of the CJEU's case law could contribute to more clarity, there is a danger that it could curb the courts' powers and give rise to additional questions or conflicting interpretations.

4.1.1.3. Rigidity of Spanish Civil Procedure

A second explanation for the high number of preliminary references is that Spanish civil procedure is quite rigid, which clashes with the more active role required of national courts under EU consumer law. The role imposed on them by the CJEU – a positive obligation to intervene, not only by applying EU consumer protection legislation *ex officio*, but also by stepping in if domestic (procedural) law offers insufficient protection – goes further than the competences attributed to Spanish civil courts.[679] The Court of Appeal (Audiencia Provincial or AP) in Barcelona has observed that Spanish civil procedure is very restrictive, and that some 'rigorisms' should be made more flexible, pursuant to the CJEU's case law.[680] In the words of another Court of Appeal, the AP in Toledo:

> 'Procedural principles must be relaxed in order to ensure that the rights conferred on consumers by [the UCTD] are real and not merely theoretical'.[681]

Spanish civil procedure has, traditionally, been characterised by a limited scope for judicial intervention, as well as a rigid notion of

678 Ángel Francisco Carrasco Perera and Maria Carmen González Carrasco, 'La doctrina casacional sobre la transparencia de las cláusulas suelo conculca la garantía constitucional de la tutela judicial efectiva' [2013] Revista CESCO de Derecho de Consumo 150.

679 Francisco Moya Hurtado de Mendoza, 'Efectividad del Derecho de la Unión Europea vs. principio constitucional de imperio de la Ley' [2017] Revista de Derecho Político 399, 411, 417.

680 AP Barcelona (Sección 15ª), judgment no. 407/2014 of 15 December 2014, JUR\2015\86196, further discussed in subsection 4.3.2 below. See also Tribunal Supremo (Sala de lo Civil), judgment no. 1916/2013 of 9 May 2013, ECLI:ES:TS:2013:1916, discussed in subsection 4.5.2 below.

681 AP Toledo (Sección 2ª), order no. 297/2018 of 12 December 2018, JUR\2019\72784, with reference to *Sánchez Morcillo* and Article 47 of the Charter. Translated from the original Spanish text, which reads, '*Los principios procesales han de flexibilizarse para viabilizar que los derechos conferidos por la Directiva ... a los consumidores sean reales y no meramente teóricos*'.

party autonomy.[682] All judicial decisions discussed in this chapter that refer to Article 47 of the Charter concern rules that restrict or exclude procedural rights of the parties and/or powers of the court. The CJEU's case law gives rise to the question of how Spanish civil court judges can reconcile their role as decentralised EU judges with traditional Spanish principles of civil procedure. An example is the dispositive principle, which entails that the parties take the initiative in civil litigation.[683] *Ex officio* control could be seen as an exception to this principle, at odds with the notion of party autonomy.[684]

The cases discussed in this chapter show that the judicial protection of consumers in Spain is determined by a continuous interplay between the legislature and the judiciary, with a strong European dimension. As a result, two procedural models have been created: one for consumers and one for other litigants.[685] The first major reform of the Spanish Code of Civil Procedure (Ley de Enjuiciamiento Civil 2000 or LEC)[686] in order to comply with the CJEU's case law on the UCTD took place in 2013. More reforms have followed. For the purposes of this book, the most relevant laws are:[687]

- Ley 1/2013,[688] which was adopted shortly after *Aziz*, and also implemented *Banif Plus Bank*.[689] The preamble refers to exceptional

---

682 Ignacio Díez-Picazo Giménez, 'Civil Justice in Spain: Present and Future, Access, Cost, and Duration' in Adrian Zuckerman (ed), *Civil Justice in Crisis: Comparative Perspectives of Civil Procedure* (Oxford University Press 1999) 388, 405; Gascón Inchausti (n 418) 122.

683 Arroyo Amayuelas (n 655) 71–72; Pérez Daudí (n 32) 161. See also subsection 2.1.2 of this book.

684 See, e.g. Maria Pía Calderón Cuadrado, 'Derechos, proceso y crisis de la justicia' (2015) 37 Revista General de Derecho Procesal 32, 37, 43; Rosa Barceló Compte, *Ventaja injusta y protección de la parte débil del contrato* (Marcial Pons 2019) 222.

685 Calderón Cuadrado (n 684) 43.

686 Ley 1/2000, de 7 de enero, de Enjuiciamiento Civil, BOE no. 7, 8 January 2000. The complete text of the LEC (in Spanish) can be accessed via: <noticias.juridicas.com/base_datos/Privado/l1-2000.html>. An English translation (made in 2015) can be found at <https://www.mjusticia.gob.es/es/areas-tematicas/documentacion-publicaciones/publicaciones/traducciones-derecho-espanol> (last accessed 3 October 2021).

687 See, for an overview, María García-Valdecasas Dorrego, *Dialogue between the Spanish Courts and the European Court of Justice Regarding the Judicial Protection of Consumers under Directive 93/13/EEC* (Fundación Registral 2018) 179–181.

688 Ley 1/2013, de medidas para reforzar la protección a los deudores hipotecarios, reestructuración de deuda y alquiler social, BOE no. 116 of 15 May 2013, p. 36373.

689 See sections 4.3 and 4.5, respectively, of this book.

financial and economic circumstances and the 'social drama' caused by foreclosures. Pursuant to its preamble, one of the aims of Ley 1/2013 was to streamline the mortgage enforcement procedure and make it more flexible, to ensure that the rights and interests of mortgage debtors were adequately protected.

- Real Decreto-ley 11/2014 (RD 11/2014),[690] which was adopted after *Sánchez Morcillo I*.[691]
- Ley 42/2015,[692] which was introduced, inter alia, to comply with *Asturcom* and *Banesto*.[693]
- Ley 5/2019,[694] which transposes the Mortgage Credit Directive[695] into Spanish law.[696]

These laws will be elaborated on further below. The dynamics are usually as follows: different courts have divergent interpretations of a set of procedural rules. When those rules are questioned in light of EU consumer law, a request for a preliminary ruling is made to the CJEU. In so far as the CJEU's ruling entails that a certain procedural arrangement is precluded, the ruling then needs to be implemented through judicial interpretation and/or legislative amendments. This, in turn, may trigger new preliminary references.

Efforts to bring Spanish procedural law into conformity with the case law of the CJEU have largely been driven by courts, in response to hesitation by the Spanish legislator.[697] As the president of the Civil Division of the Tribunal Supremo, Francisco Marín Castán, put it, the case law of the CJEU had left Spain 'without law' in the field of mortgage enforcement, therefore

---

690 Real Decreto-ley 11/2014, de medidas urgentes en materia concursal, BOE no. 217 of 6 September 2014, p. 69767.

691 See section 4.4 below.

692 Ley 42/2015, de reforma de la Ley de Enjuiciamiento Civil, BOE no. 239 of 6 October 2015, p. 90240.

693 See section 4.2 below.

694 Ley 5/2019, reguladora de los contratos de crédito inmobiliario, BOE no. 65 of 16 March 2019, p. 26329.

695 Directive 2014/17/EU on credit agreements for consumers relating to residential immovable property (OJ L060, 28 April 2014, p. 34). The European Commission had started infringement proceedings against Spain for failure to transpose the Directive in time, but the procedure was withdrawn on 17 June 2019: Case C-569/17 *European Commission v Kingdom of Spain*.

696 See section 4.3 below.

697 Carlos Teijo García and Carlos Durán Suárez, 'Crónica sobre la aplicación judicial del derecho de la UE en España (2014)' [2016] Revista Electrónica de Estudios Internacionales 18.

courts were required to resolve issues that had not yet been regulated.[698] The courts must provide effective judicial protection in practice, but the question is how they are supposed to do this if national procedural law gives no clear guidance. Pursuant to Article 5 of the Law of the Judiciary (Ley Orgánica del Poder Judicial or LOPJ),[699] Articles 1.1 and 1.6 of the Spanish Civil Code (Código Civil) and Article 1 LEC, Spanish courts must apply the law and interpret it, but they cannot create or change it.[700] Perhaps, then, it is not so surprising that Spanish courts tend to 'shield' themselves, in their decisions, behind citations from CJEU case law.[701]

4.1.2. DUALITY IN THE PROTECTION OF FUNDAMENTAL RIGHTS

A third explanation for the many preliminary references from Spain is the Tribunal Constitucional not being able or willing to play a role in a critical reassessment of the Spanish mortgage enforcement regime. Similar questions to the ones raised in *Aziz* and *Sánchez Morcillo* had already been posed to the Tribunal Constitucional, to no avail.[702] The CJEU provided a higher level of fundamental rights protection than the Tribunal Constitucional in similar cases regarding the same constellation of procedural rules. In a way, the CJEU could be seen as a 'court of last resort' to provide justice denied to mortgage debtors at the national level.[703] As Judge José Maria Fernández Seijo, who made the preliminary references to the CJEU in both *Océano* and *Aziz*,[704] remarked:

> 'It is doubtful whether Article 24 of the Constitution is of any use … therefore I ventured to take one step down and, instead of taking the route of fundamental rights, I raised an issue of consumer protection, of rights that are broader'.[705]

---

698 See <http://noticias.juridicas.com/actualidad/noticias/11185-la-jurisprudencia-del-tjue-ha-dejado-a-espana-quot%3Bsin-leyq/> (last accessed 3 October 2021).

699 Ley Orgánica 6/1985 del Poder Judicial, BOE no. 157 of 2 July 1985, p. 12666.

700 See further Nasarre-Aznar (n 677) 129.

701 See Gómez Pomar and Lyczkowska (n 660) 9–10; Juan A Mayoral, '"Government Contained?" Explaining Spanish Supreme Court's Decisions on EU Law' (Conference Paper, ECPR Conference, January 2011) <https://www.researchgate.net/publication/228543154> (last accessed 3 October 2021).

702 Case C-415/11 *Aziz* and Case C-169/14 *Sánchez Morcillo*: see subsections 4.3.2 and 4.4.2, respectively.

703 Micklitz and Reich (n 44) 805.

704 Joined Cases C-240/98 to C-244/98 *Océano*; Case C-415/11 *Aziz*.

705 In Javier Álvarez and Luis Fernando Rodríguez, *La Última Trinchera* (Planeta 2016) 107. Translated by the author from the original Spanish text, which reads, '*Te surge*

In Spain, the system of judicial review is centralised; ordinary courts are obliged to submit a question to the Tribunal Constitucional if there are doubts as to the constitutionality (and, thus, the validity) of a statutory provision, or if there are no specific legal provisions or instruments available to resolve the case.[706] The Tribunal Constitucional has a monopoly on the constitutional review of domestic law; the ordinary courts must guarantee the correct application of EU law, including the Charter.[707] Since 2015, the LOPJ has stipulated that Spanish courts and tribunals are obliged to apply EU law in conformity with the case law of the CJEU, and that civil courts have jurisdiction to hear claims arising in Spanish territory in accordance with, inter alia, EU law.[708]

It has been observed that the Tribunal Constitucional shows a certain '*apatía europea*'[709] (impassiveness or indifference) by considering an infringement of EU law as a matter of application or disapplication of the domestic legal norms in question by the ordinary courts, and not as a constitutional matter. At the same time, the Tribunal Constitucional has held that if reasonable doubt exists as to the incompatibility of national law with EU law, it is contrary to the right to due process (Article 24 of the Constitution) for an ordinary court to disapply national law without first raising a question of constitutionality (*cuestión de inconstitucionalidad*) to the Tribunal Constitucional, or making a preliminary reference to the CJEU.[710] While this seems to be in line with the principle that courts are not supposed to change the law, it raises the question as to what a Spanish civil court must do in the event of a potential conflict between domestic

---

la duda si el artículo 24 de la Constitución sirve para algo; ... así que me arriesgué a bajar un escalón y en vez de abordar un caso de derechos fundamentales me planteé un problema de tutela de los consumidores, de derechos más difusos.'

706 Ribot and Conrad (n 649) 624; Victor Ferreres Comella, *The Constitution of Spain: A Contextual Analysis* (Hart Publishing 2013) 222.

707 Ferreres Comella (n 706) 219; Albiez Dohrmann and Sánchez Lorenzo (n 639) 699. See also Camilo B Schutte, *Constitutionele rechtspraak in Spanje. Het Tribunal Constitucional en zijn jurisprudentie in hun historische context* (Shaker Publishing 1999) 195.

708 Articles 4bis and 21 LOPJ, respectively, added and amended by Ley Orgánica 7/2015, por la que se modifica la Ley Orgánica del Poder Judicial, BOE no. 174 of 22 July 2015, p. 61593.

709 Mayoral Díaz-Asensio, Berberoff Ayuda and Ordóñez Solís (n 77) 146.

710 Aida Torres Pérez, 'The Judicial Impact of European Law in Spain: ECHR and EU Law Compared' (2011) 30 Yearbook of European Law 159, 165–167. See further Encarnación Roca Trías and Susana García Couso, '¿Es real el diálogo entre tribunales? Cuestión prejudicial y control de constitucionalidad por vulneración de derechos y libertades fundamentales' [2017] Teoría y Realidad Constitucional 529.

law and EU law or EU fundamental rights.[711] The Tribunal Constitucional has framed this as a choice between the Tribunal Constitucional or the CJEU,[712] which does not seem to leave space for ordinary courts to disapply national law on their own. As Torres Pérez has observed, such a framing is problematic from the perspective of EU law, where the obligation to make a preliminary reference exists only for courts of last instance.[713] This could explain why there are so many requests for preliminary rulings from lower courts, even when they are not obliged to do so under EU law, especially since there they may be an expectation of more support from the CJEU.[714] Indeed, the Tribunal Constitucional is said to be reluctant to deal with socio-economic issues that are considered as prerogatives of the legislature and the executive.[715]

The possibility of ordinary courts making preliminary references to the CJEU, or setting aside domestic law that conflicts with directly applicable Charter provisions, challenges the role of the Tribunal Constitucional in the system of fundamental rights protection.[716] The duality between the protection of constitutional and Charter rights has led to a discussion in Spain about cooperation and coordination between the Tribunal Constitucional and the CJEU.[717] The Tribunal Constitucional itself seems to have preserved this duality by distinguishing between the supremacy of the Constitution and the primacy of EU law;[718] EU law does not enjoy constitutional status. Roca Trías has criticised this formalistic distinction and submitted that the Tribunal Constitucional should also assume its responsibility under EU law.[719] She has argued that EU law and EU fundamental rights cannot merely be placed on a par with the ECHR,

---

711 Torres Pérez (n 710) 173.

712 Tribunal Constitucional, judgment no. 241/2015 of 30 November 2015, ECLI:ES:TC:2015:241. See also Pérez Daudí (n 32) 134–135. And, in more detail, Pilar Concellón Fernández, *Dialogando con Luxemburgo: Los órganos jurisdiccionales españoles y la cuestión prejudicial (1986-2017)* (2018) 123ff <http://digibuo.uniovi.es/dspace/handle/10651/46902> (last accessed 19 October 2021). If the case law of the CJEU is sufficiently clear, and the court applies Spanish law in accordance with it, there is no violation of Article 47 of the Charter and Article 24 of the Constitution: see, e.g. AP Madrid (Sección 10ª), order no. 425/2015 of 14 December 2015, JUR\2016\15218.

713 Torres Pérez (n 710) 169–171.

714 See also subsection 4.1.1 above.

715 Casla (n 536) 294.

716 Torres Pérez (n 710) 178–179; Teijo García and Durán Suárez (n 697) 6. See also Case C-399/11 *Melloni*, discussed in subsection 2.2.2 of this book.

717 Pérez Daudí (n 32) 58.

718 Torres Pérez (n 710) 167.

719 Roca Trías and García Couso (n 710) 544. See also Pérez Daudí (n 32) 56.

which does not constitute an autonomous parameter for the Tribunal Constitucional.[720] By contrast, the Charter is binding on national courts regardless of the status accorded to it in domestic (constitutional) law.[721]

So far, the Tribunal Constitucional has limited its own role in respect of EU law to checking whether there has been an infringement of procedural safeguards, or whether the ordinary courts have applied an unreasonable and arbitrary selection of applicable rules (including EU law) that gives rise to a violation of Article 24 of the Constitution.[722] Only in such cases does it become a constitutional matter. Article 24 of the Constitution contains the right to effective judicial protection, which citizens may invoke directly.[723] But 'infringement[s] of procedural norms or guarantees' or 'procedural infringement[s]' in civil proceedings are primarily grounds for appeal before the ordinary courts (Articles 459 and 468 LEC).[724] If the judgment has become final, a so-called 'exceptional application for nullity of procedural actions' (*incidente excepcional de nulidad de actuaciones*) may be brought (Article 228 LEC).[725] In case of an alleged violation of Article 24 of the Constitution, citizens may bring an individual complaint (*recurso de amparo*) before the Tribunal Constitucional, which acts as the ultimate guarantor of national fundamental rights.[726]

---

720 Roca Trías and García Couso (n 710) 546–547. See also Torres Pérez (n 710) 166; Ribot and Conrad (n 649) 615–618.

721 See also Roca Trías and García Couso (n 710) 543.

722 See, e.g. Tribunal Constitucional, judgment no. 145/2012 of 2 July 2012, ECLI:ES:TC:2012:145; Tribunal Constitucional, judgment no. 241/2015 of 30 November 2015, ECLI:ES:TC:2014:241. For a synthesis of the Tribunal Constitucional's case law, see its judgment no. 37/2019 of 26 March 2019, ECLI:ES:TC:2019:37. See also Mayoral Díaz-Asensio, Berberoff Ayuda and Ordóñez Solís (n 77) 148.

723 Article 24 of the Spanish Constitution reads: '1. Every person has the right to obtain the effective protection of the judges and the courts in the exercise of his or her legitimate rights and interests, and in no case may he [or she] go undefended. 2. Likewise, all persons have the right of access to the ordinary judge predetermined by law; to the defence and assistance by a lawyer; to be informed of the charges brought against them; to a public trial without undue delays and with full guarantees; to the use of evidence appropriate to their defence; to not make self-incriminating statements; to not declare themselves guilty; and to be presumed innocent. The law shall determine the cases in which, for reasons of family relationship or professional secrecy, it shall not be compulsory to make statements regarding alleged criminal offences' [English translation <https://www.boe.es/legislacion/documentos/ConstitucionINGLES.pdf> (last accessed 3 October 2021)].

724 Vicente Pérez Daudí, *La protección civil de los derechos fundamentales* (Atelier 2011) 85.

725 Pérez Daudí (n 32) 143.

726 Pérez Daudí (n 724) 103.

A *recurso de amparo* against a judicial decision may provide a last resort for parties to obtain effective judicial protection. An example can be found in a case concerning mortgage enforcement and the UCTD.[727] The debtors involved complained that they should have been treated as consumers, i.e. natural persons acting for purposes outside their trade, business or profession with no link of a functional nature with a company (Article 3(b) TR-LGDCU). Therefore, their opposition against the enforcement and, later, their appeal should not have been dismissed, and their application for nullity of procedural actions should have been granted. The Tribunal Constitucional reaffirmed its position that it is not its task to control the conformity of the actions of the national (judicial) authorities with EU law. The Tribunal Constitucional must only determine whether judicial decisions are contrary to Article 24 of the Constitution. In so far as a judicial decision deliberately disregards the case law of the CJEU, it is unreasonable and arbitrary, which could, indirectly, be seen as a form of judicial review, in light of EU law. The Tribunal Constitucional held that, in this case, the CJEU's interpretation of the UCTD had, indeed, been disregarded.[728] As a consequence, the proceedings were declared null from the moment of dismissal of the initial opposition, and a new decision was required.

In a more recent decision, the Tribunal Constitucional found that the CJEU's judgment in *Banco Primus*[729] had been disregarded by a court of first instance.[730] The debtors' application for nullity of procedural actions should have been granted, or, alternatively, the court should have made a preliminary reference to the CJEU. Since it had not done so, the court had violated the primacy of EU law and the right to effective judicial protection contained in Article 24 of the Constitution. Whether this means that the Tribunal Constitucional's *apatía europea* has come to an end remains to be seen: the relation between Article 24 of the Constitution and Article 47 of the Charter is still to crystallise further.

---

727 Tribunal Constitucional, judgment no. 75/2017 of 19 June 2017, ECLI:ES:TC:2017:75.

728 In particular, the CJEU's order in Case C-74/15 *Tarcău v Banca Comercială Intesa Sanpaolo România*.

729 Case C-421/14 *Banco Primus*: see further subsection 4.4.3 below.

730 Tribunal Constitucional, judgment no. 31/2019 of 28 February 2019, ECLI:ES:TC:2019:31. See also Tribunal Constitucional, judgment no. 34/2019 of 14 March 2019, ECLI:ES:TC:2019:34, discussed in subsection 4.2.3 below.

4.1.3. OVERVIEW OF REFERENCES TO ARTICLE 47 IN SPANISH CASE LAW

The many preliminary references from Spain are a clear sign that, in the view of the referring courts, Spanish civil procedure offers insufficient protection of consumer debtors.[731] EU consumer law is said to have 'transformative capacity',[732] which resonates with the transformative function of Article 47 of the Charter. The CJEU's case law has led to a transformation of procedural rules, and the amplification of procedural rights for consumers and the powers of civil courts, although the legal framework has also become more fragmented.[733]

For this book, more than 350 decisions of the Spanish civil courts were analysed, not counting the case law of the Tribunal Constitucional. In so far as Article 47 of the Charter has become a new parameter for judicial interpretation in Spain,[734] most references to it were part of more elaborate citations of the CJEU's case law on the UCTD. This corroborates the above-mentioned observation of Spanish courts shielding themselves behind the CJEU citations. Therefore, the focus will primarily be on the original decisions that made preliminary references to the CJEU, explicitly referring to Article 47, in particular *Finanmadrid* and *Sánchez Morcillo*.[735] These are discussed in the sections corresponding to the judgments of the CJEU. The existence of a fundamental right to effective judicial protection in the Spanish Constitution may have inspired some of the references by Spanish civil courts to Article 47. A few decisions ascribe a role to Article 47 that is analogous or equivalent to Article 24 of the Constitution.[736] An important difference, of course, is that Article 47 is connected to EU consumer law; its application is limited to cases involving consumers.[737] However, a reference to Article 47 also reveals a

---

731 Mª Paz García Aburuza, 'Directiva 93/13 CEE versus Derecho Procesal Civil Español' Revista Aranzadi Doctrinal 9/2014 parte Estudio 13–15.

732 Mayoral and Torres Pérez (n 656) 729.

733 Pérez Daudí (n 32) 20; Albiez Dohrmann and Sánchez Lorenzo (n 639) 710.

734 Medina Guerrero (n 572) 279.

735 Case C-49/14 *Finanmadrid* and Case C-169/14 *Sánchez Morcillo*.

736 See, e.g. AP Madrid (Sección 10ª), order no. 425/2015 of 14 December 2015, JUR\2016\15218; AP Barcelona (Sección 15ª), judgment no. 136/2016 of 9 June 2016, JUR\2016\180303; Juzgado de Primera Instancia de Madrid, judgment no. 379/2016 of 13 October 2016, JUR\2016\237072; AP Málaga (Sección 5ª), order no. 356/2016 of 31 October 2016, JUR\2017\93140.

737 See, e.g. AP Almería (Sección 1ª), order no. 591/2017 of 19 December 2017, JUR\2018\200435, ECLI:ES:APAL:2017:781A; AP Barcelona (Sección 19ª), order no. 194/2018 of 5 July 2018, JUR\2018\210473, ECLI:ES:APB:2018:4118A; AP Girona

constitutional dimension. The prohibition of *indefensión*, i.e. a denial of the parties' rights of defence,[738] plays a central role in this respect, and will be referred to throughout this chapter.

The analysed case law touches on a range of topics that have been debated extensively in Spanish jurisprudence and legal doctrine. Recent examples are the assessment and substantive consequences of a finding of unfairness of clauses on default interest (*interés moratorio*),[739] early maturity or accelerated repayment of the loan (*vencimiento anticipado*),[740] and minimum interest rates or 'floor clauses' (*cláusulas suelo*).[741] While some of the judicial decisions that refer to the Charter also concern these issues, Article 47 has not, so far, been used to address them. The Tribunal Constitucional also considers these as substantive, not procedural, issues.[742] Therefore, these issues will only be mentioned to the extent that they are relevant for the cases discussed in this chapter. A large part of the case law relates to the mortgage enforcement regime, which has been an important topic of debate in Spain. This debate provides relevant background information, but it is not the subject of this chapter, as such, nor is it the purpose of this chapter to give an elaborate overview of all procedural issues in light of EU consumer law. The focus is on the role Article 47 has played, so far, in the reasoning of Spanish civil courts in unfair terms cases.

4.2. ACCESS TO COURT

4.2.1. INTRODUCTION: PRIVILEGED PROCEDURES

This section deals with Article 47 of the Charter in respect of consumer arbitration (in particular the case of *Asturcom*),[743] and order for payment

---

(Sección 2ª), order no. 65/2019 of 11 April 2019, JUR\2019\127067, ECLI:ES:APGI:2019:167A.

738 Further explained in subsection 4.5.1 below.

739 Joined Cases C-482/13, C-484/14, C-485/13 and C-487/13 *Unicaja*; Case C-602/13 *BBVA v Quintano Ujeta and Sánchez García*; Joined Cases C-96/16 and C-94/17 *Banco de Sabadell*.

740 Case C-70/17 *Abanca*. *Vencimiento anticipado* means that, when the debtor fails to fulfil their payment obligations, the creditor can claim the totality of the loan on the expiry of a stipulated time limit (advanced expiration date).

741 Joined Cases C-154/15, C-307/15 and C-308/15 *Gutiérrez Naranjo*. See further e.g. Arroyo Amayuelas (n 655); José Maria Fernández Seijo, *La tutela de los consumidores en los procedimientos judiciales* (Wolters Kluwer 2017); García-Valdecasas Dorrego (n 687).

742 Tribunal Constitucional, judgment no. 31/2019 of 28 February 2019, ECLI:ES:TC:2019:31.

743 Case C-40/08 *Asturcom*, discussed in subsection 3.2.2 of the preceding chapter.

procedures, which are so-called 'privileged procedures'[744] (in particular *Finanmadrid* and *Margarit Panicello*).[745] These procedures have in common that decision-making is removed from the judicial realm. It is the arbitral tribunal, specifically the court registrar (*Secretario Judicial*, currently called *Letrado de la Administración de Justicia*), not a court, that issues an arbitral award order for payment. The procedures allow creditors to obtain an enforceable title that has the same status as a judicial decision, for the purposes of enforcement, without having to follow ordinary court proceedings. Creditors just need leave to enforce the title they have obtained against the debtor, which ensures rapid debt collection for uncontested claims.[746] For those who are not familiar with Spanish civil procedure, it should be noted that the enforcement of enforceable court orders, such as judicial decisions and arbitral awards, requires court involvement.[747] The enforcing party must bring an enforcement action before the competent court. The general enforcement proceedings are governed by the rules laid down in Articles 517–570 LEC; the rules for the enforcement of mortgages and pledges are to be found in Articles 681–698 LEC.

The above-mentioned procedures entail a shift of procedural initiative: it is the *defendant*, i.e. the debtor, who must initiate adversarial (that is, *inter partes* or contentious) proceedings.[748] In principle, the case only comes before a court when the debtor challenges the claim within a relatively short time period and, even then, the space for judicial intervention (an examination of the merits of the case) is limited, if it is possible at all. All three of the cases mentioned above concern the principle of *res judicata*.[749] From the perspective of Article 47 of the Charter, this gives rise to doubts regarding the effective judicial protection of consumers. The analysed cases illustrate why it is problematic to give creditors a particularly strong

[744] AP Girona (Sección 2ª), order no. 14/2015 of 14 January 2015, JUR\2015\116526; AP Toledo (Sección 2ª), order no. 151/2017 of 2 February 2017, JUR\2017\142012; AP Almería (Sección 1ª), order no. 232/2018 of 23 May 2018, JUR\2018\201290, ECLI:ES:APAL:2018:127A. See also Aguilera Morales (n 451) 3; Díez García (n 540) 230.

[745] Case C-49/14 *Finanmadrid* and Case C-503/15 *Margarit Panicello*, discussed in subsection 3.2.3 of the preceding chapter.

[746] Luis Gómez Amigo, 'Control de las cláusulas abusivas y garantías procesales en los procesos con técnica monitoria, a la luz de la jurisprudencia reciente' [2019] Revista General de Derecho Procesal.

[747] This is different in the Netherlands, where enforceable court orders can, in principle, be enforced by the parties themselves through the engagement of a bailiff.

[748] See subsection 3.2.1 of the preceding chapter.

[749] Laid down in Articles 207.3 and 4 LEC, and introduced in subsection 3.2.2 of the preceding chapter.

procedural position vis-à-vis consumer debtors, who may not be able to exercise their rights under the UCTD and defend themselves against the enforcement of claims, some of which may be based on unfair contract terms.

The courts that made the preliminary references in *Asturcom* and *Finanmadrid*, as well as the court registrar in *Margarit Panicello*, seem to have been aware of the constitutional dimension of these cases, which was accentuated by an explicit reference to Article 47 of the Charter in the latter two cases. Both the referring court in *Finanmadrid* and the court registrar in *Margarit Panicello* referred to Article 47 to signal problems that touch upon the core of judicial protection. Neither the CJEU nor the Spanish legislature have picked up the signalling function of Article 47 in this respect; only the Tribunal Constitucional has, indirectly, by reference to *Margarit Panicello*. The referring court in *Asturcom* brought up the consumer's right of access to court and the rights of defence, but did not explicitly mention Article 47, possibly because the preliminary reference predated the Charter's entry into force and there had not yet been any CJEU judgments on the connection between Article 47 and the UCTD. The national context of the case will, nevertheless, be discussed, because it illustrates the potential empowering function of Article 47.

4.2.2. CONSUMER ARBITRATION

4.2.2.1. Consumer as Claimant or Defendant: A Crucial Difference

Article 47 of the Charter may play a role in respect of arbitration clauses in consumer contracts: (i) horizontally, as a parameter for an assessment of the validity or fairness of arbitration clauses in consumer contracts; and (ii) vertically, as an instrument to create space for such an assessment in so far as national procedural law does not provide for it.[750] *Asturcom* provides an example of a case that could have had a different outcome in respect of the latter, by reference to Article 47.

Article 47 does not seem to have played a direct role as regards the invalidity, as such, of arbitration clauses in consumer contracts under Spanish law. However, the fundamental right to effective judicial protection, as enshrined in Article 24 of the Spanish Constitution, is relevant in this regard. The Tribunal Constitucional has held that the free

[750] See also subsection 3.2.2 of the preceding chapter.

will and autonomy of the parties is the essence of arbitration; their consent is a prerequisite. Restrictions of the right of access to court are allowed for constitutionally protected reasons or objectives, as long as they are proportionate (Article 53 of the Constitution). One of these objectives, recognised by the Tribunal Constitucional, is preventing excessive litigation and unburdening the courts through facilitation of ADR. According to the Tribunal Constitucional, it is, nevertheless, contrary to Article 24 of the Constitution to prescribe arbitration as the default route.[751] As regards arbitration clauses in consumer contracts, it is dubious whether 'free will' can ever be presupposed, especially where contracts have been concluded on the basis of standard terms and conditions that are not individually negotiated. Therefore, the Spanish legislator has decided that, in the case of consumers, arbitration clauses are, generally, not allowed: if the contract that contains an arbitration clause was concluded *before* the dispute had arisen, the clause is not binding on the consumer (Article 57.4 TR-LGDCU).[752] The main reason for this is the weaker position of consumers vis-à-vis their counterparties: they cannot properly evaluate beforehand whether they want to go to arbitration, and are effectively forced to waive their legally recognised rights in this regard.[753] As a result, consumers cannot, in principle, be subjected to arbitration when they are the *defendants*.[754]

When they are the *claimants*, consumers can choose which dispute resolution mechanism they prefer: whether to submit their claim to a court or to opt for consumer arbitration. There is a special Sistema Arbitral del

---

751 Tribunal Constitucional, judgment no. 185/1987 of 18 November 1987, ECLI:ES:TC:1987:185; judgment no. 174/1995 of 23 November 1995, ECLI:ES:TC:1995:174; Tribunal Constitucional, judgment no. 352/2006 of 14 December 2006, ECLI:ES:TC:2006:352. See further Ana I Mendoza Losana, '¿Existe un derecho absoluto a accedar a los óganos jurisdiccionales en nombre de la tutela judicial efectiva?' [2017] Centro de Estudios de Consumo – Publicaciones Jurídicas 4.

752 As amended by Ley 3/2014, por la que se modifica el texto refundido de la Ley General para la Defensa de los Consumidores y Usuarios y otras leyes complementarias, aprobado por el Real Decreto Legislativo 1/2007, BOE no. 76 of 28 March 2014, p. 28967. See further Diana Marcos Francisco, 'Consumidores, sujetos privilegiados en el nuevo paradigma de justicia civil europea: medidas procesales y extraprocesales para su protección' [2015] InDret 16ff. <http://www.indret.com/pdf/1155_es.pdf> (last accessed 3 October 2021); Beka (n 32) 163–164.

753 Ley 44/2006, de 29 de diciembre, de mejora de la protección de los consumidores y usuarios, BOE no. 312 of 30 December 2006, p. 46601, preamble VII. See also Tribunal Constitucional, judgment no. 1/2018 of 11 January 2018, ECLI:ES:TC:2018:1.

754 For further background on the consumer ADR scheme in Spain, see Pablo Cortés, 'The Impact of EU Law in the ADR Landscape in Italy, Spain and the UK: Time for Change or Missed Opportunity?' (2015) 16 ERA Forum 125, 133ff.

Consumo (consumer arbitration system), which is regulated by law.[755] The Sistema was introduced in 1984 and formally established in 1993; it is regulated under the Ley de Arbitraje (Arbitration Act or LA) of 2003.[756] Article 58.1 TR-LGDCU emphasises that submission to the Sistema must be voluntary, and consent must have been expressly given. Only consumers can bring claims before the Juntas Arbitrales de Consumo (JACs), the arbitral tribunals that are part of the Sistema. The JACs are competent on the basis of a public declaration of adherence to the system by the professional party (trader); the arbitral agreement is completed when the consumer brings a claim against that party.[757] In the cases discussed below, however, the consumer was the defendant.

4.2.2.2. Asturcom *Further Explored: A Potential Empowering Function not Realised*

Before *Mostaza Claro* (2006),[758] it was unclear whether judicial control of the unfairness of the arbitration clause on which an arbitral award was based was even possible under Spanish law. Pursuant to Article 41.1 of the Ley de Arbitraje, an arbitral award can be annulled at the request of one of the parties if there is no valid arbitration agreement (Article 41.1 LA, ground (a)), or if the award is contrary to public policy (ground (f)), for example in the case of a violation of Article 24 of the Constitution due to a procedural defect.[759] In *Mostaza Claro*, the CJEU held that, in an action for annulment, the court must determine whether the arbitration agreement is invalid because it contains an unfair term, even if the consumer has not pleaded such invalidity in the course of the arbitration proceedings. This would be an annulment for lack of a

---

755 Real Decreto 636/1993, por el que se regula el sistema arbitral de consumo, BOE no. 121 of 21 May 1993, p. 15400; Real Decreto 231/2008, por el que se regula el Sistema Arbitral de Consumo, BOE no. 48 of 25 February 2008, p. 11072. See further Mª Teresa Álvarez Moreno, 'Resolución alternativa de litigios con consumidores y arbitraje de consumo' in Silvia Díaz Alabart (ed), *Manual de Derecho de consumo* (Editorial Reus 2016). The submission of disputes to arbitration other than consumer arbitration is considered to be an unfair term, except in the case of arbitration bodies established by statutory provision in respect of specific sectors or circumstances (Article 90.1 TR-LGDCU).

756 Ley 60/2003 de Arbitraje, BOE no. 309 of 26 December 2003. See also Real Decreto 231/2008, por el que se regula el Sistema Arbitral de Consumo, BOE no. 48 of 25 February 2008 (referring to Article 51 of the Constitution).

757 Álvarez Moreno (n 755) 286.

758 Case C-168/05 *Mostaza Claro*.

759 Álvarez Moreno (n 755) 296.

valid arbitration agreement (ground (a)) rather than for reasons of public policy (ground (f)).

Asturcom (2009) did not concern an action for annulment, but the enforcement of an arbitral award in default of the appearance of the consumer. The referring enforcement court – the Juzgado de Primera Instancia (Court of First Instance) in Bilbao – considered whether it should refuse to recognise and enforce the award, of its own motion. It considered the arbitration clause at issue to be unfair, because it caused a serious imbalance between the parties, and impaired the consumer's access to court and rights of defence.[760]

Both *Mostaza Claro* and *Asturcom* pertained to arbitration clauses in mobile telephone contracts that referred to the same Spanish ADR body, the Asociación Europea de Arbitraje de Derecho y Equidad (AEADE). Doubt was cast on the impartiality and independence of the arbitral tribunal, as the ADEADE was associated with the trader, and had drafted the arbitration agreement itself. Article 57.4 TR-LGDCU had not yet been amended, so arbitration clauses in contracts concluded before the disputes had arisen were still allowed, in so far as they referred to an arbitration body for a specific sector. However, the referring court in *Asturcom* still had doubts as to the unfairness of the arbitration clause at issue. The location of the AEADE was not indicated in the contract; its seat was in Bilbao, a considerable distance from the consumer's place of residence, and the costs of the arbitration proceedings almost exceeded the claimed amount.[761] Moreover, the court observed that almost all arbitral awards by the AEADE were rendered in default of appearance by the debtor.

The consumer involved had neither appeared in the arbitration proceedings nor brought an action for annulment of the arbitral award within the prescribed period of two months (Article 41.4 LA). Thus, the award had acquired the force of *res judicata* (Article 43 LA). In Spain, arbitral awards enjoy the same status as judicial decisions, for the purposes of enforcement (Article 517.2.2° LEC). The party against whom enforcement is sought can oppose it within ten days, on a limited number of grounds (Articles 556 and 559 LEC), which do not include unfair terms. Articles 551 and 552 LEC restricted the scope of judicial review to procedural requirements (not including public policy). This notwithstanding, some Spanish courts considered it possible to refuse to enforce the arbitral award when it was based on an unfair arbitration clause within the meaning of the UCTD,

---

760 Juzgado de Primera Instancia No. 4 de Bilbao, order of 4 December 2007 in case no. 1147/2007, JUR\2011\403897, ECLI:ES:JPI:2009:9A.

761 Case C-40/08 *Asturcom*, para. 25.

while other courts assessed whether the award itself was contrary to public policy, for example because of a lack of impartiality of the arbitral tribunal.[762]

But there were also courts that held that the unfairness of an arbitration clause could not be established *ex officio*, only at the request of the consumer defendant in: (a) an action for annulment; or (b) opposition to enforcement. The referring court in *Asturcom* seems to have questioned this approach, which was followed, inter alia, by its own Court of Appeal.[763] According to the AP in Bilbao, judicial intervention outside the scope of Article 552 LEC would be against legal certainty and the principle of *res judicata*: judicial protection cannot go further than what the parties demand, or what is authorised by law. This approach appears to be based on a strict interpretation of the traditional procedural principles, and the idea that courts cannot create or change the law. AG Trstenjak shared the Juzgado's doubts as to the impartiality of the arbitral tribunal and the consumer's rights of defence.[764] However, the CJEU held that the principles of equivalence and effectiveness do not automatically entail that an arbitral award with *res judicata* effect must be set aside. The Juzgado in Bilbao subsequently found that it had no other choice than to issue an enforcement order against the consumer involved.[765]

As shown in Chapter 3, Article 47 of the Charter might have led to a different conclusion. Its potential empowering function in this regard was not picked up by the CJEU. The Spanish legislature finally opted for the solution proposed by AG Trstenjak – judicial control at the enforcement stage – several years later. Ley 42/2015 confirmed the duty of *ex officio* control of unfair terms in respect of arbitral awards, with explicit reference to *Asturcom*.[766] The second transitional provision of Ley 42/2015 declares Article 552.1 LEC to be applicable in all enforcement proceedings.[767] Article 552.1 LEC now provides that the enforcement court shall examine *ex officio* whether the enforceable titles listed in Article 557.1 LEC contain

---

762 García-Valdecasas Dorrego (n 687) 47; Beka (n 32) 170.

763 See, e.g. AP Bilbao, order no. 396/08 of 6 June 2008 (not published; copy obtained from the court upon request), reversing an order in which the enforcement had been refused.

764 C-40/08 *Asturcom*, Opinion of AG Trstenjak, discussed in subsection 3.2.2 of the preceding chapter.

765 Juzgado de Primera Instancia No. 4 de Bilbao, order of 26 October 2009 in case no. 1147/2007, JUR\2011\403897, ECLI:ES:JPI:2009:9A.

766 Arroyo Amayuelas (n 655) 79.

767 Ley 42/2015, Disposición transitoria segunda: Procesos monitorios y ejecución de laudos arbitrales.

unfair terms.[768] Article 557.1 pertains to non-judicial and non-arbitral titles: strictly speaking, it does not include arbitral awards (Article 517.2.2 LEC). However, this appears to be a legislative error:[769] judicial review of arbitral awards is now possible in respect of unfair terms, regardless of any *res judicata* effect. Since it is unclear whether arbitral tribunals can exercise unfair terms control, or be obliged to do so, it should not matter whether they have already performed such control. What matters is whether or not such control has taken place in earlier *judicial* proceedings.

It should be noted that an appeal can only be brought by the *creditor* against a refusal to enforce an enforceable title (Article 552.2 LEC); the debtor cannot appeal a decision that allows the enforcement. The question as to what extent an asymmetric restriction of the right to appeal is problematic from the perspective of Article 47 will be discussed later in this chapter.[770]

4.2.3. DELEGATION OF JUDICIAL FUNCTIONS TO THE COURT REGISTRAR

4.2.3.1. Finanmadrid *Further Explored: Article 47 in its Signalling Function*

The case of *Finanmadrid* concerned the Spanish order for payment procedure (*proceso monitorio*), which is regulated by Articles 812–818 LEC. The referring enforcement court – the Juzgado de Primera Instancia No. 5 in Cartagena – found that the order for payment issued by the court registrar had acquired the force of *res judicata*. Therefore, it could no longer be examined whether the underlying contract contained any unfair terms.[771] In the decision to make a preliminary reference to the CJEU (in 2014), Article 47 of the Charter was referred to in its signalling function, to question the lack of court involvement in the procedure itself.[772] The referring court mentioned Article 47 to indicate that the procedure at stake was flawed, which led to a debate about legislative reforms at the national

768 Ley 42/2015, preamble V.

769 Arroyo Amayuelas (n 655) 79–80.

770 See section 4.4 below.

771 Case C-49/14 *Finanmadrid*, para. 24; introduced in subsection 3.2.3.2 of the preceding chapter.

772 Juzgado de Primera Instancia No. 5 de Cartagena, order of 23 January 2014 in case no. 352/2013 (not published; copy obtained from the court upon request). The national judicial decisions in the case of *Finanmadrid* have not yet been published; they are available, upon request, from the referring court.

level. Whereas the reference to Article 47 may not have been the *trigger* for these reforms, it was a clear *signal* that change was due.

> In 2006, Mr. Albán Zambrano entered into a loan agreement with Finanmadrid EFC, SA to finance the purchase of a vehicle. His wife, brother and sister-in-law were joint guarantors. After Mr. Albán failed to meet his payment obligations in 2011, Finanmadrid initiated an order for payment procedure against him as the principal debtor, and against the three guarantors. The procedure was handled entirely by a court registrar, not a judge. It is unclear why the defendants failed to appear; perhaps they did not know that they could contest the claim, or did not know on what grounds they could do so; perhaps they could not afford legal representation; or perhaps they did not have time to hire a lawyer to lodge an objection for them (within 20 days). The court registrar checked only whether the formal admissibility requirements were met, and issued an order for payment against all four defendants in 2012.

The order for payment procedure is widely used by creditors in Spain.[773] It was designed to strengthen the procedural position of creditors in respect of uncontested claims, so that they can quickly obtain an enforceable title.[774] In the case of *Banesto*,[775] the bank had argued that *ex officio* control was contrary to its right to effective judicial protection (Article 24 of the Spanish Constitution).[776] After the CJEU's judgment, however, it was clear that unfair terms control extended to this type of procedure. Article 552.1 LEC was changed to the extent that the unfairness of contract terms could be examined in the course of general enforcement proceedings.[777] Ley 42/2015 clarified that the enforcement court must do so *ex officio*.[778] It was not until Ley 42/2015 was adopted that provision was made for *ex officio* control of unfair terms in the order for payment procedure as well (Article 815.4 LEC). Before that, Spanish courts applied *Banesto* with no explicit legislative basis.[779]

---

773 See, e.g. Ley 13/2009, de reforma de la legislación procesal para la implantación de la nueva Oficina judicial, BOE no. 266 of 4 November 2009, p. 92103 (also referred to as LNOJ), preamble IV. See also Joan Picó i Junoy, 'Requiem por el proceso monitorio' (2015) 2 Justicia 523.

774 Díez-Picazo Giménez (n 682) 410; Picó i Junoy (n 773) 524.

775 Case C-618/10 *Banesto*; also discussed in subsection 3.2.3.1. On the national follow-up, see also Beka (n 32) 244–245, 316.

776 AP Barcelona, order no. 222/2012 of 29 October 2012, ECLI:ES:APB:2012:7113A. See further Beka (n 32) 241–245.

777 Ley 1/2013; see further section 4.3.3 below. See also Amayuelas (n 655) 81–82.

778 See also subsection 4.2.2 above.

779 García Aburuza (n 731) 4; Arroyo Amayuelas (n 655) 80.

The case of *Finanmadrid* predated Ley 42/2015, and *Banesto* did not, strictly speaking, pertain to the court registrar, to whom the court's competence had been delegated in 2009. As discussed in Chapter 3, *Finanmadrid* concerned four problems: the limited role of the court registrar in the procedure; the *res judicata* effect attributed to the order for payment by the enforcement court; the court registrar not being a judge; and an apparent violation of the rights of defence.[780]

The court registrar is not a judge, but a public servant who is considered to be a staff member (*dependiente*) of the Ministry of Justice.[781] The Spanish legislator had introduced a procedural reform – Ley 13/2009 – that instituted a new Oficina judicial (Judicial Office), which was meant to take over judicial functions that were not strictly constitutional, for the purpose of streamlining civil and administrative proceedings. The court registrars already supported the courts in their task of adjudicating cases on the merits and in a timely manner, but were now also attributed competences that allowed them to make decisions themselves in matters 'collateral to the jurisdictional function'.[782] For instance, the admissibility of the case was assessed by the court registrar. If one of the formal admissibility requirements was not met, the case would be put before a judge.[783]

As regards the order for payment procedure, Ley 13/2009 raised the maximum amount to 250,000 euros, to widen the scope for the handling of uncontested claims in a speedy and efficient manner.[784] Again, it was up to the court registrar to assess admissibility. Moreover, the court registrar could close the procedure by issuing an order if all formal requirements were met, and the debtor did not comply with the request for payment or failed to appear (Article 816.1 LEC). The court would only become involved if the documents indicated that the claimed amount was incorrect, or if the debtor lodged an objection within 20 days (Articles 815.3 and 818 LEC).[785] If debtors did not file an opposition, they could no longer claim restitution in subsequent proceedings (Article 816.2 LEC). Some courts, including the Juzgado in Cartagena, which made the preliminary reference in *Finanmadrid*, understood this as meaning that the order for payment

780 See subsection 3.2.3.2.

781 Article 440 LOPJ.

782 Ley 13/2009, preamble II.

783 Ley 13/2009, preamble III.

784 Ley 13/2009, preamble IV.

785 The court would also be involved if the debtor could not be located, or if they had their domicile in another jurisdiction (within Spain), which would terminate the procedure, but without prejudice to the creditor's right to make a new request: Article 813 LEC.

had *res judicata* effect, which prevented them from examining the case on the merits and performing unfair terms control.[786]

The Juzgado framed its preliminary reference to the CJEU as an issue of effective judicial protection.[787] Pursuant to Article 117 of the Spanish Constitution, justice is administered by independent judges and magistrates who are members of the judiciary, and the exercise of judicial authority is vested exclusively in courts and tribunals designated by law. In 2016 the Tribunal Constitucional held that a complete lack of judicial review of decisions of court registrars amounted to jurisdictional immunity, which is contrary to Articles 24 and 117 of the Constitution.[788] The process of 'dejudicialisation'[789] under Ley 13/2009 deprived courts of their jurisdictional competence, and parties of their access to an independent tribunal. Therefore, it could also be problematic from the perspective of Article 47 of the Charter.[790] In the words of the Juzgado in *Finanmadrid*:

> 'All this could constitute a violation of the Directive 93/13/EEC, where judicial *ex officio* control of unfair terms is not allowed – neither in the decision-making phase nor in the enforcement. It could also be contrary to the right to effective judicial protection recognised in Article 47 of the Charter of Fundamental Rights, because the order for payment procedure without opposition is a procedure in which the court does not intervene, whereas its final resolution produces the effects of *res judicata*'.[791]

In addition, the Juzgado found that the course of the proceedings jeopardised consumer debtors' right to be heard. Their only opportunity to contest the claim was in the order for payment procedure itself, by lodging an objection. If they did not make use of this opportunity, an order

---

786 Arguably erroneously: see Arroyo Amayuelas (n 655) 80; Gómez Amigo (n 746) 5.

787 Juzgado de Primera Instancia No. 5 de Cartagena, order of 23 January 2014 in case no. 352/2013 (not published; copy can be obtained from the court upon request).

788 Tribunal Constitucional, judgment no. 58/2016 of 17 March 2016, ECLI:ES:TC:2016:58. See also José Bonet Navarro, 'La necesaria reforma de la mal llamada "jura de cuentas"' [2017] Revista de Derecho UNED 73, 101; Concellón Fernández (n 712) 57–58.

789 Gascón Inchausti (n 418) 138.

790 Aguilera Morales (n 451) 5–6; Bonet Navarro (n 788) 90.

791 Juzgado de Primera Instancia No. 5 de Cartagena, order of 23 January 2014 in case no. 352/2013, para. 56. Translated from the original Spanish text, which reads, '*Todo esto podría suponer una vulneración de la Directiva 93/13/CEE, no se permite el control judicial de oficio sobre las cláusulas abusivas – ni en fase declarativa ni en ejecución. Además podría ser contrario al derecho a tutela judicial efectiva reconocido en el artículo 47 de la Carta de Derechos Fundamentales, pues el proceso monitorio sin oposición es un procedimiento en el que no interviene el Juez, sin embargo su resolución final produce efectos de cosa juzgada.*'

would be issued, without an assessment of the unfair nature of the terms of the contract on which the claim was based. The defendants needed to exercise their right to be heard within 20 days after the initiation of the procedure, otherwise it was too late. The creditor did not even have to wait until notification of the order to the defendants before requesting and dispatching the enforcement. Moreover, legal representation by both a lawyer (*abogado*) and a court representative (*procurador*) was required in order to lodge an objection.[792] Another problem in the *Finanmadrid* case itself was that only the debtor and his wife were officially notified of the order for payment procedure; the debtor had been instructed to inform the other two guarantors, but it was uncertain whether they were actually made aware of the procedure. Thus, they might not even have had an opportunity to lodge an objection.

The CJEU focused, in its judgment, on judicial control at the enforcement stage. In the meantime, Ley 42/2015 had been adopted, providing for such control in the order for payment procedure itself (Article 815.4 LEC). Ley 42/2015 also introduced a right to be heard, for both parties, within five days – legal representation was no longer required – and confirmed that there was no *res judicata* effect.[793] In addition, the court's decision could now be appealed. While it would go too far to claim that these legislative reforms were directly triggered by Article 47 (in its transformative function), they were meant to prevent *indefensión*, i.e. a denial of justice.[794] It has been said that, as a consequence, the character of the order for payment procedure has been fundamentally changed, causing it to lose its efficiency benefits, and potentially overburdening the courts.[795] In this respect, it has been observed that Article 552.1 LEC – read in conjunction with Articles 557.1 and 517.2.9 LEC, relating to enforceable procedural decisions – could have been interpreted in such a way that unfair terms control was already possible (or even mandatory) at the enforcement stage.[796] Clearly, the Juzgado in *Finanmadrid* did not share this interpretation. In its final decision, it nevertheless viewed the CJEU's judgment as allowing for an

792 Art. 818.1 LEC, read in conjunction with Art. 23.2.1° and 31.2.1° LEC: legal representation is mandatory when the claim exceeds 2,000 euros. By contrast, legal representation is not required to initiate an order for payment procedure: Art. 814.2 LEC.

793 Ley 42/2015, preamble V.

794 Gómez Amigo (n 746) 8.

795 Picó i Junoy (n 773) 525–526; Gómez Amigo (n 746) 11.

796 Aguilera Morales (n 451) 7–8; Picó i Junoy (n 773) 527. See also Case C-503/15 *Margarit Panicello*, Opinion of AG Kokott, point 52; Case C-49/14 *Finanmadrid*, Commission's written observations, para. 76.

exception, so that it could perform unfair terms control at the enforcement stage.[797]

4.2.3.2. Margarit Panicello *Further Explored: A Signal of Unconstitutionality*

The reference to Article 47 as a signal of unconstitutionality in *Finanmadrid* is not an isolated instance; it has been picked up in other cases as well. *Margarit Panicello* concerned a procedure where the door to the court was completely shut.[798] The so-called 'unpaid fee recovery procedure'[799] (*jura de cuentas* – literally 'sworn accounts'), contained in Articles 34 and 35 LEC, was specifically designed for lawyers as a pathway to recover unpaid fees from their clients. The role of the court registrar is confined to reviewing the legal services provided and determining the payable amount.[800] The decision of the court registrar is considered to be of an administrative nature: it has no substantive *res judicata* effect, yet it is binding and enforceable.[801] Until 2019, there was no administrative recourse against the decision.

> Mr. Margarit Panicello, a Spanish lawyer, was hired to represent his client in proceedings concerning the custody of her children before the Juzgado Único de Violencia sobre la Mujer (Single-Member Court dealing with matters involving violence against women) de Terrassa. In 2015, the lawyer brought a *jura de cuentas* procedure against his client for the recovery of fees. The court registrar had doubts regarding unfair contract terms and unfair commercial practices on the part of the lawyer, in particular as to information that had been given prior to the engagement about the estimated cost of his services.

The court registrar in Terrassa, who made the preliminary reference to the CJEU, distinguished the question of whether an *ex officio* examination under the UCTD (and the Unfair Commercial Practices Directive[802])

[797] Juzgado de Primera Instancia No. 5 de Cartagena, order of 11 April 2016 in case no. 352/2013 (not published; copy can be obtained from the court upon request). The default interest clause and the penalty clause were declared to be unfair, and the corresponding amounts were excluded from the claim.

[798] Case C-503/15 *Margarit Panicello*; introduced in subsection 3.2.3. See also Bonet Navarro (n 788) 85; Aguilera Morales (n 672) 5.

[799] Case C-503/15 *Margarit Panicello*, Opinion of AG Kokott, point 1.

[800] Case C-503/15 *Margarit Panicello*, Opinion of AG Kokott, para. 84.

[801] Aguilera Morales (n 451) 5–6.

[802] Directive 2005/29/EC concerning unfair business-to-consumer commercial practices in the internal market (OJ L149, 11 June 2005, p. 22).

should be possible from the question of whether the rules governing the procedure were incompatible with Article 47 of the Charter, in so far as they excluded judicial review.[803] This distinction laid bare the difference in perspective: the way in which the problem is framed – as an issue with unfair terms control or as a violation of the fundamental right to effective judicial protection – defines how it is perceived, and what the solution should be.

The preliminary reference to the CJEU was made by a court registrar rather than a court, which, as Aguilera Morales has observed, makes the reference to Article 47 particularly salient: the court registrar, who was not a judicial organ, questioned his own competence to exercise judicial functions, clearly signalling a problem from the perspective of access to court.[804] The CJEU found it had no jurisdiction, precisely due to the procedure lacking a judicial nature. This left the issue – quite unsatisfactorily – unresolved.[805]

In a judgment of 15 April 2019, the Tribunal Constitucional, nevertheless, declared the lack of judicial review of the decision of the court registrar in the *jura de cuentas* to be unconstitutional.[806] The Tribunal Constitucional referred to *Margarit Panicello* to describe the characteristics of the procedure, and the decision-making powers of the court registrar, who was not part of a judicial body. Even the grounds of opposition contained in Article 557 LEC, which included unfair terms,[807] – were assessed by the court registrar, not a court. Thus, obligations were settled between the parties in a procedure outside the judicial system. According to the Tribunal Constitucional, it was also relevant that it was always the lawyer who initiated the procedure, never the debtor. The fact that the decision lacked (substantive) *res judicata* effect, because it was given in summary proceedings, was not sufficient to guarantee judicial protection of the debtor's rights and legitimate interests. Subsequent legal action depended entirely on the debtor's initiative. The court registrar's decision was not subject to judicial review, but could still be enforced.

---

803 Case C-503/15 *Margarit Panicello*, para. 25.

804 Aguilera Morales (n 451) 13, 16. See also Bonet Navarro (n 788) 100.

805 For criticism on the CJEU's formalistic approach, see Marien Aguilera Morales, '¿Es válida la cláusula de renuncia de acciones predispuesta frente al consumidor?' in Marien Aguilera Morales (ed), *Tribunal de Justicia de la Unión Europea, justicia civil y derechos fundamentales* (Thomson Reuters Aranzadi 2020) 203.

806 See Articles 34.2 and 35.2 LEC; Tribunal Constitucional, judgment no. 34/2019 of 14 March 2019, ECLI:ES:TC:2019:34.

807 Since Ley 1/2013: see subsection 4.3.3 below.

This created a space of jurisdictional immunity that violated Articles 24 and 117 of the Constitution.

The Tribunal Constitucional appeared to share AG Kokott's view that the procedure resulted in an order of a (quasi-)judicial nature. From a constitutional perspective, the problem of jurisdictional immunity can be solved by making a means of recourse against the order available, which is what the Tribunal Constitucional has proposed, in the form of a revision (Article 454bis LEC). From the perspective of the UCTD, however, this does not address the concern, raised by Kokott, that the decision can be enforced before unfair terms control has taken place. Even if a court can perform such control, in the course of revision or at the enforcement stage, it may be too late. Therefore, a return to the situation pre-Ley 13/2009 has been proposed, which would reinstate the exclusive competence of the courts to issue payment orders. An alternative would be to bring the *jura de cuentas* procedure under the umbrella of the *proceso monitorio* or, at any rate, to apply Article 815.4 LEC by analogy in the *jura de cuentas* procedure as well.[808]

4.3. EFFECTIVE (JUDICIAL) REMEDY

4.3.1. INTRODUCTION: MORTGAGE DEBTORS AS EUROPEAN CONSUMERS

The cases in the preceding section show how it was possible for traders to circumvent judicial control by resorting to privileged procedures with little or no court involvement. A similar issue has arisen in respect of mortgage loan agreements, which has, in some cases, triggered references to Article 47 of the Charter.[809] The national background of, and follow-up events to, *Aziz* and *Sánchez Morcillo* are of special interest for the purposes of this book, and also in light of earlier decisions of the Tribunal Constitucional in similar cases.

Under Spanish procedural law, creditors have two different types of enforcement procedure at their disposal: the general enforcement procedure of Article 517 *et seq.* LEC, and the special procedure for mortgages and pledges of Article 681 *et seq.* LEC. The Spanish mortgage

808 Bonet Navarro (n 788) 103–105.

809 See, e.g. Case C-415/11 *Aziz*, para. 62; Joined Cases C-537/12 and C-116/13 *Banco Popular Español*, para. 60; Case C-169/14 *Sánchez Morcillo I*, para. 28.

enforcement regime is designed as an expeditious path towards recovery of the loan by the creditor upon default of the debtor.[810] It gives the creditor direct access to enforcement on the basis of a public deed, which constitutes an enforceable title.[811] The sale of the mortgaged property may also take place in front of a notary instead of a judge, if the parties have agreed to an extrajudicial auction (Article 129 Ley Hipotecaria).[812] The debtor's rights of defence are so severely restricted that the extrajudicial title gives the creditor a stronger instrument for enforcement than a judicial decision given in ordinary contentious proceedings.[813] From a procedural point of view, the (contractual) credit relationship has become almost ancillary to the creditor's security interests, instead of vice versa.[814]

In the wake of the 2008 financial crisis, two main problems concerning the Spanish mortgage enforcement regime came to the fore: (i) many debtors still owed significant outstanding amounts after foreclosure; and (ii) there was a lack of procedural means to remedy the numerous unfair terms in mortgage loan agreements.[815] Mortgage enforcement in Spain is separated, procedurally, from the contractual relationship between the parties, even though there is an obvious substantive connection between the creditor's security interests and the loan agreement.[816] Mortgage enforcement is considered to be an action *in rem*, not *in persona*.[817] It is subject to strict formal requirements that must be observed scrupulously, taking into account the privileged position of the mortgage holder.[818] The merits of the case, including the nullity or validity of the contract itself, are dealt with in separate declaratory proceedings on the merits, before a different (ordinary) court (Article 698.1 LEC).[819]

---

810 Anderson and Simón Moreno (n 663) 56. See also Díez García (n 540) 233, 246; Jiménez París (n 657) 986.

811 See, e.g. AP Toledo (Sección 2ª), order no. 185/2017 of 7 March 2017, JUR\2017\146402; AP Almería (Sección 1ª), order no. 52/2017 of 23 January 2017, JUR\2017\112584.

812 Ley Hipotecaria (Mortgage Act), BOE no. 58, 27 February 1946, p. 1518. Art. 129 of the Mortgage Act has been reformed by, inter alia, Ley 1/2013. See also Casla (n 536) 287.

813 Pérez Daudí (n 32) 16; Díez García (n 540) 258.

814 Díez García (n 540) 257.

815 Yolanda De Lucchi López-Tapia, 'Spanish Mortgage Foreclosure and Unfair Terms in Banking Contracts' (2015) 6 Civil Procedure Review 140, 141–142. See also González Pascual (n 514) 265–266.

816 Guillem Soler Solé, 'Ejecución hipotecaria. Limitaciones al derecho de defensa del ejecutado. Cuestión de inconstitucionalidad' [2013] Revista Xuridica Galega 13, 20.

817 AP Toledo (Sección 2ª), order no. 151/2017 of 2 February 2017, JUR\2017\142012.

818 See, e.g. AP Barcelona (Sección 16ª), order no. 283/2015 of 18 September 2015, JUR\2015\261047.

819 Arroyo Amayuelas (n 655) 75.

As discussed below, the fact that the debtor still had access to separate declaratory proceedings was deemed sufficient reason for the Tribunal Constitucional not to declare the mortgage enforcement procedure unconstitutional. The same separation between two types of proceedings was reason for the CJEU to find that the Spanish regime undermined the effective judicial protection of consumers against unfair terms.[820] The interests of creditors in effectuating their rights in an expedient manner did not justify a lack of procedural means for consumer debtors to suspend or terminate enforcement. This entailed a switch of perspective from national constitutional rights to EU consumer rights.[821] Mortgage debtors were now seen in their capacity as European consumers instead of Spanish citizens, although the underlying issues remained the same.[822] It is their status as consumers that determines their rights and underlines the need to open up rigid or restrictive rules that stand in the way of effective judicial protection.

4.3.2. *AZIZ* FURTHER EXPLORED

4.3.2.1. Referring Court: A Clear Impediment to the Exercise of Judicial Remedies

Before *Aziz*,[823] unfair terms did not constitute a ground of opposition against mortgage enforcement. In order to dispute the debt, the debtor needed to take recourse to separate declaratory proceedings, which did not (and still do not) have the effect of suspending or terminating the enforcement (Article 698.1 LEC). The only interim measure available to debtors was to ask for a retention of (part of) the amount to be paid (Article 698.2 LEC), but this would not prevent foreclosure. Debtors might be able to obtain compensation, but they would still lose their homes. The final vesting of the mortgaged property in a third party was irreversible. Once a transfer of ownership took place it would be too late, as the case

820 Case C-415/11 *Aziz*, introduced in subsection 3.3.2 of the preceding chapter.

821 Iglesias Sánchez (n 18) 971.

822 Guillem Soler Solé, 'Las ejecuciones hipotecarias en España, ante la cuestión prejudicial europea' [2013] Revista Xuridica Galega 25, 30; José Humberto Sahián, *Dimensión constitucional de la tutela de los consumidores. Progresividad y control de regresividad de los derechos de los consumidores* (doctoral thesis, Universidad Complutense de Madrid 2017) 455.

823 Case C-415/11 *Aziz*.

of *Banco Santander* showed.[824] The debtor could make a preliminary, preventive registration of an application for annulment of a mortgage (Article 131 of the Ley Hipotecaria). However, there was a significant risk that consumer debtors would not make such a registration in time, because of the rapidity of the enforcement proceedings, or because they were unaware of, or did not appreciate the extent of, their rights.[825]

> The case of *Aziz* concerned declaratory proceedings brought by Mr. Aziz against Catalunyacaixa following the sale of the mortgaged property, his family home. Mr. Aziz had failed to pay five monthly instalments. Catalunyacaixa then exercised its right to call in the totality of the mortgage loan, on the basis of an 'early maturity' or acceleration clause (*vencimiento anticipado*), and to unilaterally determine the amount of the debt. It instituted mortgage enforcement proceedings against Mr. Aziz, who did not lodge an objection. The enforcement court did not exercise unfair terms control. Mr. Aziz subsequently brought an action for a declaration seeking the annulment of the unilateral debt determination clause and nullity of the enforcement proceedings.

In *Aziz*, the referring court – the Juzgado de lo Mercantil (Commercial Court) No. 3 in Barcelona – pointed out that Mr. Aziz's failure to meet his payment obligations was neither temporarily nor quantitatively serious, and that the availability of an effective remedy for the consumer could, at least, be called into question. In its request for a preliminary ruling, the court highlighted 'both formally and substantively, a clear impediment to the consumer's exercise of rights of action or judicial remedies of such a kind as to guarantee the effective protection of his rights'.[826]

4.3.2.2. *Tribunal Constitucional on Effective Judicial Protection Pre-*Aziz

A similar question had already been put before the Tribunal Constitucional by the Juzgado de Primera Instancia No. 2 de Sabadell in 2010 by way of a *cuestión de inconstitucionalidad*.[827] The Juzgado referred not only to the debtor's fundamental right to effective judicial protection (Article 24 of the Constitution), but also to the principle of procedural equality derived from the prohibition of discrimination (Article 14), the prohibition of arbitrary

[824] Case C-598/15 *Banco Santander*: see subsection 3.3.2 of the preceding chapter.
[825] Case C-415/11 *Aziz*, paras. 56–58. See also Díez García (n 540) 247–248.
[826] See Case C-415/11 *Aziz*, para. 31 and Juzgado de lo Mercantil No. 3 de Barcelona, judgment of 2 May 2013 in case no. 13/2011, ECLI:ES:JMB:2013:21. See also Iglesias Sánchez (n 18) 967.
[827] Tribunal Constitucional, order no. 113/2011 of 19 July 2011, ECLI:ES:TC:2011:113A.

action of public authorities (Article 9) and the right to housing enshrined in Article 47 of the Constitution. Previously, in 1981, the Tribunal Constitucional had declared the Spanish mortgage enforcement regime to be in conformity with the Constitution.[828] However, the regime at issue here – in particular Articles 695 and 698 LEC – dated from 2000, thus it had not yet been tested. The Juzgado questioned the extraordinary and disproportionate limitation of grounds of opposition, which denied the debtor the possibility of challenging the contract (including the unfairness of specific terms) on which the enforcement was based, and which prevented the court from assessing all relevant circumstances of the case. Moreover, the effectiveness of a decision in the declaratory proceedings was not sufficiently guaranteed if the court could not suspend or terminate the enforcement proceedings. Thus, not all issues could be dealt with in a timely manner, which resulted in *indefensión* of the debtor.[829] In this respect, the Juzgado also pointed out the serious consequences for debtors, due to their weak economic situation.

The Tribunal Constitucional declared the *cuestión de inconstitucionalidad* inadmissible. While it acknowledged that the adversarial element of the mortgage enforcement proceedings was severely limited, it found that this did not amount to a violation of the debtor's right to effective judicial protection. It considered that there was no real dispute between the parties; the mortgage enforcement proceedings were an 'avenue of urgency' for creditors to effectuate their security rights in court. The reason the opposition grounds were restricted was that only a few exceptions could cause suspension or termination of the enforcement. The proceedings did not result in a final and binding decision and, more importantly, the door to declaratory proceedings was left open for the debtor.[830] Thus, there was no *indefensión*. The Tribunal Constitucional emphasised that the debtor had consented to the mortgage arrangement and, thus, to a limitation of his defence possibilities – an unconvincing argument in respect of non-negotiated terms, especially in consumer contracts. According to the Tribunal Constitucional, the debtor could always stop the enforcement by means of paying the instalments due, which overlooks the problem that debtors like Mr. Aziz were given mortgage loans they would most likely be unable to repay, in the first place.

---

828 Tribunal Constitucional, judgment no. 41/1981 of 18 December 1981, ECLI:ES:TC:1981:41. See also Iglesias Sánchez (n 18) 970.

829 See further Soler Solé (n 816) 25.

830 See also Díez García (n 540) 225, 231–234, 243–245.

In addition, the Tribunal Constitucional pointed out that a (hypothetical) violation of Article 24 of the Constitution depended on the violation of other constitutional rights and principles, such as the right to housing.[831] The right to housing was a guiding principle for social and economic policy, and could not give rise to a separate fundamental rights violation: the legal norms at issue merely provided for a procedural instrument to effectuate competing rights, namely the creditor's right to claim payment and the debtor's right to oppose enforcement. Here, the Tribunal Constitucional clearly did not take into account the criticism that the balance was wrong, in light of the precarious position of mortgage debtors.[832] In this respect, the approach of the Tribunal Constitucional has also been criticised for not taking the case law of the ECtHR into account on the need for procedural guarantees to ensure the protection of substantive fundamental rights, such as the right to respect for the home (Article 8 ECHR).[833]

Lastly, the Tribunal Constitucional reiterated that judicial organs are not supposed to question the constitutionality of a legislative scheme in a general or abstract way: it was neither for the courts nor the Tribunal Constitucional to formulate or assess an alternative scheme. This was said to be the exclusive competence of the legislature, which has a wide margin of freedom of choice – within the constitutional limits – that cannot and should not be restricted by the Tribunal Constitucional. In a concurring opinion, Magistrate Eugeni Gay Montalvo nevertheless warned against 'reductionism in constitutional review'. In his view, the constitutional doctrine established in 1981 could not automatically be extended to the contemporary economic and financial situation, which was radically different from the situation at the beginning of the 1980s. The legislation at issue should have been interpreted in light of the new context, because the Tribunal Constitucional should not be insensitive to the social reality to which the legal norms, values and principles of the Constitution apply.

4.3.2.3. Audiencia Provincial de Barcelona on Article 47 in the Case of Aziz

In *Aziz*, the CJEU held that the UCTD precluded national legislation that, on the one hand, did not provide for grounds of objection in mortgage enforcement proceedings based on unfair terms, and, on the other hand, did not allow the court to grant interim relief in declaratory proceedings

831 See also González Pascual (n 514) 267.
832 See subsection 4.1.2 above.
833 Díez García (n 540) 252–254; González Pascual (n 514) 260, 263.

and suspend the enforcement, if that was necessary to guarantee the full effectiveness of its final decision.[834] On 2 May 2013, the Juzgado in Barcelona gave judgment in the case of *Aziz*.[835] It considered that the function of courts was to apply and interpret the law in the context or social reality in which the dispute needed to be resolved. It referred to the public debate (political, legislative, social and economic) that had led to a process of legislative reforms, which had not been completed by the date of the judgment (Ley 1/2013 was adopted two weeks later).[836] The court's goal was to contextualise the submissions of the parties in the procedural and substantive environment of the Spanish law in force, in accordance with the UCTD.[837]

Mr. Aziz had requested that one of the terms in the mortgage loan agreement – the unilateral debt determination clause – be declared null and void, as well as requesting nullity of the enforcement proceedings. The Juzgado declared the unilateral debt determination clause and two other clauses – the acceleration clause and a default interest clause – to be unfair and, therefore, null and void. Thus, the amount claimed by the bank was not due and payable. This did not completely negate the debt incurred by the principal loan, nor did it preclude the creditor from bringing a claim in declaratory proceedings where a procedural imbalance did not exist (or at least, did not exist to same extent).[838] The Juzgado considered that the creditor had been allowed access to an enforcement regime in which the debtor could neither file an opposition based on unfair terms (Article 695.1 LEC) nor apply for interim measures in declaratory proceedings (Article 698 LEC). This had caused an irreparable harm to Mr. Aziz, but he had not claimed any damages.[839] Since the issues raised in *Aziz* concerned the Spanish mortgage enforcement system in general and, therefore, transcended the individual case, no cost order was pronounced.[840]

Both parties appealed, arguing that the Juzgado had gone beyond the ambit of the dispute. This was related to the so-called principle of 'procedural congruence' (*congruencia procesal*): that is, alignment between the submissions of the parties and the judgment of the court.[841] When there

834 Case C-415/11 *Aziz*, para. 59.
835 Juzgado de lo Mercantil No. 3 de Barcelona, judgment of 2 May 2013 in case no. 13/2011, ECLI:ES:JMB:2013:21.
836 See subsection 4.3.3 below.
837 Judgment of Juzgado (n 835), paras. 4.3–4.4.
838 Judgment of Juzgado (n 835), para. 12.6 and 12.8.
839 Judgment of Juzgado (n 835), paras. 11.6, 12.3 and 12.7.
840 Judgment of Juzgado (n 835), para. 13.5.
841 Pérez Daudí (n 32) 94; Barceló Compte (n 684) 218–219.

is no such alignment, so-called *incongruencia* occurs. Like *res judicata*, procedural congruence is a mandatory principle of civil procedure, aimed at legal certainty within the process.[842] Mr. Aziz argued there was *incongruencia* because no decision had been given on his request for nullity of the enforcement proceedings. The bank alleged that the Juzgado had awarded more than had been claimed; Mr. Aziz had only asserted the unfairness of one clause, not three.

On 15 December 2014, the AP in Barcelona held that, although Mr. Aziz was right, from a formal point of view, there was no substantive *incongruencia*. The judgment at first instance must be read as dismissing his request for nullity of the enforcement proceedings. The foreclosure had already taken place; it was unclear who presently had possession over the property and, therefore, the consequences of such nullity would be unclear as well.[843] The AP also dismissed the bank's allegation of *incongruencia*. Mr. Aziz had, indeed, requested nullity of the enforcement, which meant that the court could examine all contractual terms on which it was based *ex officio* without violating the principle of procedural congruence.[844]

In this respect, the AP referred to Article 47 of the Charter to underline that the requirements of a fair trial had been observed, including the principle of procedural congruence and the right to be heard.[845] This is one of the few self-standing references to Article 47 in Spanish case law, and will be explored further below.[846]

The AP in Barcelona, ultimately, came to a different conclusion to the Juzgado. It did not find the terms at issue to be unfair, except the default interest clause. Even if there was *incongruencia*, this would not improve the legal position of Mr. Aziz. He had failed to meet his payment obligations; therefore, the bank could reasonably assume that it was entitled to terminate the contract and initiate the enforcement. To prevent the foreclosure, Mr. Aziz could have complained to the bank and/or paid the instalments due, but he did neither.[847] The judgment of the Juzgado was reversed, and the AP Barcelona ordered a recalculation of interest. In this respect, the

842 AP León (Sección 1ª), judgment no. 192/2017 of 19 May 2017, JUR\2017\171244, ECLI:ES:APLE:2017:536.

843 AP Barcelona (Sección 15ª), judgment no. 407/2014 of 15 December 2014, JUR\2015\86196, paras. 16–22. See also the judgment of Juzgado (n 835), para. 12.9.

844 Judgment of AP Barcelona (n 843), para. 52.

845 Judgment of AP Barcelona (n 843), paras. 24–26; see further subsection 4.5.2 below.

846 See subsection 4.5.2 below.

847 Judgment of AP Barcelona (n 843), paras. 76–79.

CJEU's judgment was a pyrrhic victory for Mr. Aziz. He brought a cassation appeal, but the Tribunal Supremo has not taken up his case.[848]

4.3.3. IMPLEMENTATION AND FOLLOW-UP

4.3.3.1. A New Opposition Ground and an Empowering Function of Article 47?

The CJEU found that the UCTD precluded the procedural rules at issue in *Aziz*, but it did not prescribe a specific solution, let alone invent a new remedy.[849] The judgment presented the Spanish legislature with two options: (a) expand the grounds for opposition in the enforcement proceedings; or (b) allow the court, in declaratory proceedings, to provide interim relief and suspend the enforcement.[850] The first option was chosen. Ley 1/2013 introduced a new opposition ground in Article 695.1.4 LEC, based on unfair terms.[851] This opposition leads to suspension of the enforcement proceedings until the parties have been heard and a decision has been taken (Article 695.2 LEC). This has made the enforcement proceedings slightly more adversarial, but only in respect of unfair terms. If the opposition succeeds, the enforcement is terminated in so far as it is based on the unfair term(s) at issue; in all other cases, it will be continued without the application of the unfair term(s) (Article 695.3 LEC).

Ex officio control was introduced in the general enforcement proceedings (Articles 552.1 and 557.1.7 LEC), but not specifically in the *mortgage*

848 José Maria Fernández Seijo, 'Lights and shadows in the *Aziz* case' in Chantal Mak and Betül Kas (eds), *Civil Courts and the European Polity: The Constitutional Role of Private Law Adjudication in Europe* (Hart Publishing, forthcoming 2022).

849 See also subsection 3.3.2 of the preceding chapter.

850 See, e.g. AP Girona (Sección 2ª), order no. 116/2015 of 10 March 2015, JUR\2015\153253; AP Almería (Sección 1ª), order no. 206/2016 of 9 May 2016, JUR\2017\86409.

851 The revised Article 695.1 LEC reads as follows: 'In proceedings under this chapter, an objection to enforcement by the party against whom enforcement is sought may be admitted only if it is based on the following grounds: (1) Extinction of the security or the secured obligation … (2) An error in determining the amount due … (3) In the case of enforcement against movable property mortgaged or property subject to a non-possessory pledge, the existence of another pledge, movable-property or immovable-property mortgage on, or seizure of, that property registered before the charge giving rise to the procedure, which must be proved by means of the corresponding certificate from the Registry. (4) The unfairness of a contractual term constituting the grounds for enforcement or that has determined the amount due' [English translation taken from Case C-169/14 *Sánchez Morcillo I*, para. 9].

enforcement proceedings. However, it seems clear that Article 552.1 LEC should apply there as well.[852] According to the AP in Barcelona, the new opposition ground provides an extra opportunity for the consumer's defence, in addition to *ex officio* control: one does not exclude the other.[853] There is still some debate as to whether the debtor should be able to file an opposition and/or the enforcement court should be able to perform unfair terms control (*ex officio*) at *any stage* of the enforcement, not just at the beginning, with due observance of the right to be heard.[854] According to the AP in Toledo, *ex officio* control in the enforcement proceedings should be possible until a final decision has been given. It referred to *Sánchez Morcillo* and Article 47 to justify a flexible approach, and held that this did not run counter to the principle of legal certainty.[855] This could be seen as an example of an empowering function: a function that will be discussed further in respect of *Sánchez Morcillo*.

Ley 1/2013 contains a transitional provision to the effect that the legislative amendments would be applicable to enforcement proceedings that were pending at the moment of its entry into force. Where the time period of ten days for filing an opposition had already elapsed, debtors had one month after the publication of Ley 1/2013 to formulate an extraordinary opposition on the basis of unfair terms. The CJEU found it problematic that debtors had not been notified individually of this possibility, in light of the rights of defence, legal certainty, and the protection of legitimate expectations.[856] Ley 5/2019 clarified that a new period of ten days started running from the moment of personal notification of this possibility to the debtor, which was required to take place within 15 days of the Ley's entry into force.[857]

In cases where the enforcement is taking place extrajudicially, Ley 1/2013 stipulates that the notary must stay the extrajudicial auction

---

852 Arroyo Amayuelas (n 655) 76.

853 Judgment of AP Barcelona (n 843), cited above, para. 45. See also AP Barcelona (Sección 17ª), order no. 372/2015 of 26 November 2015, JUR\2016\101861.

854 Pérez Daudí (n 32) 69; Faustino Cordon Moreno, *Acción colectiva y acción individual para la tutela de los derechos de los consumidores* [2016] Centro de Estudios de Consumo – Publicaciones Jurídicas. See also AP Valencia (Sección 6ª), order no. 255/2017 of 27 June 2017, JUR\2018\25068, ECLI:ES:APV:2017:3327A.

855 AP Toledo (Sección 2ª), order no. 297/2018 of 12 December 2018, JUR\2019\72784.

856 The CJEU has held that a one-month time limit could not be imposed on consumers without a personal notification: Case C-8/14 *BBVA*, para. 38. See also Medina Guerrero (n 572) 275–277.

857 This possibility only applies to enforcement proceedings that were pending when Ley 1/2013 entered into force; proceedings initiated afterwards are governed by the new provisions (transitional provision 3).

of property if one of the parties brings a case before a court alleging that the mortgage loan agreement on which it is based is unfair (Article 129.2/f Ley Hipotecaria, with reference to Article 695.1.4 LEC). The notary must also notify the parties of (potentially) unfair terms in the mortgage loan agreement, so that they can take legal action.[858] There is – at least in theory – a register of terms that have been declared invalid by final judicial decisions; notaries cannot declare contractual terms unfair themselves, even though their main role is to control the legality of the transaction.[859]

It should be noted that Article 695 LEC was not specifically written for the benefit of consumers: it pertains to all kinds of mortgage debtors. At first sight, the amendments are not limited to unfair terms in consumer contracts. However, courts do interpret it as such: only consumers (within the meaning of the TR-LGDCU) can rely on them.[860] Professionals and companies can invoke the unfairness of standard terms under the LCGC, but only in ordinary (declaratory) proceedings.[861] This does not lead to *indefensión*.[862] If a party is erroneously considered not to be a consumer and is, therefore, wrongfully denied a judicial remedy, this might nevertheless constitute a violation of Article 24 of the Constitution.[863] Here, the protection offered by Article 24 of the Constitution goes beyond the scope of Article 47 of the Charter read in conjunction with the UCTD, which is in line with Article 47's accessory character.

4.3.3.2. *No Interim Relief Contrary to Article 47?*

There is still no direct link between the enforcement proceedings and the declaratory proceedings of Article 698 LEC, which could be viewed as problematic from the perspective of effective judicial protection. Article 698 LEC even expressly prohibits any suspensory effect of the declaratory proceedings (see also Article 565 LEC). It has been argued that this provision is contrary to Article 47 of the Charter read in conjunction

858 See also subsection 3.3.2.3 of the preceding chapter.

859 Anderson and Simón Moreno (n 663) 68. Because the notary does not exercise a judicial function, there is arguably no conflict with Article 117 of the Spanish Constitution: Díez García (n 540) 257.

860 See, e.g. AP Las Palmas (Sección 5ª), order no. 189/2014 of 22 July 2014, JUR\2015\9437. See also subsection 4.1.3 above and the case law cited there.

861 See, e.g. AP Castellón (Sección 3ª), order no. 185/2015 of 3 September 2015, JUR\2015\271187; AP Girona (Sección 2ª), order no. 52/2016 of 9 February 2016, JUR\2016\192307.

862 AP Girona (Sección 2ª), order no. 274/2014 of 18 December 2014, JUR\2015\81699; AP Girona (Sección 2ª), order no. 185/2015 of 6 May 2015, JUR\2015\166350.

863 See subsection 4.1.2 above.

with the UCTD.[864] According to the AP in Madrid, the court must do everything in its power to ensure the full effectiveness of the UCTD: this requires suspension of the enforcement proceedings until a decision has been taken in the declaratory proceedings.[865] The AP in Madrid referred to the CJEU's judgments in *Aziz* and *Sánchez Morcillo* and, thus, indirectly to Article 47, which again fulfilled an empowering function by authorising the court to disregard Article 698 (and Article 565) LEC and, thus, move in the direction of an eliminatory function. According to the AP in Granada, however, courts cannot suspend the enforcement without a legislative basis, not even in the interest of consumer protection.[866] The purpose of opposition in mortgage enforcement proceedings is to terminate the enforcement, not to suspend it; the aim of the declaratory proceedings is to compensate the debtor, not to undo the effects of the enforcement.[867]

It has been argued that the Spanish legislator should have opted for suspension of the enforcement in the declaratory proceedings, in addition to, or even instead of, expanding the opposition grounds in the mortgage enforcement proceedings.[868] The expansion of the grounds changed the nature of the mortgage enforcement proceedings, which now involve additional contractual and consumer law issues.[869] The court in the declaratory proceedings could be seen as a better forum for addressing the (alleged) unfairness of contract terms, because this court is where debtors are supposed to exercise their rights of defence and contest the claim on the merits.[870]

There is no legislative provision that prescribes *ex officio* control by ordinary courts in declaratory proceedings.[871] Pérez Daudí has argued

864 See, e.g. Case C-380/15 *Garzón Ramos*, with explicit reference to Article 47 of the Charter. See also Iglesias Sánchez (n 600) 964. This case did not fall within the competence of the CJEU, because it concerned mortgage enforcement proceedings against a real estate agent that had financed the purchase of the property. The consumers who lived there were third parties, who could not challenge the mortgage or the enforcement. This illustrates the lack of defence possibilities in the Spanish mortgage enforcement system, not only for mortgage debtors, but also for third parties such as tenants: Díez García (n 540) 236.

865 AP Madrid (Sección 10ª), order no. 223/2015 of 9 July 2015, JUR\2015\186525.

866 AP Granada (Sección 3ª), order no. 208/2015 of 11 December 2015, JUR\2016\114214; AP Granada (Sección 3ª), order no. 135/2016 of 30 June 2016, JUR\2016\222262; AP Granada (Sección 3ª), order no. 10/2017 of 31 January 2017, JUR\2017\91912. See also AP Almería (Sección 1ª), order no. 118/2017 of 9 March 2017, JUR\2017\157110.

867 See also Díez García (n 540) 239–240, 245, 250.

868 Díez García (n 540) 215.

869 Medina Guerrero (n 572) 269.

870 See also Micklitz (n 339) 642.

871 Arroyo Amayuelas (n 655) 74.

that these courts should be able to interfere in pending enforcement proceedings, on the basis of Article 721 LEC, with due regard to the rights of defence.[872] Article 721 LEC provides that the parties may request interim measures that are necessary to ensure the effectiveness of the judicial protection sought, but that the court may not adopt such measures *ex officio*. There is a risk that consumers will not expressly apply for interim relief, because they are unaware of, or do not appreciate the extent of, their rights.[873]

Some courts have ordered suspension of the enforcement as a preventive measure, but only in cases where enforcement proceedings had not yet been initiated.[874] A legislative solution, proposed by Díez García, would be to automatically suspend enforcement proceedings when declaratory proceedings are brought regarding the same case.[875] The declaratory proceedings could then be seen as an extension of the enforcement proceedings, and all other issues that do not constitute a ground of opposition can be raised in the declaratory proceedings.[876] Of course, this would make the enforcement proceedings less attractive for creditors, which might explain why the Spanish legislator does not seem to have considered such a profound solution. Thus, the implementation of *Aziz* could be seen as incomplete, and causing only more legal uncertainty,[877] as confirmed by further preliminary references on this issue.[878]

4.3.3.3. Consequences for Enforcement?

A follow-up question to consider is to what extent it would have helped Mr. Aziz if the mortgage enforcement proceedings could have been suspended and/or the terms at issue had been deemed unfair. According to the Juzgado, the consequence of its finding of unfairness was that all three clauses should be declared null and void, and that the claimed amount should not be due and payable.[879] By contrast, the AP in Barcelona found

---

872 Pérez Daudí (n 32) 90.

873 See also Case C-568/14 *Fernández Oliva*, paras. 33–35.

874 Pérez Daudí (n 32) 88–89.

875 Díez García (n 540) 256. See also Barral-Viñals (n 6) 94.

876 AP Barcelona (Sección 15ª), judgment no. 407/2014 of 15 December 2014, JUR\2015\86196, para. 49.

877 Medina Guerrero (n 572) 269; Pérez Daudí (n 32) 90. See also 2019 Max Planck report (n 33), p. 53.

878 See, e.g. the above-mentioned cases C-380/15 *Garzón Ramos* and C-568/14 *Fernández Oliva*.

879 Juzgado de lo Mercantil No. 3 de Barcelona, judgment of 2 May 2013 in case no. 13/2011, ECLI:ES:JMB:2013:21, para. 12.8.

that nullity of the enforcement proceedings could not be proclaimed; the amount owed by Mr. Aziz should simply be recalculated.

As regards (default) interest clauses, it could be argued that the debt should be recalculated: the nullity of certain terms does not automatically render the entire contract invalid.[880] If the clause is not the basis of the enforcement, and the enforcement proceedings have not yet been concluded, they may proceed (Article 695.3 LEC).[881] In respect of the two other clauses at issue in *Aziz*, it could be argued that the enforcement should have been terminated. When a unilateral debt determination clause is declared to be null and void, this means that the creditor was not entitled to unilaterally determine the amount owed by the debtor. The expedited enforcement procedure is an action *in rem*, directed against the assets of the debtor and based on certainty of the claimed amount.[882] Thus, the creditor should be barred from the procedure. This does not mean the debtor is 'off the hook', but the creditor loses a procedural advantage.[883]

The same could be argued as regards acceleration clauses, in so far as a debtor's non-compliance with their payment obligations does not warrant early termination. There were different readings of the CJEU's judgment in *Abanca*, and these reveal tension between the consumer debtor's right to effective judicial protection and the creditor's security interests.[884] When an unfair (and, thus, invalid) acceleration clause is struck from a loan agreement, it seems obvious that the creditor can no longer claim the entire loan in the enforcement proceedings.[885] However, the Tribunal Supremo

880 AP Tarragona (Sección 1ª), order no. 64/2013 of 10 June 2013, JUR\2014\294027; AP Castellón (Sección 3ª), order no. 175/2014 of 10 September 2014, JUR\2015\52954. See also Barral-Viñals (n 6) 94.

881 AP Barcelona (Sección 13ª), order no. 210/2014 of 6 October 2014, JUR\2014\295342.

882 AP Toledo (Sección 2ª), order no. 185/2017 of 7 March 2017, JUR\2017\146402. See also Barral-Viñals (n 6) 81.

883 Barral-Viñals (n 6) 83.

884 Case C-70/17 *Abanca*. The CJEU seems to have (erroneously) presumed that removal of an unfair acceleration clause from the loan agreement meant that the continued existence of the contract was no longer possible, leaving space for the referring court to examine whether the consumer would then be exposed to particularly unfavourable consequences, and to replace the clause with the new wording of the legislative provision on which the clause is based (para. 64).

885 It also seems obvious that the loan agreement can continue to exist without the term: Francesco de Elizalde, 'Partial Invalidity for Unfair Terms? CJEU in *Abanca* – C-70 & 179/17' [2019] Journal of European Consumer and Market Law 147; Anderson and Simón Moreno (n 663) 58. See, e.g. AP Toledo (Sección 2ª), order no. 663/2017 of 1 December 2017, JUR\2018\64957, ECLI:ES:APTO:2017:377A; AP Toledo (Sección 2ª), order no. 31/2019 of 28 January 2019, JUR\2019\128090,

has allowed enforcement on the basis of Article 693.2 and Article 24 of Ley 5/2019, if the statutory requirements are met.[886] After *Aziz*, the minimum period that the creditor must wait to get access to the enforcement proceedings is for the debtor to be in default of three monthly instalments (Article 693.1 LEC); in cases concerning mortgaged residential properties of natural persons, the period is at least 12 months. Even after termination of the enforcement procedure because of an unfair acceleration clause, new proceedings can be brought. Apparently, such a termination does not have *res judicata* effect.[887]

4.4. EQUALITY OF ARMS

4.4.1. INTRODUCTION: ASYMMETRIC RIGHTS OF APPEAL IN MORTGAGE ENFORCEMENT PROCEEDINGS

The discussion above shows that the CJEU's case law cannot solve all systemic dysfunctions in Spanish procedural law.[888] The outcome in the case of *Aziz* illustrates that the harsh consequences of 'predatory lending' cannot be addressed fully through increased procedural protection of consumer debtors. Moreover, Article 47 of the Charter is not a universal remedy: its functions only manifest themselves on the national level in

ECLI:ES:APTO:2019:68A. The Spanish government seems to have argued differently before the CJEU: Case C-70/17 *Abanca*, Opinion of AG Szpunar, point 114; see also Candida Leone, 'Case Note *Abanca Corporación Bancaria, S.A. v Alberto García Salamanca Santos*' [2020] Revue européenne de droit de la consommation 317. Leone observes that it is, ultimately, for the consumer to decide whether to opt for invalidity of the contract, with reference to Case C-260/18 *Dziubak v Raiffeisen Bank International*.

886 Tribunal Supremo (Sala de lo Civil), judgment no. 463/2019 of 11 September 2019, ECLI:ES:TS:2019:2761. The question of whether this interpretation was compatible with the Charter was declared inadmissible, because it was not clear how this was relevant for the resolution of the case at hand: Case C-92/16 *Bankia v Rengifo Jiménez and Felix Caixa*, paras. 33–38.

887 Case C-486/16 *Bankia v Sánchez Martínez and Sánchez Triviño*, paras. 35 and 49. According to the Tribunal Supremo, Article 552.3 LEC does not apply, because the enforcement is based on a mandatory statutory provision (Article 24 of Ley 5/2019), not on the unfair acceleration clause. Article 552.3 LEC stipulates that once a decision that terminates the enforcement proceedings becomes final, the creditor only has recourse to ordinary proceedings, unless *indefensión* has occurred, which is a ground for nullity of the decision: see, e.g. AP Málaga (Sección 5ª), order no. 311/2015 of 12 November 2015, JUR\2016\84863.

888 Iglesias Sánchez (n 600) 973; García Aburuza (n 731) 13–15; Barral-Viñals (n 6) 95.

so far as it is used by courts to justify the application or disapplication of procedural rules in certain ways.

The case of *Sánchez Morcillo* and its follow-up events provide another example of the imperfect trialogue between Spanish civil courts, the CJEU and the Spanish legislature.[889] It can be regarded as proof that the efforts of the Spanish government to upgrade the procedural framework of mortgage enforcement proceedings to EU standards have been insufficient.[890] After the CJEU's judgment in *Aziz*, a new ground of opposition was included in Article 695.1.4 LEC.[891] It could be said that this removed the procedural disadvantage for consumer debtors, but it also shifted the problem to the appeal phase. Article 695.4 LEC contained an asymmetric restriction of the right to appeal for mortgage debtors, which was justified by the privileged position of the mortgage holder.[892] Mortgage enforcement proceedings are not considered to be fully adversarial. There was (and still is) no procedural connection with ordinary proceedings on the merits: the enforcement can go ahead once the debtor's opposition against it is dismissed, or when the decision to terminate the enforcement has been overturned on appeal. Thus, the problem of irreversibility has not been completely resolved after *Aziz*.

As discussed in Chapter 3, *Sánchez Morcillo I* could be seen as an example of how Article 47 of the Charter – read in conjunction with the UCTD – and effectiveness may lead to a different outcome.[893] From an effectiveness perspective, unfair terms control (*ex officio*) at first instance could be sufficient. Article 47 requires equality of arms, which means, in unfair terms cases, that consumers must also be able to bring an appeal. In this respect, it must be noted that, in Spain, appeal is not considered to be a second chance to litigate the case. The ambit of the dispute is limited: a party cannot present new claims or defences on appeal,[894] due to the other party's right to be heard, since the other party has not been given the opportunity to respond to these claims or defences at first instance.[895] The first instance is the initial and essential phase of the process and

[889] Case C-169/14 *Sánchez Morcillo I* and Case C-539/14 *Sánchez Morcillo II* (pertaining to the same dispute), introduced in subsection 3.4.2 of the preceding chapter.

[890] Gómez Pomar and Lyczkowska (n 661) 110–111. See also Díez García (n 540) 235; Jiménez París (n 657) 986.

[891] See subsection 4.3.3 above.

[892] Medina Guerrero (n 572) 272.

[893] See also Moya Hurtado de Mendoza (n 679) 411.

[894] Díez-Picazo Giménez (n 682) 391.

[895] AP Almería (Sección 1ª), order no. 471/2017 of 24 October 2017, JUR\2018\201909, ECLI:ES:APAL:2017:1035A.

provides the core of judicial protection; the right to appeal (in civil proceedings) is not a constitutional guarantee.[896] This could be another explanation for why the preliminary reference in *Sánchez Morcillo I* was framed as an issue of equality of arms, rather than the lack of an effective remedy.[897]

4.4.2. *SÁNCHEZ MORCILLO I* FURTHER EXPLORED

4.4.2.1. Tribunal Constitucional: Access to Court of First Instance Guaranteed

In *Sánchez Morcillo*, it was the referring court that raised the reference to Article 47 of the Charter. It is interesting to note that the request for a preliminary ruling was made on 2 April 2014, only three weeks after the Tribunal Constitucional had dismissed a *cuestión de inconstitucionalidad* regarding Article 695.4 LEC.

In November 2013, the Juzgado de Primera Instancia No. 7 in Avilés had posed two *cuestiónes de inconstitucionalidad* regarding Article 695.4 LEC. It had pointed out that the lack of an opportunity for the debtor to appeal would make it difficult to remedy the consequences of mortgage enforcement. According to the Juzgado, the discriminatory and unequal treatment of the parties to the proceedings constituted a violation of Articles 14 and 24 of the Constitution. However, the Tribunal Constitucional found, in its judgment of 10 March 2014, that the procedural requirement of *juicio de relevancia* had not been met.[898] This requirement means, in short, that the validity of the norm in question must be relevant to, or necessary for, the outcome of the case.[899] No decision had yet been given in the enforcement proceedings at hand, so appeal was not yet at issue. Moreover, it was not clear, in advance, that the debtor's objection would be dismissed. It appeared that the Juzgado had anticipated the debtor's intention to appeal without considering other options, such as termination

---

896 AP Lleida (Sección 2ª), order no. 55/2013 of 25 March 2013, JUR\2014\294266.

897 See also subsection 3.4.1 of the preceding chapter.

898 Tribunal Constitucional, order no. 70/2014 of 10 March 2014, ECLI:ES:TC:2014:70A. See also Tribunal Constitucional, order no. 71/2014 of 10 March 2014, ECLI:ES:TC:2014:71A; Tribunal Constitucional, order no. 111/2014 of 8 April 2014, ECLI:ES:TC:2014:111A, Tribunal Constitucional, order no. 112/2014 of 8 April 2014, ECLI:ES:TC:2014:112A and Tribunal Constitucional, order no. 113/2014 of 8 April 2014, ECLI:ES:TC:2014:113A.

899 Díez García (n 540) 218.

of the proceedings, or the route offered by Article 698 LEC. Therefore, the question was hypothetical and premature.

This strict interpretation by the Tribunal Constitucional led to a paradox: the enforcement court, at first instance, could not pose a *cuestión de inconstitucionalidad*, but neither could appellate courts, precisely because there was no possibility of appeal for the debtor.[900] In the case of *Sánchez Morcillo*, the AP in Castellón circumvented this paradox by making the preliminary reference before declaring the appeal inadmissible. It considered that the CJEU's answer to the question of whether Article 695.4 LEC was compatible with Article 7 of the UCTD, and Article 47 of the Charter, was necessary to determine whether the appeal was admissible and, thus, whether the case could proceed or not.[901] Needless to say, if the appeal was inadmissible, the Court of Appeal would not be able to exercise *ex officio* control of unfair terms either. The AP in Castellón also found that it was the court of highest instance in this case, because no cassation appeal would be available before the Tribunal Supremo against a decision dismissing the appeal.

The adoption of such an approach is unlikely to have led to a different outcome before the Tribunal Constitucional: in a later judgment, given only five days after the CJEU's judgment in *Sánchez Morcillo I*, but without any reference to that judgment, the Tribunal Constitucional added that the debtor had had access to a court of first instance, so there had been no violation of Article 24 of the Constitution.[902] The debtor had taken up the opportunity to raise objections in the enforcement proceedings, and so could claim compensation in separate, ordinary proceedings. Again, the Tribunal Constitucional did not distinguish between different types of mortgage debtors.

4.4.2.2. Audiencia Provincial Castellón: An Unjustified Procedural Advantage

The case law of the Tribunal Constitucional had provided a reason for the AP in Castellón to make a preliminary reference to the CJEU in

[900] Díez García (n 540) 221–222.

[901] The AP in Alava had come to a similar conclusion: either the appeal was inadmissible because it had been brought by the debtor, or it was admissible because Article 694.4 LEC (old) was contrary to the right to a fair trial and equality of arms: AP Álava (Sección 1ª), order no. 94/2014 of 24 September 2014, JUR\2014\255268.

[902] Tribunal Constitucional, order no. 206/2014 of 22 July 2014, ECLI:ES:TC:2014:206A.

Sánchez Morcillo.[903] Neither the consumer debtors nor the court of first instance had referred to the existence of unfair terms in the mortgage loan agreement.[904] It was the AP in Castellón itself that had brought up Article 47 of the Charter; a reference to the UCTD had only been added following an observation by one the parties.[905]

> When Mr. Sánchez Morcillo and Ms. Abril García (the debtors) had failed to meet their payment obligations, BBVA had demanded accelerated repayment of the entire loan and initiated mortgage enforcement proceedings. The debtors' opposition to the enforcement had been dismissed. Under Spanish procedural law, consumer debtors could not bring an appeal, even if the enforcement was based on unfair terms in the loan agreement, or due to the court's failure to perform *ex officio* control. Mr. Sánchez Morcillo and Ms. Abril García, nevertheless, had tried to bring an appeal before AP Castellón.

According to the AP in Castellón, the enforcement initiated by the bank appeared to have been based on at least one unfair term, concerning a default interest rate of 19 per cent per year (15 per cent higher than the statutory interest rate in Spain at the time). In this case, the debtors could not have based their opposition on unfair terms, because it had been filed on 12 March 2013, two months before Ley 1/2013 entered into force. Pursuant to Article 695.4 LEC, appeal could only be lodged by the creditor against the termination of the enforcement and/or the disapplication of an unfair term. Consumer debtors could not bring an appeal against a rejection of their opposition. Separate declaratory proceedings would not suspend the enforcement. The AP in Castellón observed that this was problematic, in light of *Aziz*, and contrary to Article 47 of the Charter:

> 'This court considers that the aforementioned Article 695.4 of the Code of Civil Procedure [LEC] is incompatible with the right to a fair trial and equality of arms set forth in Article 47 of the Charter of Fundamental Rights of the European Union'.[906]

---

903 AP Castellón (Sección 3ª), order of 2 April 2014, JUR\2014\179524.

904 The debtors' opposition was based on the alleged lack of an enforceable title, due to a formal defect and the court's lack of competence. See also Case C-169/14 *Sánchez Morcillo I*, View of AG Wahl, point 26.

905 Speech by Mr. Alejandro Rubio González, (former) State Attorney (n 213). See also subsection 2.2.2 of this book.

906 Translated from the original Spanish text, which reads, 'Este tribunal considera que el citado art. 695.4 de la Ley de Enjuiciamiento Civil es incompatible conel derecho a un juicio equitativo y en igualdad de armas enunciado en el artículo 47 de la Carta de Derechos Fundamentales de la Unión Europea.'

The AP in Castellón used Article 47 as an additional argument to explain why Ley 1/2013 was still insufficient, from the perspective of the effective judicial protection of consumers under the UCTD. It drew attention to the procedural advantage enjoyed by the creditor, which was, in its view, unjustified. Article 47 aims to ensure a balance between the parties to the proceedings, which – according to the AP in Castellón – entailed that each party must be able to bring an appeal under the same conditions. The reference to Article 47, thus, fulfilled a strengthening function in respect of consumers' procedural rights, but also an empowering function as to the role of courts. The principle of equality of arms amplified the duty of the national legislator and courts to counterbalance consumers' weaker position in the procedural realm.[907] Such an empowering function has been picked up by other courts as well, for example in the above-mentioned decision of the AP in Toledo;[908] *Sánchez Morcillo* seems to have paved the way.

4.4.3. IMPLEMENTATION AND FOLLOW-UP

4.4.3.1. A Transformative Function of Article 47, to a Certain Extent

The CJEU gave its judgment in *Sánchez Morcillo I* on 17 July 2014. It held that Article 7 UCTD, read in conjunction with Article 47 of the Charter, precluded the asymmetric restriction of the right to appeal at issue. The transformative function of Article 47 has already been highlighted, in Chapter 3; this has certain limitations, as the national follow-up developments show. Real Decreto-ley 11/2014 of 5 September 2014 amended Article 695.4 LEC: mortgage debtors are now allowed to bring an appeal against a decision dismissing their objection on the basis of unfair terms.[909] In the preamble of RD 11/2014 (VI), explicit reference

---

907 Medina Guerrero (n 572) 273.

908 AP Toledo (Sección 2ª), order no. 297/2018 of 12 December 2018, JUR\2019\72784, discussed in subsection 4.3.3 above. See, for another example, AP Almería (Sección 1ª), order no. 426/2017 of 25 September 2017, JUR\2018\200338, ECLI:ES:APAL:2017:727A. The AP in Almeria referred to the inequality of arms between consumers and traders as an argument for *ex officio* control in mortgage enforcement proceedings, with due regard for the right to be heard.

909 The revised Article 695.4 LEC reads as follows: 'An appeal may lie against the order discontinuing enforcement or disapplying an unfair term or rejecting the opposition on the ground laid down in paragraph 1(4) of the present article. Save in those circumstances, no appeal shall lie against orders adjudicating upon the objection to

was made to the CJEU's judgment. Some appellate courts that applied the new Article 695.4 LEC also referred to the principle of equality of arms to explain why the amendment had been made.[910] RD 11/2014 contained a transitional provision to the effect that the new Article 695.4 LEC was applicable to enforcement proceedings that had not yet been concluded by means of a transfer of possession to the party that acquired the property. In cases where the debtors' objection had been dismissed, the debtors had a period of one month after the day that RD 11/2014 entered into force to bring an appeal on the basis of the new Article 695.4 LEC.[911] Ley 9/2015 changed this period to two months after its entry into force.[912]

After the CJEU's judgment in *Sánchez Morcillo I*, the AP in Castellón found that it could still not examine the appeal on the merits. The recent legislative reform had not addressed the uncertainty: pursuant to the new Article 695.4 LEC, appeal was only possible against a ruling of the court at first instance dismissing an objection based on unfair terms. In the case of Mr. Sánchez Morcillo, no such objection had been raised, which meant that the new Article 695.4 LEC did not apply either.[913] Therefore, the appeal was, strictly speaking, still not admissible, and the Court of Appeal could not exercise *ex officio* control of unfair terms. This would apply not only to Mr. Sánchez Morcillo, but to all consumers in his situation. The AP in Castellón decided to make a second preliminary reference to the CJEU.[914] In addition to Article 47 of the Charter, the AP raised the

enforcement referred to in the present article and the effects of those orders shall be confined exclusively to the enforcement proceedings in which they are made' [English translation taken from Case C-539/14 *Sánchez Morcillo II*, para. 8]. Strictly speaking, neither 'discontinuing enforcement' or 'disapplying an unfair term' is the same as 'rejecting the opposition', which is why the latter was added to Article 695.4 LEC by Ley 9/2015 (see below): AP Valencia (Sección 9ª), order no. 123/2015 of 25 February 2015, JUR\2015\124382; AP Valencia (Sección 9ª), order no. 460/2014 of 11 September 2014, JUR\2015\51381. See also Roca Trías and García Couso (n 710) 531.

910 See, e.g. AP Lleida (Sección 2ª), order no. 36/2015 of 26 February 2015, JUR\2015\158435; AP Valencia (Sección 9ª), order no. 455/2014 of 8 September 2014, JUR\2015\51807.

911 See, e.g. AP Barcelona (Sección 16ª), order no. 168/2015 of 19 May 2015, JUR\2015\160073.

912 Ley 9/2015, de medidas urgentes en materia concursal, BOE no. 125 of 26 May 2015, p. 43874. Questions have been raised as to the constitutionality of making the calculation of this period dependent on the publication of RD 11/2014 in the BOE, given the requirement of personal notification of the enforcement to the debtor: Medina Guerrero (n 572) 278.

913 See also AP Tarragona (Sección 3ª), order of 30 September 2014, JUR\2015\43480; AP Castellón (Sección 3ª), order no. 216/2015 of 30 September 2015, JUR\2015\271027.

914 AP Castellón (Sección 3ª), order of 21 November 2014, JUR\2015\5684.

right to housing (Article 34 of the Charter) and the right to family life (Article 7 of the Charter). Unfortunately, the CJEU did not provide any further assistance.[915] In its final decision of 3 September 2015 in *Sánchez Morcillo I*,[916] the AP found that it, inevitably, had to dismiss the appeal.

In a way, the empowering function of Article 47 was cut short by the legislative amendment. In this respect, it is interesting to note that the AP in Castellón had already started allowing appeals by consumer debtors in enforcement proceedings on 29 July 2014, less than two weeks after the CJEU's first judgment. The AP referred, in this respect, to the judgment, and to Article 47 of the Charter, as well as the primacy of EU law and the obligation of national courts to set aside conflicting provisions of national law.[917] These appeals were declared admissible despite the fact that Article 695.4 LEC had not yet been amended. Other courts, such as the APs in Barcelona and Pontevedra, also allowed appeals that had been brought before the entry into force of RD 11/2014, with reference to Article 47 of the Charter.[918] In a case where the opposition of the consumer debtors as to the unfairness of a default interest clause had been successful, i.e. the opposition had not been dismissed, the AP in Barcelona still allowed an appeal against the ruling, because the appeal challenged the consequences of the unfairness. The court of first instance had ordered a recalculation of the debt and interest, but the consumer debtors had claimed there was no interest due at all. The AP Barcelona agreed with the debtors and held that the appeal was admissible, in light of the 'tenor' of the CJEU's judgment in *Sánchez Morcillo I*. The AP also referred to the need to ensure access to justice, to reasons of procedural economy, and to the above-mentioned transitional provision that established retroactivity in favour of consumers.[919] Thus, it went beyond the CJEU's judgment in *Sánchez Morcillo II*, and the AP in Castellon's final decision in that case.

---

915 Case C-539/14 *Sánchez Morcillo II*.

916 AP Castellón (Sección 3ª), order no. 187/2015 of 3 September 2015, JUR\2015\271900, ECLI:ES:APCS:2015:91A.

917 AP Castellón (Sección 3ª), order no. 171/2014 of 29 July 2014, JUR\2015\10598, ECLI:ES:APCS:2014:55A. The Commission had also suggested this possibility in its written observations, paras. 70 and 72.

918 AP Pontevedra (Sección 1ª), order no. 148/2014 of 28 July 2014, JUR\2014\225714; AP Barcelona (Sección 17ª), order no. 259/2014 of 3 September 2014, JUR\2014\295502, referring to the case of *Von Colson* (n 264); AP Barcelona (Sección 4ª), order no. 196/2014 of 18 September 2014, JUR\2014\297187; AP Granada (Sección 3ª), order no. 162/2014 of 22 September 2014, JUR\2015\2137.

919 AP Barcelona (Sección 1ª), order no. 253/2014 of 26 September 2014, JUR\2015\10332. See also AP Barcelona (Sección 13ª), order no. 221/2014 of 16 October 2014,

By contrast, the AP in Madrid has defended a strict interpretation of Article 695.4 LEC. It has considered that a maximalist interpretation should be avoided, for the sake of consumer protection, because it would have the paradoxical consequences of limiting consumers' access to mortgage credit and taking away certain advantages of mortgage enforcement that Ley 1/2013 awards them, such as the guarantee that their properties will not be sold for less than a certain percentage of their estimated value.[920] However, it could be argued that it should be up to the debtor to decide which course of action to take;[921] if they bring an appeal, it is clearly with the objective of terminating the enforcement.

Spanish procedural law still does not put appellate proceedings on a par with proceedings at first instance.[922] Firstly, if consumer debtors do not file an opposition, it seems that they forfeit the right to appeal; the new Article 695.4 LEC does not give them a right to appeal against an *ex officio* finding that the terms at issue are not unfair.[923] Secondly, consumers only have the option to appeal in mortgage enforcement proceedings; asymmetric appeal rights still exist in the general enforcement proceedings.[924] Thirdly, an appeal does not suspend the enforcement procedure, unless the debtor can demonstrate that this would cause irreparable harm.[925] The AP in Barcelona did not see this situation as incompatible with the UCTD and/or Article 47 of the Charter, because unfair terms control is supposed to take place (*ex officio*) at first instance, regardless of opposition by the debtor.[926] And, fourthly, if an appeal is at least partially successful, no cost order is ordered against the losing party (Article 398.2 LEC). According to the

---

JUR\2014\294909; AP Lleida (Sección 2ª), order no. 36/2015 of 26 February 2015, JUR\2015\158435; AP Valencia (Sección 6ª), order no. 188/2015 of 8 September 2015, JUR\2016\130308; AP Barcelona (Sección 16ª), order no. 385/2015 of 17 December 2015, JUR\2016\47092.

920 AP Madrid (Sección 10ª), order no. 452/2016 of 22 December 2016, JUR\2017\25699. See also Tribunal Supremo (Sala de lo Civil), judgment no. 463/2019 of 11 September 2019, ECLI:ES:TS:2019:2761, discussed in subsection 4.3.3 above.

921 According to settled CJEU case law, account must be taken of the intention expressed by the consumer as to whether or not she prefers to rely on the system of protection under the Directive: see, e.g. Case C-19/20 *IW and RW v Bank BPH*, para. 47.

922 Gascón Inchausti (n 418) 124.

923 Jiménez París (n 657) 986.

924 See subsection 4.2.2 above.

925 Articles 561.3 and 567 LEC; Díez García (n 540) 239. See also AP Madrid (Sección 10ª), order no. 8/2017 of 16 January 2017, JUR\2017\61994; AP Almería (Sección 1ª), order no. 118/2017 of 9 March 2017, JUR\2017\157110.

926 AP Barcelona (Sección 17ª), order no. 372/2015 of 26 November 2015, JUR\2016\101861.

AP in Guipúzcoa, this is not a violation of the right to effective judicial protection, as guaranteed by Article 47 of the Charter: it does not impede access to court, because the 'loser pays' principle applies at first instance if the claim is awarded fully (Article 394.1 LEC), and the consumers involved can obtain restitution of advantages wrongly obtained by the trader.[927] However, if the consumers lose at first instance, and have to bring an appeal to correct this, they will have to bear the costs, which may have a deterrent effect.[928]

4.4.3.2. Res Judicata *Effect of a Decision in the Enforcement Proceedings?*

The question arises as to whether the 'tenor' of the CJEU's judgment in *Sánchez Morcillo I* should have entailed that appeals brought by consumers in the same situation as Mr. Sánchez Morcillo were admissible. When the opposition was filed, unfair terms were not yet recognised as a ground of opposition, let alone as a ground of appeal. The court of first instance did not rule until 19 June 2013, i.e. after the entry into force of Ley 1/2013, which meant that it could (and should) have examined the terms of the mortgage loan agreement *ex officio* and/or given Mr. Sánchez Morcillo the opportunity to supplement his grounds of opposition.[929] It could be argued that the court's failure to do so should not be held against the consumer,[930] or that this amounts to *indefensión*, if it cannot be remedied.[931] This could constitute a violation of Article 47 of the Charter, which requires an effective remedy for infringements of EU (consumer) rights.

In Spain, a so-called 'virtual' *res judicata* effect means that it is no longer possible to debate issues that *could have been* the subject of previous proceedings between the same parties that have resulted in a final decision; it is binding upon those parties, for reasons of legal certainty and

---

927 AP Guipúzcoa (Sección 2ª), order no. 229/2019 of 20 March 2019, JUR\2019\172545, ECLI:ES:APSS:2019:355.

928 Request for a preliminary ruling in Case C-385/20 *EL and TP v Caixabank* (pending).

929 Carrasco Perera and Lyczkowska (n 540) 4. Perhaps the court of first instance did not do so because Article 552.1 LEC had not been expressly declared to be applicable in mortgage enforcement proceedings: see also subsection 4.2.2 above and Case C-169/14 *Sánchez Morcillo I*, para. 39.

930 See also Tribunal Supremo, judgment no. 3373/2017 of 27 September 2017, ECLI:ES:TS:2017:3373, para. 4.3: 'Resultaría paradójico que una medida destinada a la protección del consumidor, como es el control de oficio de la abusividad contractual, pudiera acabar perjudicándole si no se ejerce por el tribunal.'

931 See, e.g. AP Valencia (Sección 6ª), order no. 255/2017 of 27 June 2017, JUR\2018\25068, ECLI:ES:APV:2017:3327A, as well as the judgment of the Tribunal Constitucional discussed below.

procedural economy, and to avoid contradictory decisions.[932] It needs to be mentioned, as a side note, that virtual *res judicata* is a slightly different issue from that which was at stake in *Duarte Hueros*: that case was about the possibility (or otherwise) of introducing new grounds at a later stage in the same instance (*preclusión procesal*, or procedural preclusion).[933] Virtual *res judicata* concerns the status of a judicial decision in *subsequent* proceedings, and the possibility (or otherwise) of bringing a new claim.

Before *Aziz*, the Tribunal Constitucional had held that a decision in mortgage enforcement proceedings did not have substantive *res judicata* effect.[934] The question arose as to whether, after the adoption of Ley 1/2013 and RD 11/2014, such a decision had virtual *res judicata* effect, in the sense that debtors could no longer bring an objection against unfair terms in subsequent declaratory proceedings. On the one hand, it could be argued that there should be no *res judicata* effect, because both types of proceedings have different objectives.[935] On the other hand, the Tribunal Supremo held, in 2014, that if debtors had had the opportunity to file an opposition but had not done so, they were, indeed, precluded from bringing declaratory proceedings and claiming nullity of the enforcement.[936] In the *Aziz* case, the AP in Barcelona considered that the court's power of *ex officio* control could not go so far as to defy the principle of *res judicata*, which forms the core of the right to effective judicial protection:

> 'Neither our legal system nor that of any other country around us could accept the abolition of that principle, which constitutes an essential guarantee of the functioning of justice and is part of the core of the right to effective judicial protection enshrined in Article 24 of the Constitution, to the same extent as it is in Article 6 ECHR and Article 47 of the Charter'.[937]

---

932 Jiménez París (n 657) 987–988. See also Case C-32/12 *Duarte Hueros v Autociba and Automóviles Citroën España*, Opinion of AG Kokott, point 9.

933 Case C-32/12 *Duarte Hueros v Autociba and Automóviles Citroën España*. See also Pérez Daudí (n 32) 69; Gascón Inchausti (n 418) 123–124.

934 See subsection 4.3.2 above.

935 Díez García (n 540) 237. See also subsection 4.3.3 above.

936 Tribunal Supremo (Sala de lo Civil), judgment no. 4617/2014 of 24 November 2014, ECLI:ES:TS:2014:4617; see also AP Granada (Sección 3ª), order no. 208/2015 of 11 December 2015, JUR\2016\114214. The transitional provisions of Ley 1/2013, RD 11/2014 or Ley 9/2015 could be seen as an exception to *res judicata* effect: AP Barcelona (Sección 16ª), order no. 35/2015 of 5 February 2015, JUR\2015\115541.

937 AP Barcelona (Sección 15ª), judgment no. 407/2014 of 15 December 2014, JUR\2015\86196, para. 86. Translated from the original Spanish text, which reads, '*Ni nuestro ordenamiento jurídico ni el de ningún otro país de nuestro entorno podrían aceptar la derogación de ese principio, que constituye una garantía esencial del funcionamiento de la jurisdicción y está incluido en el núcleo esencial del derecho a la*

In the case of Mr. Aziz, Ley 1/2013 had not yet entered into force at the time of the enforcement proceedings and, therefore, virtual *res judicata* was not an issue.[938] The court was not precluded from exercising unfair terms control in the declaratory proceedings. However, after *Banco Primus* (2017),[939] which concerned an extraordinary opposition brought by the debtor under Ley 1/2013, it appears that it no longer matters whether unfair terms *could have been* raised earlier. What matters is that there is no (virtual) *res judicata* in so far as an assessment of unfair terms has not been conducted. The Tribunal Supremo followed the CJEU judgment by concluding that it was still possible to raise the issue of unfair terms in subsequent declaratory proceedings, where it was not yet clear that there was a duty of *ex officio* control, or that unfair terms constituted an opposition ground.[940]

The Tribunal Constitucional recently confirmed that an application for nullity of procedural actions would be possible, too.[941] The court that had dismissed the application for nullity had found that *Banco Primus* neither had retroactive effect nor provided a reason for revision of the original decision. The Tribunal Constitucional, however, ruled that the original decision's *res judicata* effect should be disregarded. Even if the debtors had not filed an opposition, they had made an application for nullity, and the court should perform unfair terms control *ex officio* unless that had already taken place, which was not the case here. Whether *Banco Primus* had retroactive effect did not matter, because the application for nullity had been made after the CJEU's judgment had come out. If the court was in doubt, it should have made a preliminary reference to the CJEU.

In the case of Mr. Sánchez Morcillo, unfair terms had not been the subject of the enforcement proceedings. The decision, thus, lacked *res judicata* effect, because the court of first instance did not exercise *ex officio* control, and the appeal was declared inadmissible.[942] From the perspective of effective judicial protection, the most important factor was that the court's failure to perform unfair terms control (*ex officio*) could

---

tutela efectiva que consagra el artículo 24.1 CE, en la misma medida en la que lo está en el artículo 6 del Convenio Europeo de Derechos Humanos y en el artículo 47 de la Carta de Derechos.' See also Pérez Daudí (n 32) 48.

938 Judgment of AP Barcelona (n 843), para. 87.

939 Case C-421/14 *Banco Primus*.

940 Tribunal Supremo (Sala de lo Civil), judgment no. 3373/2017 of 27 September 2017, ECLI:ES:TS:2017:3373, para. 5.1. See also Pérez Daudí (n 32) 83–84.

941 Tribunal Constitucional, judgment no. 31/2019 of 28 February 2019, ECLI:ES:TC:2019:31.

942 See also Pérez Daudí (n 32) 83–84.

be remedied by giving consumers like Mr. Sánchez Morcillo an actual opportunity to exercise their rights.

4.5. RIGHT TO BE HEARD

4.5.1. INTRODUCTION: THE PROHIBITION OF *INDEFENSIÓN*

If litigants are denied the opportunity to present their cases before decisions are taken that adversely affect their interests, this may constitute violation of Article 47 of the Charter.[943] This is very similar to the prohibition of *indefensión* laid down in Article 24 of the Spanish Constitution.

Indefensión occurs when a party is denied the right to defend their rights and legitimate interests by exercising their right of action and/or right to be heard.[944] It is not tied to unfair terms control; it extends to all elements that are decisive for the case.[945] The prohibition of *indefensión* is a powerful instrument, because it may lead to the nullity of all subsequent procedural actions, including judicial decisions, a consequence that is not prescribed by Article 47. *Indefensión* may be invoked in an ordinary appeal on the basis of a procedural breach.[946] The appellate court may then declare procedural actions null, and send the case back to the court of first instance.[947] If the judicial decision has already become final, *indefensión* may be the basis for an exceptional application for nullity of procedural actions,[948] which must be brought within 20 days after a party becomes aware of the procedural breach, or within five years after notification of the decision. There is no possibility of appeal.

In the context of the UCTD, the situation of consumers like Mr. Sánchez Morcillo could amount to *indefensión*, in so far as the consumer does not

943 See subsection 2.1.2.4 and section 3.5 of this book.

944 See, e.g. Mª Immaculada Sánchez Barrios, 'La acción como derecho a la tutela efectiva' [2010] Justicia: Revista de derecho procesal 167, 180.

945 See also AP Madrid (Sección 14ª), order no. 33/2015 of 18 February 2015, JUR\2015\100490.

946 Article 459 LEC; Pérez Daudí (n 32) 67, 73. See, e.g. AP Valencia (Sección 11ª), order no. 67/2017 of 23 February 2017, JUR\2017\130297; AP Sevilla (Sección 6ª), order no. 311/2015 of 17 December 2015, JUR\2016\58585.

947 See, e.g. AP Las Palmas (Sección 5ª), order no. 243/2014 of 2 October 2014, JUR\2015\56330; AP Las Palmas (Sección 5ª), order no. 96/2015 of 30 March 2015, JUR\2015\120970; AP Valencia (Sección 11ª), order no. 67/2017 of 23 February 2017, JUR\2017\130297.

948 See also subsection 4.1.2 above.

have at least one possibility to challenge an enforcement based on unfair terms. The AP in Valencia, for instance, has held that there was *indefensión* because the court of first instance had failed to perform *ex officio* control, which obviously affects the position of consumers negatively.[949] There may also be *indefensión* in the scenario that the court has performed *ex officio* control, but not given the parties the chance to present their views about the unfair nature of the term(s) at issue and the consequences of a finding of unfairness.[950] In such a case, the AP in Barcelona held that the bank could not invoke the *res judicata* effect of a previous decision in enforcement proceedings against the consumer debtor who had not been heard. This would have been contrary to Article 24 of the Spanish Constitution and Article 47 of the Charter, as interpreted by the CJEU in *Banif Plus Bank*.[951]

The generative function of Article 47 in *Banif Plus Bank*[952] translates into national procedural law. Prior to *Banif Plus Bank*, there was no explicit provision for a right to be heard, in the procedures discussed in this chapter. In light of the decision in that case, however, the right to be heard must now be observed in all proceedings that concern potentially unfair contract terms, regardless of their privileged or expedited nature. It could be argued that the right to be heard is so fundamental that it does not stem from any legislative provisions, or from the case law of the CJEU.[953] Nevertheless, codification of the requirements following from Article 47 was deemed necessary by the Spanish legislature.[954] Ley 1/2013 and Ley 42/2015, which introduced *ex officio* control in general enforcement procedures and order for payment procedures, added a stipulation that if the court finds any potentially unfair terms, it will hear the parties within five days, and take a decision within another five days (see Articles 552.1 LEC and 815.4 LEC, respectively). Furthermore, the mortgage enforcement procedure was also amended: the enforcement must be suspended, and the parties summoned to be heard by the court within 15 days (Article 695.2 LEC).[955] It has even

[949] AP Valencia (Sección 6ª), order no. 255/2017 of 27 June 2017, JUR\2018\25068, ECLI:ES:APV:2017:3327A.

[950] AP Málaga (Sección 5ª), order no. 311/2015 of 12 November 2015, JUR\2016\84863.

[951] AP Barcelona (Sección 11ª), order no. 39/2019 of 6 February 2019, JUR\2019\49202, ECLI:ES:APB:2019:279A.

[952] Case C-472/11 *Banif Plus Bank*, discussed in subsection 3.5.2 of the preceding chapter.

[953] AP Málaga (Sección 5ª), order no. 335/2015 of 15 December 2015, JUR\2016\83571.

[954] The AP in Lleida found that it could not determine the procedural path that courts of first instance must follow on the basis of *Banif Plus Bank*, and that legislative changes implementing *Aziz* could not be anticipated: AP Lleida (Sección 2ª), order no. 55/2013 of 25 March 2013, JUR\2014\294266.

[955] Ley 8/2013, de rehabilitación, regeneración y renovación urbanas, BOE no. 153 of 27 June 2013, p. 6938.

been codified in Article 83(1) TR-LGDCU that the court must hear the parties when it finds that a contractual term is unfair (Ley 3/2014).

The prohibition of *indefensión* may be invoked by both consumers and traders.[956] If their rights to be heard are not observed, this is not only a formal defect, but also leads to substantive *indefensión*: the decision has been based on legal and factual elements that the parties have not been able to respond to.[957] This argument is often used successfully by traders, when seeking to have a decision repealed after one of their terms has been declared unfair.[958]

4.5.2. TRIBUNAL SUPREMO ON ARTICLE 47: A RECONCILIATORY APPROACH

Indefensión typically occurs when the court has awarded either more than has been claimed (*ultra petita*) or something other than that which has been claimed (*extra petita*), without giving the parties a chance to respond.[959] As a result, the parties' submissions and the court's decision are not aligned: there is *incongruencia*, i.e. no procedural congruence. As the case of *Aziz* shows, *incongruencia* does not necessarily mean that there is *indefensión*: both Mr. Aziz and the bank had (and made use of) actual opportunities to defend their rights.[960] In such a case, there is not necessarily a fundamental

956 AP Málaga (Sección 5ª), order no. 207/2016 of 15 June 2016, JUR\2016\240828.

957 AP Alicante (Sección 8ª), order no. 24/2018 of 12 March 2018, JUR\2018\162684, ECLI:ES:APA:2018:174A; AP Valencia (Sección 6ª), order no. 255/2017 of 27 June 2017, JUR\2018\25068, ECLI:ES:APV:2017:3327A; AP Málaga (Sección 5ª), order no. 335/2015 of 15 December 2015, JUR\2016\83571; AP Málaga (Sección 5ª), order no. 311/2015 of 12 November 2015, JUR\2016\84863. This does not go so far as to give the bank a separate opportunity to respond to the recalculation of amounts, where they have already been heard on the nullity of unfair terms: AP Málaga (Sección 5ª), order no. 207/2016 of 15 June 2016, JUR\2016\240828.

958 See, e.g. AP Las Palmas (Sección 5ª), order no. 207/2014 of 12 September 2014, JUR\2015\55184; AP Lleida (Sección 2ª), order no. 46/2015 of 9 March 2015, JUR\2015\121304; AP Lleida (Sección 2ª), order no. 158/2016 of 27 October 2016, JUR\2017\51706; AP Las Palmas (Sección 5ª), order no. 276/2017 of 17 October 2017, JUR\2018\123083, ECLI:ES:APGC:2017:504A; AP Alicante (Sección 8ª), order no. 24/2018 of 12 March 2018, JUR\2018\162684, ECLI:ES:APA:2018:174A (within the framework of an order for payment procedure); AP Barcelona (Sección 11ª), order no. 38/2019 of 6 February 2019, JUR\2019\49570, ECLI:ES:APB:2019:275A.

959 Pérez Daudí (n 32) 94–96. See, e.g. AP Vizcaya (Sección 5ª), judgment no. 250/2013 of 30 September 2013, JUR\2014\144762.

960 See also subsection 4.3.2 above.

rights violation if the decision is not entirely aligned.[961] *Incongruencia* may, nevertheless, constitute an infringement of Article 24 of the Constitution. It could be said, by analogy, that it also violates Article 47 of the Charter. In the words of the AP in Madrid:

> 'It cannot simply be held that … we proceed to declare some clauses unfair; that is, without facilitating a contentious debate and with a surprise decision, while we forget that Article 47 of the European Charter of Fundamental Rights also proclaims the right to effective judicial protection without producing *indefensión*'.[962]

The AP in Barcelona also read a requirement of procedural congruence into Article 47 of the Charter:

> 'In our view, it is inconceivable that the dispositive principle could be derogated from by the requirement of the effectiveness of EU law, because this principle also informs EU law through the Charter of Fundamental Rights, in particular the recognition of private property rights therein (Article 17), which includes the right to dispose of rights, and the right to the effective protection [of those rights] (Article 47), which includes the right of action. It also encompasses the right to a fair trial, which has, amongst its prerequisites, procedural congruence, and the right to be heard must be observed effectively'.[963]

The AP in Barcelona elaborated that there is a difference between initiating civil proceedings, which only the parties can do, and determining the object of the proceedings on the basis of the cause of action and the claim,

---

961 See, e.g. Tribunal Supremo (Sala de lo Civil), judgment no. 1916/2013 of 9 May 2013, ECLI:ES:TS:2013:1916, discussed below.

962 AP Madrid (Sección 10ª), order no. 452/2016 of 22 December 2016, JUR\2017\25699. Translated from the original Spanish text which reads, '*[N]o puede pretenderse, sin más, que … procedamos a declarar abusivas algunas cláusulas, id est, sin facilitar la contradicción procesal y con una respuesta sorprensiva, olvidando que también el artículo 47 de la Carta Europea de los Derechos Fundamentales proclama el derecho a la tutela judicial efectiva sin producción de indefensión.*'

963 AP Barcelona (Sección 15ª), judgment no. 407/2014 of 15 December 2014, JUR\2015\86196, para 26. Translated from the original Spanish text, which reads, '*Creemos que es inconcebible que el principio dispositivo pueda considerarse derogado por exigencia de la efectividad del derecho comunitario porque ese dispositivo o de la demanda informa también el derecho comunitario a través de la Carta de Derechos Fundamentales de la Unión Europea, y particularmente del reconocimiento en la misma del derecho de propiedad privada (artículo 17), que incluye el derecho de disponer de los derechos y del derecho a la tutela efectiva (artículo 47), que incluye el derecho de acción. Y también incluye el derecho a un proceso equitativo, que exige entre sus presupuestos que se trate de un proceso congruente y en el que se respete la contradicción efectiva.*'

which is a matter of interpretation for the court.[964] As long as there is a link between the clause(s) at issue and the claim and/or the parties' allegations, the assessment of unfairness and declaration of nullity are within the ambit of the dispute.[965] The AP in Barcelona's approach can be seen as an attempt to reconcile the rigidities of civil procedure with the requirements of effective consumer protection under the UCTD. It aims to resolve, by reference to the parties' rights to be heard, the (perceived) tension between *ex officio* control and procedural congruence. Article 47 of the Charter fulfils a *reconciliatory function*, whereby it operates as a hinge between EU and national exigencies.[966] Indeed, it could be argued that there is no conflict at all, as long as the parties get their 'day in court': both parties have the opportunity to present their views, and adapt their arguments, if necessary, and the court's decision can, subsequently, be based on the parties' submissions.[967]

Another example of how Article 47 has been used to reconcile a more active role of the court with traditional features of civil procedure can be found in the judgment of the Tribunal Supremo of 9 May 2013 on so-called *cláusulas suelo* (floor clauses). The Tribunal Supremo gave this judgment in a collective action brought by the Asociación de Usuarios de los Servicios Bancarios (AUSBANC) against four Spanish banks.[968]

> *Cláusulas suelo*, which were widely used by credit providers in Spain in their standard terms and conditions, establish a minimum rate below which the variable interest rate cannot fall (usually 2.75–4 per cent). The Tribunal Supremo

964 Judgment of AP Barcelona (n 843), paras. 30–31.

965 Judgment of AP Barcelona (n 843), paras. 39 and 41. One of the judges argued, in a concurring opinion, that the bank's allegation of *incongruencia* was not relevant, because the *ex officio* obligation of the court to protect consumers against unfair terms was mandatory and part of public policy, and so it applied regardless of the consumer's position in the proceedings.

966 The term 'reconciliatory approach' is derived from Schebesta (n 253) 862. See also Bech Serrat (n 251) 12. In the words of Schebesta, 'Rather than framing an issue as a conflict between European and national exigencies, it creates an overlap, a fiction, of a single norm expressed on both levels.' Other authors have also used the term 'reconcile' in respect of competing demands of EU and national law: see, e.g. Wilman (n 68) 935; Van Gerven (n 10) 530.

967 Carrasco Perera and González Carrasco (n 678) 150–152. See also Jordi Nieva Fenoll, 'La actuación de oficio del juez nacional europeo' [2017] Justicia 181, 204–205. The AP in Malaga found that there would be no *indefensión* as long as its decision was based on the parties' submissions: AP Málaga (Sección 6ª), order no. 182/2016 of 16 March 2016, AC/2016/1219.

968 Tribunal Supremo (Sala de lo Civil), judgment no. 1916/2013 of 9 May 2013, ECLI:ES:TS:2013:1916.

> found that *cláusulas suelo* in themselves were lawful, but it formulated a list of six circumstances in which those clauses could be unfair for lack of transparency.[969] The Tribunal Supremo ordered the defendant banks to eliminate those clauses from their contracts concluded with consumers. However, the Tribunal Supremo also held that a finding of invalidity did not have retroactive effect: neither judicial decisions with the force of *res judicata* were affected, nor payments that had been made before the judgment was published. Thus, consumers could only claim restitution of amounts overpaid *after* the date of publication of the judgment. This constituted a temporal limitation of the right to full restitution under Spanish law (see, in particular, Article 1303 of the Código Civil). One of the considerations of the Tribunal Supremo was that retroactive effect would give rise to serious economic repercussions; *cláusulas suelo* were widespread and their use had been tolerated for a long time.[970] The CJEU held on 21 December 2016 that Articles 6 and 7 UCTD precluded the adoption of such a temporal limitation in national case law.[971]

In its judgment of 9 May 2013, the Tribunal Supremo cited *Banif Plus Bank* and referred to Article 47 of the Charter, in respect of the principle of *audi alteram partem*.[972] It stressed the need for coordination between the duty to guarantee the effectiveness of the UCTD, on the one hand, and procedural congruence, on the other, by means of facilitating the parties to exercise their rights to be heard in the course of the proceedings.[973] In the words of the Tribunal Supremo:

> 'In so far as it is necessary to achieve the effectiveness of EU law in unfair terms cases, the courts must temper the classic rigidities of civil procedure in such a way that, in the analysis of the potentially unfair nature of the clauses that may be declared null and void, the formal structure of recourses need not be adjusted. The ruling need not be adjusted exactly to the claim either, provided that the parties have had the chance to be heard on the arguments that determine the qualification of the clauses as unfair'.[974]

---

969 See further Francesco de Elizalde, 'The Rain in Spain Does Not Stay in the Plain – Or How the Spanish Supreme Court Ruling of 25 March 2015, on Minimum Interest Rate Clauses, affects European Consumers' [2015] Journal of European Consumer and Market Law 184.

970 See also Joined Cases C-154/15, C-307/15 and C-208/15 *Gutiérrez Naranjo*, para. 24.

971 Joined Cases C-154/15, C-307/15 and C-208/15 *Gutiérrez Naranjo*, para. 75.

972 Tribunal Supremo (Sala de lo Civil), judgment no. 1916/2013 of 9 May 2013, ECLI:ES:TS:2013:1916.

973 See also AP Valencia (Sección 11ª), judgment no. 586/2013 of 30 December 2013, AC\2014\415; AP Guipúzcoa (Sección 3ª), judgment no. 292/2016 of 1 December 2016, JUR\2017\64956.

974 Judgment of the Tribunal Supremo (n 972), para. 130. Translated from the original Spanish text, which reads, '*[E]n la medida en que sea necesario para lograr la eficacia*

Ironically, it has been argued that *indefensión* occurred in the *AUSBANC* case when it was before the Tribunal Supremo, because the claim was awarded on grounds that had not been part of the debate between the parties – in short, the lack of transparency of *cláusulas suelo*.[975]

The same reconciliatory approach has been followed by most Spanish civil courts.[976] Only a few courts have seen the right to be heard as a limitation of the duty of *ex officio* control.[977] Most have seen it as a precondition to being able to adjudicate the case on the merits. The notion of adversarial or contentious proceedings forms part of a fair trial; it means that the parties must be able to present their views on all elements of fact and law on which the court's decision will be based.[978] Some courts have referred to Article 47 to emphasise the consumer's autonomy: it is ultimately the consumer who decides whether the term at issue should be declared unfair or not.[979]

The introduction of an (extra) opportunity for the parties to present their views in respect of unfair terms has made the above-mentioned expedited procedures slightly more adversarial. This has met with criticism,

---

del Derecho de la Unión, en los supuestos de cláusulas abusivas, los tribunales deban atemperar las clásicas rigideces del proceso, de tal forma que, en el análisis de la eventual abusividad de las cláusulas cuya declaración de nulidad fue interesada, no es preciso que nos ajustemos formalmente a la estructura de los recursos. Tampoco es preciso que el fallo se ajuste exactamente al suplico de la demanda, siempre que las partes hayan tenido la oportunidad de ser oídas sobre los argumentos determinantes de la calificación de las cláusulas como abusivas.'

975 Carrasco Perera and González Carrasco (n 678) 148ff.

976 See, e.g. AP Valencia (Sección 6ª), judgment no. 53/2016 of 2 February 2016, JUR\2016\145999; AP Vizcaya (Sección 5ª), judgment no. 250/2013 of 30 September 2013, JUR\2014\144762; AP Guipúzcoa (Sección 3ª), judgment no. 292/2016 of 1 December 2016, JUR\2017\64956; AP Las Palmas (Sección 5ª), order no. 6/2016 of 11 January 2016, JUR\2016\65926; AP Valencia (Sección 11ª), judgment no. 586/2013 of 30 December 2013, AC/2014/415.

977 See, e.g. AP Málaga (Sección 6ª), order no. 182/2016 of 16 March 2016, AC/2016/1219, with reference to *Banif Plus Bank* and Article 47 of the Charter; AP Alicante (Sección 8ª), judgment no. 295/2016 of 28 October 2016, JUR\2016\265901.

978 AP Madrid (Sección 14ª), order no. 33/2015 of 18 February 2015, JUR\2015\100490; AP Valencia (Sección 11ª), judgment no. 586/2013 of 30 December 2013, AC/2014/415; AP Barcelona (Sección 1ª), judgment no. 104/2016 of 11 March 2016, JUR\2016\120913; AP Barcelona (Sección 11ª), order no. 48/2014 of 20 March 2014, JUR\2014\296437; AP Santa Cruz de Tenerife (Sección 1ª), order no. 171/2013 of 17 December 2013, JUR\2015\9254; AP Alicante (Sección 8ª), judgment no. 295/2016 of 28 October 2016, JUR\2016\265901.

979 See, e.g. AP Almería (Sección 1ª), order no. 154/2017 of 30 March 2017, JUR\2018\200420, ECLI:ES:APAL:2017:679A; AP Almería (Sección 1ª), order no. 426/2017 of 25 September 2017, JUR\2018\200338, ECLI:ES:APAL:2017:727A.

because it has fundamentally changed the nature of these procedures.[980] However, it has also been welcomed, because it allows the court to align its decision with the parties' submissions by hearing them first; it is about giving due regard to the parties' positions rather than limiting the court's power to raise new factual or legal grounds.[981] In this respect, Article 47 of the Charter may be seen as the counterpart of *ex officio* control. Both lead to a more balanced procedure in unfair terms cases:[982] consumer rights under the UCTD are protected, alongside the parties' rights of defence. The prohibition of *indefensión*, which can be read into Article 47, justifies an active court that facilitates the litigating parties. This can be seen as a form of open constitutionalisation: it shows how Article 47 may be used to open up rigid or restrictive rules with due regard for the principles underpinning civil procedure.

4.5.3. THE OTHER SIDE OF ARTICLE 47: THE *CLÁUSULAS SUELO* SAGA

4.5.3.1. Third-Party Effects of a Collective Action

The notion of *indefensión* has internal and external aspects: internal, in the sense that *indefensión* must be prevented within the process; and external, in the sense that an extension of the effects of a decision to third parties who have not participated in the process may amount to *indefensión*. An example of the latter can be found in one of the cases that resulted in the CJEU's *Irles López* judgment of 21 December 2016 on *cláusulas suelo*, where a question was posed on Article 47 of the Charter.[983] This touches on the relevance of collective actions for individual actions regarding the same subject matter. Questions have also been raised as to the *res judicata* effect of judicial decisions given before 21 December 2016 that run counter to the judgment of the CJEU. The cases discussed in this subsection reveal the other side (*altera parte*) of Article 47: it can be used as an argument for the judicial protection of traders, which may create tension with the Directive's full effectiveness, and the rights of individual consumers.

---

980 See also subsections 4.2.3 and 4.3.3 above.

981 AP Vizcaya (Sección 5ª), judgment no. 250/2013 of 30 September 2013, JUR\2014\144762.

982 AP Guipúzcoa (Sección 3ª), judgment no. 292/2016 of 1 December 2016, JUR\2017\64956, para. 130.

983 Case C-305/18 *Irles López* (part of the CJEU's judgment in Joined Cases C-154/15, C-307/15 and C-308/15 *Gutiérrez Naranjo*).

The Tribunal Supremo judgment of 9 May 2013 in the *AUSBANC* case was positive for consumers in so far as it declared *cláusulas suelo* to be unfair, in certain circumstances. However, the judgment also contained a temporal limitation that restricted the right to full restitution of interest paid after 9 May 2013. The referring court in *Irles López* questioned whether this limitation could also be extended to individual actions, with regard to Article 47 of the Charter.[984] On 25 March 2015, the Tribunal Supremo held that such an extension was, indeed, possible.[985] A similar link between collective and individual actions was assumed with regard to a different collective action, brought by the Asociación de Usuarios de Bancos Cajas y Seguros de España (ADICAE) against 72 financial institutions, seeking an injunction prohibiting the continued use of *cláusulas suelo*.[986] Several courts decided to stay proceedings brought by individual consumers against the same financial institutions, pending the outcome of the *ADICAE* case.[987] This gave rise to concerns as to the effective judicial protection of consumers. Collective actions are an exception to the rule that litigants can invoke only their own subjective rights and legitimate interests in court, not those of others.[988] The effects of a decision in a collective action may be extended to individual consumers who were not a party to those proceedings, to the extent that it may benefit them.[989] However, the temporal limitation at issue here was detrimental to consumers.

Therefore, the question of the referring court – the AP in Alicante – in *Irles López* was whether the temporal limitation of the restitutory effects of a finding of unfairness of *cláusulas suelo* could automatically be extended to individual actions. The financial institutions alleged that such an extension was possible, and the Tribunal Supremo confirmed this in its above-mentioned judgment of 25 March 2015. The AP in Alicante, nevertheless, had doubts as to the compatibility of the case law of the

---

984 AP Alicante (Sección 8ª), order of 15 June 2015 in case 661/2013, JUR\2015\190491, para. 91.

985 Tribunal Supremo (Sala de lo Civil), judgment no. 1280/2015 of 25 March 2015, ECLI:ES:TS:2015:1280.

986 This ultimately resulted in a judgment of the Juzgado de lo Mercantil nº 11 de Madrid, judgment no. 53/2016 of 7 April 2016, ECLI:ES:JMM:2016:53.

987 Pérez Daudí (n 32) 119, 122–123.

988 Judgment of Tribunal Supremo in *AUSBANC* (n 968), para. 57. On the role of consumer associations and collective redress in the Spanish legal system, see further Maria Teresa Alonso Pérez, Francesco de Elizalde and Regina Garcimartín Montero, 'An Interdisciplinary View of Enforcement and Effectiveness of Spanish Consumer Law' in Geneviève Saumier and Hans-W Micklitz (eds), *Enforcement and Effectiveness of Consumer Law* (Springer 2018) 600–601, 605–608.

989 Case C-472/10 *Invitel*.

Tribunal Supremo with Article 47 of the Charter. It considered that the effectiveness of the collective action did not justify a limitation that would be to the detriment of the rights of third parties: in this case, consumers.[990] In so far as a judicial decision might affect parties that were not involved in the proceedings leading up to it, concerns as to *indefensión* may arise. The CJEU did not answer the question, presumably because it had already quashed the temporal limitation in its judgment of 21 December 2016.[991]

After the CJEU judgment, the Tribunal Supremo reversed its case law and held that its judgment of 9 May 2013 did not produce substantive *res judicata* effect for individual consumers.[992] The reason for this was that the individual consumers were not parties to the collective action, and that the objective and the effects of a collective action were different from those of an individual action. The Tribunal Supremo adhered to the list of circumstances that rendered *cláusulas suelo* unfair. Financial institutions can still allege, in a concrete case, that a *cláusula suelo* was not unfair. The AP in Pontevedra has held it would be contrary to the principle of equality of arms if the creditor did not have this possibility, with reference to *Banif Plus Bank*.[993]

Moreover, the AP in Leon has found that, if the creditor appeals a finding of unfairness, the Court of Appeal cannot quash a temporal limitation *ex officio*. This would follow from the so-called prohibition of *reformatio in peius*, a mandatory norm of procedural law which entails that an appeal cannot put the appellant – in this case, the creditor – in a worse position (Article 465.6 LEC).[994] According to the AP in Leon, it could not revise a decision at first instance to the detriment of the appellant bank, because the consumer had not challenged the temporal limitation in appeal. *Banif Plus Bank* merely required courts to inform consumers of their rights and observe the adversarial principle.[995] Later, the AP in Leon clarified that, in

990 AP Alicante (Sección 8ª), order of 15 June 2015 in case 661/2013, JUR\2015\190491, para. 92.

991 Joined Cases C-154/15, C-307/15 and C-308/15 *Gutiérrez Naranjo*, para. 76.

992 See, e.g. Tribunal Supremo (Sala de lo Civil), judgment no. 477/2017 of 24 February 2017, ECLI:ES:TS:2017:477; Tribunal Supremo (Sala de lo Civil), judgment no. 3028/207 of 20 July 2017, ECLI:TS:2017:3028.

993 AP Pontevedra (Sección 1ª), judgment no. 568/2016 of 12 December 2016, JUR\2017\8971.

994 AP León (Sección 1ª), judgment no. 446/2017 of 19 December 2017, JUR\2018\38156, ECLI:ES:APLE:2017:1270.

995 See also, and more in depth, AP León (Sección 1ª), judgment no. 346/2017 of 13 October 2017, JUR\2018\277847, ECLI:ES:APLE:2017:998.

contentious proceedings, the court cannot take decisions for consumers when they present their case: it is not the court's task to be inquisitorial and/or specify the grounds of appeal.[996] This view reflects the rigidity of Spanish civil procedure and the divide between proceedings at first and second instances.

According to the Tribunal Supremo, disregarding the prohibition of *reformatio in peius* in favour of the *ex officio* application of EU law would be contrary to the right to effective judicial protection, as guaranteed by Article 24 of the Spanish Constitution and Article 47 of the Charter.[997] This is another example of a traditional principle of civil procedure being defended by reference to Article 47,[998] without properly considering or justifying the negative consequences for the effective judicial protection of individual consumer rights. It seems arbitrary that *ex officio* control in appeals should depend on which party loses at first instance. The question of whether this interpretation of the prohibition of *reformatio in peius* is reconcilable with the UCTD is currently pending before the CJEU.

4.5.3.2. Res Judicata *Effect of Decisions Predating the CJEU Judgment on* Cláusulas Suelo

Since *Sales Sinués*, it has been clear that collective actions for an injunction have a different purpose and character from individual actions for compensation or restitution.[999] According to the CJEU, the need to ensure consistency between judicial decisions does not justify a stay of individual actions pending a collective action. The Tribunal Constitucional has, subsequently, held that, from a constitutional perspective, there is no obligation to stay individual actions with a view to individual rights protection. It would hamper the effective exercise of consumer rights to

996 AP León (Sección 1ª), judgment no. 308/2017 of 23 July 2018, JUR\2018\282480, ECLI:ES:APLE:2018:891; AP León (Sección 1ª), judgment no. 344/2018 of 26 September 2018, JUR\2018\302054, ECLI:ES:APLE:2018:982.

997 Case C-869/19 *L v Unicaja Banco* (pending).

998 See also AP Barcelona (Sección 15ª), judgment no. 407/2014 of 15 December 2014, JUR\2015\86196 on *res judicata* and the dispositive principle (cited in sections 4.4.3 and 4.5.2 above); AP Madrid (Sección 10ª), order no. 452/2016 of 22 December 2016, JUR\2017\25699 on procedural congruence (cited in section 4.5.2).

999 Joined Cases C-381/14 and C-385/14 *Sales Sinués*. On this topic, see also Fabrizio Cafaggi and Stephanie Law, 'Unfair Contract Terms – Effect of Collective Proceedings' in Evelyne Terryn, Gert Straetmans and Veerle Colaert (eds), *Landmark Cases of EU Consumer Law: In Honour of Jules Stuyck* (Intersentia 2013) 659.

impose the outcome of a collective action on individual consumers; this could even be contrary to Article 24 of the Constitution.[1000]

In many individual cases where the proceedings were not stayed, a final and binding decision was given prior to the CJEU judgment of 21 December 2016 with respect to the temporal limitation. This gave rise to the question as to whether the *res judicata* effect of such a decision undermined the effective judicial protection of the consumers involved; in a sense, they had been punished for having brought a claim early on. It has been argued that this runs counter to Article 47 of the Charter, and that respecting the *res judicata* effect of such decisions undermines the effective judicial protection of consumers under the UCTD.[1001]

The balance between the principle of *res judicata* and the effective judicial protection of consumers under the UCTD is unclear. The CJEU has held that national courts are not required to disregard national procedural rules conferring finality on judicial decisions, even if those decisions would violate EU law.[1002] That being said, the CJEU has ruled several times on the scope of *res judicata*, inter alia in *Banco Primus*.[1003] Moreover, the CJEU held in *Finanmadrid* that the mere fact that the consumer had not challenged the claim (in time) did not justify the absence of judicial control.[1004] Thus, the effectiveness of the UCTD warranted an exception to the principle of *res judicata*.

The question was whether consumers who had already obtained final decisions in their cases could still claim full restitution (i.e. of amounts paid before and after 9 May 2013), or whether the decision's (formal and substantive) *res judicata* effect prevented this. This question pertained to the situation where the court had found the *cláusula suelo* to be unfair, but had applied the temporal limitation, as promulgated by the Tribunal Supremo. There had been neither *indefensión* nor inertia on the part of the consumer; on the contrary, the consumer had, proactively, brought a claim for restitution. Thus, *Banco Primus* and *Finanmadrid* were of little help here. This, paradoxically, meant that a consumer who did not make use

---

[1000] Tribunal Constitucional, judgment no. 148/2016 of 19 September 2016, ECLI:ES:TC:2016:148. See further Pérez Daudí (n 32) 124–125; Cordon Moreno (n 854).

[1001] Bech Serrat (n 251) 13, 54. See also AP Madrid (Sección 10ª), order no. 101/2016 of 17 March 2016, JUR\2016\89139; AP Álava (Sección 1ª), judgment no. 110/2017 of 6 March 2017, JUR\2017\135437.

[1002] See, e.g. Joined Cases C-154/15, C-307/15 and C-308/15 EU *Gutiérrez Naranjo*, para. 68.

[1003] Case C-421/14 *Banco Primus*, discussed in subsection 4.4.3 above.

[1004] Case C-49/14 *Finanmadrid*, para. 54.

of an opportunity to assert their rights derived from the UCTD would be better off than a consumer who did so, and consequently found themselves bound by a decision with *res judicata* effect.[1005]

The Tribunal Supremo has held that the *res judicata* effect of judicial decisions given before 21 December 2016 must be respected.[1006] A new CJEU judgment is not a ground for revision under Spanish law,[1007] and, according to the prevailing doctrine in Spain, it does not constitute a new ground for setting aside *res judicata*.[1008] However, in so far as civil procedure has a compensatory function, this – together with Article 47 of the Charter – may warrant a more flexible approach towards *res judicata*.[1009] The formal *res judicata* effect of the decision could be left intact; only its substantive *res judicata* effect would need to be disregarded when a new claim is brought.[1010] The reason for this would be that consumers should not be punished for courts failing to take proper account of EU law. Decisions being given while the compatibility of the temporal limitation with EU law was debatable, and/or proceedings not being stayed pending the preliminary reference before the CJEU, could be seen as violations of consumers' right to effective judicial protection.[1011] As Rott has observed, the trader's expectations of getting away with a breach of EU consumer law can hardly be classified as legitimate and worthy of protection.[1012]

1005 See, e.g. AP León (Sección 1ª), judgment no. 192/2017 of 19 May 2017, JUR\2017\171244, ECLI:ES:APLE:2017:536 for a strict interpretation.

1006 Tribunal Supremo (Sala de lo Civil), order no. 2684/2017 of 4 April 2017, ECLI:ES:TS:2017:2684A.

1007 See Article 510 LEC and Article 5bis LOPJ.

1008 See also Pérez Daudí (n 32) 110–111, 140.

1009 Bech Serrat (n 251) 37, 55.

1010 Pérez Daudí (n 32) 116. See also Jesús Sánchez García, 'Efectos procesales y sustantivos derivados de la sentencia del Tribunal de Justicia de la Unión Europea de 21 de diciembre de 2016' [2017] Revista de Derecho vLex.

1011 Pérez Daudí (n 32) 146. See, for a different view, AP Lleida (Sección 2ª), order no. 55/2013 of 25 March 2013, JUR\2014\294266. According to the AP in Lleida, there was no legal basis to suspend enforcement proceedings while awaiting the CJEU's decision in *Aziz*.

1012 Rott (n 98) 198. In the wake of the *cláusulas suelo* saga, Real Decreto 1/2017 de medidas urgentes de protección de consumidores en materia de cláusulas suelo (BOE no. 18 of 21 January 2017, p. 5379) was adopted to facilitate the out-of-court settlement of consumer claims. However, more than half of those claims have been declared inadmissible, or been dismissed by the financial institutions in question: Aguilera Morales, '¿Es válida la cláusula de renuncia de acciones predispuesta frente al consumidor?' (n 805) 26. Aguilera Morales addresses a follow-up issue, namely whether a clause that stipulates the consumer has relinquished the right to bring an action is valid.

4.6. INTERIM CONCLUSION: THE ROLE OF ARTICLE 47 IN SPANISH CASE LAW

In Spanish unfair terms cases, courts mainly refer to Article 47 of the Charter as part of a broader reference to CJEU case law, which is used to justify a certain interpretation of procedural rules, for example suspension of mortgage enforcement proceedings until a decision is taken in the declaratory proceedings, or to explain why rules have been changed, for example the introduction of a possibility of appeal for consumer debtors. For Spanish civil courts, a reference to Article 47, read in conjunction with the UCTD, appears to be one possible avenue for expanding consumers' procedural rights, creating more space for judicial intervention, and triggering legislative reforms to that effect. In this respect, it may fulfil not only a strengthening or empowering function, but also a signalling and even a transformative function – with some important delimitations.

In *Sánchez Morcillo* and *Finanmadrid*, Article 47 was used to signal systemic issues: a procedural inequality in mortgage enforcement proceedings, and a delegation of judicial functions in the order for payment procedure, respectively. Both cases had a constitutional dimension; they concerned the justiciability of consumer rights and the availability of a remedy for procedural breaches. Effective judicial protection cannot be guaranteed if the ambit of the dispute is too limited and/or the courts are sidelined completely. In *Sánchez Morcillo*, the Tribunal Constitucional's views on access to court and the system of recourse in appeal were perceived to be too narrow, in light of the imbalance between the parties, both substantively and procedurally. In a way, the CJEU has taken up a role that the Tribunal Constitucional would not fulfil, although *Sánchez Morcillo II* shows the limits of how far the CJEU is able or willing to go. Article 47's accessory character is not its only constraint: even though it authorises national civil courts to set aside legislative provisions, or to go against their own Supreme Court, it is unlikely they will do so without backup from the Tribunal Constitucional, or the CJEU itself.

The case law analysed in this chapter, nevertheless, shows that Article 47 transcends both the UCTD's effectiveness and *ex officio* control of unfair terms. Whereas the CJEU in *Finanmadrid* did not engage with the constitutional dimension at all, and strictly adhered to the question of whether unfair terms control was possible at some stage of the proceedings, the referring court had also questioned whether court registrars could exercise an adjudicative function, in the first place. Moreover, at case level, there seemed to be a potential situation of *indefensión* under Article 24 of the Spanish Constitution, i.e. a violation of the rights of the defence, which could also run counter to Article 47 of the Charter.

The prohibition of *indefensión* has another component: the court's decision must align with the parties' submissions. The parties must get an opportunity to present their views, and the court must take those views into account. In the expedited procedures discussed in this chapter, tension becomes visible between a more active role for the court, on the one hand, and party autonomy, procedural economy and legal certainty (procedural congruence and *res judicata*), on the other. In the event of a (perceived) conflict, Article 47 may fulfil a reconciliatory function. Observance of the parties' rights to be heard is a way to avoid *indefensión*, and to ensure a more balanced procedure. However, a few cases have been discussed in which Article 47 was invoked to tip the balance back to the side of traders.

The analysed case law reveals the boundaries of Article 47 as an interpretive or explanatory tool. For every decision that gives a broad interpretation of the applicable procedural rules, there is another that interprets the same rules in a restrictive manner. And, even in case of a broad interpretation, consumers may find themselves without an effective remedy in practice, like Mr. Aziz. The clash between those courts adhering to a strict application of the law and those attempting to expand the scope for judicial intervention provides another explanation for the continuous stream of preliminary references from Spain.

Moreover, the different legislative solutions chosen for different types of procedures reveal the 'patchwork' nature of the LEC in general: it does not provide a comprehensive framework for the adjudication of consumer cases. There does not appear to be much room for Spanish civil courts to interpret the law in a consumer-friendly spirit: the empowering function of Article 47 is, apparently, not strong enough to change that.

CHAPTER 5

ARTICLE 47 IN UNFAIR TERMS CASES IN THE NETHERLANDS

This chapter examines the role of Article 47 of the Charter in Dutch unfair terms cases. The number of references to Article 47 by civil courts in the Netherlands is low compared to Spain. This does not mean that effective judicial protection is not an issue. The CJEU's case law on the UCTD has given rise to various procedural questions, in particular as to the implementation of the *ex officio* doctrine. This chapter starts with an overview of these questions, as well as possible explanations for the low number of references to Article 47 by Dutch civil courts (section 5.1). It then proceeds with an analysis of the few unfair terms cases where an explicit reference to Article 47 has been made (section 5.2). These cases reveal both a signalling and a rhetorical function of Article 47: they show the courts' awareness of the fundamental rights at stake and the persuasive authority of Article 47, especially in respect of norms with a protective purpose. Several cases concern the level and scope of judicial protection in unfair terms cases; these give a broad interpretation of available remedies, but do not mention Article 47 (section 5.3).

Furthermore, parallels can be drawn between Dutch and Spanish cases on the role of courts of appeal: these cases include, inter alia, *Asbeek Brusse* – until recently the only Dutch preliminary reference on the UCTD – and *Sánchez Morcillo*, one of the key judgments on Article 47 read in conjunction with the UCTD (section 5.4). Finally, the impact of Article 47 of the Charter via *Banif Plus Bank* and *Asbeek Brusse*, in respect of the right to be heard, is discussed (section 5.5).

5.1. BACKGROUND: A LIMITED ROLE OF ARTICLE 47 IN DUTCH UNFAIR TERMS CASES

5.1.1. IMPACT OF THE UCTD ON DUTCH CIVIL PROCEDURE

Consumer protection is considered to be a socio-economic component of Dutch private law, which mostly finds its expression in substantive rules of contract law. It has been linked to the notion of compensation for inequality between the parties (*ongelijkheidscompensatie*),[1013] which, in Dutch legal literature, is often referred to in the areas of labour law and administrative (procedural) law. The 1992 Civil Code (Burgerlijk Wetboek or BW) introduced an open norm containing a test for standard contract terms and conditions (Article 6:233 BW, which refers to terms that are 'unreasonably burdensome' or 'excessively onerous'). The debate has largely been concentrated on the interpretation and application of this open norm, in light of the UCTD. An unfair term can be declared null and void (unenforceable or non-binding); the Supreme Court of the Netherlands (Hoge Raad) has also confirmed that such a term may be annulled by courts, of their own motion.[1014] Furthermore, there is a 'blacklist' of specific clauses in consumer contracts that are deemed to be unfair (Article 6:236 BW), and a 'grey list' of clauses that are presumed to be unfair unless proven otherwise (Article 6:237 BW).

The Dutch legislator has been criticised for half-hearted or indecisive drafting when implementing EU consumer law, leaving it entirely up to the courts to interpret and apply the law.[1015] The CJEU's case law has not

---

1013 Jac Rinkes, 'Ontwikkelingen in het consumentenrecht' [2009] Contracteren 56, 57; Ruth de Bock, *Tussen waarheid en onzekerheid: Over het vaststellen van feiten in de civiele procedure* (Kluwer 2011) 124; Jan Biemans and Alex Geert Castermans, *Barmhartigheid in het burgerlijk recht. Bespiegelingen over de grenzen aan kredietverlening en een bijdrage aan het behoud van bestaanszekerheid* (Uitgeverij Paris 2017) 21, 90.

1014 Hoge Raad, judgment of 13 September 2013, ECLI:NL:HR:2013:691, NJ 2014, 274 m.nt. HB Krans (*Heesakkers/Voets*), para. 3.7.3. In his case note, Krans refers to a special 'European' application of the ground for annulment in Article 6:233 BW.

1015 Roland de Moor, 'Procesrechtelijke beschouwingen van de tweede gratis-mobieltjes-uitspraak van de Hoge Raad' [2016] Tijdschrift voor Consumentenrecht en handelspraktijken 232, 232–233. See also Charlotte Pavillon, *Open normen in het Europees consumentenrecht. De oneerlijkheidsnorm in vergelijkend perspectief* (Kluwer 2011) 2–3. In Case C-144/99 *Commission of the European Communities v Kingdom of the Netherlands*, the CJEU found that the UCTD had not been fully transposed into Dutch law. A settled judicial interpretation of legislative provisions that are not

been codified in the Netherlands; no amendments have been made to the Dutch Code of Civil Procedure (Wetboek van Burgerlijke Rechtsvordering or Rv) so far. It is up to the judiciary to implement the *ex officio* doctrine ('*ambtshalve toetsing*') in practice, but until 2013 the Hoge Raad did not provide much guidance either.[1016] In 2010, a report was published by a special working group of the National Consultation Committee on Civil Law of the District and Subdistrict Courts (Landelijk overleg vakinhoud civiel en kanton van de rechtbanken or LOVCK), containing detailed guidelines for the *ex officio* application of EU consumer law, in particular the UCTD, by lower courts. Second and third versions of the LOVCK Report were published in 2014 and 2018, respectively.[1017] The Report, in its various versions, was intended to formulate a common judicial position, but it has not been endorsed by appellate courts, and the Hoge Raad is silent about its status. Nevertheless, the Report is said to have contributed to a 'culture shift' in the adjudication of consumer cases.[1018] It contains recommendations to all lower courts dealing with consumer cases, with extensive references to CJEU case law on the UCTD. While the Report, thus, facilitates judicial protection in unfair terms cases, it does not expressly mention the Charter.

The reception of the *ex officio* doctrine in the Netherlands has already been discussed, in detail, by other scholars.[1019] For the purposes of this book, only the key judgments on the role of Dutch civil courts in unfair terms cases will be mentioned.

---

precise and clear enough is not sufficient to attain the results envisaged by the Directive (paras. 20–21).

1016 See, e.g. Pavillon (n 1015) 135. There are no specific provisions for consumers in the Dutch Code of Civil Procedure, with a few exceptions concerning competence (Article 101 Rv) and forum choice (Article 108 Rv).

1017 The Report's full title is *Ambtshalve toetsing III. Herzien rapport van de LOVCK&T redactieraad*, May 2018. The report will hereinafter be referred to as '2018 LOVCK Report'. It can be found (in Dutch) at <https://www.rechtspraak.nl/SiteCollection Documents/rapport-at-III-31-juli-2018.pdf> (last accessed 19 October 2021).

1018 Opinion of AG Valk of 12 July 2019, ECLI:NL:PHR:2019:769 (StAR), point 3.16. See also Alain Ancery and Bart Krans, 'Consumer Protection and EU-Driven Judicial Activism in the Netherlands' in Anna Nylund and Magne Strandberg (eds), *Civil Procedure and Harmonisation of Law* (Intersentia 2019) 126, 136–137.

1019 See, e.g. Ancery (n 32); Arthur Hartkamp, '*Ex Officio* Application in Case of Unenforceable Contracts or Contract Clauses: EU Law and National Laws Confronted' in Louise Gullifer and Stefan Vogenauer (eds), *English and European Perspectives on Contract and Commercial Law, Essays in Honour of Hugh Beale* (Hart Publishing 2014); Ewoud Hondius, 'Unfair Contract Terms and the Consumer: ECJ Case Law, Foreign Literature, and Their Impact on Dutch Law' [2016] European Review of Private Law 457.

In *Heesakkers/Voets* (2013), a leading judgment following the CJEU's judgment in *Asbeek Brusse*,[1020] the Hoge Raad provided guidance for the interpretation of Dutch law in a manner consistent with the CJEU's case law on the UCTD. The judgment predates most CJEU references to Article 47 of the Charter, but, like the LOVCK Report, it addresses the ways in which Dutch civil courts must ensure effective judicial protection under the UCTD. The case revolved around three main procedural issues: the scope for *ex officio* control of unfair terms in, firstly, appeal proceedings and, secondly, default proceedings, where the role of the court is usually more limited, as well as the powers of the court to gather information. Voets, who had been contracted by Heesakkers to carry out construction work in his home, brought a claim for payment of an outstanding amount, plus contractual interest. The claim was awarded in Voets' favour, both at first instance, and on appeal. On appeal before the Hoge Raad, Heesakkers no longer contested Voets' main claim, but he complained that the Court of Appeal (Gerechtshof) had granted contractual interest without performing unfair terms control *ex officio*: the interest clause had not been challenged in the appeal before the Gerechtshof. In short, the Hoge Raad held that the duty of *ex officio* control did apply in appeal proceedings, where the court is competent to examine compliance with national rules of public policy; Article 6 of the UCTD is considered to be equivalent to such rules.[1021] The same applies in default proceedings. If the necessary factual and legal information is available for the court to suspect that a clause may fall within the scope of the UCTD, and, therefore, be unfair, the court must investigate this, even if it has not been brought up by any of the parties themselves. The court must take the measures of inquiry that are needed to ensure the full effectiveness of the UCTD.[1022] The court must also observe the principle of *audi alteram partem* and allow the parties to further specify or amend their positions.[1023] If the court finds a term to be unfair, it must annul the term *ex officio*, unless the consumer opposes the term's inapplicability.

The *ex officio* doctrine has an impact on other procedural issues, such as evidence and the burden of proof. In 2012, the Hoge Raad held

1020 Case C-488/11 *Asbeek Brusse*; see further subsection 5.4.1 below.

1021 Hoge Raad, judgment of 13 September 2013, ECLI:NL:HR:2013:691 (*Heesakkers/Voets*), paras. 3.6.3, 3.9.2 and 3.6.1. See also Madeleine van Rossum and Emma van der Minne, 'De (on)mogelijkheid van ambtshalve toetsing van het Unierecht in hoger beroep' [2017] Tijdschrift voor de Procespraktijk 98, 101.

1022 Judgment of Hoge Raad (n 1021), para. 3.9.1. See also Hoge Raad 10 July 2015, ECLI:NL:HR:2015:1866, para. 3.7.

1023 Judgment of Hoge Raad (n 1021), para. 3.9.2. See further section 5.5 below.

that, in principle, it is the consumer who must invoke, and if necessary prove, a term's unfairness.[1024] According to the LOVCK Report, this is irreconcilable with the duty of *ex officio* control set out in the CJEU's case law (and elaborated on in *Heesakkers/Voets*).[1025] If a term is on the blacklist of unfair standard terms and conditions in consumer contracts, its use cannot be justified under any circumstances.[1026] If a term is on the grey list, it is presumed to be unfair, unless proven otherwise by the trader. If the term is on neither list, the court can still request the trader to explain why the term is not unfair, in the circumstances of the case. It can also do so where the consumer has not invoked the term's unfairness. The court can ask traders to submit their general terms and conditions to the court, if they have not yet done so: if a trader refuses, the court can presume those terms to be unfair.[1027]

After *Heesakkers/Voets, ex officio* control has remained contentious, in particular in the course of judicial review of arbitral awards, and appellate proceedings.[1028] The more active role required from courts under EU consumer law has caused tension with, in particular, the notion of party autonomy. There is also tension between this role and the need for efficiency, both from the perspective of traders and creditors who wish to quickly obtain an enforceable court order, and with reference to the costs of the administration of justice.[1029] That being said, the need for 'strategic' references to the CJEU has not yet manifested itself in Dutch law.[1030] Since 2012 Dutch civil courts can also opt to make a preliminary reference to the Hoge Raad instead, which can provide guidance on the application of (EU) consumer law in the Dutch legal system.[1031]

1024 Hoge Raad, 21 September 2012, ECLI:NL:HR:2012:BW6135 (*Van Marrum/Wolff*), para. 2.4, discussed further in subsection 5.2.1 below.

1025 2018 LOVCK Report, p. 77.

1026 Marco Loos, *Algemene voorwaarden* (Boom Juridische Uitgevers 2018) 169.

1027 2018 LOVCK Report, p. 37. See also Loos (n 1026) 170.

1028 See further subsections 5.2.2 and 5.4.1.

1029 2018 LOVCK Report, p. 41. See also Ancery (n 32) 134, 139.

1030 Jasper Krommendijk, 'Van Middelburg tot Almelo. Het hoe en waarom van prejudiciële vragen aan het Hof van Justitie van de Europese Unie door Nederlandse lagere rechters' (2018) 39 Recht der Werkelijkheid 7, 12–13.

1031 See, e.g. Hoge Raad, 12 February 2016, ECLI:NL:HR:2016:236 (*Lindorff/Nazier*); Hoge Raad, 8 November 2019, ECLI:NL:HR:2019:1731 (*Intermaris*). Two recent preliminary references to the CJEU concern the substantive legal consequences of a finding of unfairness, not the role of courts in the proceedings. Therefore, they will not be discussed in the present chapter. Gerechtshof Amsterdam, 5 March 2019, ECLI:NL:GHAMS:2019:657 and Gerechtshof Den Haag, 2 April 2019, ECLI:NL:GHDHA:2019:630.

5.1.2. LACK OF REFERENCES TO ARTICLE 47 IN DUTCH CASE LAW

5.1.2.1. Low Visibility of Article 47, Despite its Discursive Value

Article 47 of the Charter plays a much less visible role in unfair terms cases in the Netherlands than it does in Spain. Most procedural issues that have arisen in the context of the UCTD are not constitutionalised, i.e. they have not been approached from a fundamental rights perspective – with the notable exception of arbitration clauses in consumer contracts. Conversely, infringements of procedural safeguards or due process requirements are not consumerised, i.e. they have not specifically been connected with substantive (EU) consumer law. On the one hand, there might be no need to refer to Article 47 if there are other means available to achieve the required level of judicial protection: in particular, consistent interpretation of existing (procedural) rules. On the other hand, the scarce references to Article 47 in Dutch case law might also be a result of the Dutch civil courts' lack of awareness of, or hesitation about, the Article's potential functions – possibly because the Netherlands does not have a constitutional tradition.[1032]

The only instances in which the Dutch civil courts have explicitly referred to Article 47 of the Charter in unfair terms cases pertain to arbitration clauses. Perhaps it is not surprising that effective judicial protection as a fundamental rights issue emerges in cases about contractual terms that *exclude* the consumer's right to take legal action or exercise any other legal remedy (Annex, Article 1(q) of the UCTD). Certain terms can make it *more difficult* for consumers to exercise their rights in court,[1033] for example prohibitions on assignation of their claims to third parties,[1034] or clauses that impose a burden of proof on the consumer that would not

[1032] T Barkhuysen, AW Bos and F Ten Have, 'Een verkenning van de betekenis van het Handvest van de grondrechten van de Europese Unie voor het privaatrecht. Deel 2: De verhouding van het Handvest tot het EVRM en de meerwaarde van het Handvest' [2011] Nederlands Tijdschrift voor Burgerlijk Recht 547. It may take some time before the CJEU's case law on Article 47 of the Charter reaches Dutch courts: Leon Timmermans, 'Het doeltreffendheidsbeginsel na *Puškár*. Een toekomst binnen het kader van het beginsel van effectieve rechtsbescherming?' in Henri de Waele, Jasper Krommendijk and Karin Zwaan (eds), *Tien jaar EU-Grondrechtenhandvest in Nederland* (Wolters Kluwer) 11.7.

[1033] See, e.g. Joined Cases C-537/12 and C-116/13 *Banco Popular Español*, paras. 70–71; Case C-415/11 *Aziz*, paras. 73–74.

[1034] See, e.g. Rechtbank Oost-Brabant, 28 June 2018, ECLI:NL:RBOBR:2018:3169; Rechtbank Noord-Holland, 17 April 2019, ECLI:NL:RBNHO:2019:3323.

otherwise apply.[1035] However, such terms do not make it *impossible* for consumers to appear in court.[1036] Arbitration clauses, by contrast, do not determine the content of consumer rights or how they can be exercised, but take away the possibility of exercising these rights in court altogether.

The low number of references to Article 47 in Dutch case law might signify that, on a systemic level, the justiciability of consumer rights under the UCTD has been sufficiently ensured. No violations of Article 47 of the Charter appear to have been established yet. However, this could be an 'unknown unknown': it cannot be ascertained from judicial decisions alone whether there are flaws in the system that have remained invisible, so far.[1037] Moreover, framing the question as whether or not there has been a violation of Article 47 is too black and white, in light of the functions, identified in the previous chapters, that a reference to Article 47 may play in judicial reasoning. Article 47 has discursive value, and it may serve as an 'interpretative device'[1038] for open norms in private law and civil procedure, as the cases discussed in this chapter will show.

5.1.2.2. Space for Judicial Intervention

The justiciability of the rights that consumers derive from the UCTD appears to be less of an issue in the Netherlands than in Spain. There are no indications that fundamental interests are insufficiently protected, or that there is an 'enforcement deficit' in respect of mandatory statutory provisions.[1039] Dutch civil courts seem to have more (*ex officio*) powers than their Spanish counterparts, for example to take measures of

1035 See, e.g. Gerechtshof Amsterdam, 2 April 2019, ECLI:NL:GHAMS:2019:1109; Hoge Raad 28 September 2018, ECLI:NL:HR:2018:1800. A term reversing the burden of proof to the detriment of the consumer does not automatically qualify as unfair, but it must be examined whether the term at issue alters the consumer's legal position by removing or hindering their procedural rights: *Lovasné Tóth*, paras. 49 and 56. See, for more examples, JML van Duin, 'Effectieve rechtsbescherming van consumenten door de civiele rechter: een procesrechtelijk perspectief' [2019] Tijdschrift voor de Procespraktijk 138, 142.

1036 See also the differentiation proposed in subsection 3.3.1 of Chapter 3 of this book.

1037 See also Roland de Moor, 'Hoe effectief is onze consumentenbescherming?' [2017] Tijdschrift voor Consumentenrecht en handelspraktijken 154, 156.

1038 T Barkhuysen, AW Bos and F Ten Have, 'Een verkenning van de betekenis van het Handvest van de grondrechten van de Europese Unie voor het privaatrecht. Deel 1: De inhoud, de juridische status en het toepassingsbereik van het Handvest, in het bijzonder in horizontale verhoudingen' [2011] Nederlands Tijdschrift voor Burgerlijk Recht 479.

1039 Opinion of AG Drijber of 23 February 2018, ECLI:NL:PHR:2018:154, points 63–64.

investigation, especially in uncontested claims.[1040] Restrictive procedural conditions that affect Article 47 of the Charter's core components may also be less prevalent in Dutch law than in Spanish law, or may even be absent altogether. For instance, a Dutch court's *failure* to perform *ex officio* control in default proceedings is not the same as a Spanish court's *inability* to do so in mortgage enforcement proceedings. While the Dutch court could assess unfair terms, the Spanish court could not. Moreover, when there is still an opportunity for the consumer to oppose or appeal the court's decision, there is no violation of the right to an effective judicial remedy, as such. A separate order for payment procedure, such as exists in Spain, which combines restrictive procedural conditions with a limited scope for judicial intervention, does not exist in the Netherlands.[1041] There are no strict limitations on the debtor's grounds for challenging mortgage enforcement in the Netherlands either. Thus, there is more space for judicial intervention, without the need to set procedural rules aside, or to make legislative changes.

Dutch civil procedure, in general, appears to be less rigid than in Spain.[1042] Procedural rules are to be applied by civil courts in a 'deformalised' manner, in order to provide flexibility and manageability.[1043] The deformalisation of procedural law is said to have shifted the focus to the

---

1040 Hoge Raad, judgment of 13 September 2013, ECLI:NL:HR:2013:691 (*Heesakkers/Voets*), para. 3.9.1; see further subsection 5.3.1 of this chapter. On the active role of the court in contentious civil proceedings, see, e.g. Ruth de Bock, 'Feitenonderzoek tijdens de mondelinge behandeling' in Dineke de Groot and Hans Steenbergen (eds), *De mondelinge behandeling in civiele zaken* (Boom Juridische Uitgevers 2019) 185.

1041 The (European) small claims procedure is not necessarily expedited: there is room for contestation, an exchange of written arguments and an oral hearing: see also Rechtbank Amsterdam, 9 March 2020, ECLI:NL:RBAMS:2020:1477.

1042 As Hartkamp has observed, in a case note on Case C-32/12 *Duarte Hueros*, Spanish civil procedure is very consumer-unfriendly compared to Dutch civil procedure. In the Netherlands, a change of claim would have been possible, or a new claim could have been brought after the initial one had been dismissed, because the rules on *res judicata* are less strict: see Arthur Hartkamp, 'Ambtshalve toepassing van Europees consumentenrecht. Een nieuw hoofdstuk: de richtlijn consumentenkoop' [2015] Ars Aequi 222.

1043 Menno Bruning, 'Over redelijke wetstoepassing en hanteerbaarheid van het Nederlands privaatrecht. Mogelijkheden en grenzen in de rechtsvormede rechtspraak op grond van de billijkheid' in Ruben de Graaff and others (eds), *Rechtsvorming door de Hoge Raad* (Ars Aequi Libri 2016) 97–98; Ivo Giesen, *Beginselen van burgerlijk procesrecht* (Wolters Kluwer 2015) 500. See also Vincent Lindijer, *De goede procesorde. Een onderzoek naar de betekenis van de goede procesorde als normatief begrip in het burgerlijk procesrecht* (Kluwer 2006) 518–519. Lindijer makes a comparison between due process requirements and other (open) norms and doctrines, such as the 'abuse of law' ('*misbruik van bevoegdheid*') criterion.

rationale of the norms at issue, and the reasonable interests of the parties that deserve (judicial) protection.[1044] The interpretation of procedural rules by Dutch civil courts can be justified by reference to (unwritten) principles of due process (*goede procesorde*) and a proper administration of justice (*behoorlijke rechtspleging*), in the development of which Article 6 ECHR is said to have played an important role.[1045]

It could, nevertheless, be argued that Article 47 of the Charter has more normative power, because it has direct effect: it can serve as a basis on which legislative provisions can be set aside. This is not possible on the basis of unwritten principles, nor on the basis of the Dutch Constitution, which contains a prohibition of constitutional review (Article 120). There is no constitutional court in the Netherlands, and courts are prohibited from exercising constitutional review of primary legislation (statutes).[1046] Parliament is expected to assess the constitutionality of new legislation during the legislative process. There is a national equivalent of Article 6 ECHR and Article 47 of the Charter: Article 17 of the Dutch Constitution (Grondwet) recognises the right of access to court.[1047] However, the prohibition of constitutional review entails that private parties have to rely on national procedural law for the effectuation of their rights.[1048] The direct effect of Article 47 stems from EU law itself, and not from the Constitution, which distinguishes it from the direct effect that applies to Article 6 ECHR in the Dutch legal order.[1049] Article 94 of the Constitution gives precedence to directly effective international provisions, such as Article 6 ECHR, over colliding national norms, including the

1044 Lindijer (n 1043) 626.

1045 Giesen (n 1043) 50–51.

1046 Jerfi Uzman, Tom Barkhuysen and Michiel L Van Emmerik, 'The Dutch Supreme Court: A Reluctant Positive Legislator?' in Allan R Brewer-Carías (ed), *Constitutional Courts as Positive Legislators* (Cambridge University Press 2011) 645. See also Ruben de Graaff, 'Prescription. A Private-Law Concept at the Forefront of Fundamental Rights Protection' in Clementine Breedeveld-de Voogd and others (eds), *Core Concepts in the Dutch Civil Code, Continuously in Motion. BW Krant Jaarboek no. 30* (Wolters Kluwer 2016) 146–148.

1047 Article 17 of the Dutch Constitution reads, 'No one may be prevented against their will from being heard by the courts to which they are entitled to apply under the law' [English translation: <https://www.government.nl/binaries/government/documents/regulations/2012/10/18/the-constitution-of-the-kingdom-of-the-netherlands-2008/the-constitution-of-the-kingdom-of-the-netherlands-2008.pdf> (last accessed 3 October 2021)].

1048 Carla Sieburgh, 'Waarom het Unierecht de invloed van grondrechten op het privaatrecht aanjaagt en versterkt' [2015] THEMIS 3, 6.

1049 Uzman, Barkhuysen and Van Emmerik (n 1046) 673–674.

Constitution itself.[1050] Both Article 47 of the Charter and Article 6 ECHR empower Dutch courts to set aside conflicting provisions of national law, in concrete cases. In addition, civil courts can disapply statutory provisions on the basis of reasonableness and fairness (Article 6:2(2) BW),[1051] sometimes in cases that could be understood as involving fundamental rights, i.e. examples of hidden constitutionalisation.[1052] They may, nevertheless, be reluctant to do so, especially where the legislative or executive branches have a margin of discretion.[1053] Moreover, legality review on the basis of EU law is relatively new in private law,[1054] which might be another explanation for reluctance on the part of Dutch civil courts to apply Article 47 of the Charter.

5.1.2.3. Assumption that Article 47 of the Charter and Article 6 ECHR are Interchangeable

Dutch civil courts generally assume that Article 47 of the Charter and Article 6 ECHR are interchangeable,[1055] an assumption that does not do justice to Article 47's connection to EU rights.[1056] In a case concerning State liability for an alleged failure of the Hoge Raad (Civil Division) to make a preliminary reference to the CJEU, the Hague Court of Appeal expressly held that 'Article 6 ECHR corresponds with Article 47 of the Charter'.[1057] In another case concerning an alleged violation of the right

1050 Article 94 of the Constitution reads, 'Statutory regulations in force within the Kingdom shall not be applicable if such application is in conflict with provisions of treaties or of resolutions by international institutions that are binding on all persons.'

1051 Article 6:2(2) BW reads, 'A rule in force between a creditor and a debtor by virtue of law, common practice or a juridical act does not apply as far as this would be unacceptable, in the circumstances, by standards of reasonableness and fairness' [Translation: <http://www.dutchcivillaw.com/civilcodebook066.htm> (last accessed 3 October 2021)].

1052 Ruben de Graaff, 'De betekenis van de redelijkheid en billijkheid voor de bescherming van grondrechten' [2016] THEMIS 202, 213; Floor Bakker, *Billijkheidsuitzonderingen. Het wegens bijzondere omstandigheden buiten toepassing laten van wettelijke voorschriften in individuele gevallen* (Wolters Kluwer 2018) 148–149.

1053 De Graaff (n 1052) 206; Bakker (n 1052) 81–83.

1054 Carla Sieburgh, 'Het EU-Handvest van de Grondrechten en het algemene vermogensrecht. De (potentiële) betekenis van het Handvest voor rechtsverhoudingen tussen particulieren' in Janneke Gerards, Henri de Waele and Karin Zwaan (eds), *Vijf jaar bindend EU-Grondrechtenhandvest. Doorwerking, consequenties, perspectieven* (Wolters Kluwer 2015) 510.

1055 See also Barkhuysen, Bos and Ten Have (n 1032).

1056 See also subsection 2.2.2 of this book.

1057 Gerechtshof Den Haag, 25 October 2016, ECLI:NL:GHDHA:2016:2984, para. 4.3.

to adjudication within a reasonable time in a European small claims procedure, the District Court of The Hague also used the term 'corresponds', to describe the relationship between the two instruments.[1058] In both cases, the reference to the ECHR made sense because of the special relevance of ECtHR case law for State liability under EU law.[1059]

The same assumption as to the interchangeability of Article 6 ECHR and Article 47 of the Charter is made in 'horizontal' cases between two private parties, for instance in respect of jurisdiction[1060] or challenges concerning the judge's impartiality,[1061] as well as in relation to court fees and the right of access to court.[1062] Alleged violations of fair trial rights in concrete cases are generally adjudicated under the umbrella of Article 6 ECHR, not Article 47 of the Charter, even where the case might, at first sight, seem to fall within the scope of EU consumer law.[1063] Perhaps Dutch civil courts do not see a clear need to refer to Article 47 of the Charter, as a result of the ECHR being more ingrained in Dutch legal practice. The requirements of Article 47, which are less crystallised, might be perceived as not going beyond those of Article 6 ECHR and, thus, having little or no added value. Moreover, fragmentation of procedural protection according to subject matter may be considered as undesirable.[1064] The ECHR is not only older than the Charter, but its application is also unconnected to EU law and, therefore, more general. The majority of references to Article 47 of the Charter in civil cases are trans-substantive, as well, i.e. lacking a clear link to EU law.

In most cases, Dutch civil courts seem to mention Article 47 of the Charter almost as an afterthought. A notable exception is a recent case on

---

1058 Rechtbank Den Haag, 23 November 2016, ECLI:NL:RBDHA:2016:14190, para. 4.15.

1059 See, e.g. ECtHR 8 April 2014, Appl. No. 17120/09 *Dhahbi v Italy* on the failure to make a preliminary reference; Case C-385/07 *Der Grüne Punkt*, paras. 177–179, on the reasonable time requirement.

1060 Rechtbank Oost-Brabant, 31 January 2013, ECLI:NL:RBOBR:2013:BZ0842.

1061 Gerechtshof Den Haag, 25 November 2014, ECLI:NL:GHDHA:2014:3833; Rechtbank Zutphen, 12 January 2012, ECLI:NL:RBZUT:2012:BV1679. In these cases, the link with EU law and, thus, the applicability of Article 47 of the Charter was not immediately obvious. See also Rechtbank Den Haag, 6 June 2018, ECLI:NL:RBDHA:2018:6463, para. 4.32.

1062 See, e.g. Gerechtshof Arnhem-Leeuwarden, 3 July 2014, ECLI:NL:GHARL:2014:5450; Rechtbank Zutphen, 4 January 2012, ECLI:NL:RBZUT:2012:BV6245.

1063 See, e.g. Hoge Raad, 8 November 2019, ECLI:NL:HR:2019:1731 (*Intermaris*) (further discussed in subsection 5.2.2 below); Hoge Raad, 8 February 2019, ECLI:NL:HR:2019:207; Gerechtshof Den Haag, 12 March 2019, ECLI:NL:GHDHA:2019:453.

1064 See, e.g. Charlotte Vrendenbarg, *Proceskostenveroordeling en toegang tot de rechter in IE-zaken: regelingen over proceskosten getoetst aan het EU-recht* (Wolters Kluwer 2018) 62; Krans (n 236) 582.

cost orders in the area of data protection, where the Court of Appeal in 's-Hertogenbosch referred prominently to Article 47, to justify a deviation from the 'loser pays' principle normally adhered to in Dutch procedural law.[1065] This shows that Article 47 can have an impact on the application of procedural rules in a case concerning rights derived from EU law. The Court of Appeal concluded that the applicant, who had made an application under the Dutch Data Protection Act,[1066] could not be ordered to pay the costs of the defendant bank, even though he had lost the case on the merits.[1067] The applicant was a natural person who had exercised his rights under EU law, in the form of the Data Protection Directive. In this respect, the Court of Appeal cited *Puškár*,[1068] a CJEU judgment that concerned the costs of administrative proceedings preceding judicial review: those costs cannot be excessively high. It found that a cost order would impede the applicant's position, and obstruct the exercise of the right to an effective remedy before a court of law (Article 47 of the Charter).

The absence of a link with EU law in other Dutch cases on Article 47 could be an intentional 'spillover effect'.[1069] However, it also raises the question of whether Dutch civil courts are sufficiently aware of the link between substance and procedure in the adjudication of unfair terms cases, as highlighted in the CJEU's case law on the UCTD. Article 47 of the Charter requires effective judicial protection of consumer rights under the UCTD. It follows from the CJEU's case law that the position of consumers as weaker parties must also be taken into consideration from a procedural

---

1065 Gerechtshof 's-Hertogenbosch, 1 February 2018, ECLI:NL:GHSHE:2018:363. In a similar case, the District Court of The Hague adopted a more formal understanding of the right of access to court (Article 47 of the Charter): the applicant could exercise this right, and had actually done so, but the District Court found that the applicant had caused unnecessary legal costs by making two almost identical applications and then withdrawing them at the last minute, while indicating that this would not end the dispute. Thus, a cost order was warranted: Rechtbank Den Haag, 28 June 2019, ECLI:NL:RBDHA:2019:6302, paras. 2.34–2.35.

1066 The Wet Bescherming Persoonsgegevens (WBP) implemented Directive 95/46/EC on the protection of individuals with regard to the processing of personal data and on the free movement of such data (Data Protection Directive).

1067 Judgment of 1 February 2018 (n 1065), paras. 3.8.3–3.8.5. The applicant was not exempted from paying court fees: Gerechtshof 's-Hertogenbosch, 18 January 2018, ECLI:NL:GHSHE:2018:166, paras. 2.5–2.6.

1068 Case C-73/16 *Puškár*, paras. 54–60 and 75–76. See also subsection 2.1.2.1 of this book.

1069 The Dutch Council of State has held that the importance of access to an independent judicial tribunal also requires that, in cases *outside* the scope of Article 6 ECHR and Article 47 of the Charter, exceptions may have to be made to strict admissibility requirements on the basis of court fees: decision of 6 March 2013, cited by Opinion of AG Wesseling-van Gent of 4 December 2015, ECLI:NL:PHR:2015:2663, point 2.19.

perspective. For instance, it could be argued that, in consumer cases, the deterrent effect of costs should also be accounted for, and that *ex officio* control cannot fully compensate for this: if no legal action is brought, the case does not come before a court.[1070] Either way, the tendency to view procedural safeguards as trans-substantive is not consonant with the connection between substantive and procedural protection of EU consumer rights. This connection becomes visible, not only in respect of arbitration clauses and access to court (section 5.2), but also in cases where effective judicial protection requires a broad interpretation of judicial remedies (sections 5.3 and 5.4). Whereas Dutch civil courts seem to have found solutions for procedural issues without referring to Article 47, this does not mean that the fundamental rights dimension of consumer adjudication might not become relevant in future cases.

5.2. ACCESS TO COURT

5.2.1. ARBITRATION CLAUSES IN CONSUMER CONTRACTS

5.2.1.1. Van Marrum/Wolff: *Eliminatory Function of Article 47 in its Horizontal Dimension*

The case of *Van Marrum/Wolff* is cited as an example of the use of the Charter as a source of inspiration for the interpretation of open norms, in this case Article 6:233(a) BW.[1071] It shows that Article 47 of the Charter may be triggered when consumers are deprived of their rights of access to court, due to unfair arbitration clauses. In so far as Article 47 – in its horizontal dimension[1072] – was used, in this case, as a parameter to assess the unfairness of arbitration clauses in consumer contracts, it could be ascribed an eliminatory function. The Court of Appeal that adjudicated the case deemed such clauses to be unfair, even though they were not on the blacklist at the time.[1073] Article 47, thus, provided a justification for going

---

1070 See also subsection 3.2.4 of this book. On the potential implications for cost orders in consumer cases, see further JML van Duin, 'Wie betaalt de rekening? De kostenveroordeling in de context van het EU-consumentenrecht' [2018] Tijdschrift voor Consumentenrecht en handelspraktijken 177.

1071 See, e.g. Sieburgh (n 1054) 507; Jessy Emaus, 'Rechten, beginselen en horizontale directe werking van de grondrechten uit het EU-Handvest' [2015] Nederlands Tijdschrift voor Burgerlijk Recht 67, 67.

1072 See also subsections 2.2.2, 3.2.2 and 4.2.2 of this book.

1073 Gerechtshof Leeuwarden, 5 July 2011, ECLI:NL:GHLEE:2011:BR2500 (*Van Marrum/Wolff*).

beyond what was strictly required by national provisions implementing the UCTD.

Van Marrum/Wolff was a case between a consumer (Wolff) and a construction company (Bouwbedrijf Van Marrum BV). The consumer brought a claim for faulty performance against the company, which then invoked an arbitration clause in the General Terms and Conditions for Contracting Work in the Construction Sector 1992. At first instance, the Leeuwarden District Court had held that the arbitration clause was unfair within the meaning of Article 6:233(a) BW. The clause had not been individually negotiated, and its purpose was to prevent or obstruct the consumer from bringing a claim (Annex, Article 1(q) of the UCTD).[1074] The company lodged an interim appeal before the Leeuwarden Court of Appeal, and argued that, at that time, the Dutch legislature had deliberately left arbitration clauses off the blacklist, because the quality and independence of arbitration as a means of alternative dispute resolution in consumer cases was sufficiently guaranteed.

The Leeuwarden Court of Appeal considered that it was not constrained by the Dutch legislator's considerations. Instead, it had to take the wording and purpose of the UCTD into account, in order to comply with its obligation to ensure the Directive's full effect (Article 288(3) TFEU).[1075] Its finding that arbitration clauses, in general, were unfair nevertheless went beyond what was required by the Directive (or its Annex), which makes the reference to Article 47 of the Charter all the more interesting.[1076] It implies that the link between the fundamental right of access to court and EU consumer law might warrant a higher level of protection. The Court of Appeal noted that arbitration clauses withhold from consumers the court protection assigned to them by law, often without them having had the opportunity to negotiate their contracts, and without them being aware that they are being deprived of their rights of access to court.[1077] The Court of Appeal found that arbitration may have certain disadvantages for consumers, compared to proceedings before a State court: there are no equivalent safeguards in relation to the independence of the arbiter, or for the application of national and EU law, notwithstanding the (presumed) expertise of the arbitral tribunal, in this case the Arbitration Board for the

---

1074 Rechtbank Leeuwarden, 15 July 2009, ECLI:NL:RBLEE:2009:BJ2957 (*Van Marrum/ Wolff*).

1075 Judgment of Gerechtshof Leeuwarden (n 1073), para. 3.6.

1076 The Court of Appeal's judgment was followed (at least once), by Rechtbank Leeuwarden, 3 August 2011, ECLI:NL:RBLEE:2011:BR4256.

1077 Judgment of Gerechtshof Leeuwarden (n 1073), para. 3.10.

Building Industry in the Netherlands (Raad van Arbitrage voor de Bouw). Moreover, consumers could be deterred from invoking their rights by the higher costs involved, or the distance between their place of residence and the seat of the arbitral tribunal, regardless of whether they were claimants or defendants.

The question of whether, and under what conditions, arbitration clauses in consumer contracts are to be considered as unfair has been the subject of debate. In his Opinion in *Van Marrum/Wolff*, AG Spier noted a 'growing aversion' to arbitration clauses in consumer contracts,[1078] but he dismissed the Court of Appeal's robust approach. He tentatively concluded that arbitration clauses were not, as such, unacceptable, but that in consumer contracts they should, in principle, be considered unfair. It would then be up to the trader to prove that the arbitration clause was not unfair, in the special circumstances of the case.[1079] According to Spier, the company in question had not brought forward any facts or circumstances that could support such a conclusion.[1080]

Unlike the Court of Appeal and AG Spier, the Hoge Raad refused to anticipate the blacklisting or 'grey listing' of arbitration clauses. It quashed the judgment on the ground that the Court of Appeal should have taken the special circumstances of the case into account instead of using objective reasoning that was applicable to all arbitration clauses in consumer contracts.[1081] Remarkably, the Hoge Raad did not pay express attention to the exclusive effect of arbitration clauses and any concerns to which this may give, in light of the right of access to court. It also ruled that it is, in principle, the consumer who must prove that the arbitration clause at issue is unfair.[1082] This is a peculiar ruling, not only because it is usually the trader who invokes the arbitration clause, and upon whom the onus to prove its validity should, therefore, fall,[1083] but also, and especially, because of the duty of *ex officio* control.

1078 Opinion of AG Spier of 11 May 2012, ECLI:NL:PHR:2012:BW6135 (*Van Marrum//Wolff*), para. 3.35.1, with reference to, inter alia, Case C-168/05 *Mostaza Claro*.

1079 Opinion of AG Spier (n 1078), paras. 3.36, 3.40.1 and 3.40.2.

1080 Opinion of AG Spier (n 1078), paras. 3.49 and 3.59.2.

1081 Hoge Raad, 21 September 2012, ECLI:NL:HR:2012:BW6135 (*Van Marrum/Wolff*), paras. 3.4–3.5. What would have happened after the judgment was quashed, had the case been pursued, remains a matter for conjecture. Upon inquiry, the lawyer who represented Van Marrum in this case affirmed that the heirs of Mr. Wolff decided not to pursue the case.

1082 Judgment of Hoge Raad (n 1081), para. 3.4.

1083 See also Rechtbank Rotterdam, 18 May 2011, ECLI:NL:RBROT:2011:BQ5670, para. 4.6.

5.2.1.2. *Signalling Function Ahead of Legislative Change*

Since 2015, arbitration clauses have been blacklisted: they are considered to be unfair, unless consumers are given a period of *one month* from the moment an arbitration clause is invoked against them to decide whether they would prefer to go to court instead (Article 6:236(n) BW).[1084] According to the Dutch legislator, the main reason for blacklisting arbitration clauses that leave no choice for consumers is that consumers would otherwise be deprived, without being aware of it and/or against their will, of the court protection assigned to them by law.[1085] The Dutch legislator referred, inter alia, to *Asturcom*[1086] and *Van Marrum/Wolff*. In this respect, the *Van Marrum/Wolff* decision could be seen as an example of a reference to Article 47 in its signalling function, ahead of legislative change.

In the meantime, the Amsterdam Court of Appeal had already followed the Leeuwarden Court of Appeal, with reference to Article 47 of the Charter.[1087] In addition to the disadvantages of arbitration pointed out by the court in Leeuwarden, the court in Amsterdam considered that the costs of arbitration were much higher than the costs of ordinary civil proceedings, and that it did not seem plausible that arbitral proceedings would have been significantly faster, in this case. According to the court, it did not matter whether the arbitration clause was part of the general terms and conditions or the contract itself, as long as it could be characterised as a standard term falling within the scope of unfair terms control. Neither did it matter that the clause at issue had been negotiated with consumer organisations, because each individual case needed to be assessed on its own merits; there could, nevertheless, still be circumstances that rendered the clause unfair, for instance when the consumer did not get a real opportunity to make an informed choice at the time of concluding the contract.[1088]

1084 Article 6:236(n) BW reads, in English translation (<http://www.dutchcivillaw.com/civilcodebook066.htm> (last accessed 3 October 2021)): 'The following stipulations in the applicable standard terms and conditions are deemed to be unreasonably burdensome for [consumers]: … a stipulation which provides for the settlement of a dispute other than by a court with jurisdiction pursuant to law, unless it still allows the [consumer] to choose for a settlement of the dispute by the court with jurisdiction pursuant to law and this choice can be made within a period of at least one month after the [trader] has invoked the stipulation in writing.'

1085 Kamerstukken (Parliamentary Papers) II, 2012/2013, 33 611, no. 3, p. 7. See also Opinion of AG Hartlief of 6 July 2018, ECLI:NL:PHR:2018:788, point 5.31.

1086 Case C-40/8 *Asturcom*, discussed in subsection 3.2.2.

1087 Gerechtshof Amsterdam, 17 April 2012, ECLI:NL:GHAMS:2012:BX3835.

1088 See further subsection 5.2.2 below.

Both Courts of Appeal relied on Article 47 of the Charter as one of the reasons for deeming arbitration clauses in consumer clauses to be unfair. Some lower courts arrived at the same conclusion merely by referring to the UCTD's (non-binding) Annex.[1089] Other lower courts arrived at the opposite conclusion, considering that arbitration clauses could only be deemed unfair if the special circumstances of the case led to that conclusion.[1090] Pavillon has, nevertheless, argued that there are no circumstances, either abstract or concrete, that could justify a restriction of consumers' rights of access to court by removing their choice between arbitration and a State court in advance. In her view, the restriction of this right, and the corresponding lack of guarantees of a fair trial and/or the application of national and EU (consumer) law, should be decisive: these 'objective' disadvantages go beyond the individual consumer.[1091]

Now that arbitration clauses in consumer contracts have been blacklisted, the question arises of whether there is still a role for Article 47 of the Charter in the assessment of the fairness or unfairness of such clauses.[1092] The blacklist emphasises the absence of consent, rather than making a comparison between arbitration and court proceedings, as such. Consumers waive judicial protection if they do not object within one month after an arbitration clause has been invoked against them. However, the mere fact that an arbitration clause respects the one-month period does not automatically make it valid.[1093] The circumstances of the case remain relevant, such as the question of whether the consumers have been informed about their rights, and whether the arbitration proceedings are sufficiently balanced. Here, Article 47 of the Charter might still play a role, in particular in respect of the rights of defence.[1094]

1089 See, e.g. Rechtbank Amsterdam, 17 December 2008, ECLI:NL:RBAMS:2008:BH1368, para. 3.4.

1090 See, e.g. Rechtbank Gelderland, 10 April 2013, ECLI:NL:RBGEL:2013:CA0523.

1091 C.M.D.S. Pavillon, case note on Gerechtshof Leeuwarden, 5 July 2011, ECLI:NL:GHLEE:2011:BR2500 (*Van Marrum/Wolff*). (2012) 19 Tijdschrift voor Bouwrecht 98-106, para. 8.

1092 Heidi van Ginkel, *Het arbitragebeding in algemene voorwaarden* (Celsus juridische uitgeverij 2013) 46–48.

1093 Opinion of AG Valk of 12 July 2019, ECLI:NL:PHR:2019:769 (*Intermaris*), points 3.22 and 3.29. See also Dorien Thiescheffer, *E-court naast overheidsrechtspraak. Online rechtspraak als alternatieve geschilbeslechting en de garanties voor consumenten* (Celsus juridische uitgeverij 2018) 66.

1094 See also Thiescheffer (n 1093) 108.

5.2.1.3 Pharma Slovakia*: A Rhetorical Function of Article 47*

The question arises as to what extent Article 47 of the Charter warrants a restrictive interpretation of the parties' intentions to submit a dispute to arbitration, in the context of the UCTD. It could be argued that when a consumer does not object to arbitration, this is not the same as tacitly accepting, let alone expressly agreeing to it.[1095] In this respect, the consumer's weaker position plays an important role, as opposed to non-consumer cases, where the parties are presumed to have equal knowledge and bargaining power. The extra scrutiny exercised towards arbitration clauses in consumer cases may be extended to other weaker parties, as demonstrated by *Pharma Slovakia*, a case between a limited partnership and one of its partners.[1096] Again, this goes beyond what is required by the UCTD or the national provisions implementing the Directive.

The partner involved had brought a claim against the company for payment of benefits. After the company invoked an arbitration clause in the partnership agreement, the court of first instance had ruled that it was not competent to hear the claim. In appeal, it was argued by the partner, who challenged the arbitration clause, that both the clause itself and the intention of the parties should be interpreted restrictively, in light of the right of access to court.[1097] The partner also invoked the UCTD, (or, rather, its consequential effect (*reflexwerking*), because, strictly speaking, the UCTD was not applicable).[1098] The Court of Appeal of Arnhem-Leeuwarden considered that the position of the partner was similar to that of a consumer, in terms of knowledge and bargaining power. Moreover, the court found that the arbitration clause at issue was comparable to a standard term, because it was not a core term, and had not been individually negotiated. But, given the circumstances of the case, the clause did not lead to a significant imbalance between the parties (within the meaning

---

1095 See, e.g. Rechtbank Amsterdam, 25 January 2019, ECLI:NL:RBAMS:2019:1339, para. 3.6. See also Marte Knigge and Pauline Ribbers, 'Arbitrage, afstand van recht en artikel 6 EVRM' (2017) 20 Tijdschrift voor Arbitrage 35; Thiescheffer (n 1093) 70.

1096 Gerechtshof Arnhem-Leeuwarden, 11 July 2017, ECLI:NL:GHARL:2017:5961 (*Pharma Slovakia*), para. 6.20.

1097 Gerechtshof Amsterdam, 1 March 2011, ECLI:NL:GHAMS:2011:BR1722, para. 2.10. See also Rechtbank Rotterdam, 18 May 2011, ECLI:NL:RBROT:2011:BQ5670, para. 4.5.

1098 On *reflexwerking*, see further Alain Ancery and Charlotte Pavillon, 'Processuele aspecten van reflexwerking van consumentenrecht' (2014) 145(7026) Weekblad voor privaatrecht, notariaat en registratie 647; Carlotta Rinaldo, 'Beyond Consumer Law – Small Enterprises, Independent Contractors and Other Professional Weak Parties' (2019) 15 European Review of Contract Law 227.

of Article 3 UCTD and Article 1(q) of the Annex):[1099] the clause referred to the Dutch Arbitration Institute (NAI), an independent and impartial arbitral institution with sufficient expertise; costs and distance were not a problem; and the appellant had not contested the fact that arbitration clauses are common in partnership agreements.

The Court of Appeal of Arnhem-Leeuwarden found the approach taken in *Van Marrum/Wolff* to be too 'categorical'.[1100] It held that, while Article 47 of the Charter and Article 17 of the Constitution both safeguard the fundamental right of access to court, Article 17 allowed for an exception, in the event of consent (see also Article 1021.1 Rv). The requirement of consent was met if there was a valid arbitration agreement, even in the case of an arbitration clause that was comparable to a standard term. This seems to imply that Article 47 of the Charter would call for more scrutiny, although it was, strictly speaking, not applicable in this case. The reference to Article 47 was more than just ornamental: it showed awareness of the fundamental right at stake, and has persuasive authority as to the rationale of judicial protection, in this context. It, thus, fulfils a *rhetorical function*,[1101] which could be seen as a weaker version of Article 47's signalling function; it does not question the existing norms as such. Furthermore, it has spillover effect: the parallel with consumers and the lack of consent may inspire a closer examination of factors that could render an arbitration clause unfair.[1102] Such a spillover effect would show how Article 47 also has the potential to increase judicial protection outside the scope of the UCTD.

5.2.2. *INTERMARIS* CASE: INTENSITY OF JUDICIAL REVIEW OF ARBITRAL AWARDS

In 2019, the Amsterdam District Court made a preliminary reference to the Hoge Raad in a case pertaining to a private arbitration institute

---

1099 In this respect, the Court of Appeal referred to Hoge Raad, 21 April 2017, ECLI:NL:HR:2017:773, paras. 3.5.4–3.5.6.

1100 Gerechtshof Arnhem-Leeuwarden, 11 July 2017, ECLI:NL:GHARL:2017:5961 (*Pharma Slovakia*), para. 6.21.

1101 Derived from Smits (n 363) 24; Cherednychenko (n 67) 505. Cherednychecnko refers to a 'weak indirect horizontal effect of fundamental rights', which 'ensures that the values underlying fundamental rights are respected in contract law' and, thus, 'contributes to the development of contract law rules with a view to protecting the weaker party, but at the same time preserves the leading role of contract law in deciding disputes between private parties'.

1102 See also Rechtbank Gelderland, 20 July 2016, ECLI:NL:RBGEL:2016:4868, para. 2.9; Rechtbank Gelderland, 20 March 2019, ECLI:NL:RBGEL:2019:1175.

(Stichting Intermaris). The case concerned judicial review of arbitral awards and consumers' fundamental rights of access to court, albeit without explicitly mentioning Article 47 of the Charter. It, nevertheless, showed how a reference to the right of access to court may have an empowering function in respect of the role of courts, similar to the reference to Article 47 by AG Trstenjak in her opinion in *Asturcom*.

The differences between this case and *Van Marrum/Wolff* were twofold. In *Intermaris*: (i) the consumer was the *defendant*; and (ii) judicial review took place *ex post*, i.e. when the arbitration had already taken place and resulted in an arbitral award. Under Dutch law, if no action for annulment of an arbitral award is brought within three months, it becomes final, and its enforcement can only be refused where the arbitral proceedings or the award itself are prima facie contrary to public policy.[1103] Leave for enforcement of an arbitral award is usually granted *ex parte*, i.e. without hearing the other party, and the request is only dealt with summarily. This does not account for unfair terms control, which extends to arbitral awards. There were doubts as to how intensive the judicial review of arbitral awards should be in consumer cases, and what should happen in the case of a lack of information about the course of the arbitration proceedings. More specifically, the question was to what extent the court must be able to verify that the one-month period of Article 6:236(n) BW has been observed, and that the consumer has been sufficiently informed about the differences between arbitration and court proceedings, particularly in terms of costs, and the possibilities of opposing or appealing the final award or decision.[1104] In the course of enforcement proceedings, the court normally receives the arbitral award only, and does not carry out an elaborate examination. This means that the court, usually, will not have information about any irregularities in the arbitral proceedings, nor will it engage in a thorough investigation. Often, it cannot be ascertained from the award itself whether it has been based on an unfair arbitration clause, and sometimes not even whether it involves a *consumer* defendant.

In the *Intermaris* case, the Hoge Raad held that the fundamental nature of the right of access to court entailed that the court should check, if necessary *ex officio*, whether the one-month period had been observed.[1105] In this respect, a distinction can be made between the potential unfairness

---

1103 Articles 1063.2 and 1065.1(e) Rv.

1104 Rechtbank Amsterdam, 27 February 2019, ECLI:NL:RBAMS:2019:1338, paras. 3.6–3.7 and 3.11.

1105 Hoge Raad, 8 November 2019, ECLI:NL:HR:2019:1731 (*Intermaris*), para. 2.8.7.

of an arbitration clause, and other (substantive) terms on which the claim is based.[1106] *Ex officio* control of the latter is based on public policy as a prima facie ground to refuse enforcement of the arbitral award at issue. An unfair arbitration clause, by contrast, results in an invalid arbitration agreement. The Hoge Raad, thus, allowed for a broader scope of judicial review, with due regard to the parties' right to be heard.[1107]

For creditors, arbitration may provide an alternative route for debt collection that is easier, faster and cheaper than the judicial system. As a recent controversy about a private foundation called e-Court showed,[1108] several aspects of this may be problematic, from the perspective of Article 47 of the Charter. e-Court provided an online arbitration tool, which was used by professional creditors to quickly obtain an enforceable title. In some cases, the power to submit disputes to e-Court was unilateral, i.e. only the trader could do so, which could be seen as running counter to the principle of equality of arms. Moreover, the time limit for the consumer to submit a defence was very short (approximately one week), and the one-month period for the consumer to object to an arbitration clause being invoked against them was not always observed.[1109] If no defence was submitted, a standardised award would be generated, which merely referred to the case file for the claimed amount and other case-specific information.[1110] There were also concerns as to e-Court's independence: its business model was based on large numbers of cases brought by the same creditors ('repeat players'). An action for annulment of an arbitral award issued by e-Court against a consumer would hardly ever be initiated by the consumer in question.[1111] The solution proposed by the 2018 LOVCK Report was that the court must refuse to grant leave for enforcement if the award appears to be based on an unfair arbitration clause, or if it cannot be verified that unfair terms control has taken place.

[1106] Hoge Raad (n 1105), para. 2.5.5. See also Opinion of AG Valk (n 1093), point 4.20.

[1107] Hoge Raad (n 1105), para. 2.5.7. The Supreme Court had already held that the fundamental nature of the right of access to court entailed that the question of whether a valid arbitration agreement has been concluded must, ultimately, be answered by a court: Hoge Raad, 26 September 2014, ECLI:NL:HR:2014:2837, para. 4.2.

[1108] For this subsection, the main source is an article published (in Dutch) by investigative journalists Karlijn Kuijpers, Thomas Muntz and Tim Staal, 'Vonnis te koop' (2018) 3 De Groene Amsterdammer 28, available at <https://www.groene.nl/artikel/vonnis-te-koop> (last accessed 3 October 2021). See further Thiescheffer (n 1093); Emma van Gelder, 'Online Dispute Resolution: een veelbelovend initiatief voor toegang tot het recht?' [2018] Maandblad voor Vermogensrecht 262.

[1109] Rechtbank Amsterdam, 30 January 2018, ECLI:NL:RBAMS:2018:419.

[1110] Rechtbank Amsterdam, 27 March 2017, ECLI:NL:RBAMS:2017:2427.

[1111] Thiescheffer (n 1093) 70.

The necessary information must be provided in the arbitral award itself, possibly substantiated with documents from the case file.[1112]

In his Opinion in *Intermaris*, AG Valk asserted that the fundamental nature of the right of access to court entailed that the court's examination of an arbitration clause cannot be limited to a summary investigation.[1113] In this respect, Valk referred to *Asturcom*, but mentioned only Article 6 ECHR, not Article 47 of the Charter. The court must check whether the arbitration clause contains the mandatory period of (at least) one month, and whether this period has been observed in practice. The mere fact that the arbitral award itself confirms that this period has been observed is not sufficient in this regard.[1114] The court must also examine other circumstances that may render the term unfair, even if the one-month period has been observed.[1115] The court must respect the trader's right to be heard, whether or not the consumer defendant has entered an appearance.[1116] If the court finds that the arbitration clause is, indeed, unfair and/or the one-month period has not been observed, enforcement of the award must be refused.[1117]

The Hoge Raad followed the AG's Opinion in *Intermaris*, by reference to the effective judicial protection of consumers under the UCTD.[1118] The broadened scope for judicial review in the course of enforcement of arbitral awards is reminiscent of the Spanish (and Polish) cases discussed in Chapters 3 and 4.[1119] In the absence of an order for payment procedure, creditors in the Netherlands have resorted to arbitration as a pragmatic solution for bulk debt collection cases.[1120] However, arbitration should not turn into an avenue for creditors to deprive consumers of their rights, including the right to effective judicial protection guaranteed by Article 47 of the Charter. It is not only about ensuring compliance with the UCTD, but also – and even more compellingly – about guaranteeing

---

1112 2018 LOVCK Report, pp. 73–79.

1113 Opinion of AG Valk of 12 July 2019, ECLI:NL:PHR:2019:769 (*Intermaris*), points 1.4, 4.20 and 6.2(a).

1114 Opinion of AG Valk (n 1113), points 6.2 (i), (k) and (l).

1115 Opinion of AG Valk (n 1113), point 6.2 (o).

1116 Opinion of AG Valk (n 1113), points 6.2 (c) and (d).

1117 Opinion of AG Valk (n 1113), points 6.2 (h), (m) and (n).

1118 Judgment of Hoge Raad (n 1105), paras. 2.5.5 and 2.8.4.

1119 See, in particular, Case C-49/14 *Finanmadrid*; Case C-503/15 *Margarit Panicello;* Case C-176/17 *Profi Credit Polska;* and Case C-623/17 *PKO Bank Polski*, all discussed in section 3.2 of this book.

1120 Willemien Netjes and Arno R Lodder, 'E-Court – Dutch Alternative Online Resolution of Debt Collection Claims: A Violation of the Law or Blessing in Disguise?' [2019] International Journal of Online Dispute Resolution 70, 114.

the consumer's fundamental right of access to court. Article 47 provides a legal argument for judicial protection; it is not solely a matter of policy or politics, but a signal in a broader debate on the role of courts in light of EU (consumer) law.

5.3. EFFECTIVE (JUDICIAL) REMEDY

5.3.1. THE NOTION OF EFFECTIVE LEGAL OR JUDICIAL PROTECTION IN DUTCH LAW

The notion of effective legal or judicial protection (*effectieve rechtsbescherming*), as such, has not played a major role in Dutch unfair terms cases, let alone as a fundamental right. According to Giesen, it is not yet a principle of Dutch civil procedure: in his view there is no clear distinction between this notion and the right of access to court. At the same time, he has acknowledged that, in the context of EU law, effective judicial protection is broader: it also encompasses an effective remedy.[1121]

Indeed, previous chapters have shown that Article 47 of the Charter – read in conjunction with the UCTD – requires the availability of judicial remedies against, inter alia, the enforcement of claims by creditors against consumer debtors. Unlike in Spain, there is no separate order for payment procedure in the Netherlands. The debate about judicial review of arbitral awards, nevertheless, shows how creditors in the Netherlands are looking for alternative routes to obtain enforceable titles against consumer debtors. It would go beyond the scope of this book to examine to what extent this is caused by *ex officio* control of unfair terms in default proceedings, where the role of the court is usually limited to an examination of whether: (i) the procedural requirements have been met; and (ii) the claim does not appear to be unlawful or unfounded (Article 139 Rv). Some courts exercise extra scrutiny when 'repeat players', i.e. creditors that bring large numbers of claims, are involved.[1122] Repeat players may count on the fact that many consumer debtors do not contest claims, either because they are unaware of their rights, or for other reasons, such as the threat of high costs in

1121 Giesen (n 1043) 99–100.

1122 de Moor (n 1015) 234; Alain Ancery and Cindy Seinen, 'Vorderingen in b2c-verstekken: toetsen of toewijzen?' [2015] Tijdschrift voor Civiele Rechtspleging 77, 84–85; Cindy Seinen, 'De waarheidsplicht en de geraden gevolgtrekking anno 2020: een zoektocht naar proportionaliteit' [2020] Tijdschrift voor Civiele Rechtspleging 33, 39–40.

relation to the claimed amounts. Not only could this lead to the settlement of unfounded claims, for example claims that are, at least partially, based on unfair terms, it could also undermine the substantive and procedural rights of consumer defendants, due to their status as weaker parties.[1123] Courts try to put a check on this by dismissing claims when they are not sufficiently substantiated,[1124] and/or by issuing a higher costs order on the basis of 'abuse of process' (*misbruik van procesrecht*).[1125] Since this is a broader issue than effective judicial protection under the UCTD, it suffices here to observe that (further) dejudicialisation of the debt collection process could be problematic, in light of Article 47.[1126]

In the Netherlands, neither the UCTD nor Article 47 of the Charter play any significant role in the context of mortgage enforcement. An inquiry into the reasons behind this would fall outside the scope of this book. As we saw in Chapter 4, the Spanish mortgage cases arose in a specific socio-economic context. A similar flood of cases did not occur in the Netherlands, or at least not on the same scale. Perhaps Dutch judges and legal practitioners have not realised that the duty of unfair terms control (*ex officio*) extends to enforcement disputes; perhaps the existing procedural safeguards and level of judicial protection are generally considered to be sufficient.[1127] In this respect, one could argue that, if there is no (apparent) violation of Article 47 of the Charter, there is no need to refer to the Article. This would, however, reflect too narrow a view on the functions of a reference to Article 47.

1123 Rechtbank Amsterdam, 27 March 2020, ECLI:NL:RBAMS:2020:2002, para. 5. See also Case C-618/10 *Banesto*, discussed in subsection 3.2.3 of this book.

1124 On the basis of Articles 21 and 111 Rv. See, e.g. Rechtbank Amsterdam, 9 November 2018, ECLI:NL:RBAMS:2018:7770; Rechtbank Den Haag, 2 July 2019, ECLI:NL:RBDHA:2019:7920. Seinen has observed this does not constitute a violation of the right of access to court (Article 47 of the Charter): Seinen (n 1122) 38.

1125 See, e.g. Rechtbank Limburg, 26 July 2017, ECLI:NL:RBLIM:2017:7453; Rechtbank Amsterdam, 16 October 2017, ECLI:NL:RBAMS:2017:7577.

1126 See also subsections 3.2.3 and 4.2.3 of this book. See further van Duin (n 1035) 142.

1127 See, e.g. a case concerning interest rates where the bank's right to enforcement was examined without any reference to EU consumer law: Rechtbank Rotterdam, 11 May 2016, ECLI:NL:RBROT:2016:6438. In a case note on *Sánchez Morcillo*, Mak refers to a decision of the District Court in Amsterdam where the bank's conduct – resorting to mortgage enforcement at a time of crisis – was deemed an 'abuse of rights' (*misbruik van recht*): Rechtbank Amsterdam, 13 May 2013, ECLI:NL:RBAMS:2013:CA0869. As Mak points out, this pertained to the exercise of (contractual) rights rather than the potential unfairness of standard terms and conditions in the mortgage loan agreement: C Mak, 'Noot Bij HvJ EU 17 Juli 2014, C-169/14 *Sánchez Morcillo*' EHRC 2014/234.

5.3.2. PERSUASIVE AUTHORITY IN RESPECT OF NORMS WITH A PROTECTIVE PURPOSE

5.3.2.1. SEBA*: An Expansive Interpretation of Remedies*

The rhetorical function of a reference to Article 47 shows the Article's persuasive authority, which extends to the notion of effective judicial protection. An example can be found in the so-called *SEBA* case, which concerned a collective action in the context of the UCTD. Consumer protection organisations do not enjoy the same level of judicial protection as individual consumers.[1128] But, in his Opinion on the *SEBA* case, AG Wissink used *effectieve rechtsbescherming* as one of the arguments for a flexible, consumer-friendly interpretation of statutory provisions providing for two distinct types of legal remedies (in the sense of causes of action).[1129] Even though the case did not concern a fundamental rights issue, it indirectly enhanced the effective judicial protection of consumers. This could be seen as a spillover effect of EU consumer law into the realm of national law.

The Hoge Raad has adopted *effectieve rechtsbescherming* as a criterion, at national level, to assess the admissibility of collective actions: combining or grouping the interests of different parties together must promote efficient and effective legal protection against an infringement of those interests.[1130] In the Explanatory Memorandum on the introduction of collective actions in Dutch law (Article 3:305a BW), it is observed that 'efficient' refers, in this context, to procedural economy, and 'effective' to the effective enforcement of norms that aim to protect a certain group of interested parties.[1131] Whilst this criterion does not stem directly from EU law, it shows that Dutch civil courts are familiar with reasoning based on such notions. It may serve as an argument to justify a certain solution and/or to fill a legislative gap, especially when norms with a protective

---

1128 See also subsection 3.4.3 of this book. On the same issue, see Freerk Vermeulen and Tanja Schasfoort, 'Ambtshalve toetsing aan Unierecht ten gunste van belangenorganisaties?' [2017] Tijdschrift voor Civiele Rechtspleging 89.

1129 Opinion of AG Wissink of 22 January 2016, ECLI:NL:PHR:2016:3 (*SEBA*).

1130 See, e.g. Hoge Raad, 11 December 1987, ECLI:NL:HR:1987:AC2270. The criterion is also applied in collective actions (partially) pertaining to standard terms and conditions in consumer contracts, see, e.g. Gerechtshof Amsterdam, 11 July 2013, ECLI:NL:GHAMS:2013:1966; Rechtbank Den Haag, 28 October 2015, ECLI:NL:RBDHA:2015:12213.

1131 Kamerstukken (Parliamentary Papers) II, 1992/1993, 22 486, no. 3, p. 5.

purpose are at stake, and/or no effective judicial remedy would otherwise be available.[1132]

The *SEBA* case was brought by a foundation representing the interests of holders of a long-term ground lease in Amsterdam (Stichting Erfpachters Belang Amsterdam or SEBA), as well as a number of individual leaseholders, against the city of Amsterdam. There was a dispute about the validity of the rent revision clause in the general conditions of the ground lease. The rent was revised unilaterally between 2006 and 2009, based on the binding decisions of experts. The claimants had argued that the clause allowing for unilateral revision was unfair. In the actions brought by the individual leaseholders, the Amsterdam Court of Appeal had annulled the clauses at issue. In the collective action, however, the Court had referred the case to the Court of Appeal in The Hague. Pursuant to Article 6:240 BW, this Court of Appeal has exclusive jurisdiction to issue declaratory judgments: injunctions that specific stipulations are unfair.[1133] Such declaratory judgments may contain additional prohibitions on the use or promotion of the stipulations at issue. If the party who uses these stipulations keeps using them, they are voidable by any other person who enters into a contract with that party (Article 6:243 BW).

Because most underlying contracts had been concluded before 31 December 1994, the case largely fell outside the temporal scope of the UCTD. In respect of contracts concluded in 2000, however, the Hoge Raad interpreted Article 6:233 BW in conformity with the Directive. It held that the possibility of an action on the basis of Article 6:240 BW did not preclude a collective action, within the meaning of Article 3:305a BW.[1134] An action based on Article 6:240 called for a preventive, abstract assessment resulting in a judgment that can be invoked by third parties. By contrast, an action based on Article 3:305a pertained to concrete legal relationships between the defendant and its contractual counterparties, whose interests were represented collectively.[1135] AG Wissink submitted

[1132] Giesen (n 1043) 94–96, with reference to, e.g. Hoge Raad, 27 November 2009, ECLI:NL:HR:2009:BH2162, paras. 14.11.1–14.11.2 (*World Online*). See also, e.g. Gerechtshof Arnhem-Leeuwarden, 28 August 2018, ECLI:NL:GHARL:2018:7753; Gerechtshof Arnhem-Leeuwarden, 5 February 2019, ECLI:NL:GHARL:2019:1060.

[1133] The provision is an implementation of Directive 2009/22/EC on injunctions for the protection of consumers' interests (OJ L110, 1 May 2009, p. 30).

[1134] Hoge Raad, 29 April 2016, ECLI:NL:HR:2016:769 (*SEBA*), paras. 4.6.2–4.6.3.

[1135] On the third-party effect of collective actions, see also subsection 4.5.3 of this book. See further Charlotte Pavillon, 'De derdenwerking van collectieve acties tegen onredelijke bedingen in het licht van de Europese rechtspraak' [2016] Tijdschrift voor Consumentenrecht en handelspraktijken 160.

that the distinction between the two types of actions should, therefore, not be applied too strictly: they were not mutually exclusive, and should not be split up between two different courts.[1136]

The Hoge Raad adopted this proposed solution.[1137] This shows how the notion of effective judicial protection may serve as a justification for an expansive interpretation of the remedies available to consumer protection organisations, which leads, in turn, to a higher level of protection than that prescribed by EU consumer law. A comparable mechanism is visible in an earlier case, where the Hoge Raad adopted a lenient approach towards the interruptive effect of a collective action on the basis of Article 3:305a BW, in respect of running limitation periods.[1138] It held that this interruptive effect should extend to all individual claims falling within the scope of the collective action, in the interests of the efficient and effective legal protection that the collective action aimed to achieve.

That there was no reference to Article 47 of the Charter does not mean that cases like these cannot fall within its scope. Prescriptive periods are not beyond the reach of EU law and, therefore, neither are they beyond the reach of Article 47.[1139] According to the CJEU, consumers must have the opportunity to become aware of their rights before the period begins to run or expires.[1140] In the *SEBA* case, there was no apparent

1136 Opinion of AG Wissink of 22 January 2016, ECLI:NL:PHR:2016:3 (*SEBA*), point 9.12.4.

1137 The case was referred to the Court of Appeal in The Hague for further adjudication of the individual actions and the collective action, together: Gerechtshof Den Haag, 19 September 2017, ECLI:NL:GHDHA:2017:2894. SEBA also brought a new, separate action on the basis of Article 6:240 BW before the Court of Appeal in The Hague, in respect of the general conditions of the ground lease that the City of Amsterdam enacted in 2016: see Gerechtshof Den Haag, 12 March 2019, ECLI:NL:GHDHA:2019:453.

1138 Hoge Raad, 9 October 2015, ECLI:NL:HR:2015:3018, para. 3.5.4

1139 See, e.g. Case C-616/18 *Cofidis v YU, ZT*, Opinion of AG Kokott in C-616/18 *Cofidis*, points 64 and 85; Case C-485/19 *Profi Credit Slovakia*, para. 54; Joined Cases C-776/19 to C-782/19 *BNP Paribas Personal Finance*, para. 29. On prescriptive periods in the context of the UCTD, see further Charlotte Pavillon, 'Beter ten hele gedwaald dan ten halve gekeerd? De verjaring van de sanctie op oneerlijke bedingen' [2019] Weekblad voor privaatrecht, notariaat en registratie 621; Daniël Stein, 'Verjaring en Unierecht' in Valérie Tweehuysen and Steven Bartels (eds), *Verjaring* (Wolters Kluwer 2020). On the fundamental rights dimension of prescription, see De Graaff (n 1046) 144–145. De Graaff observes that it may be difficult to determine the required (minimum) level of protection when one party's fundamental right of access to court must be balanced against another fundamental right, or against other interests, such as legal certainty and the other party's legitimate expectations.

1140 See, e.g. Joined Cases C-698/18 and C-699/18 *SCRaiffeisen Bank and BRD Groupe Société Generale*, para. 67. Under the Romanian rules at issue, a period of three years started to run from the date of full performance of the contract, irrespective of whether consumers were, or reasonably could have been, aware of their rights.

violation: the limitation period expired three years after the day that the unfairness of a specific clause was invoked (in a collective action or by an individual consumer), i.e. it started running when the consumer could have become aware of its unfair nature, and could have brought a legal action.[1141] Moreover, it did not apply if the unfairness was invoked as a defence,[1142] which, according to AG Wissink, extended to *ex officio* control in cases concerning claims against consumers. In such cases, effective judicial protection as a fundamental right did not come into play either.[1143] However, this might be different if time limits were too short to enable consumers to prepare and bring effective actions, or if their procedural rights were otherwise excessively restricted, as discussed in Chapter 3.

5.3.2.2. Lindorff/Nazier: *Spillover Effect to Purely National Matters*

Another example of the rhetorical value of the notion of effective judicial protection can be found in *Lindorff/Nazier*, a case concerning mobile phone subscriptions with an 'all-in price' including a 'free' device.[1144] The Hoge Raad held that Dutch courts were obliged to exercise *ex officio* control in respect of both Article 7:61(2) BW, which implements the Consumer Credit Directive,[1145] and Article 7A:1576 BW on purchase in instalments, even though the latter Article is not of European origin. The Hoge Raad put Article 7A:1756 BW on an equal footing with Article 7:61 BW for the sake of manageability, and effective protection of consumer interests.[1146] According to the Hoge Raad, a violation of the requirements of Article 7:61(2) BW could lead to annulment of the contract, even though the law did not define a separate sanction.[1147] The Hoge Raad emphasised the importance of ensuring *effectieve rechtsbescherming* for consumers, if necessary of the court's own motion, tailored to the circumstances of the case, and with due regard for the right to be heard.[1148] In the words of the Hoge Raad, 'provisions that are aimed at the

---

1141 Articles 6:235(4) and 3:51(1) BW.

1142 Article 3:51(3) BW.

1143 Opinion of AG Wissink of 22 January 2016, ECLI:NL:PHR:2016:3 (*SEBA*), para. 10.8. See also Gerechtshof Den Haag, 12 March 2019, ECLI:NL:GHDHA:2019:453, para 2.14, which referred to Article 6 ECHR instead of Article 47 of the Charter.

1144 Hoge Raad, 12 February 2016, ECLI:NL:HR:2016:236 (*Lindorff/Nazier*).

1145 Directive 2008/48/EC on credit agreements for consumers (OJ L133, 22 May 2008, p. 66).

1146 Judgment of Hoge Raad (n 1144), paras. 3.11.1 and 3.11.2.

1147 Judgment of Hoge Raad (n 1144), para. 3.7.3.

1148 Judgment of Hoge Raad (n 1144), paras. 3.8.2, 3.9 and 3.11.1.

protection of consumers' require adequate measures ensuring effective judicial protection.[1149]

The solution adopted by the Hoge Raad did not follow from the principles of equivalence and effectiveness, because the case concerned purely national provisions. The maxim *ubi ius, ibi remedium* – where there is a right, there must be a remedy – also has persuasive authority in cases falling outside the scope of EU law.[1150] Ancery and Seinen have observed that, in the context of consumer law, this notion can even be a more compelling argument for *ex officio* control than public policy.[1151] The Hoge Raad used it in *Lindorff/Nazier* to reinforce an active role for courts,[1152] and to justify application of the remedy of annulment in the absence of a specific legislative provision. It may, thus, provide a justification for 'spontaneous harmonisation',[1153] where it is used as an argument to expand *ex officio* control to purely national matters.

In a later (non-consumer) case, however, the Hoge Raad expressly linked the duty of *ex officio* control (on appeal) to the public policy character of national provisions that did not stem from EU law.[1154] The question is whether such provisions purport to protect public interests of such a fundamental nature that their enforcement should not be hampered by procedural restrictions. This appears to be a stricter test than the one applied in *Lindorff/Nazier*. The Hoge Raad reiterated this formula in the above-mentioned *Intermaris* case, in respect of a national provision on debt collection charges (Article 6:96(6) BW). While this provision was intended to protect consumers, it did not concern public policy or EU law.[1155] Thus, there are limits to the spillover effect discussed in this section.

The debate on what effective judicial protection entails in consumer cases, and when *ex officio* control is required, is far from settled.

1149 Judgment of Hoge Raad (n 1144), para. 3.8.2.

1150 See also Giesen (n 1043) 95. As observed by the Deputy Procurator General Langemeijer and Advocate General Wissink at the Supreme Court in the famous *Urgenda* case, effective judicial protection requires that norms are upheld, and that rights can *actually* be enforced in court: Opinion of 13 September 2019, ECLI:NL:PHR:2019:887 (*Urgenda*), point 4.197.

1151 Ancery and Seinen (n 1122) 78. See also Opinion of AG Wissink of 21 December 2012, ECLI:NL:PHR:2012:BY7854 (*Heesakkers/Voets*), points 3.19 and 3.36; Opinion of AG Wissink of 23 September 2016, ECLI:NL:PHR:2016:938, point 3.45.

1152 See also, e.g. Gerechtshof Arnhem-Leeuwarden, 4 September 2018, ECLI:NL:GHARL:2018:7970, para. 4.4.

1153 Marco Loos, *Spontane harmonisatie in het contracten- en consumentenrecht* (Vossiuspers 2006); Krans (n 236) 585.

1154 Hoge Raad, 1 June 2018, ECLI:NL:HR:2018:818.

1155 Hoge Raad, 8 November 2019, ECLI:NL:HR:2019:1731 (*Intermaris*), para. 2.9.3. AG Valk had argued for *ex officio* control, to ensure consistency between European and national law: Opinion of AG Valk, points 5.4 and 6.4.

As Hartkamp has noted,[1156] problems seem mainly to arise in special procedures such as the enforcement of arbitral awards, or in appellate proceedings. The latter will be discussed in the next section.

5.4. EQUALITY OF ARMS

5.4.1. *EX OFFICIO* CONTROL WITHIN THE AMBIT OF THE DISPUTE ON APPEAL

5.4.1.1. Asbeek Brusse*: No Systemic Issue with Justiciability on Appeal*

The case law as regards appellate proceedings shows how Dutch civil courts, and the Hoge Raad in particular, have found ways to ensure the effective judicial protection of consumers without resorting to Article 47 of the Charter.

A question that came up in *Asbeek Brusse* was what was required from the Court of Appeal in view of the fact that it was the court of second instance in respect of adjudication of the case.[1157] In appellate proceedings, the ambit of the dispute is strictly limited to the part(s) of the judgment against which objections have been raised.[1158] Until *Asbeek Brusse*, it was unclear whether, and to what extent, courts of appeal could, or should, perform *ex officio* control; there is a delicate balance between observing the strict (albeit largely judge-made) rules governing appellate proceedings and ensuring the UCTD's full effectiveness.[1159]

Asbeek Brusse concerned a claim based on a residential tenancy agreement that provided for the payment of rent due, contractual interest and a penalty for late payments. At first instance, the claim was granted. The tenants brought an appeal, arguing that the penalty should be

---

1156 Arthur Hartkamp, 'De verhouding tussen twee Europese "remedies": lidstaataansprakelijkheid en ambtshalve toepassing van de richtlijn oneerlijke bedingen' [2016] Ars Aequi 658, 662.

1157 Case C-488/11 *Asbeek Brusse*, also discussed in subsection 3.4.2 of this book.

1158 Parts that are not challenged obtain *res judicata* effect, encompassing both formal *res judicata* ('*kracht van gewijsde*'), i.e. they are deemed final and irrevocable, and substantive *res judicata* ('*gezag van gewijsde*'), i.e. they are binding between the parties. See further Pieter Frans Lock, 'Ambtshalve toetsing in hoger beroep: Over de omvang van het hoger beroep en het door de grieven ontsloten gebied' [2014] Tijdschrift voor Civiele Rechtspleging 45.

1159 Ancery (n 32) 134, 139.

mitigated, but without invoking the clause's potential unfairness, which, if established, would free them from being bound by its effects.[1160] The Amsterdam Court of Appeal made a preliminary reference to the CJEU to ask whether the case fell within the scope of the UCTD (the CJEU found that it did), whether the Court of Appeal must perform *ex officio* control (the CJEU found that it must), and whether it could mitigate the penalty instead of disapplying it (the CJEU found that it could not). In respect of *ex officio* control, the CJEU held this to be a matter of equivalence, i.e. the Court of Appeal must perform unfair terms control where it has the power to examine, of its own motion, any grounds for invalidity of contract terms – because they are contrary to public policy or a mandatory statutory provision – that are clearly apparent from the elements submitted at first instance.[1161] In a follow-up judgment, the Amsterdam Court of Appeal declared the penalty clause to be unfair. After it had given the parties the opportunity to present their views on the contractual interest clause,[1162] it also declared that clause to be unfair; only the main claim was awarded, plus statutory interest. Although statutory interest had not been (explicitly) claimed, the Court of Appeal held that such a claim was implicit, on the basis of the landlord's submissions in this regard.[1163]

A comparison between (the national implementation of) *Asbeek Brusse* and *Sánchez Morcillo*[1164] reveals two important differences. Firstly, under Dutch law, the grounds of appeal are not restricted to the extent that unfair terms can no longer be raised on appeal. For the question of whether a judicial decision can be appealed, it is irrelevant whether unfair terms control has taken place at first instance or not. In *Asbeek Brusse*, the appeal itself was admissible; the question concerned the ambit of the dispute in the concrete case. Secondly, Dutch courts of appeal can perform unfair terms control *ex officio*, because they have this power on the basis of public policy. Thus, in principle, there is redress available for a procedural breach at first instance; there is no systemic issue with the justiciability of consumer rights on appeal, as such. Again, this might explain why there is no need to refer to Article 47, in this context.

1160 Gerechtshof Amsterdam, 13 September 2013, ECLI:NL:GHAMS:2013:CA1825.

1161 Case C-488/11 *Asbeek Brusse*, para. 45; see also subsection 3.4.2 of this book.

1162 Gerechtshof Amsterdam, 21 January 2014, ECLI:NL:GHAMS:2014:950.

1163 Gerechtshof Amsterdam, 29 July 2014, ECLI:NL:GHAMS:2014:5414.

1164 Case C-169/14 *Sánchez Morcillo*, discussed in subsections 3.4.2 and 4.4.2 of this book.

5.4.1.2. Ebecek/Stichting Trudo: *Ambit of the Dispute and Role of the Court on Appeal*

After *Asbeek Brusse*, the Hoge Raad confirmed, in *Heesakkers/Voets*, that courts of appeal were obliged to perform *ex officio* control of unfair terms falling within the ambit of the dispute.[1165] It further clarified the meaning of 'ambit of the dispute' in *Ebecek/Stichting Trudo*,[1166] another case about a penalty clause in a residential tenancy agreement. The court of first instance had not found the clause to be unfair. On appeal, the tenant requested that the judgment be quashed and the claim dismissed in its entirety. The Court of Appeal in 's-Hertogenbosch did not re-examine the alleged unfairness of the penalty clause, because no specific objection had been lodged against the finding of the court of first instance: the tenant had only asked for mitigation of the penalty. The tenant brought an appeal before the Hoge Raad on the ground that the Court should, nevertheless, have performed *ex officio* control.

The Hoge Raad distinguished the area opened up by the appellant's objections (*het door de grieven ontsloten gebied*) from the ambit of the dispute (*grenzen van de rechtsstrijd*).[1167] The latter, which was a matter of interpretation, determined what the court should decide on. In *Trudo*, the penalty clause was not specifically mentioned in the objections, but it *was* part of the ambit of the dispute: the appeal challenged the part of the judgment that granted the claim, which was based on the penalty clause at issue.[1168] This meant that this part of the judgment had not obtained *res judicata* effect and, therefore, fell within the ambit of the dispute. Thus, the Court of Appeal should have performed unfair terms control (*ex officio*). This is in line with later CJEU case law: what matters is whether the terms fall within the ambit of the dispute, which they do if they form the basis of the claim.[1169]

A potential problem could arise if the consumer did not contest the penalty, meaning that the penalty clause would fall outside the ambit of

---

1165 Hoge Raad, 13 September 2013, ECLI:NL:HR:2013:691 (*Heesakkers/Voets*), para. 3.6.3; see also subsection 5.2.1 above. See also Opinion of AG Wissink of 10 April 2015, ECLI:NL:PHR:2015:455, points 3.20–3.22, followed in Hoge Raad, 10 July 2015, ECLI:NL:HR:2015:1866, paras. 3.6–3.9.

1166 Hoge Raad, 26 February 2016, ECLI:NL:HR:2016:340, NJ 2017/214 m.nt. HB Krans (*Ebecek/Stichting Trudo*).

1167 Judgment of Hoge Raad (n 1166), paras. 3.4.2–3.4.3.

1168 Judgment of Hoge Raad (n 1166), para. 3.5. See also Ancery and Krans (n 1018) 138.

1169 Case C-511/17 *Lintner v UniCredit Bank Hungary*, para. 44. Whether or not the terms were applied or executed, in practice, is irrelevant: Case C-602/13 *BBVA*, para. 50; Case C-421/14 *Banco Primus*, para. 73.

the dispute.[1170] This would be at odds with the need to ensure effective judicial protection, especially if, at first instance, no unfair terms control at all has taken place. The court's failure to do so (*ex officio*) is not a matter of the UCTD's effectiveness on a systemic level, but, rather, the incorrect application of procedural rules in a concrete case. There is a parallel with *Sánchez Morcillo*, where the question arose of how such a failure – or a procedural breach – could be remedied, if not by a court of appeal. An additional issue is that no appeal can be brought in cases where the value of the claim does not exceed 1,750 euros.[1171]

In his Opinion on *Heesakkers/Voets*, AG Wissink had mentioned the possibility of unfair terms control in the course of enforcement proceedings, but he also observed that this would be less efficient, from the perspective of procedural economy. More importantly, it would require the consumer to actively oppose the enforcement.[1172] Another possibility could be for the consumer to bring new proceedings, although this would also require the consumer to take further legal action. The case of *Banco Primus* suggests that the *res judicata* effect of the original judgment does not cover unfair terms that have not yet been the subject of examination by a court.[1173] Otherwise, the only remedies left would be the professional liability of the consumer's lawyer – if they had legal representation, which is often not the case – or State liability. As observed earlier,[1174] it is questionable whether this constitutes an effective remedy against unfair terms and/or a procedural breach: it lets the trader 'off the hook'.

5.4.2. CALLS FOR A MORE TAILORED APPROACH

There is another important parallel between *Asbeek Brusse* and *Sánchez Morcillo*. In both cases, consideration was given to the type of contract at issue: a tenancy agreement and a mortgage loan agreement, respectively, which both pertained to housing. In *Asbeek Brusse*, the CJEU considered

---

1170 M Nieuwenhuijs and MEA Möhring, 'Vindt de consumentenbescherming haar grens in het appelprocesrecht?' [2016] Tijdschrift voor Civiele Rechtspleging 87, 90.

1171 Article 332 Rv.

1172 Opinion of AG Wissink of 21 December 2012, ECLI:NL:PHR:2012:BY7854 (*Heesakkers/Voets*), point 3.31.

1173 Case C-421/14 *Banco Primus*; see subsection 4.4.3 of the preceding chapter. This also applies if it cannot be derived from the original (default) judgment that unfair terms control has taken place: Rechtbank Amsterdam 29 November 2019, ECLI:NL:RBAMS:2019:8803.

1174 See subsection 2.2.1.2 of Chapter 2, with reference to Case C-168/15 *Tomášová*.

that 'the consequences of the inequality existing between the parties are aggravated by the fact that, from an economic perspective, such a [residential tenancy] contract relates to an essential need of the consumer, namely to obtain lodging, and involves sums which most frequently, for the tenant, represent one of the most significant items in his budget, while, from a legal perspective, this is a contract which, as a general rule, is covered by complex national rules about which individuals are often poorly informed'.[1175] Socio-economic factors such as the right to housing also played a role in both *Sánchez Morcillo* and *Kušionová*.[1176] The substantive imbalance between the parties, especially when the case concerns the family home, can be exacerbated even further by procedural inequalities. This underlines that the importance of procedural guarantees and, in particular, equality of arms, is also applicable to appeals.

The question arises as to what circumstances – such as the type of contract at issue, the significance of what is at stake (such as the family home), or whether the consumer has legal representation – are relevant for the degree to which courts should compensate for the weaker position of consumers, from a procedural point of view. The court does not have to make up fully for total inertia on the part of a consumer who does not make use of available judicial remedies in a concrete case.[1177] However, consumers' failure to exercise their rights in court cannot always be imputed to inertia. For example, if the terms at issue were not found to be unfair at first instance, as was the case in *Trudo*, this could deter consumers from raising a specific objection on appeal: they might believe there is no chance of success anyway. Therefore, the fact that no specific objection is lodged is not sufficient to give rise to an assumption that the consumer waives the protection offered by the UCTD.[1178] The argument that consumers have mandatory legal representation on appeal, and so can no longer be presumed to be unaware of their rights, is not convincing either.[1179] If anything, a requirement to have legal representation could be an additional procedural obstacle for consumers. Therefore, after *Trudo*, the only reason for not performing *ex officio* control that remains is that

---

1175 Case C-488/11 *Asbeek Brusse*, para. 32.

1176 Case C-169/14 *Sánchez Morcillo* and C-34/13 *Kušionová*: see subsections 3.3.2 and 3.4.2 of this book, respectively.

1177 See subsections 3.2.2 and 3.2.3 of Chapter 3.

1178 Opinion of AG Wissink of 30 October 2015, ECLI:NL:PHR:2015:2703 (*Ebecek/Stichting Trudo*), points 3.24.2–3.25.2.

1179 Opinion of AG Wissink (n 1178), point 3.20.4. See also Case C-497/13 *Faber*, para. 47.

circumstances exist whereby the terms at issue are not part of the ambit of the dispute.[1180]

Calls have, nevertheless, been made for a more tailored approach, based on the concrete circumstances of the case.[1181] In his Opinion on *Heesakkers/Voets*, AG Wissink pointed out that the UCTD presumes that there is an imbalance between the parties, but that, in practice, the contrast may not be as black and white.[1182] The position of Voets – the professional party in this case, a small enterprise – was not too different from that of a consumer. In this respect, a distinction could be made between 'one-shotters' and 'repeat players': the latter have the advantage of knowledge and resources.[1183] While the degree of inequality *in concreto* is not relevant, from the perspective of the CJEU's case law, this has met with some criticism,[1184] which reveals tension between categorical protection and a case-specific proposition. The position of traders that make use of general terms and conditions should also be considered, the criticism goes, and consumers should not be given undue procedural advantages.

However, effective judicial protection of consumers is not aimed at giving them undue procedural advantages: the aim is to restore the balance. It would go too far to question the court's impartiality when it helps the consumer by applying EU consumer law and/or compensating for inequality. The court acts as a 'counterweight', to ensure the application of mandatory law;[1185] this does not change the substance of the law itself, nor does it influence the court's substantive assessment.[1186] As observed earlier, there is no one-on-one relationship between the procedural position of one party and the substantive position of the other.[1187] Moreover, the

1180 See also Gerechtshof Den Haag, 19 September 2017, ECLI:NL:GHDHA:2017:2894 (*SEBA*), para. 2.3.

1181 See, e.g. Ancery and Pavillon (n 1098); Vermeulen and Schasfoort (n 1128); Biemans and Castermans (n 1013) 102–103.

1182 Opinion of AG Wissink of 21 December 2012, ECLI:NL:PHR:2012:BY7854 (*Heesakkers/Voets*), point 3.16.

1183 Marc Galanter, 'Why the "Haves" Come out Ahead: Speculations on the Limits of Legal Change' (1974) 9 Law & Society Review 95, 107. See also Judith Resnik, 'Access to Justice, Access to Knowledge, and Economic Inequalities in Open Courts and Arbitrations' (2018) 96 North Carolina Law Review 101, 103.

1184 Alain Ancery, 'Ambtshalve toepassing van consumentenbeschermend EU-recht' [2013] Maandblad voor Vermogensrecht 329, 338–339; Vermeulen and Schasfoort (n 1128) 95.

1185 Beka (n 32) 140–141.

1186 See also ECtHR 20 December 2018, Appl. No. 22853/15 *Merkantil*, para. 66.

1187 See subsection 3.5.2 of Chapter 3. For a discussion of other arguments intrinsic to Dutch civil procedure – such as the prohibition of *reformatio in peius*, which entails

trader's position must also be taken into account. If anything, Article 47 of the Charter makes it clear that the court must observe fundamental procedural guarantees for both parties; in particular, the trader's right to be heard.

5.5. RIGHT TO BE HEARD

In Dutch unfair terms cases, the right to be heard is the most visible of the procedural rights guaranteed by Article 47 of the Charter, even if it is not referred to explicitly. Before *Banif Plus Bank*,[1188] Dutch civil courts rarely made any (explicit) reference to the principle of *audi alteram partem* (*hoor en wederhoor*), in the context of the UCTD. Of course, this does not mean that this principle was not observed. On the contrary, it is one of the most fundamental principles underpinning Dutch civil procedure.[1189] It was only in mid-2013 – after the judgment in *Banif Plus Bank*, which refers to Article 47 of the Charter, and *Asbeek Brusse* – that courts started explicitly referring to *hoor en wederhoor* for both parties: the consumer and the trader.[1190]

This was related to the implementation of the *ex officio* doctrine. In the 2014 version of the LOVCK Report,[1191] *Banif Plus Bank* was cited to emphasise that courts, when exercising *ex officio* control, must observe the principle of *audi alteram partem*. The consumer must be given the opportunity to make a choice between annulment and preservation of the clause at issue, and the trader must be given the chance to respond, and to argue why the clause is not unfair in the circumstances of the case, even if

that an appellant (the trader, in this case) cannot be put in a worse position by their own appeal – see Opinion of AG Wissink on *Heesakkers/Voets* (n 1182), point 3.25ff. According to AG Wissink, the effective protection of consumer rights outweighs these arguments (point 3.39).

1188 Case C-472/11 *Banif Plus Bank*, discussed in subsection 3.5.2.

1189 Giesen (n 1043) 310. See also Ancery (n 32) 30. The principle of *audi alteram partem* is codified in Article 19 Rv.

1190 See, e.g. Rechtbank Midden-Nederland, 26 June 2013, ECLI:NL:RBMNE:2013:3393, para. 3.16; Gerechtshof 's-Hertogenbosch, 15 November 2013, ECLI:NL:GHSHE:2013:5206, para. 4.3.4; Gerechtshof Arnhem-Leeuwarden, 10 December 2013, ECLI:NL:GHARL:2013:9446, para. 4.2; Rechtbank Amsterdam, 18 December 2013, ECLI:NL:RBAMS:2013:9891, para. 4.11; Gerechtshof Amsterdam, 25 February 2014, ECLI:NL:GHAMS:2014:1580, para. 3.7.3; Rechtbank Amsterdam, 23 July 2014, ECLI:NL:RBAMS:2014:5421, para. 2.5; Gerechtshof Arnhem-Leeuwarden, 1 August 2017, ECLI:NL:GHARL:2017:6578, para. 5.5.

1191 Mentioned in subsection 5.1.1 above; see pp. 17–18 of the Report.

there is a suspicion that the clause is unfair because it is on the blacklist.[1192] The Hoge Raad adopted similar reasoning in *Heesakkers/Voets*.[1193] The (implicit) impact of Article 47 on the adjudication of unfair terms cases by Dutch civil courts is, thus, a qualification, or fine-tuning, of *ex officio* control in light of the UCTD. It shows how, just as in Spain, the generative function of Article 47 translates into national procedural law.

Just like in Spain, a violation of the right to be heard is often invoked by traders in unfair terms cases in the Netherlands when they challenge judicial decisions that are unfavourable to them. Several judgments have been called into question because the outcome, arguably, constituted a 'surprise decision'.[1194] Such a surprise decision is often the result of a court basing its decision on information in the case file that was not part of the debate between the parties and/or the ambit of the dispute.

Usually, an alleged violation of the right to be heard can still be remedied, as long as the proceedings are still pending, and have not resulted in a decision with formal *res judicata* effect. For instance, in a case where the Court of Appeal found the initial claim to have been based on an anti-speculation clause in a deed of transfer falling within the scope of the UCTD, it ordered an oral hearing before a full bench. It held that one of the purposes of appellate proceedings was to repair any mistakes made by the court of first instance. There was no longer a violation of the right to be heard, because the parties did have sufficient opportunities, on appeal, to substantiate their positions.[1195]

In this respect, it is relevant to consider at what precise stage of the proceedings the exchange of arguments is supposed to take place. In the above-mentioned *SEBA* case, the Hoge Raad held that the parties must be able to express their views about the court's intended *investigation* into the applicability of the UCTD and the unfairness of the term(s) at issue.[1196] The 2018 LOVCK Report states that the parties must be heard

1192 See also 2018 LOVCK Report, pp. 22 and 42, where it is added that, in default proceedings, it will suffice for the court to inform the claimant (trader), provided, of course, that consumer defendant has been duly notified of the proceedings.

1193 Hoge Raad, 13 September 2013, ECLI:NL:HR:2013:691 (*Heesakkers/Voets*), para. 3.9.1. See also Gerechtshof Arnhem-Leeuwarden, 10 September 2013, ECLI:NL:GHARL:2013:6635, para. 7.8 and Opinion of AG Wissink of 30 October 2015, ECLI:NL:PHR:2015:2703 (*Ebecek/Stichting Trudo*), point 3.8.1.

1194 See, e.g. Gerechtshof 's-Hertogenbosch, 24 September 2013, ECLI:NL:GHSHE:2013:4346, para. 11.13; Opinion of AG Wissink of 5 April 2019, ECLI:NL:PHR:2019:346, point 5.43. See also de Moor (n 1015) 234; Vermeulen and Schasfoort (n 1128) 93.

1195 Gerechtshof Arnhem-Leeuwarden, 18 August 2015, ECLI:NL:GHARL:2015:6097, paras. 3.9 and 3.12.

1196 Hoge Raad, 29 April 2016, ECLI:NL:HR:2016:769 (*SEBA*), para. 5.1.8.

in the case of an intended *annulment*,[1197] which suggests that this can be done after the court's provisional assessment. It is hard to see how the court could ask relevant questions at the oral hearing, or allow the parties to submit additional documents, if it cannot make a provisional assessment. According to the CJEU, the principle of *audi alteram partem*, as guaranteed by Article 47 of the Charter, entails that:

> '[W]here the national court, *after* establishing, on the basis of the matters of fact and law at its disposal, or which were communicated to it following the measures of inquiry which it undertook of its own motion, that a term comes within the scope of the Directive, finds, *following* an assessment made of its own motion, that that term is unfair, it is, as a general rule, required to inform the parties to the dispute of that fact and to invite each of them to set out their views on that matter, with the opportunity to challenge the views of the other party'.[1198] [emphasis added]

Indeed, when a party is accused of an infringement of EU law, it must get an opportunity to respond to all the elements on which the court's decision will be based, before the final *judgment* is rendered.[1199] This is in line with the CJEU's reading of Article 47 of the Charter.

It has been observed that *ex officio* control of unfair terms has a price in terms of procedural efficiency.[1200] If it only takes place on appeal, and not at first instance, it means that the parties lose out on first instance, and the exchange of arguments is postponed until a later stage of the proceedings. This may cause a significant delay, or come at the cost of a well-considered debate between the parties. It has also been contended that Article 6 ECHR and Article 47 of the Charter prevent courts from taking decisions based on legal or factual elements that the trader was not, and did not have to be, prepared for.[1201] These objections show the other side of Article 47, which approaches the adjudication of unfair terms cases from a due process perspective. Effective judicial protection of both parties could be understood as the court guiding the exchange of arguments between them in a concrete and detailed manner, thereby facilitating the decision-making process. The right to be heard is not only a due process

1197 2018 LOVCK Report, p. 22.
1198 Case C-472/11 *Banif Plus Bank*, para. 31.
1199 See also Gerechtshof Arnhem-Leeuwarden, 23 August 2016, ECLI:NL:GHARL:2016:6736, para. 3.12 (in a non-consumer case).
1200 Vermeulen and Schasfoort (n 1128) 93. See also Ancery (n 32) 155–158.
1201 Vermeulen and Schasfoort (n 1128) 93.

requirement: it also enables the court to provide justice for both parties by taking all circumstances of the case into account.[1202] This is reminiscent of the reconciliatory function of Article 47, which leads to a more balanced procedure.[1203]

Still, the question can be asked, more balanced for whom?[1204] Chapter 4 shows how Article 47 may be used to defend traditional principles of civil procedure without properly considering how they might prevent courts from restoring the balance for consumers, or otherwise affect the effective judicial protection of individual consumer rights. Courts should, therefore, be wary of how and why Article 47 is being invoked, by whom, and to what end.

5.6. INTERIM CONCLUSION: THE ROLE OF ARTICLE 47 IN DUTCH CASE LAW

Dutch civil courts rarely refer to Article 47 of the Charter. In the context of the UCTD, procedural issues are dealt with almost exclusively within the framework of *ex officio* control. In the Netherlands, the CJEU's case law has been implemented mostly through judge-made law, i.e. consistent interpretation of (open) norms and a consumer-friendly application of procedural rules that determine the powers of the court, in particular in default and appellate proceedings (see, for example, *Trudo*) and judicial review of arbitral awards (*Intermaris*). In general, unfair terms cases are not constitutionalised. The only references to Article 47, in this context, were made in respect of arbitration clauses in consumer contracts, before such clauses were blacklisted, and (more implicitly) in relation to the right to be heard.

In *Van Marrum/Wolff*, Article 47 was one of the parameters in the substantive unfairness assessment of an arbitration clause, which could be seen as an instance of its eliminatory function, but only horizontally, i.e. in the contractual relationship between the parties. It could also be perceived as a signal to the legislature that arbitration clauses should be included in the blacklist of unfair terms. Dutch civil courts have not yet

1202 Pavillon (n 1015) 124. Opinion of AG Wissink of 21 December 2012, ECLI:NL:PHR:2012:BY7854 (*Heesakkers/Voets*), points 3.18 and 3.30.

1203 See subsection 4.5.3 of this book.

1204 As Kennedy has observed, rights arguments may mediate between law and policy where they explain and justify rules, but their supposedly objective character may also reduce rights arguments to a question of balancing: Kennedy (n 364) 320.

engaged in legality reviews on the basis of Article 47. Whereas they have strived for a unified approach towards *ex officio* control, they do not seem to have recognised the different rationale of effective judicial protection as an EU fundamental right. This could be due to several factors: perhaps there really is no need for them to do so, perhaps they are reluctant because of the lack of a constitutional tradition in the Netherlands, or perhaps they do not see the (added) value of Article 47 vis-à-vis Article 6 ECHR, as, for example, the *Intermaris* case suggests. In this respect, they have tended to overlook that the link between substantive and procedural protection of consumers under the UCTD might warrant a higher level of protection, or at least extra scrutiny on the part of the courts. In this respect, Article 47 of the Charter could fulfil an empowering function.

The notion of effective judicial protection has persuasive authority: courts use it as an argument for giving an expansive interpretation of legislative provisions, especially when norms with a protective purpose are concerned. In so far as a reference to Article 47 shows awareness of the fundamental rights at stake, it could fulfil a rhetorical function, where it provides a reason for going beyond what a strict application of the law would otherwise require. In addition, it might reveal a focus on the need to ensure due process in a concrete case. This gets obscured by an exclusive emphasis on *ex officio* control. There is, nevertheless, a danger of Article 47 being turned into an argument for curtailing the effective judicial protection of individual consumer rights, which courts should be wary of. Moreover, a case-by-case approach may conceal the need to remedy structural imbalances in the civil justice system and, in particular, potentially problematic aspects of litigation against consumer defendants. Procedural protection is not entirely trans-substantive, which is exactly what makes Article 47 of the Charter stand out – something that Dutch civil courts do not seem to (fully) acknowledge.

CHAPTER 6
CONCLUSION
The Many Colours of Article 47

6.1. SYNTHESIS: ARTICLE 47 IN UNFAIR TERMS CASES

6.1.1. A CHAMELEON-LIKE PROVISION

This book addresses the functions of references to Article 47 of the EU Charter of Fundamental Rights by the CJEU, and by Spanish and Dutch civil courts, in the context of the UCTD. European citizens all have the right to effective judicial protection of the rights and freedoms that EU law confers on them, including the rights derived from consumer protection legislation. They act in their capacities as consumers on a day-to-day basis, and enter into contracts based on standard terms and conditions. There is a wide variety of terms, and an equally wide variety of ways in which these can be unfair, possibly with far-reaching consequences, for example by imposing excessive interest rates or severely limiting procedural rights. In unfair terms cases, gaps and obstacles in national procedural laws have come to light that prevent consumers from exercising their rights vis-à-vis traders and/or prevent national courts from protecting those rights effectively. The availability of effective judicial protection is, apparently, not self-evident.

Article 47 safeguards the fundamental right to an effective remedy before an independent and impartial tribunal established by law, for everyone whose EU rights and freedoms are violated. At first sight, Article 47 confirms a universal maxim: where there is a right, there must be a remedy – a means of recourse to enforce the right, or to obtain redress for an infringement of the right. Its application in practice, however, is more ambiguous. This book paints a picture of Article 47 as a chameleon-like provision, corresponding to a mosaic of functions that it may fulfil, in the context of the UCTD. It is multifaceted, and the analysed case law shows that its implications are influenced by the applicable factual, legal and national contexts. How it manifests itself depends, inter alia, on the (substantive and procedural) rights it is pertaining to, and the national setting in which it is being applied. This book seeks to answer the question of how and why courts make references to Article 47 in unfair terms cases. What can such references achieve?

In this chapter, three key findings will be presented. Firstly, there is a discrepancy between the wide ramifications that Article 47 could, in theory, have, and its application in practice (section 6.2). Different views have been expressed on the (added) value of effective judicial protection as an EU fundamental right, ranging from cautionary or dismissive to optimistic and hopeful. Article 47 has important features that distinguish it from the notion of (full) effectiveness in EU law, which curtails the procedural autonomy of the EU Member States. It holds the promise of autonomous procedural safeguards with direct effect. Some of its core components are less homogenous to the principle of effectiveness, in particular the right of access to court and the right to be heard, but also the principle of equality of arms. Article 47 has an accessory, open-ended character; here lies both its main constraint and its strength. On the one hand, its application is confined to EU law, and it does not prescribe specific remedies. On the other, it has the potential to go beyond a minimum level of protection and transcend the effectiveness of specific EU instruments such as the UCTD. The analysed case law, nevertheless, shows that, despite the high number of references in cases concerning the Directive, Article 47 has played only a modest role, so far, in the adjudication of unfair terms cases. An alleged infringement of one of its core components may trigger its application, but it has not yet been used to set a positive standard beyond the broad requirement of justiciability (that consumers must have genuine opportunities to exercise their rights in court, and that courts must be able to adjudicate those rights).

Secondly, a focus on the CJEU's case law gives only a one-sided representation of the functions of Article 47: it is only part of the picture. There is no juxtaposition between references to Article 47 by the CJEU and by national civil courts (section 6.3). Dutch courts do not approach the procedural protection of consumers as a fundamental rights issue. By contrast, Spanish civil courts have recognised a constitutional dimension in cases where the availability of judicial remedies for consumers was excluded or severely limited, which resulted in a denial of justice. This dimension may get lost when Article 47 gets conflated with the principle of effectiveness in the CJEU's case law. The Spanish experience makes clear that Article 47 has discursive value in respect of the courts' responsibility to protect substantive EU rights, as well as to ensure observance of procedural safeguards, which have been given further content in the context of the UCTD. There is a need to restore not only the transactional balance but also procedural equality.

Thirdly – and this is where the primary significance of a reference to Article 47 lies in a concrete case (section 6.4) – it may enhance the visibility of systemic issues by highlighting gaps and obstacles in, and creating spaces for, the effective judicial protection of EU (consumer) rights at the national level. Article 47 must entail more than effectiveness, if its core components are to be taken seriously. However, these conclusions are nuanced. Rather than being a universal remedy, Article 47 provides a starting point for a debate on the choice and design of remedies and procedures, in light of EU consumer law and fundamental rights.

6.1.2. OVERVIEW OF FUNCTIONS, WITH EXAMPLES FROM THE ANALYSED CASE LAW

In Chapter 2, an overview was given of several functions ascribed to Article 47 of the Charter in legal doctrine, and this distilled them into five main categories. In Chapters 3, 4 and 5, evidence of these functions was found in the analysed case law, but not to an extent that proves that Article 47 has become a yardstick or standard for national procedural law. In all five categories, there are examples of cases that display some of the indicators identified in section 2.6; these cases can, thus, be placed on a spectrum between conceptualisations of Article 47 as largely parallel to effectiveness (the first category) and Article 47 as a positive standard (the fifth category):

Table 3 Overview of the functions of Article 47 in case law

	Function (label)	Indicators
1.	LEGITIMISING FUNCTION	– Reference to Article 47 merely serves as legitimation for CJEU interference – Parallel or supplementary to effectiveness; other functions cannot be (clearly) discerned
	Example:	– CJEU *Profi Credit*,[1205] in combination with strengthening function (see below)

(continued)

[1205] Case C-167/17 *Profi Credit Polska*; see subsection 3.2.4 of this book.

Table 3 *continued*

	Function (label)	Indicators
2.	STRENGTHENING FUNCTION	Reinforcing effectiveness, but may go further: – Express recognition of (and restriction of) core components of Article 47 as fundamental rights issue – Rights-based: focus on procedural rights – Emphasis on consumer's perspective: availability of recourse
	Examples:	– CJEU *Profi Credit Polska*: confirms and consolidates *Banesto* and *Finanmadrid*[1206] (access to court as fundamental rights issue) – CJEU *Kušionová*:[1207] confirms and consolidates *Aziz* (effective (judicial) remedy as fundamental rights issue)
	EMPOWERING FUNCTION	Overlap with strengthening function, but: – Court-centred: focus on responsibility of courts – Emphasis on court's perspective: power or duty to intervene
	Examples:	– CJEU *Dunai*:[1208] mandate of national courts to provide effective remedy – Spain: AP Madrid on suspension of mortgage enforcement proceedings post-*Aziz*[1209] – Spain: AP Barcelona on admissibility of appeal by consumer debtor in mortgage enforcement proceedings[1210]
3.	SIGNALLING FUNCTION	– Court could have opted to refer to effectiveness but referred (instead or additionally) to Article 47 to signal an issue in the design of procedure – More than ornamental: potential fundamental rights violation indicates seriousness – Aim is to make deliberation explicit and/or to trigger debate (trialogue) about the need for change
	Examples:	– Referring court in *Finanmadrid*:[1211] delegation of judicial competencies as separate fundamental rights issue
	TRANSFORMATIVE FUNCTION	Overlap with signalling function, but: – Reference to Article 47 (is a factor that) triggers debate about an upgrade of national procedural law
	Example:	– Manifested at national level in *Sánchez Morcillo*:[1212] Spanish case before the CJEU on equality of arms in appeals

(continued)

[1206] Case C-618/10 *Banesto* and C-49/14 *Finanmadrid*; see subsection 3.2.3 of this book.

[1207] Case C-34/13 *Kušionová*; see subsection 3.3.2 of this book.

[1208] Case C-118/17 *Dunai*; see subsection 3.3.3 of this book.

[1209] AP Madrid (Sección 10ª), order no. 223/2015 of 9 July 2015, JUR/2015/186525; see subsection 4.3.3 of this book. Case C-415/13 *Aziz* is also discussed in subsection 3.3.2.

[1210] AP Barcelona (Sección 4ª), order no. 196/2014 of 18 September 2014, JUR/2014/297187; AP Barcelona (Sección 1ª), order no. 253/2014 of 26 September 2014, JUR/2015/10332; see subsection 4.4.3 of this book.

[1211] C-49/14 *Finanmadrid*; see subsections 3.2.3 and 4.2.3 of this book.

[1212] Case C-169/14 *Sanchez Morcillo I* and Case C-539/14 *Sánchez Morcillo II* (pertaining to the same dispute); see subsection 3.4.2 and section 4.4 of this book.

Table 3 *continued*

	Function (label)	Indicators
4.	Eliminatory function	- Separate test from effectiveness, although outcome may be the same - Not necessarily a higher threshold, but different rationale - Vertical: basis to set restrictive procedural rules aside (judicial review) - Horizontal: parameter for substantive assessment of unfair terms (judicial control)
	Examples:	- CJEU *Aqua Med*[1213] (vertical dimension) - The Netherlands: *Van Marrum/Wolff*[1214] (horizontal dimension)
5.	Generative function	- Article 47 as separate source of positive requirements - Compliance with autonomous procedural safeguards may go *against* effectiveness
	Example:	- CJEU *Banif Plus Bank*:[1215] gives content to right to be heard (see also the impact on Spanish and Dutch procedural law) - Various examples from Spain and the Netherlands on reception of *Banif Plus Bank* at the national level[1216]

Source: Compiled by the author.

More importantly, two new functions of a reference to Article 47 were found in the Spanish and Dutch case law:

Table 3 **Overview of the functions of Article 47 in case law continued**

	Function (label)	Indicators
6.	Reconciliatory function	- Article 47 as a hinge between EU and national exigencies to resolve (perceived) tension
	Examples:	- Spain: Tribunal Supremo in *AUSBANC*[1217] and AP Barcelona in the *Aziz* case[1218]
7.	Rhetorical function	- Reference to Article 47 shows awareness of the fundamental right at stake, but does not question existing norms, as such - Argument for an expansive interpretation of national law (higher level of protection)
	Example:	- The Netherlands: *Pharma Slovakia*[1219]

Source: Compiled by the author.

1213 Case C-266/18 *Aqua Med*; see subsection 3.2.4 of this book.

1214 Gerechtshof Leeuwarden, 5 July 2011, ECLI:NL:GHLEE:2011:BR2500; see subsection 5.2.1 of this book.

1215 Case C-472/11 *Banif Plus Bank*; see subsection 3.5.2 of this book.

1216 Sections 4.5 and 5.5, respectively, of this book.

1217 Tribunal Supremo (Sala de lo Civil), judgment no. 1916/2013 of 9 May 2013, ECLI:ES:TS:2013:1916; see subsection 4.5.2 of this book.

1218 AP Barcelona (Sección 15ª), judgment no. 407/2014 of 15 December 2014, JUR/2015/86196; see subsection 4.5.2 of this book.

1219 Gerechtshof Arnhem-Leeuwarden, 11 July 2017, ECLI:NL:GHARL:2017:5961; see subsection 5.2.1 of this book.

This overview is not exhaustive. Comprehensive summaries of the case law analyses can be found in the interim conclusions of the corresponding chapters. Separate functions could not be discerned in all cases, for various reasons – for instance, because the reference to Article 47 was not adopted by the CJEU, or because it was purely ornamental. This corroborates the finding of discrepancies between the functions of Article 47 in theory and in practice: the Article does not always live up to its (potential) discursive value. The overview also reveals divergence between the functions of Article 47 in the case law of the CJEU, and in the case law of the Spanish and Dutch civil courts. Its empowering function, particularly discernible in CJEU cases, is not really picked up by national courts, with a few exceptions.

Furthermore, the two additional functions – a reconciliatory function and a rhetorical function – do not fit seamlessly into any of the other five categories. This also shows that the (added) value of Article 47 is, ultimately, determined by the meaning attached to it by courts themselves, as reflected in their decisions.

6.2. ARTICLE 47 IN CJEU CASE LAW: DISCREPANCY BETWEEN THEORY AND PRACTICE

6.2.1. ARTICLE 47 AS ENHANCED EFFECTIVENESS

The CJEU's case law on the UCTD acknowledges the importance of justiciability, in a broad sense. It has uncovered procedural issues that transcend the UCTD and highlight the importance of effective judicial protection. Various authors have drawn attention to Article 47's potential to reinforce a rights-based, court-centred approach, where it may call for extra scrutiny – from the CJEU, but also, and especially, from national courts that must provide effective judicial protection in cases falling within the scope of EU consumer law. When Article 47 is read in conjunction with the UCTD, the link between substantive and procedural protection changes its colours. The mere existence of a remedy is not enough: the remedy must also be effective in light of the Directive, which aims to restore the balance between consumers and traders. The CJEU has, repeatedly, affirmed the 'obligation to protect' on the part of courts that follows from Article 47. This supports the claim put forward by, inter alia, Reich, Gerstenberg and Collins[1220] that, at least in theory, Article 47 intensifies the responsibility

[1220] See subsection 2.5.1 of this book.

of national courts as European courts. It may strengthen the procedural rights of citizens in their capacities as European consumers and holders of EU rights. It may also empower courts, as protectors of those rights, to give remedy-oriented interpretations of the applicable procedural rules, or to set conflicting norms aside (see, for example, *Dunai*).

The CJEU's references to Article 47 in unfair terms cases indicate a focus on the availability of judicial remedies under reasonable procedural conditions (see, for example, *Profi Credit*). While this may legitimise further CJEU interference in national (procedural) law, it is hard to identify the distinguishing features of Article 47 in the CJEU's case law. Article 47 is not used in its eliminatory or generative functions as such, i.e. as a separate test or source of positive requirements, with the exception of the right to be heard. Article 47 is mostly applied as an enhanced form of effectiveness, for example where it is referred to in respect of the need for an 'effective procedural path' to obtain a substantive remedy (*Sziber*), in light of the obligations of the Member States and their national courts to ensure that unfair terms are not binding on consumers, and to provide 'adequate and effective means' to that end (Articles 6 and 7 of the UCTD).

Article 47 gives content to procedural guarantees, in light of the UCTD. For instance, an asymmetric appeal prohibition in mortgage enforcement proceedings against consumer debtors was found to be contrary to the principle of equality of arms (*Sánchez Morcillo*). As such, Article 47 may amplify the compensatory function of civil procedure in consumer litigation. This is legitimated by the need to ensure substantive protection under the UCTD. However, the CJEU has not provided any further guidance as to what constitutes an effective judicial remedy in this context, for example what time limits are acceptable. Article 47 may preclude procedural conditions that are too restrictive, but it does not prescribe which conditions would be reasonable instead. Chapter 3 reveals the kind of deference to be expected from the CJEU, given its institutional position, Article 47's constraints, and a functional approach towards proceduralisation under the UCTD. The CJEU appears to view Article 47 not only as accessory in character, but also ancillary: it enhances substantive consumer protection, not procedural protection, as such.

6.2.2. A MISMATCH BETWEEN EFFECTIVENESS AND A FUNDAMENTAL RIGHTS PERSPECTIVE

At the same time, the analysis in this book corroborates a mismatch between the CJEU's focus on ensuring the effectiveness of EU law, and an

EU fundamental rights perspective. Conflating Article 47 with effectiveness may obfuscate the real issue: a shortfall in judicial remedies or procedural safeguards, irrespective, or on top of, a lack of substantive protection. This, in turn, may exacerbate the subordinated position of consumers vis-à-vis traders, which is all the more salient where they risk losing their family homes in the course of mortgage enforcement proceedings (see, for example, *Kušionová*). A reference to the Charter marks a problem with judicial protection (Article 47) – in this case, in view of the right to housing (Article 7) – that is more profound than just a failure to perform *ex officio* control of unfair terms. The case law on expedited procedures shows how restrictive procedural rules that are generally legitimate may become problematic when they are considered in light of the risk that consumers are prevented or deterred from going to court. As a result, courts may be circumvented or completely sidelined.

The case of *Finanmadrid* exemplifies that a procedural breach can constitute a separate violation of Article 47, which, nevertheless, remains underexposed in the CJEU's judgment. *Ex officio* control cannot compensate entirely for procedural inequalities between consumers and traders, either de facto, in terms of the knowledge or financial means required to take legal action, or *de jure*, in terms of (insufficient) judicial remedies. It does not remedy the preclusive effect of procedural obstacles, such as a constellation of time limits and costs, per se. Article 47 pertains to the availability and accessibility of effective judicial remedies for infringements of substantive *and* procedural rights. It does not necessarily have to entail a higher threshold than effectiveness, or lead to a different outcome, but it provides a different rationale for judicial protection. Whether it is excessively difficult, or virtually impossible, for consumers to exercise their substantive rights – in court or otherwise – is a different question from whether an 'excessive restriction' of the procedural requirements of Article 47 has occurred (see *Aqua Med*). The latter question places emphasis on respect for the core components of Article 47, rather than on the effective enforcement of EU consumer law. Article 47 is not merely instrumental: its rule of law connotation goes beyond the objectives of specific instruments of EU law. Judicial protection can be seen both as a process, and a goal in and of itself. Article 47 has normative content and intrinsic value: it is more than a function of the limitations placed on the Member States' procedural autonomy.[1221] Indeed, it holds the promise of autonomous procedural

[1221] See Case C-61/14 *Orizzonte Salute*, Opinion of AG Jaäskinen, cited in subsection 2.5.2 of this book.

safeguards or, rather, hybrids, consisting of diversified rules at the national level that conform to certain EU-wide, judge-made standards, reflecting Van Cleynenbreugel's observation of guided deference by the CJEU.[1222]

The contrasting dynamics between Article 47 and effectiveness become visible in cases like *Banif Plus Bank*, where the duty of *ex officio* control is qualified by the fundamental rights, of both consumers and traders, to be heard. Another example can be found in the case of *Asturcom*. As the Opinion of AG Trstenjak shows, Article 47 can support the argument that there should always be a form of judicial control, in order to prevent consumers from being deprived of their rights of access to court and/or rights of defence. A similar argument can be made in respect of the delegation of judicial functions to court registrars, for example the power to issue orders for payment (see the referring court in *Finanmadrid*). In this respect, it could be helpful to differentiate between rules that regulate the course of judicial proceedings and rules that impinge on Article 47's core components. The latter may give rise to a self-standing violation of Article 47, as the 'excessive restriction' test in *Aqua Med* seems to imply. The starting point matters: Article 47 warrants the observance of procedural rights and safeguards in and of themselves, rather than focusing primarily on the justification of rules in light of the aim of consumer protection, as against, for example, the aim of ensuring a swift debt enforcement.

Notwithstanding Article 47's potential to increase the visibility of effective judicial protection as an EU fundamental right, the CJEU's case law hardly puts it into action, or is, at most, ambivalent. Chapters 2 and 3 revealed how this ambivalence affects the impact of Article 47 on Spanish and Dutch law.

6.3. ARTICLE 47 IN SPANISH AND DUTCH CASE LAW

The references to Article 47 by the CJEU, and by the Spanish and Dutch civil courts, converge to the extent that they show how Article 47 may justify an interpretation of national procedural law in such a way as to expand consumers' procedural rights and/or the scope for judicial intervention. Such references to Article 47 may also have a signalling effect by indicating

1222 See subsection 2.4.2 of this book.

possible fundamental rights violations, which highlights the seriousness, as well as the urgency, of remedying the consequences.

However, the analysis in this book shows divergence between the CJEU and the analysed national case law in three important aspects. Firstly, at the national level, Article 47's empowering function is not as strong as it might seem. Spanish and Dutch civil courts seem hesitant to disregard or supplement procedural rules on the basis of Article 47 alone, without CJEU backup. Secondly, while the CJEU's case law on Article 47 could be construed as a cautious attempt at open constitutionalisation, the fundamental rights dimension remains largely hidden, in Dutch unfair terms cases. For Spain, it is the opposite: the cases referring to Article 47 have a clear constitutional background. But interpretations of national procedural law diverge, and some courts have adopted an outright restrictive approach towards the effective judicial protection of individual consumer rights. Thirdly, the CJEU's instrumental approach towards consumer protection under the UCTD, on a systemic level, creates tension with the more tailored approach followed in concrete cases before national civil courts. This emphasises the importance of making clear what conflicting rights and interests are at stake, and how these should be balanced against each other.

6.3.1. SPAIN: A CLEAR CONSTITUTIONAL DIMENSION

The references to Article 47 in Spanish unfair terms cases can only be understood against the background of the many requests for preliminary references that Spanish civil courts have made to the CJEU. In the aftermath of the 2008 financial crisis, Spanish civil courts have reframed issues affecting vulnerable debtors as issues of consumer protection under the UCTD. They have pinpointed deficiencies in the national procedural framework, which are especially problematic where a lack of substantive protection also exists. The analysed case law demonstrates how a shortfall in judicial protection in (expedited) procedures involving consumers can be problematic, in itself. In addition to aggravating the substantive imbalance, it may also allow creditors to circumvent judicial control, and enforce claims against consumers that are either based on unfair terms or otherwise unfounded. This undermines the Directive's effectiveness, and may result in denials of justice, if consumers are effectively denied the opportunity to exercise their rights. The fact that rights originating in EU law are at stake adds an extra layer, which triggers the applicability of Article 47 of the Charter. Thus, consumer adjudication in Spain has acquired a clear constitutional dimension.

The case of *Sánchez Morcillo* forms a striking example. The referring court (re)formulated its question under the UCTD to bring in Article 47. The fundamental rights angle of this case was informed by the Tribunal Constitucional's formalistic approach towards the procedural rights of mortgage debtors. This shows that there were motives on the table other than solely the need to protect consumers against unfair terms: a reference to Article 47 may indicate the need to redress structural imbalances in the civil justice system. It adds a different perspective to the principle of effectiveness, and resonates with national constitutional language. The CJEU seems to have acknowledged this by explicitly adopting the reference to Article 47, and by condemning the asymmetric position of consumers and traders as regards the right of appeal, in light of the principle of equality of arms.

Sánchez Morcillo exemplifies a trialogue between national courts, the CJEU and the national legislature on the level and scope of effective judicial protection for consumers. The CJEU's case law has led to legislative reforms in Spain, which, in turn, have changed the course of the procedures at issue, and could be seen as hybridisation in the procedural sphere, in so far as cases fall within the scope of the UCTD (*Sánchez Morcillo II*). This reflects Article 47's transformative potential, whereby it results in an upgrade of national procedural law, as envisaged by Gerstenberg and Reich. A reference to Article 47 in its signalling function may even be instrumental, in its own way, as a means of achieving an ulterior goal, for example to set a reform into motion, with the aim of opening up rigid procedural rules that limit the court's space to offer a solution in a concrete case. Where Article 47 operates as a correction mechanism, this also reminds us of the leverage function of fundamental rights in private law.

The signalling function of Article 47 is more than symbolic: the implication that a fundamental rights violation must be prevented or remedied has persuasive authority in judicial reasoning. As such, Article 47 has an empowering function, whereby it can provide an argument for an expansive interpretation of national procedural law. For instance, the AP in Barcelona allowed an appeal brought by consumer debtors in mortgage enforcement proceedings before the law was changed, for which *Sánchez Morcillo* paved the way. And, after *Aziz*, the AP in Madrid found that the prohibition of suspension of mortgage enforcement proceedings while declaratory proceedings were pending ran counter to Article 47.

Other courts, however, have reached different, sometimes contradictory decisions. These lay bare the scattered nature of the manner in which the CJEU's case law has been received in the Spanish legal system. Article 47 has not been embraced across the board as a tool to enhance the effective judicial protection of consumers. On the contrary, Article 47 is sometimes invoked in defence of procedural principles such as *res judicata*, without giving sufficient consideration or justification as to how this may negatively affect the protection of individual consumer rights. Spanish civil courts struggle to reconcile the CJEU's case law with the 'classic rigidities of civil procedure'.[1223] The active role that courts are required to take fits uncomfortably with the principle that it is the parties who take the procedural initiative and determine the ambit of the dispute. Interestingly, the AP in Barcelona, in the *Aziz* case, and the Tribunal Supremo, in a landmark decision on *cláusulas suelo*, resorted to Article 47 to coordinate between this principle and *ex officio* control. Here, Article 47 fulfilled a reconciliatory function by resolving the (perceived) tension between EU and national exigencies. The court's task is to facilitate the litigating parties, and to uphold their subjective rights. The parties must have an opportunity to exercise their rights, and to present their views, so that the court can take a decision based on their submissions. Giving them the chance to be heard respects their autonomy and avoids a denial of justice (*indefensión*).

6.3.2. THE NETHERLANDS: NO CONSTITUTIONALISATION OF CONSUMER CASES

In the Netherlands, the right to be heard, as guaranteed by Article 47 of the Charter, has also been invoked to emphasise that the court must take the position of each party, and the circumstances of the case, into account when it performs *ex officio* control. The impact of Article 47 has mostly been indirect: there are still very few explicit references to it in Dutch unfair terms cases. In Chapter 5, it was discussed how Dutch civil courts seem to have found other ways to ensure effective judicial protection of consumers under the UCTD, inter alia through a coordinated approach taken by lower courts towards consistent interpretation of procedural norms. The Hoge Raad has provided guidance, in particular as regards the

[1223] Tribunal Supremo (Sala de lo Civil), judgment no. 1916/2013 of 9 May 2013, ECLI:ES:TS:2013:1916, cited in subsection 4.5.2.

role of the court in default and appellate proceedings. This could explain why Dutch civil courts are less inclined to look for solutions in EU law.

In so far as procedural issues are constitutionalised, it is within the scope of Article 6 ECHR, a trans-substantive provision that guarantees a minimum level of protection. While Article 47 of the Charter has obtained its own identity, due to the link with EU law, Dutch civil courts have mistakenly assumed that Article 6 ECHR and Article 47 of the Charter are interchangeable. In the high-profile *Intermaris* case on judicial review of arbitral awards in consumer cases, only Article 6 ECHR was referred to, despite a clear connection to consumers' fundamental right of access to court, a necessary prerequisite for judicial intervention. In the few cases that have contained a reference to Article 47, it has been mentioned in the same breath as Article 6 ECHR and/or Article 17 of the Dutch Constitution.

However, there are indications that such a reference is not just ornamental. A few Courts of Appeal went beyond what was required by the UCTD's effectiveness and held that arbitration clauses in consumer contracts must be considered as unfair, before they were placed on the statutory blacklist. These Courts used Article 47 in its empowering function, i.e. as an extra argument to reinforce their reasoning as to why access to court should not be excluded in advance. It was one of the parameters in the substantive unfairness assessment of arbitration clauses, and a reason to eliminate them from consumer contracts. In a way, this could also be seen as an instance of its signalling function: a call for blacklisting arbitration clauses, ahead of legislative change. A weaker form of use of Article 47 is a reference to it in its rhetorical function: the applicable norms are not questioned, as such, but the reference to Article 47 shows awareness of the fundamental right at stake (*Pharma Slovakia*).

Interestingly, Dutch civil courts have used the notion of 'effective judicial protection' as a justification for an expansive, consumer-friendly interpretation of remedies, even outside the scope of EU law. This notion may be a powerful argument to stress the link between substantive and procedural protection, especially in respect of norms with a protective purpose. Courts must provide both types of protection – if necessary, of their own motion – with due regard for the parties' rights to be heard, and within the ambit of the dispute.

Unlike in Spain, the CJEU's case law on the UCTD has not been codified in the Netherlands, leaving courts more flexibility. However, there is, arguably, a lack of clarity or predictability in respect of the ways in which procedural safeguards are observed. When the court performs *ex officio* control, this may lead to questions as to the extent of the parties' rights to be heard, or complaints that this causes unacceptable delays. More importantly, a case-by-case approach may hide patterns – which can only be discovered through samples of individual judgments – in the ways that courts deal with systemic issues, for example the deterrent effect of costs. A reference to Article 47 may not only contribute to the visibility of such issues, but also empower courts, as well as litigants, to overcome them. A judgment by the Court of Appeal in 's-Hertogenbosch – albeit in a data protection case – exemplifies how Article 47 could be used to signal to citizens that the prospect of a cost order should not discourage them from exercising their EU rights in court.[1224]

The mismatch between the principle of effectiveness and an EU fundamental rights approach could partly explain why Dutch civil courts seldom refer to Article 47. A technocratic reading of the CJEU's case law obscures the rationale of effective judicial protection, in the context of the UCTD. Article 47 emphasises the systemic responsibility of courts to address not only situational, but also structural, problems, especially where consumers are prevented or deterred from going to court. In this respect, Article 47 could give a European dimension to the debate on access to justice, and the prevention of opportunistic debt collection practices, in the Netherlands, too.

6.3.3. DIFFERENCES BETWEEN SPAIN AND THE NETHERLANDS

Several factors, both legal and non-legal, that could explain the differences between the Spanish and Dutch case law, are discussed in this book. The high number of references, in Spain, to Article 47 of the Charter was partly a response to a social emergency, as well as a reflection of the formalistic approach of the legislature and the highest courts. Pleas have been made for more flexibility towards procedural rules and principles, which would require a change of the law or allow courts to interpret the law in a consumer-friendly spirit. In the Netherlands, the space to interpret the law in this spirit was already there, or at least it could be done without legislative change. Instead of going against higher courts, lower courts cooperated to develop detailed guidelines on the application of the *ex officio* doctrine in Dutch law. Thus, arguably, they did not need to resort

1224 Gerechtshof 's-Hertogenbosch, 1 February 2018, ECLI:NL:GHSHE:2018:363; see subsection 5.1.2 of this book.

to fundamental rights to provide effective judicial protection in consumer litigation 'within the system'. In Spain, the structure of the dialogue (or trialogue) has been different, because the legislature has been involved, and the relationship between courts has been more discordant, when it comes to EU consumer law.

Moreover, Dutch civil courts have not questioned the applicable procedural rules, as such. Consumers' procedural rights and the scope for judicial intervention are not as restricted in the Netherlands as they are in Spain. Procedural inequalities between creditors and consumer debtors may exist, in practice, but they are not explicitly ingrained in the law itself. This makes an important difference to how substantive rights can be exercised and effectuated. In so far as there is tension between procedural principles such as party autonomy, and the effectiveness of the UCTD, the latter generally prevails. By contrast, Spanish civil courts seem to have experienced more difficulties in reconciling the two, in light of the rigidity of Spanish civil procedure.

Unlike in Spain, there is no centralised system of constitutional review in the Netherlands. Dutch civil courts, thus, have no need to justify themselves, from a constitutional point of view, by shielding themselves behind CJEU citations. The application of EU consumer law, and more specifically the UCTD, is not seen as a fundamental rights issue. Only consumer arbitration has been constitutionalised, and, even then, only to some extent. Interestingly, from the perspective of Article 47 and the right of access to court, consumers enjoy a higher level of protection in Spain, where arbitral proceedings against consumer defendants are not possible at all. And, in a way, Spanish consumers seem to be better protected against mortgage enforcement based on unfair terms: judicial control is guaranteed by law, despite the expedited nature and otherwise limited scope of the proceedings. This is another example of a systemic issue that transcends the Directive, but might have been overlooked in the Netherlands, due to the focus on *ex officio* control and public policy that has dominated the Dutch debate. Court involvement comes with certain safeguards: Article 47 may have persuasive authority in this respect, as the Spanish case law makes clear.

6.4. JUSTICE FOR BOTH

To conclude, Article 47 of the Charter is a chameleon-like provision: it requires further interpretation, depending on the context in which it is applied. It can blend in effectively, but it can also stand on its own merits: where it is placed on the spectrum between these positions depends on the court that refers to it. Through a comparison of Spanish and Dutch case law, this book has shown that Article 47's (added) value, in practice, is in the eye of the beholder: Spanish civil courts appreciate its functions differently from their Dutch counterparts.

The Spanish case law shows that a reference to Article 47, even in a single case, may enhance the visibility of systemic problems with the justiciability of EU consumer rights. In this respect, Tridimas and Gentile[1225] have pointed out that fundamental rights language might have a strong signalling effect. How an issue is framed matters for the way that it is approached and resolved. While the CJEU appears to be concerned, primarily, with the UCTD's effectiveness, other issues have come to light that touch on the fundamental right to effective judicial protection as such. By conceiving these as constitutional issues, Spanish civil courts have highlighted shortfalls that were more profound than a failure to perform unfair terms control, in particular a lack of access to judicial remedies for consumers.

The categorical protection of consumers as weaker parties requires courts to compensate for a substantive (i.e. transactional) imbalance, as well as for procedural inequalities. Calls have, nevertheless, been made for a more tailored approach, i.e. a true balancing of the rights and interests at stake, in the circumstances of the case. A narrow vision of effective judicial protection focuses on the court's active role for the benefit of consumers; a broad understanding also accounts for due process, as an end in itself. At the same time, the Spanish experience teaches us that, even from a due process perspective, the problem is not overprotection of consumers. Spanish procedural law seems to systematically favour traders, creditors and 'repeat players' by endorsing their privileged positions. Within the framework of the UCTD, their rights to be heard may qualify the court's *ex officio* powers or duties, but Article 47 should not be used as an argument to preserve existing inequalities. 'Justice for both', to borrow Eleanor Roosevelt's words,[1226] means that structural imbalances should be identified as such, and removed or compensated for as much as possible.

To the extent that there is still a 'civil justice gap' in unfair terms cases, it exists on the side of consumers, not on the side of traders. In this respect,

[1225] See subsection 2.5.2 of this book.

[1226] 'Justice cannot be for one side alone, but must be for both': 'My Day', 14 October 1947, The Eleanor Roosevelt Papers Digital Edition (2017).

Article 47's (unfulfilled) potential lies in its discursive value. Courts may use Article 47 to openly deliberate about perceived tensions between EU and national law, propose possible solutions and, thus, contribute to closing the gap. Article 47 may provide a new source of inspiration: even if it only reaffirms pre-existing rights and principles, it recognises effective judicial protection as an EU fundamental right. Concerns of overextension, in the sense that Article 47 would be capable of expanding the CJEU's competences, or blurring the boundaries of judicial lawmaking, seem, so far, to be unfounded. Rather, Article 47 provides an anchor point for the discourse on effective judicial protection, especially where conflicting rights and interests are at stake.

Article 47's chameleon-like nature suits an approach of guided deference by the CJEU, which leaves room for interpretation and balancing by national civil courts. Article 47 is an open provision, rooted in EU law, that does not impose specific solutions from above, but empowers courts and litigants from below. It pushes for a broad view on the role of civil courts that reconciles national (procedural) law with an EU consumer law perspective. Article 47 seems to leave space to take other factors into account next to the objectives of the UCTD, such as the proper administration of justice, but this should not come at the cost of depriving private parties of effective judicial protection. Article 47 is less instrumental – less alien to private law and civil procedure – than the principle of effectiveness, because it recognises that individual rights deserve protection, in and of themselves. As such, it seems to fit better into the private law discourse than it does in the effectiveness paradigm. Rather than being an incursion on party and procedural autonomy, Article 47 may provide a route that is more in harmony with the role and reasoning of civil courts.

For the viability of Article 47 as an EU-wide standard, however, further guidance or clarification as to what effective judicial protection entails is crucial. Article 47 can be both a shield and a sword: what matters is in whose hands it is put – strengthening what, or empowering whom? Article 47's chameleon-like nature could transform into capriciousness if it were to be used as a counterargument against restoring the balance for consumers. Therefore, this book concludes by concurring with calls made for open constitutionalisation to openly address questions about the balance struck at different levels. Otherwise, the fundamental rights aspects of consumer adjudication will remain invisible, or allow only for a reductionist approach that does not do justice to the rationale of effective judicial protection, in this context. The courts bringing effective judicial protection into practice, must show the colours of Article 47.

BIBLIOGRAPHY

Adinolfi A, 'The "Procedural Autonomy" of Member States and the Constraints Stemming from the ECJ's Case-Law: Is Judicial Activism Still Necessary?' in Hans-Wolfgang Micklitz and Bruno De Witte (eds), *The European Court of Justice and the Autonomy of the Member States* (Intersentia 2012)

Aguilera Morales M, '¿*Quo vadis* "jura de cuentas"? ¿*quo vadis* Europa? El estatus y función de los Secretarios Judiciales a examen por el TJUE' [2017] 41 Revista General de Derecho Procesal 6–7

——, 'TJUE, proceso civil y tutela del consumidor: repaso de un año que termina y previsiones en torno a otro que comienza' [2018] 44 Revista General de Derecho Procesal 29

——, '¿Es válida la cláusula de renuncia de acciones predispuesta frente al consumidor?' in Marien Aguilera Morales (ed), *Tribunal de Justicia de la Unión Europea, justicia civil y derechos fundamentales* (Thomson Reuters Aranzadi 2020)

Albiez Dohrmann KJ and Sánchez Lorenzo S, 'National Perspectives: Spain' in Karl Riesenhuber (ed), *European Legal Methodology* (Intersentia 2017)

Alonso Pérez MT, de Elizalde F and Garcimartín Montero R, 'An Interdisciplinary View of Enforcement and Effectiveness of Spanish Consumer Law' in Geneviève Saumier and Hans-W Micklitz (eds), *Enforcement and Effectiveness of Consumer Law* (Springer 2018)

Álvarez J and Fernando Rodríguez L, *La última trinchera* (Planeta 2016)

Álvarez Moreno MT, 'Resolución alternativa de litigios con consumidores y arbitraje de consumo' in Silvia Díaz Alabart (ed), *Manual de Derecho de consumo* (Editorial Reus 2016)

Ancery A, *Ambtshalve toepassing van EU-recht* (Kluwer 2012)

——, 'Ambtshalve toepassing van consumentenbeschermend EU-recht' [2013] Maandblad voor Vermogensrecht 329

Ancery A and Krans B, 'Consumer Protection and EU-Driven Judicial Activism in the Netherlands' in Anna Nylund and Magne Strandberg (eds), *Civil Procedure and Harmonisation of Law* (Intersentia 2019)

Ancery A and Pavillon C, 'Processuele aspecten van reflexwerking van consumentenrecht' (2014) 145(7026) Weekblad voor privaatrecht, notariaat en registratie 647

——, 'De rechterlijke lijdelijkheid in rook opgegaan? De ambtshalve toepassing van de consumentenkoopregels nader toegelicht' [2015] Maandblad voor Vermogensrecht 243

Ancery A and Seinen C, 'Vorderingen in b2c-verstekken: toetsen of toewijzen?' [2015] Tijdschrift voor Civiele Rechtspleging 77

Anderson M and Simón Moreno H, 'The Spanish Crisis and the Mortgage Credit Directive: Few Changes in Sight', in Esther Arroyo Amayuelas and Miriam Anderson (eds), *The Impact of the Mortgage Credit Directive in Europe – Contrasting Views From Member States* (Europa Law Publishing 2017)

Aronstein I, *Remedies for Infringements of EU Law in Legal Relationships between Private Parties* (Wolters Kluwer 2019)

Arroyo Amayuelas E, 'No vinculan al consumidor las cláusulas abusivas: del Derecho civil al procesal y entre la prevención y el castigo' in Esther Arroyo Amayuelas and Ángel Serrano de Nicolás (eds), *La Europeización del Derecho privado: cuestiones actuales* (Marcial Pons 2016)

——, 'Mortgage Credit in Spain' [2017] Journal of European Consumer and Market Law 132

Bakker F, *Billijkheidsuitzonderingen. Het wegens bijzondere omstandigheden buiten toepassing laten van wettelijke voorschriften in individuele gevallen* (Wolters Kluwer 2018)

Barceló Compte R, *Ventaja injusta y protección de la parte débil del contrato* (Marcial Pons 2019)

Barkhuysen T, *Artikel 13 EVRM: effectieve nationale rechtsbescherming bij schending van mensenrechten* (Koninklijke Vermande 1998)

Barkhuysen T, Bos AW and Ten Have F, 'Een verkenning van de betekenis van het Handvest van de grondrechten van de Europese Unie voor het privaatrecht. Deel 1: De inhoud, de juridische status en het toepassingsbereik van het Handvest, in het bijzonder in horizontale verhoudingen' [2011] Nederlands Tijdschrift voor Burgerlijk Recht 479

——, 'Een verkenning van de betekenis van het Handvest van de grondrechten van de Europese Unie voor het privaatrecht. Deel 2: De verhouding van het Handvest tot het EVRM en de meerwaarde van het Handvest' [2011] Nederlands Tijdschrift voor Burgerlijk Recht 547

Barral-Viñals I, 'Aziz Case and Unfair Contract Terms in Mortgage Loan Agreements: Lessons to Be Learned in Spain' (2015) 4 Penn State Journal of Law & International Affairs 69

Bartl M, 'Internal Market Rationality, Private Law and the Direction of the Union: Resuscitating the Market as the Object of the Political' (2015) 21 European Law Journal 572

Bartl M and Leone C, 'Minimum Harmonisation after *Alemo-Herron*: The Janus Face of EU Fundamental Rights Review' (2015) 11 European Constitutional Law Review 140

Beal K, '*Ubi Ius, Ibi Remedium*: Do the Union Courts have the "Latin for Judging"' [2015] Judicial Review 115

Bech Serrat JM, 'Cláusulas suelo y autonomía procesal en la Unión Europea: ¿por qué no hacer una excepción a la cosa juzgada?' [2018] InDret <https://www.raco.cat/index.php/InDret/article/view/332601>

Beijer M, 'Active Guidance of Fundamental Rights Protection by the Court of Justice of the European Union: Exploring the Possibilities of a Positive Obligations Doctrine' (2015) 8 Review of European Administrative Law 127

——, *The Limits of Fundamental Rights Protection by the EU: The Scope for the Development of Positive Obligations* (Intersentia 2017)

Beka A, *The Active Role of Courts in Consumer Litigation: Applying EU Law of the National Courts' Own Motion* (Intersentia 2018)

Benöhr I, *EU Consumer Law and Human Rights* (1st edn., Oxford University Press 2013)

Biemans J and Castermans AG, *Barmhartigheid in Het Burgerlijk Recht. Bespiegelingen over de Grenzen Aan Kredietverlening En Een Bijdrage Aan Het Behoud van Bestaanszekerheid* (Uitgeverij Paris 2017)

Birks P, 'Rights, Wrongs and Remedies' (2000) 20 Oxford Journal of Legal Studies 1

Bobek M, 'Why There is no Principle of "Procedural Autonomy" of the Member States' in Hans-Wolfgang Micklitz and Bruno De Witte (eds), *The European Court of Justice and the Autonomy of the Member States* (Intersentia 2012)

de Bock R, *Tussen waarheid en onzekerheid: Over het vaststellen van feiten in de civiele procedure* (Kluwer 2011)

——, 'Feitenonderzoek tijdens de mondelinge behandeling' in Dineke de Groot and Hans Steenbergen (eds), *De mondelinge behandeling in civiele zaken* (Boom Juridische Uitgevers 2019)

Bonet Navarro J, 'La necesaria reforma de la mal llamada "jura de cuentas"' [2017] Revista de Derecho UNED 73

Bosch Grau J and Escolar I, *El secuestro de la justicia: Virtudes y problemas del sistema judicial* (Roca Editorial de Libros 2018)

Bruning M, 'Over redelijke wetstoepassing en hanteerbaarheid van het Nederlands privaatrecht. Mogelijkheden en grenzen in de rechtsvormede rechtspraak op grond van de billijkheid' in Ruben de Graaff and others (eds), *Rechtsvorming door de Hoge Raad* (Ars Aequi Libri 2016)

Bustos Gisbert R, 'La aplicación judicial de la CDFUE' [2017] Teoría y Realidad Constitucional 333

Cafaggi F, 'On the Transformations of European Consumer Enforcement Law: Judicial and Administrative Trialogues, Instruments and Effects', in Fabrizio Cafaggi and Stephanie Law (eds), *Judicial Cooperation in European Private Law* (Edward Elgar Publishing 2017)

——, 'Towards Collaborative Governance of European Remedial and Procedural Law?' (2018) 19 Theoretical Inquiries in Law 235

Cafaggi F and Iamiceli P, 'The Principles of Effectiveness, Proportionality and Dissuasiveness in the Enforcement of EU Consumer Law: The Impact of a Triad on the Choice of Civil Remedies and Administrative Sanctions' (2017) 25 European Review of Private Law 575

Cafaggi F and Law S, 'Unfair Contract Terms – Effect of Collective Proceedings' in Evelyne Terryn, Gert Straetmans and Veerle Colaert (eds), *Landmark Cases of EU Consumer Law: In Honour of Jules Stuyck* (Intersentia 2013)

Calderón Cuadrado MP, 'Derechos, proceso y crisis de la justicia' [2015] 37 Revista General de Derecho Procesal 32

Caponi R and Nowak JT, 'Access to Justice' in Burkhard Hess and Stephanie Law (eds), *Implementing EU Consumer Rights by National Procedural Law. Luxembourg Report on European Procedural Law: Volume II* (Beck 2019)

Carrasco Perera ÁF and González Carrasco MC, 'La doctrina casacional sobre la transparencia de las cláusulas suelo conculca la garantía constitucional de la tutela judicial efectiva' [2013] Revista CESCO de Derecho de Consumo 150

Carrasco Perera ÁF and Lyczkowska K, 'STJUE de 17 de Julio de 2014, *Asunto* C-169/14, Banco Bilbao Vizcaya Argentaria: un nuevo (y esta vez defectuoso) pronunciamiento del TJEU sobre el procedimiento hipotecario español' [2014] Revista CESCO de Derecho de Consumo 1

Caruso D, 'Fairness at a Time of Perplexity' in Stefan Vogenauer and Stephen Weatherill (eds), *General Principles of Law: European and Comparative Perspectives* (Hart Publishing 2017)

Casla K, 'The Rights We Live in: Protecting the Right to Housing in Spain through Fair Trial, Private and Family Life and Non-Retrogressive Measures' (2016) 20 The International Journal of Human Rights 285

Cherednychenko O, *Fundamental Rights, Contract Law and the Protection of the Weaker Party* (European Law Publishers 2007)

——, 'The EU Charter of Fundamental Rights and Consumer Credit: Towards Responsible Lending?' in Hugh Collins (ed), *European Contract Law and the Charter of Fundamental Rights* (Intersentia 2017)

Cherednychenko O and Reich N, 'The Constitutionalization of European Private Law: Gateways, Constraints, and Challenges' [2015] European Review of Private Law 797

Claes M, *The National Courts' Mandate in the European Constitution* (doctoral thesis, Maastricht University 2004)

Van Cleynenbreugel P, 'Judge-Made Standards of National Procedure in the Post-Lisbon Constitutional Framework' (2012) 37 European Law Review 90

Collins H, 'The Constitutionalization of European Private Law as a Path to Social Justice?' in Hans-W Micklitz (ed), *The Many Concepts of Social Justice in European Private Law* (Edward Elgar Publishing 2011)

——, 'On the (In)Compatibility of Human Rights Discourse and Private Law' in Hans-W Micklitz (ed), *Constitutionalization of European Private Law* (Oxford University Press 2014)

——, 'The Revolutionary Trajectory of EU Contract Law towards Post-National Law', in Sarah Worthington, Andrew Robertson and Graham Virgo (eds), *Revolution and Evolution in Private Law* (Hart Publishing 2018)

Colombi Ciacchi A, 'European Fundamental Rights, Private Law, and Judicial Governance' in Hans-W Micklitz (ed), *Constitutionalization of European Private Law* (Oxford University Press 2014)

——, 'European Fundamental Rights and Private Law: The Dutch System in the Context of Different Legal Families' in Bettina Heiderhoff, Sebastian Lohsse and

Reinier Schulze (eds), *EU-Grundrechte und Privatrecht: EU Fundamental Rights and Private Law* (Nomos 2016)
Concellón Fernández P, *Dialogando con Luxemburgo: Los órganos jurisdiccionales españoles y la cuestión prejudicial (1986–2017)* (2018) <http://digibuo.uniovi.es/dspace/handle/10651/46902>
Cordon Moreno F, *Acción colectiva y acción individual para la tutela de los derechos de los consumidores* [2016] Centro de Estudios de Consumo – Publicaciones Jurídicas
Cortés P, 'The Impact of EU Law in the ADR Landscape in Italy, Spain and the UK: Time for Change or Missed Opportunity?' (2015) 16 ERA Forum 125
Della Negra F, 'The Uncertain Development of the Case Law on Consumer Protection in Mortgage Enforcement Proceedings: *Sánchez Morcillo* and *Kušionová*' (2015) 52 Common Market Law Review 1009
Díez García H, 'Igualdad de Armas y Tutela Judicial Efectiva En El Art. 695.4 LEC Tras El Real Decreto-Ley 11/2014, de 5 de Septiembre: Crónica de Una Reforma Legislativa Anunciada (de Los AATC 70/2014, 71/2014, 111/2014, 112/2014 y 113/2014 a La STJUE de 17 de Julio de 2014)' [2014] Derecho Privado y Constitución 247
Díez-Picazo Giménez I, 'Civil Justice in Spain: Present and Future, Access, Cost, and Duration' in Adrian Zuckerman (ed), *Civil Justice in Crisis: Comparative Perspectives of Civil Procedure* (Oxford University Press 1999)
Domurath I, *Consumer Vulnerability and Welfare in Mortgage Contracts* (Hart Publishing 2017)
Dougan M, *National Remedies before the Court of Justice* (Hart Publishing 2004)
——, 'The Vicissitudes of Life at the Coalface: Remedies and Procedures for Enforcing Union Law before the National Courts' in Paul Craig and Gráinne De Búrca (eds), *The Evolution of EU Law* (Oxford University Press 2011)
Dubos O, 'The Origins of the Proceduralisation of EU Law: A Grey Area of European Federalism' (2015) 8 Review of European Administrative Law 7
Van Duin JML, 'Metamorphosis? The Role of Article 47 of the EU Charter of Fundamental Rights in Cases Concerning National Remedies and Procedures under Directive 93/13/EEC' [2017] Journal of European Consumer and Market Law 190
——, 'Wie betaalt de rekening? De kostenveroordeling in de context van het EU-consumentenrecht' [2018] Tijdschrift voor Consumentenrecht en handelspraktijken 177
——, 'Effectieve rechtsbescherming van consumenten door de civiele rechter: een procesrechtelijk perspectief' [2019] Tijdschrift voor de Procespraktijk 138
Van Duin JML and Leone C, 'The Real (New) Deal: Levelling the Odds for Consumer-Litigants' [2019] European Review of Private Law 1227
Düsterhaus D, 'Judicial Coherence in the Area of Freedom, Security and Justice – Squaring Mutual Trust with Effective Judicial Protection' (2015) 8 Review of European Administrative Law 151
Ebers M, *Rechte, Rechtsbehelfe Und Sanktionen Im Unionsprivatrecht* (Mohr Siebeck 2016)

Eidenmüller H and Fries M, 'Against False Settlement: Designing Efficient Consumer Rights Enforcement Systems in Europe' in Hans-W Micklitz and Andrea Wechsler (eds), *The Transformation of Enforcement: European Economic Law in a Global Perspective* (Hart Publishing 2016)

Eilmansberger T, 'The Relationship between Rights and Remedies in EC Law: In Search of the Missing Link' (2004) 41 Common Market Law Review 1199

Ellingsen HK, 'Effective Judicial Protection of Individual Data Protection Rights: *Puškár*' (2018) 55 Common Market Law Review 1879

de Elizalde F, 'The Rain in Spain Does Not Stay in the Plain – Or How the Spanish Supreme Court Ruling of 25 March 2015, on Minimum Interest Rate Clauses, affects European Consumers' [2015] Journal of European Consumer and Market Law 184

——, 'Partial Invalidity for Unfair Terms? CJEU in *Abanca* – C-70 & 179/17' [2019] Journal of European Consumer and Market Law 147

Emaus J, 'Rechten, beginselen en horizontale directe werking van de grondrechten uit het EU-Handvest' [2015] Nederlands Tijdschrift voor Burgerlijk Recht 67

Engström J, *The Europeanisation of Remedies and Procedures through Judge-Made Law – Can a Trojan Horse Achieve Effectiveness?* (European University Institute 2009)

——, 'The Europeanization of Remedies and Procedures – the Principle of Effective Judicial Protection in the Swedish Judicial Habitat' (2011) 23 European Review of Public Law 577

——, 'The Principle of Effective Judicial Protection after the Lisbon Treaty. Reflection in the Light of Case C-279/09 *DEB Deutsche Energiehandels- Und Beratungsgesellschaft MbH*' (2011) 4 Review of European Administrative Law 53

Ervo L, 'Party Autonomy and Access to Justice', in Laura Ervo, Minna Gräns and Antti Jokela (eds), *Europeanization of Procedural Law and the New Challenges to Fair Trial* (Europa Law Publishing 2009)

Esteban de la Rosa F, 'The Treatment of Unfair Terms in the Process of Foreclosure in Spain: Mortgage Enforcement Proceedings in the Aftermath of the ECJ's "Ruling of the Evicted"' [2015] Zeitschrift für Europäisches Privatrecht 366

Faber W and Martinson C, 'Can Ownership Limit the Effectiveness of EU Consumer Contract Law Directives? A Suggestion to Employ a "Functional Approach"' [2019] Austrian Law Journal 85

Fejős A and Willett C, 'Consumer Access to Justice: The Role of the ADR Directive and the Member States' (2016) 24 European Review of Private Law 33

Fernández Seijo JM, *La tutela de los consumidores en los procedimientos judiciales* (Wolters Kluwer 2017)

——, 'Lights and shadows in the *Aziz* case' in Chantal Mak and Betül Kas (eds), *Civil Courts and the European Polity: The Constitutional Role of Private Law Adjudication in Europe* (Hart Publishing, forthcoming 2022)

Ferreres Comella V, *The Constitution of Spain: A Contextual Analysis* (Hart Publishing 2013)

Frantziou E, 'The Horizontal Effect of the Charter of Fundamental Rights of the EU: Rediscovering the Reasons for Horizontality' (2015) 21 European Law Journal 657

——, *The Horizontal Effect of Fundamental Rights in the European Union – A Constitutional Analysis* (Oxford University Press 2019)

Galanter M, 'Why the "Haves" Come out Ahead: Speculations on the Limits of Legal Change' (1974) 9 Law & Society Review 95

García Aburuza MP, 'Directiva 93/13 CEE versus Derecho Procesal Civil Español' Revista Aranzadi Doctrinal 9/2014 parte Estudio 13–15

García-Valdecasas Dorrego M, *Dialogue between the Spanish Courts and the European Court of Justice Regarding the Judicial Protection of Consumers under Directive 93/13/EEC* (Fundación Registral 2018) 179–181

Garot MJ, 'Acerca del concepto de "independencia judicial" en la reciente jurisprudencia del Tribunal de Justica de la Unión Europea' in Marien Aguilera Morales (ed), *Tribunal de Justicia de la Unión Europea, justicia civil y derechos fundamentales* (Thomson Reuters Aranzadi 2020)

Gascón Inchausti F, 'Between Reform and Dejudicialization: Current Trends in Spanish Civil Litigation' in Alan Uzelac and Remco van Rhee (eds), *Transformation of Civil Justice* (Springer International Publishing 2018)

van Gelder E, 'Online Dispute Resolution: een veelbelovend initiatief voor toegang tot het recht?' [2018] Maandblad voor Vermogensrecht 262

Gerstenberg O, 'Constitutional Reasoning in Private Law: The Role of the CJEU in Adjudicating Unfair Terms in Consumer Contracts' [2015] European Law Journal 599

Van Gerven W, 'Of Rights, Remedies and Procedures' (2000) 37 Common Market Law Review 501

Van Gestel R and Micklitz H-W, 'Revitalizing Doctrinal Legal Research in Europe: What About Methodology?' EUI Law Working Papers 2011/05

Giesen I, *Beginselen van burgerlijk procesrecht* (Wolters Kluwer 2015)

van Ginkel H, *Het arbitragebeding in algemene voorwaarden* (Celsus juridische uitgeverij 2013)

Gómez Amigo L, 'Control de las cláusulas abusivas y garantías procesales en los procesos con técnica monitoria, a la luz de la jurisprudencia reciente' (2019) 49 Revista General de Derecho Procesal

Gómez Pomar F and Lyczkowska K, 'Spanish Courts, the Court of Justice of the European Union and Consumer Law. A Theoretical Model of Their Interaction' (2014) 4 InDret 6 <www.indret.com/pdf/1093.pdf>

——, 'Spanish Courts, the European Court and Consumer Law: Some Thoughts on Their Interaction' in Fabrizio Cafaggi and Stephanie Law (eds), *Judicial Cooperation in European Private Law* (Edward Elgar Publishing 2017)

González Pascual M, 'Social Rights Protection and Financial Crisis in Europe. The Right to Housing in Spain: a Cautionary Tale' (2016) 9 Inter-American and European Human Rights Journal 260

de Graaff R, 'De betekenis van de redelijkheid en billijkheid voor de bescherming van grondrechten' [2016] THEMIS 202

——, 'Prescription. A Private-Law Concept at the Forefront of Fundamental Rights Protection' in Clementine Breedeveld-de Voogd and others (eds), *Core Concepts in the Dutch Civil Code, Continuously in Motion. BW Krant Jaarboek no. 30* (Wolters Kluwer 2016)

Grundmann S, 'The Fault Principle as the Chameleon of Contract Law: A Market Function Approach' (2009) 107 Michigan Law Review 1583

Gutiérrez de Cabiedes Hidalgo P and Cantero Gamito M, 'Spain' in Irina Domurath, Guido Comparato and Hans-W Micklitz (eds), *The over-indebtedness of European consumers: a view from six countries* (EUI LAW 2014/10) <http://cadmus.eui.eu//handle/1814/32451>

van Harten H, *Autonomie van de nationale rechter in het Europees recht: een verkenning van de praktijk aan de hand van de Nederlandse Europeesrechtelijke rechtspraak over de vestigingsvrijheid en het vrijedienstenverkeer* (doctoral thesis, University of Amsterdam 2011)

Hartkamp A, 'The Effect of the EC Treaty in Private Law: On Direct and Indirect Horizontal Effects of Primary Community Law' [2010] European Review of Private Law 527

——, '*Ex Officio* Application in Case of Unenforceable Contracts or Contract Clauses: EU Law and National Laws Confronted' in Louise Gullifer and Stefan Vogenauer (eds), *English and European Perspectives on Contract and Commercial Law: Essays in Honour of Hugh Beale* (Hart Publishing 2014)

——, 'Ambtshalve toepassing van Europees consumentenrecht. Een nieuw hoofdstuk: de richtlijn consumentenkoop' [2015] Ars Aequi 222

——, 'De verhouding tussen twee Europese "remedies": lidstaataansprakelijkheid en ambtshalve toepassing van de richtlijn oneerlijke bedingen' [2016] Ars Aequi 658

——, *European Law and National Private Law: Effect of EU Law and European Human Rights Law on Legal Relationships between Individuals* (2nd edn., Intersentia 2016)

Havu K, 'EU Law in Member State Courts: Adequate Judicial Protection and Effective Application: Ambiguities and Nonsequiturs in Guidance by the Court of Justice?' (2016) 8 Contemporary Readings in Law and Social Justice 158

Hazelhorst M, *Free Movement of Civil Judgments in the European Union and the Right to a Fair Trial* (TMC Asser Press 2017)

Heiderhoff B, 'Die Selbstbeschränkung des Anwendungsbereichs der EU-Charte in Art. 51 und die Ausbildung eines anerkennungsrechtlichen europäischen ordre public', in Bettina Heiderhoff, Sebastian Lohsse and Reinier Schulze (eds), *EU-Grundrechte und Privatrecht/EU Fundamental Rights and Private Law* (Nomos 2016)

Hess B and Law S (eds), *Implementing EU Consumer Rights by National Procedural Law. Luxembourg Report of European Procedural Law: Volume II* (Beck 2019)

Hesselink M, 'A European Legal Method? On European Private Law and Scientific Method' (2009) 15 European Law Journal 20

Hodges C, 'Consumer Protection and Procedural Justice', in Evelyne Terryn, Gert Streatmans and Veerle Colaert (eds), *Landmark Cases of EU Consumer Law – In Honour of Jules Stuyck* (Intersentia 2013)

van Hoek A, 'CJEU – *Pammer and Alpenhof* – Grand Chamber, 7 December 2010, Joined Cases 585/08 and 144/09' [2012] European Review of Contract Law 93
——, 'Eén voor allen en allen voor één: individuele versus collectieve handhaving van het consumentenrecht in het IPR' [2016] Ars Aequi 957
Hofmann H, 'Article 47 – Right to an Effective Remedy. D. Analysis. III. Specific Provisions (Meaning)' in Steve Peers and others (eds), *The EU Charter of Fundamental Rights: A Commentary* (Hart Publishing 2014)
Hondius E, 'Unfair Contract Terms and the Consumer: ECJ Case Law, Foreign Literature, and Their Impact on Dutch Law' [2016] European Review of Private Law 457
Howells G and Weatherill S, *Consumer Protection Law* (Routledge 2005)
Iglesias Sánchez S, 'The Court and the Charter: The Impact of the Entry into Force of the Lisbon Treaty on the ECJ's Approach to Fundamental Rights' (2012) 49 Common Market Law Review 1565
——, 'Unfair Terms in Mortgage Loans and Protection of Housing in Times of Economic Crisis: *Aziz v. Catalunyacaixa*' (2014) 51 Common Market Law Review 955
Jaremba U, *National Judges as EU Law Judges: The Polish Civil Law System* (Martinus Nijhof Publishers 2014)
Jiménez París T, 'El incidente de oposición en la ejecución hipotecaria por existencia de cláusulas abusivas y las SSTJUE de 17 de julio de 2014 y 21 de enero de 2015' [2015] Revista Crítica de Derecho Inmobiliario 982/1004
Józon M, 'Unfair Contract Terms Law in Europe in Times of Crisis: Substantive Justice Lost in the Paradise of Proceduralisation of Contract Fairness' [2017] Journal of European Consumer and Market Law 157
Kamphorst A, 'The Right to a Fair Trial in Online Consumer Dispute Resolution' [2019] Journal of European Consumer and Market Law 175
Kelemen RD, 'The Impact of the Court of Justice on the European Law Enforcement Architecture', in Hans-W Micklitz and Andrea Wechsler (eds), *The Transformation of Enforcement. European Economic Law in Global Perspective* (Hart Publishing 2016)
Kenna P and Simón Moreno H, 'Towards a Common Standard of Protection of the Right to Housing in Europe through the Charter of Fundamental Rights' (2019) 25 European Law Journal 608
Kennedy D, *A Critique of Adjudication* (Harvard University Press 1997)
Knigge M and Ribbers P, 'Arbitrage, afstand van recht en artikel 6 EVRM' (2017) 20 Tijdschrift voor Arbitrage 35
——, 'Waiver of the Right to Set-Aside Proceedings in Light of Article 6 ECHR: Party-Autonomy on Top?' (2017) 34 Journal of International Arbitration 775
Krans B, *Nederlands burgerlijk procesrecht en materieel EU-recht* (Kluwer 2010)
——, 'EU Law and National Civil Procedure Law: An Invisible Pillar' (2015) 23 European Review of Private Law 567
Krommendijk J, 'Is There Light on the Horizon? The Distinction between *Rewe* Effectiveness and the Principle of Effective Judicial Protection in Article 47 of the Charter after Orizzonte' (2016) 53 Common Market Law Review 1395

——, 'Van Middelburg tot Almelo. Het hoe en waarom van prejudiciële vragen aan het Hof van Justitie van de Europese Unie door Nederlandse lagere rechters' (2018) 39 Recht der Werkelijkheid 7

——, 'De civiele kamer en de prejudiciële procedure: kritisch doch loyaal aan het Hof van Justitie' [2019] Tijdschrift voor Civiele Rechtspleging 1

Kuijer M, 'Fundamental Rights Protection in the Legal Order of the European Union', in Adam Lazowski and Steven Blockmans (eds), *Research Handbook on EU Institutional Law* (Elgar Publishing 2016)

Leczykiewicz D, '"Effective Judicial Protection" of Human Rights after Lisbon: Should National Courts Be Empowered to Review EU Secondary Law?' (2010) 35 European Law Review 326

——, '"Where Angels Fear to Tread": The EU Law of Remedies and Codification of European Private Law' [2012] European Review of Contract Law 47

——, 'Horizontal Application of the Charter of Fundamental Rights' (2013) 38 European Law Review 479

Lenaerts K, 'The Rule of Law and the Coherence of the Judicial System of the European Union' (2007) 44 Common Market Law Review 1625

——, 'The Court of Justice of the European Union and the Protection of Fundamental Rights' [2011] Polish Yearbook of International Law 79

Lenaerts K and others, *EU Procedural Law* (Oxford University Press 2014)

Leone C, 'Case Note *Abanca Corporación Bancaria, SA v Alberto García Salamanca Santos*' [2020] Revue européenne de droit de la consommation 317

——, *The missing stone in the Cathedral: of unfair terms in employment contracts and coexisting rationalities in European contract law* (doctoral thesis, University of Amsterdam 2020)

Lindijer V, *De goede procesorde. Een onderzoek naar de betekenis van de goede procesorde als normatief begrip in het burgerlijk procesrecht* (Kluwer 2006)

Lock PF, 'Ambtshalve toetsing in hoger beroep: Over de omvang van het hoger beroep en het door de grieven ontsloten gebied' [2014] Tijdschrift voor Civiele Rechtspleging 45

Loos M, *Spontane harmonisatie in het contracten- en consumentenrecht* (Vossiuspers 2006)

——, 'Access to Justice in Consumer Law' (2015) 36 Recht der Werkelijkheid 113

——, 'Enforcing Consumer Rights through ADR at the Detriment of Consumer Law' [2016] European Review of Private Law 61

——, *Algemene voorwaarden* (Boom Juridische Uitgevers 2018)

Loos M and Luzak J, 'Wanted: A Bigger Stick. On Unfair Terms in Consumer Contracts with Online Service Providers' (2016) 39 Journal of Consumer Policy 63

De Lucchi López-Tapia Y, 'Spanish Mortgage Foreclosure and Unfair Terms in Banking Contracts' (2015) 6 Civil Procedure Review 140

Luzak J, 'You Too Will Be Judged: Erga Omnes Effect of Registered Unfair Contract Terms in Poland' (2017) 6 Journal of European Consumer and Market Law 120

Mak C, *Fundamental Rights in European Contract Law* (Kluwer Law International 2008)

——, 'Judgment of the Court (First Chamber) of 6 October 2009, *Asturcom Telecomunicaciones SL v Cristina Rodríguez Nogueira*, Case C-40/08' [2010] European Review of Contract Law 437

——, 'Rights and Remedies. Article 47 EUCFR and Effective Judicial Protection in European Private Law Matters' in Hans-Wolfgang Micklitz (ed), *'The Constitutionalization of European Private Law' (Collected Courses EUI Summer School)* (Oxford University Press 2014) <http://ssrn.com/abstract=2126551>

——, 'Unchart(er)ed Territory: EU Fundamental Rights and National Private Law' in Arthur Hartkamp and others (eds), *The Influence of EU Law on National Private Law* (Kluwer 2014)

——, 'Noot Bij HvJ EU 17 Juli 2014, C-169/14 *Sánchez Morcillo*' EHRC 2014/234

Marco Molina J, 'Spanish Law in 2010–2012: The Influence of European Union Law and the Impact of the Economic Crisis' (2013) 6 Journal of Civil Law Studies 401

Marcos Francisco D, 'Consumidores, sujetos privilegiados en el nuevo paradigma de justicia civil europea: medidas procesales y extraprocesales para su protección' [2015] InDret 16 <http://www.indret.com/pdf/1155_es.pdf>

Martín Faba JM, 'El juez de la ejecución hipotecaria puede apreciar de oficio la abusividad de una clásula ...' [2017] Centro de Estudios de Consumo – Publicaciones Jurídicas

Mayoral Díaz-Asensio JA, Berberoff Ayuda D and Ordóñez Solís D, 'El juez español como juez de la Unión Europea' [2013] Revista española de derecho europeo 127

Mayoral JA, '"Government Contained?" Explaining Spanish Supreme Court's Decisions on EU Law' <https://www.researchgate.net/publication/228543154>

Mayoral JA and Torres Pérez A, 'On Judicial Mobilization: Entrepreneuring for Policy Change at Times of Crisis' (2018) 40 Journal of European Integration 719

McGregor L, 'Alternative Dispute Resolution and Human Rights: Developing a Rights-Based Approach through the ECHR' (2015) 26 European Journal of International Law 607

Medina Guerrero M, 'Derecho a la vivienda y desahucios: la protección del deudor hipotecario en la jurisprudencia del TJUE' [2015] Teoría y Realidad Constitucional 261

Mendoza Losana AI, '¿Existe un derecho absoluto a accedar a los óganos jurisdiccionales en nombre de la tutela judicial efectiva?' [2017] Centro de Estudios de Consumo – Publicaciones Jurídicas

Micklitz H-W, 'The ECJ between the Individual Citizen and the Member States: A Plea for a Judge-Made European Law on Remedies' in Hans-W Micklitz and Bruno de Witte (eds), *The European Court of Justice and the Autonomy of the Member States* (Intersentia 2012)

——, '*Mohamed Aziz* – Sympathetic and Activist, but Did the Court Get It Wrong?' in Anna Sodersten and Joseph HH Weiler, *When the ECJ Gets it Wrong* (European Constitutional Law Network 2013)

——, 'Unfair Contract Terms – Public Interest Litigation before European Courts' in Evelyne Terryn, Gert Straetmans and Veerle Colaert (eds), *Landmark Cases of EU Consumer Law: In Honour of Jules Stuyck* (Intersentia 2013)

——, 'The Transformation of Enforcement in European Private Law: Preliminary Considerations' [2015] European Review of Private Law 491

——, 'The Consumer: Marketised, Fragmentised, Constitutionalised' in Dorota Leczykiewicz and Stephen Weatherill (eds), *The Images of the Consumer in EU Law: Legislation, Free Movement and Competition Law* (Hart Publishing 2016)

——, 'The Constitutional Transformation of Private Law Pillars through the CJEU' in Hugh Collins (ed), *European Contract Law and the Charter of Fundamental Rights* (Intersentia 2017)

Micklitz H-W and Reich N, 'The Court and Sleeping Beauty: The Revival of the Unfair Contract Terms Directive (UCTD)' (2014) 51 Common Market Law Review 771

Miller LL, 'The Use of Case Studies in Law and Social Science Research' (2018) 14 Annual Review of Law and Social Science 381

de Moor R, 'Procesrechtelijke beschouwingen van de tweede gratis-mobieltjes-uitspraak van de Hoge Raad' [2016] Tijdschrift voor Consumentenrecht en handelspraktijken 232

——, 'Hoe effectief is onze consumentenbescherming?' [2017] Tijdschrift voor Consumentenrecht en handelspraktijken 154

Moya Hurtado de Mendoza F, 'Efectividad del Derecho de la Unión Europea vs. principio constitucional de imperio de la Ley' [2017] Revista de Derecho Político 399

Nasarre-Aznar S, '"Robinhoodian" Courts' Decisions on Mortgage Law in Spain' (2015) 7 International Journal of Law in the Built Environment 127

Nicola F and Tichadou E, '*Océano Grupo*: A Transatlantic Victory for the Consumer and a Missed Opportunity for European Law', *EU Law Stories. Contextual and Critical Histories of European Jurisprudence* (Cambridge University Press 2017)

Nieuwenhuijs M and Möhring MEA, 'Vindt de consumentenbescherming haar grens in het appelprocesrecht?' [2016] Tijdschrift voor Civiele Rechtspleging 87

Nieva Fenoll J, 'La actuación de oficio del juez nacional europeo' [2017] Justicia 181

Netjes W and Lodder A, 'e-Court – Dutch Alternative Online Resolution of Debt Collection Claims: A Violation of the Law or Blessing in Disguise?' [2019] International Journal of Online Dispute Resolution 70

Nolan D and Robertson A, 'Rights and Private Law' in Donal Nolan and Andrew Robertson (eds), *Rights and Private Law* (Hart Publishing 2012)

Nowak JT, 'De bevoegdheid van EU-lidstaten voor de aanname van regels van nationaal procesrecht: grenzen in de rechtspraak van het Hof van Justitie' in Nicolas Cariat and Janek Tomasz Nowak (eds), *Le droit de l'Union européenne et le juge belge – Het recht van de Europese Unie en de Belgische rechter* (Bruylant 2015)

——, 'Considerations on the Impact of EU Law on National Civil Procedure: Recent Examples from Belgium' in Vesna Lazić and Steven Stuij (eds), *International Dispute Resolution: Selected Issues in International Litigation and Arbitration (Short Studies in Private International Law)* (TMC Asser Press 2018)

Oderkerk M, 'The Need for a Methodological Framework for Comparative Legal Research – Sense and Nonsense of "Methodological Pluralism" in Comparative Law' (2015) 79 Rabels Zeitschrift für ausländisches und internationales Privatrecht 589

Oomen B, 'The Contested Homecoming of Human Rights in the Netherlands' (2013) 31 Netherlands Quarterly of Human Rights 41

Östlund A, *Effectiveness versus Procedural Protection: Tensions Triggered by the EU Law Mandate of Ex Officio Review* (Nomos 2019)

Pavillon C, *Open normen in het Europees consumentenrecht. De oneerlijkheidsnorm in vergelijkend perspectief* (Kluwer 2011)

——, 'De derdenwerking van collectieve acties tegen onredelijke bedingen in het licht van de Europese rechtspraak' [2016] Tijdschrift voor Consumentenrecht en handelspraktijken 160

——, 'Beter ten hele gedwaald dan ten halve gekeerd? De verjaring van de sanctie op oneerlijke bedingen' [2019] Weekblad voor privaatrecht, notariaat en registratie 621

Pech L and Sayers D, 'Article 47 – Right to an Effective Remedy. D. Analysis. VII–VIII. Article 47(2)' in Steve Peers and others (eds), *The EU Charter of Fundamental Rights: A Commentary* (Hart Publishing 2014)

Pérez Daudí V, *La protección civil de los derechos fundamentales* (Atelier 2011)

——, *La protección procesal del consumidor y el orden público comunitario* (Atelier 2018)

Perriello LE, 'Right to Housing and Unfair Contract Terms' [2018] Journal of European Consumer and Market Law 96

Picó i Junoy J, 'Requiem por el proceso monitorio' (2015) 2 Justicia 523

Półtorak N, *European Union Rights in National Courts* (Wolters Kluwer 2015)

Prechal S, 'The European Acquis of Civil Procedure: Constitutional Aspects' (2014) 19 Uniform Law Review 179

——, 'The Court of Justice and Effective Judicial Protection: What Has the Charter Changed?' in Christophe Paulussen and others (eds), *Fundamental Rights in International and European Law: Public and Private Law Perspectives* (TMC Asser Press 2015)

Prechal S and Widdershoven R, 'Redefining the Relationship between "*Rewe*-Effectiveness" and Effective Judicial Protection' (2011) 4 Review of European Administrative Law 31

Ramos Muñoz D, 'Fundamental Rights and Private Law – A Blueprint for Analysis with Spanish Eyes', in Bettina Heiderhoff, Sebastian Lohsse and Reinier Schulze (eds), *EU-Grundrechte und Privatrecht / EU Fundamental Rights and Private Law* (Nomos 2016)

Reich N, 'More Clarity after "*Claro*"? Arbitration Clauses in Consumer Contracts as an ADR (Alternative Dispute Resolution) Mechanism for Effective and Speedy Conflict Resolution, or as "Deni de Justice"?' [2007] European Review of Contract Law 41

——, 'The Principle of Effectiveness and EU Private Law' in Ulf Bernitz, Xavier Groussot and Felix Schulyok (eds), *General Principles of EU Law and European Private Law* (Kluwer Law International 2013)

——, *General Principles of EU Civil Law* (Intersentia 2014)

——, 'Party Autonomy and Consumer Arbitration in Conflict: A "Trojan Horse" in the Access to Justice in the E.U. ADR-Directive 2013/11?' (2015) 4 Penn State Journal of Law & International Affairs 290

Resnik J, 'Access to Justice, Access to Knowledge, and Economic Inequalities in Open Courts and Arbitrations' (2018) 96 North Carolina Law Review 101

Ribot J and Conrad J, 'National Report: Spain' in Gert Brüggemeijer, Aurelia Colombi Ciacchi and Giovanni Comandé (eds), *Fundamental Rights and Private Law in the European Union, Volume I: A Comparative Overview* (Cambridge University Press 2010)

Riesenhuber K, 'Interpretation of EU Secondary Law' in Karl Riesenhuber (ed), *European Legal Methodology* (Intersentia 2017)

Rinaldo C, 'Beyond Consumer Law – Small Enterprises, Independent Contractors and Other Professional Weak Parties' (2019) 15 European Review of Contract Law 227

Rinkes J, 'Ontwikkelingen in het consumentenrecht' [2009] Contracteren 56

Roca Trías E and García Couso S, '¿Es real el diálogo entre tribunales? Cuestión prejudicial y control de constitucionalidad por vulneración de derechos y libertades fundamentales' [2017] Teoría y Realidad Constitucional 529

van Rossum M and van der Minne E, 'De (on)mogelijkheid van ambtshalve toetsing van het Unierecht in hoger beroep' [2017] Tijdschrift voor de Procespraktijk 98

Rott P, 'The Court of Justice's Principle of Effectiveness and its Unforeseeable Impact on Private Law Relationships' in Dorota Leczykiewicz and Stephen Weatherill (eds), *The Involvement of EU Law in Private Law Relationships* (Hart Publishing 2013)

Sabaté I, 'The Spanish Mortgage Crisis and the Re-Emergence of Moral Economies in Uncertain Times' (2016) 27 History and Anthropology 107

Safjan M and Düsterhaus D, 'A Union of Effective Judicial Protection: Addressing a Multi-Level Challenge through the Lens of Article 47 CFREU' (2014) 33 Yearbook of European Law 3

Sahián JH, *Dimensión constitucional de la tutela de los consumidores. Progresividad y control de regresividad de los derechos de los consumidores* (doctoral thesis, Universidad Complutense de Madrid 2017) <https://eprints.ucm.es/43562/>

Sánchez Barrios MI, 'La acción como derecho a la tutela efectiva' [2010] Justicia: Revista de derecho procesal 167

Sánchez García J, 'Efectos procesales y sustantivos derivados de la sentencia del Tribunal de Justicia de la Unión Europea de 21 de diciembre de 2016' [2017] Revista de Derecho vLex <http://vlex.com/vid/efectos-procesales-sustantivos-derivados-656589369>

Sanna G, 'Article 47 of the EU Charter of Fundamental Rights and Its Impact on Judicial Cooperation in Civil and Commercial Matters' in Giacomo Di Federico (ed), *The EU Charter of Fundamental Rights* (Springer 2011)

Schebesta H, 'Does the National Court Know European Law? A Note on *Ex Officio* Application after *Asturcom*' [2010] European Review of Private Law 847

——, 'Procedural Theory in EU Law' in Kai Purnhagen and Peter Rott (eds), *Varieties of European Economic Law and Regulation: Liber Amicorum for Hans Micklitz* (Springer 2014)

Schmid C, 'The Instrumentalist Conception of the Acquis Communautaire in Consumer Law and its Implications on a European Contract Law Code' [2005] European Review of Contract Law 211

Schutte CB, *Constitutionele rechtspraak in Spanje. Het Tribunal Constitucional en zijn jurisprudentie in hun historische context* (Shaker Publishing 1999)

Scott C, 'Enforcing Consumer Protection Laws' in Geraint Howells, Ian Ramsay and Thomas Wilhelmsson (eds), *Handbook of Research on International Consumer Law* (Edward Elgar Publishing 2010)

Seinen C, 'De waarheidsplicht en de geraden gevolgtrekking anno 2020: een zoektocht naar proportionaliteit' [2020] Tijdschrift voor Civiele Rechtspleging 33

Serrano de Nicolás A, 'Control notarial de las cláusulas abusivas en los préstamos hipotecarios' in Esther Arroyo Amayuelas and Ángel Serrano de Nicolás (eds), *La Europeización del Derecho privado: cuestiones actuales* (Marcial Pons 2016)

Sieburgh C, 'Legitimiteit van de confrontatie van Europees recht en burgerlijk recht van nationale origine', *Controverses rondom legaliteit en legitimatie* (Kluwer 2011)

——, 'Principles in Private Law: From Luxury to Necessity – Multi-Layered Legal Systems and the Generative Force of Principles' (2012) 22 European Review of Private Law 295

——, 'Het EU-Handvest van de Grondrechten en het algemene vermogensrecht. De (potentiële) betekenis van het Handvest voor rechtsverhoudingen tussen particulieren' in Janneke Gerards, Henri de Waele and Karin Zwaan (eds), *Vijf jaar bindend EU-Grondrechtenhandvest. Doorwerking, consequenties, perspectieven* (Wolters Kluwer 2015)

——, 'Waarom het Unierecht de invloed van grondrechten op het privaatrecht aanjaagt en versterkt' [2015] THEMIS 3

Smits JM, 'Constitutionalisering van het vermogensrecht', *Preadviezen uitgebracht voor de Nederlandse Vereniging voor Rechtsvergelijking* (Kluwer 2003)

Snijders H, 'Openbare orde, rechtspersonen en mensenrechten' [2014] Nederlands Juristenblad 1174

Soler Solé G, 'Ejecución hipotecaria. Limitaciones al derecho de defensa del ejecutado. Cuestión de inconstitucionalidad' [2013] Revista Xuridica Galega 13

——, 'Las ejecuciones hipotecarias en España, ante la cuestión prejudicial europea' [2013] Revista Xuridica Galega 25

Solomon JM, 'What is Civil Justice' [2010] William & Mary Law School Scholarship Repository – Faculty Publications. Paper 1149

Stein D, 'Verjaring en Unierecht' in Valérie Tweehuysen and Steven Bartels (eds), *Verjaring* (Wolters Kluwer 2020)

Storskrubb E, *Civil Procedure and EU Law: A Policy Area Uncovered* (Oxford University Press 2008)

Teijo García C and Durán Suárez C, 'Crónica sobre la aplicación judicial del derecho de la UE en España (2014)' [2016] Revista Electrónica de Estudios Internacionales <http://www.reei.org/index.php/revista/num31/cronicas/cronica-sobre-aplicacion-judicial-derecho-ue-espana-2014>

Thiescheffer D, *E-court naast overheidsrechtspraak. Online rechtspraak als alternatieve geschilbeslechting en de garanties voor consumenten* (Celsus juridische uitgeverij 2018)

Timmermans L, 'Het doeltreffendheidsbeginsel na *Puškár*. Een toekomst binnen het kader van het beginsel van effectieve rechtsbescherming?' in Henri de Waele, Jasper Krommendijk and Karin Zwaan (eds), *Tien jaar EU-Grondrechtenhandvest in Nederland* (Wolters Kluwer)

Tjong Tjin Tai E, 'Effectiviteitsbeginsel en nationaal privaatrecht' [2011] Weekblad voor privaatrecht, notariaat en registratie 790

Torres Pérez A, *Conflicts of Rights in the European Union: A Theory of Supranational Adjudication* (Oxford University Press 2009)

——, 'The Judicial Impact of European Law in Spain: ECHR and EU Law Compared' (2011) 30 Yearbook of European Law 159

Tridimas T, 'Bifurcated Justice: The Dual Character of Judicial Protection in EU Law' in Allan Rosas, Egil Levits and Yves Bot (eds), *The Court of Justice and the Construction of Europe: Analyses and Perspectives on Sixty Years of Case-law* (Springer 2013)

Tridimas T and Gentile G, 'The Essence of Rights: An Unreliable Boundary?' (2019) 20 German Law Journal 794

Trstenjak V and Beysen E, 'European Consumer Protection Law: *Curia Semper Dabit Remedium*?' (2011) 48 Common Market Law Review 95

Tulibacka M, 'Europeanization of Civil Procedure: In Search of a Coherent Approach' (2009) 46 Common Market Law Review 1527

——, 'Proceduralisation of EU Consumer Law and its Impact on European Consumers' (2015) 8 Review of European Administrative Law 51

Ugartemendia Eceizabarrena JI, 'La eficacia entre particulares de la Carta de Derechos Fundamentales de la Unión Europea a la luz de la jurisprudencia del Tribunal de Justicia' [2017] Teoría y Realidad Constitucional 361

Uzman J, *Constitutionele remedies bij schending van grondrechten: over effectieve rechtsbescherming, rechterlijk abstineren en de dialoog tussen rechter en wetgever* (Kluwer 2013)

Uzman J, Barkhuysen T and Van Emmerik ML, 'The Dutch Supreme Court: A Reluctant Positive Legislator?' in Allan R Brewer-Carías (ed), *Constitutional Courts as Positive Legislators* (Cambridge University Press 2011)

Vermeulen F and Schasfoort T, 'Ambtshalve toetsing aan Unierecht ten gunste van belangenorganisaties?' [2017] Tijdschrift voor Civiele Rechtspleging 89

Vernadaki Z, 'Civil Procedure Harmonization in the EU: Unravelling the Policy Considerations' (2013) 9 Journal of Contemporary European Research 298

——, *EU Civil Procedure and Access to Justice after the Lisbon Treaty: Perspectives for a Coherent Approach* (doctoral thesis, University College London 2013) <http://discovery.ucl.ac.uk/1399838/>

Von Danwitz T, 'The Rule of Law in the Recent Jurisprudence of the ECJ' (2014) 35 Fordham International Law Journal 1311

Vranken J, 'Methodology of Legal Doctrinal Research' in Mark van Hoecke (ed), *Methodologies of Legal Research: Which Kind of Method for What Kind of Discipline* (Hart Publishing 2010)

Vrendenbarg C, *Proceskostenveroordeling en toegang tot de rechter in IE-zaken: regelingen over proceskosten getoetst aan het EU-recht* (Wolters Kluwer 2018) <http://hdl.handle.net/1887/58468>

Wagner G, 'Harmonisation of Civil Procedure: Policy Perspectives' in XE Kramer and CH van Rhee (eds), *Civil Litigation in a Globalising World* (Springer/TMC Asser Press 2012)

Walkila S, *Horizontal Effect of Fundamental Rights in EU Law* (Europa Law Publishing 2016)

Ward A, 'Article 47 – Right to an Effective Remedy. E. Evaluation' in Steve Peers and others (eds), *The EU Charter of Fundamental Rights: A Commentary* (Hart Publishing 2014)

Weatherill S, Vogenauer S and Weingerl P, 'Private Autonomy and Protection of the Weaker Party' in Stefan Vogenauer and Stephen Weatherill (eds), *General Principles of Law: European and Comparative Perspectives* (Hart Publishing 2017)

Werbrouck J, 'Another Brick in the Wall: The Court's Judgment in *KdG/Susan Kuijpers*, 17 May 2018 [C-147/16]' [2019] European Review of Private Law 135

Whittaker S, 'Who Determines What Civil Courts Decide? Private Rights, Public Policy and EU Law' in Dorota Leczykiewicz and Stephen Weatherill (eds), *The Involvement of EU Law in Private Law Relationships* (Hart Publishing 2013)

Wielsch D, 'The Function of Fundamental Rights in EU Private Law' (2014) 10 European Review of Contract Law 365

Wilhelmsson T, 'Unfair Contract Terms' in Geraint Howells, Christian Twigg-Flesner and Thomas Wilhelmsson, *Rethinking EU Consumer Law* (Routledge 2018)

Wilman F, *Private Enforcement of EU Law Before National Courts* (Edward Elgar Publishing 2015)

——, 'The end of the absence? the growing body of EU legislation on private enforcement and the main remedies it provides for' (2016) 53 Common Market Law Review 887

Wrbka S, *European Consumer Access to Justice Revisited* (Cambridge University Press 2015)

Zglinski J, 'Doing Too Little or Too Much? Private Law Before the European Court of Human Rights' (2018) 37 Yearbook of European Law 1

Zuckerman A, 'Justice in Crisis: Comparative Dimensions of Civil Procedure', in Adrian Zuckerman (ed), *Civil Justice in Crisis: Comparative Perspectives of Civil Procedure* (Oxford University Press 1999)

INDEX

ABOUT THE AUTHOR

Dr. J.M.L. (Anna) van Duin is Assistant Professor of Private Law and Digital Justice at the University of Amsterdam. She is Deputy Director of the Amsterdam Centre for Transformative Private Law (ACT) and Editor of the Dutch Journal of Civil Procedure (*Tijdschrift voor Civiele Rechtspleging*). After graduating from Leiden University and the University of Oxford, she worked as a litigator for six years. She has authored several publications on consumer law and access to justice and participated in EU-funded projects on judicial cooperation and fundamental rights.

www.ingramcontent.com/pod-product-compliance
Ingram Content Group UK Ltd.
Pitfield, Milton Keynes, MK11 3LW, UK
UKHW021827100926
8556IPUK00003B/198